Clinical Neuropsychology of Alcoholism

Robert G. Knight

and

Barry E. Longmore
University of Otago
Dunedin
New Zealand

LEA **LAWRENCE ERLBAUM ASSOCIATES, PUBLISHERS** LEA
Hove (UK)   Hillsdale (USA)

Lawrence Erlbaum Associates Ltd., Publishers
27 Palmeira Mansions
Church Road
Hove
East Sussex, BN3 2FA
UK

British Library Cataloguing in Publication Data

A catalogue record of this book is available from the British Library

ISBN 0-86377-327-3 (Hbk)
     0-86377-338-9 (Pbk)

Printed and bound by BPC Wheatons Ltd., Exeter

To Fiona and Sam,
and to
Ione, Kieran, and Jamie

Contents

PART 2: ALCOHOL AND THE NERVOUS SYSTEM

Series Preface

From being an area primarily on the periphery of mainstream behavioural and cognitive science, neuropsychology has developed in recent years into an area of central concern for a range of disciplines. We are witnessing not only a revolution in the way in which brain–behaviour–cognition relationships are viewed, but a widening of interest concerning devlopments in neuropsychology on the part of a range of workers in a variety of fields. Major advances in brain-imaging techniques and the cognitive modelling of the impairments following brain damage promise a wider understanding of the nature of the representation of cognition and behaviour in the damaged and undamaged brain.

Neuropsychology is now centrally important for those working with brain-damaged people, but the very rate of expansion in the area makes it difficult to keep up with findings from current research. The aim of the *Brain Damage, Behaviour and Cognition* series is to publish a wide range of books which present comprehensive and up-to-date overviews of current developments in specific areas of interest.

These books will be of particular interest to those working with the brain-damaged. It is the editors' intention that undergraduates, postgraduates, clinicians and researchers in psychology, speech pathology and medicine will find this series a useful source of information on important current developments. The authors and editors of the books in this series are experts in their respective fields, working at the forefront of contemporary research. They have produced texts which are accessible and scholarly. We thank them for their contribution and their hard work in fulfilling the aims of the series.

CC and DJM
Sydney, Australia and Ipswich, UK
Series Editors

Brain Damage, Behaviour and Cognition
Developments in Clinical Neuropsychology

Series Editors
Chris Code, University of Sydney, Australia
Dave Müller, Suffolk College of Higher and Further Education, UK

Published titles

Preface

Abuse of alcohol is a major health problem in most parts of the world. Despite the profusion of research publications, dependence on alcohol has no known aetiology, and no certain treatment. It is a disorder where the disastrous family, legal, and employment consequences are compounded by medical complications and neurological damage. In this book we are primarily concerned with the way alcohol affects the brain. Our intention is to describe advances in the neuropsychology of alcoholism in a way that makes this work accessible to clinicians from a variety of disciplines who treat people with alcohol-related problems. Our particular concern, however, is to provide a relevant background in research and practice in this area for clinical psychologists and neuropsychologists whose professional work brings them into contact with clients who abuse alcohol.

The brain changes caused by excessive use of alcohol have been investigated from a range of perspectives. Biomedical researchers have focused on changes in the biological functioning and the structure of the brain, using an increasingly sophisticated array of techniques, including neuroradiological scanning, electrophysiological recordings, and measurement of regional cerebral blood flow. To this can be added the data that have come from the postmortem examination of the brains of alcoholics who have shown varying degrees of organic damage in life. Neurotoxic impairment of the brain is not the only potentially harmful effect of alcohol; damage to all the major organs of the body has been reported, and these effects often accentuate neurological changes. A knowledge of the organic basis of the changes in the brain caused by alcoholism is a necessary background to evaluating psychological deficits.

The task of neuropsychologists is, most fundamentally, to determine how these biological changes impact on psychological function, especially on cognition. For the clinician, there is the added objective of translating this knowledge into a practical understanding of how these deficits affect the everyday functioning of individual clients. There is no doubt that a history of severe alcohol dependence may result in profound and sometimes irreversible cognitive dysfunctions. Neuropsychologists are interested in the relationship between these effects and concomitant alterations in the brain, because they shed light on how the brain works. Another issue for neuropsychologists is whether there are subtle changes in cognitive functioning that present in the early stages of alcohol abuse or a consequence of heavy social drinking. This research has implications for the management of alcohol abusers and for public education about alcohol. In addition, neuropsychologists have been concerned with outlining the pattern of cognitive deficits in alcoholics and in determining whether some functions of the brain are more vulnerable to alcohol than others. In all this work there is a need to be familiar with the essentials of experimental methods and the limitations of the currently available neuropsychological tests.

Many people assisted in the preparation of this book. We are grateful to Jocelyn Burke, Mary Hamilton, Geoff Lowe, Alan Parkin, and Bruce Spittle, who provided helpful comments on sections of the manuscript. We are grateful also for the practical support, advice, and encouragement of Hamish Godfrey, Graeme Hammond-Tooke, Paul Mullen, and Geoff White. Part of the manuscript was prepared while one of us (RGK) was on leave at the School of Psychology, Flinders University of South Australia, and thanks are due to the School for making the visit a pleasant and productive time. We would like to acknowledge the support we have received in conducting our research work over the years from numerous people involved in the care of brain damaged alcoholics in Dunedin, including Tony Braam, Jan Collins, Roy Hughes, David Menkes, and Wayne Rickerby, and also the Alcoholic Liquor Advisory Council of New Zealand. Special thanks are due to Mary-Anne Jensen and Irene Lovell, who typed the manuscript, Kally Barton for her invaluable clerical assistance, and Steve Bush for his artistic talents. Lastly, we would like to thank all the many people who have given their time to participate in our studies of the effects of alcohol; we are most appreciative of your interest and efforts.

Robert Knight
Barry Longmore
1993

CHAPTER ONE

Introduction

On this planet, ethanol is probably almost as old as life itself but in the universe it is probably much older. Large amounts have recently been detected adrift in the constellation Sagittarius.

Lieber (1982, p. xi)

The history of alcohol use extends back thousands of years. There is no record of where or how fermented drinks were first made, but few of the preliterate peoples did not discover or encounter alcohol at some stage of their development. Indeed only the indigenous peoples of Tierra del Fuego, the aboriginal tribes of Australia, and groups of Eskimos, did not learn about alcohol. In Europe, it is likely that mead made from honey was the earliest form of alcoholic drink. No doubt, however, ethanol was produced from whatever was available—fruit, berries, cacti, and tubers. With its ability to induce a sense of transcendent euphoria, alcohol came to be associated with times of celebration. Thus drinking came to be an integral part of ceremonies associated with rites of passage, the making of magic, the promotion of fertility, and preparations for war.

The ancient civilizations of the Middle East, the Babylonians, Hebrews, Sumerians, and Egyptians, left behind written inscriptions and frescoes providing us with evidence of a flourishing trade in wine and of their knowledge of the consequences of drunkenness. The benefits that flowed from drinking were lauded; the troubles that it provoked lamented. Alcohol has been a part of the Judaeo-Christian culture since the earliest times

1

and there are numerous references to it in the Bible. In Genesis, one of Noah's first acts on alighting from the Ark was to till the ground and plant a vineyard. He was, however, innocent of some of the properties of the grape, which left him naked and drunk in his tent, to be discovered by his sons. Also to be found in Genesis is the story of how the daughters of Lot used wine to render their father senseless, before they lay with him to preserve his line. In the Old Testament we see both the beneficent and evil effects of alcohol. In Proverbs (31: 6–7) the power of alcohol to provide solace is recorded: "Give strong drink to them that are sad: and wine to them that are grieved in the mind: Let them drink, and forget their want, and remember their sorrow no more". There are also dire warnings: "Look not upon the wine when it is yellow, when the colour thereof shineth in the glass: it goeth in pleasantly. But in the end it will bite like a snake, and will spread abroad poison like a basilisk" (Proverbs 23: 31–35). It is also apparent that the Hebrews knew of the toxic effect of alcohol. The woman Hannah is observed moving her mouth in prayer without uttering words, and mistaken for a drunkard hallucinating.

In the world of the ancient Greeks, both mead and wine were well known. According to legend it was Dionysus, sometimes known as Bacchus, who brought them wine. The votaries of Dionysus were given to rituals of frantic ecstasy, in which alcohol played a part, giving them a sense of being at one with the god. Dionysus is often represented in opposition to Apollo, who exemplified the qualities of discipline, rationality, and purity. Drunkenness features on occasion in Greek writings. Antipater of Thessalonica writes, for example, of the cunningness of the habitual inebriate. Paton (1916, p. 455) quotes Antipater telling of the woman Bacchylis, known as "the sponge of Bacchus", who once addressed the goddess Demeter in this manner:

"If I can escape from the wave of this pernicious fever, for the space of a hundred suns I will drink but fresh water and avoid Bacchus and wine". But when she was quit of her illness on the very first day she devised this dodge. She took a sieve, and looking through its close meshes, saw even more than a hundred suns.

Elsewhere, this dedication is recorded: "Xenophon, the toper, dedicates his empty cask to thee Bacchus. Receive it kindly for it is all he has" (Paton, 1916, p. 341). Drunkards were artful in the pursuit of their addiction and left impecunious as a result. In addition to the psychosocial effects, the Greek physician Hippocrates also recorded the medical consequences. Amongst his *Aphorisms* he states that "If a drunk man suddenly becomes speechless in a fit, he will die after convulsions unless a fever ensues or unless, upon recovering from his hangover, he regain his voice" (Lloyd, 1978, p. 222). Elsewhere he teaches, with considerable justification, that "A shivering fit and delerium following excessive drinking are bad" (Lloyd, 1978, p. 231).

Viticulture was known to the Romans from the time of the founding of the city (Jellinek, 1976). Wine was celebrated by the Latin poets, and an evocative picture of the extravagant banqueting and drinking habits of rich freedmen is to be found in the *Satyricon* of Petronius. Seneca (p. 273) rails against the drinking bouts of his time in his *Epistle on Drunkenness:*

> What glory is there in carrying too much liquor? When you have won the prize, and the other banqueters, sprawling asleep or vomiting, have declined your challenge to still other toasts; when you are the last survivor of the revels; when you have vanquished everyone by your magnificent show of prowess and there is no man who has proved himself of so great capacity as you—you are vanquished by the cask.

Many of the most prominent citizens of that time were notable drunkards, including the general Sulla, Mark Anthony, and Tiberius Claudius Nero. Of Anthony, Seneca (p. 273) wrote:

> Mark Anthony was a great man, a man of distinguished ability; but what ruined him and drove him into foreign habits and un-Roman vices if it was not drunkenness and—no less potent that wine—the love of Cleopatra?

The Romans spread their knowledge and practice of viticulture both East, to the regions that were to form the Byzantine empire, and West through Europe. Cultivation of the grape occurred throughout Gaul and the Rhone valley, eventually crossing the channel to Britain (Sournia, 1990). To the North, the Germanic people brewed and consumed in great quantities beer made from barley and mead. Throughout the Middle Ages, wine drinking became increasingly popular in Europe. Wine was prescribed by doctors for its medicinal properties and cultivated extensively by the Church. The glories of wine were celebrated; the medical perils of excessive consumption were largely unknown. Typical of the medieval Latin lyrics exalting the pleasures of drinking are those found in the *Carmina Burana*, an anthology of such songs, thought to have been compiled at the monastery of Benedictbeureu, during the thirteenth century.

By the thirteenth century the Arabs had learned to distil ethanol from wine, which acquired the Latin name *spiritus* or *aqua vitae*. From the beginning of the sixteenth century, knowledge of the distillation of alcohol became widespread, and with it the opportunity to drink alcohol in the strength of 50% by volume, as compared with the strength of wine, which varied from 10–15%. The Dutch learned to make gin from grain and juniper berries and exported this skill and the product to England. Each nation distilled a preferred spirit: whisky in Scotland, vodka in Russia, arak in the Mediterranean countries, and schnapps in Germany. By the beginning of the eighteenth century the scale of drunkenness caused by gin and other spirits in England was becoming a matter of grave concern. Gin was blamed for the evils of poverty, disease, criminality, and chaos in family life. London was populated with numerous gin houses and there was widespread drunkenness among the poor and the rich. A compelling image of the time is Hogarth's "Gin Lane" with its debauched woman and abused child. With the advent of the industrial revolution came a greater concern for the physical effects of alcohol on productivity; no longer was drinking considered to be a way of enhancing the performance of the manual labourer. The tremors associated with inebriation, which Hippocrates and Galen had observed, were now labelled *delerium tremens* by Sutton, who, in 1813, observed this symptom in the sailors he ministered to, although he was unaware that the cause was alcohol abuse.

In response to the pervasive drunkenness and the associated civil problems in the early part of the nineteenth century, several temperance organisations were founded. The medical profession became increasingly aware of the damage that alcohol caused; the relationship between alcohol abuse and liver disease was established, and descriptions of the medical consequences of alcohol entered the literature. Benjamin Rush, often regarded as the father of American psychiatry, inveighed against alcohol, which he saw as undermining the fabric of colonial America. In 1784 he published a monograph entitled *An Inquiry into the Effects of Ardent Spirits on the Human Mind and Body*, drawing the attention of his colleagues to the ubiquitous social and organic damage caused by drunkenness. The public concern with inebriety is highlighted by the title of a pamphlet circulated at the time, which described America "as becoming a nation of drunkards" (Sournia, 1990).

The diagnosis of alcoholism was first used by the Swedish physician Magnus Huss, in his *Alcoholismus chronicus*, published simultaneously in Sweden and Germany in 1849. He lectured extensively on the threat that alcohol posed to the human body and to traditional Swedish values, based on his extensive clinical experience and travels throughout Europe. He characterised alcoholism as being both a mental and a physical disorder, and recognised the widespread organ damage caused by ethanol. Throughout the nineteenth century a scattering of medical and scientific publications described the chronic effects of alcohol abuse, but not until the latter part of the century was the body of work sufficient for the scientific study of the consequences of alcohol to be regarded as clearly established (Keller, 1966). By that time, the effect of chronic alcoholism on cognition was widely recognised (Blandford, 1884, pp. 67–68):

> After years of habitual drinking, drinking which may hardly have amounted to intoxication, far less to delerium tremens, we may perceive the mind weakening, memory failing, and the dotage of premature age coming on; and not infrequently with the decrepitude of mental power, we notice some amount of body paralysis, which slowly advances at the same time ...

The concern of this book is with the changes in the brain caused by alcohol and the consequent changes in neuropsychological functioning that come with these lesions. The research we will be concerned with dates from the time in the late nineteenth century when Wernicke and Korsakoff first described the brain lesions they found in the brains of their chronic alcoholic patients. Wernicke's encephalopathy has come to be solely associated with alcoholism, although the first of the cases he described in 1881 was of a 20-year-old seamstress, who developed symptoms of ophthalmoplegia, ataxia, and drowsiness as a consequence of sulphuric acid poisoning. His other cases, however, involved chronic alcoholism. One was a woman who was admitted with delerium, hallucinations, and ophthalmoplegia, who died after 6 days in hospital. On autopsy, lesions were identified in the periventricular area and Wernicke (1881, p. 48) described her neurological condition as "an independent, inflammatory, acute nuclear disease in the region of the optic nerves".

In 1887, Korsakoff provided the first detailed account of patients with an irreversible amnesic disorder associated with alcoholic peripheral nerve disease, which he called polyneuritic psychosis (Korsakoff, 1955). He identified the disorder in both alcoholic and non-alcoholic subjects and surmised that a common pathology and aetiology caused the disease. Many reports of memory disorder in alcoholism predated those of Korsakoff, a fact which he himself acknowledged, citing Magnus Huss as one such forerunner. However, the comprehensive nature of Korsakoff's description has ensured that there has been no challenge to his primary position in recognising this condition (Victor, Adams, & Collins, 1971). Korsakoff's view was that the amnesia was principally the result of cortical atrophy, and neither he nor Wernicke recognised the link between the two disorders they had identified. The history of the clinical description of chronic amnesia in alcoholism from the 1880s features the gradual appreciation of the link between Wernicke's encephalopathy and Korsakoff's amnesia and the discussion of the possible aetiological basis.

In formulating a cause for the aetiology of Wernicke's disease, and by implication, Korsakoff's syndrome, nutritional insufficiency was soon seen to have an important role. The study of beriberi in the 1880s, led to the identification of vitamin B_1 (thiamine) deficiency as the root cause. In 1886, the Japanese navy succeeded in eradicating beriberi by adding fresh foods, fish, and vegetables to their sailors' diet of polished rice. Experimental studies with pigeons showed that thiamine deficiency caused neural degeneration, and research with human volunteers showed that diets depleted of thiamine caused reversible confusion and memory loss (Spillane, 1947). An increasing body of clinical and experimental evidence pointed to thiamine deficiency as causing alcoholic encephalopathy. This association was strengthened by DeWardener and Lennox's (1947) report on 52 cases of encephalopathy occurring in malnourished prisoners held in Singapore from 1942 to 1945. No less than 70% of their cases also had the classic physical symptoms of beriberi; these symptoms, and the mental confusion, were banished by injections of thiamine. DeWardener and Lennox described the condition as "cerebral beriberi".

By the turn of the century, medical practitioners had come to appreciate that alcohol caused a variety of medical disorders. These included gastritis, cirrhosis and degeneration of the liver, pancreatitis, hypertension, cardiomyopathy, and an increased risk of certain cancers, as well as damage to the central nervous system. Concern at the considerable menace posed by alcohol to public health, as well as to the social fabric, led to a variety of legislative experiments designed to enforce abstinence. In the United States, prohibition won legislative approval with the addition in 1920 of the eighteenth amendment to the Constitution. Prohibition, however, proved a failure from the outset and by 1933 it was clear that this attempt at legislating abstinence had failed. Only unambiguous religious teaching, as in the Koran or the Buddhist lay ethic, seems sufficient to motivate sobriety, at least amongst believers.

With establishment of psychology as a laboratory science in the 1890s came the first attempts to study the changes in cognition caused by alcohol using the methods of experimental psychology. In 1896 Kraepelin studied the perceptual processes of amnesic alcoholics using the tachistoscope. Talland (1965) describes a variety of experimental studies carried out during the period 1900 to 1915 by Brodmann, Ranschburgh, Schneider, and others. In an early report, Wechsler (1917) described results from a study of five amnesic alcoholics using the procedures that were later to be the basis for his well-known memory battery. He found that chronic amnesics performed normally on the Digit Span test, but were grossly impaired on measures of paired-associate learning; he characterised amnesia in terms of a failure to form new associations.

THE STRUCTURE OF THE BOOK

This book is divided into four Parts.

Part 1

In Part 1 we describe the medical and neurological conditions that result from alcohol abuse, and neuropsychological approaches to assessing deficits in alcohol-impaired clients. As we have already seen, there has been a gradually increasing awareness of the toxic effects of alcohol. Alcoholism has been seen to promote a range of serious physical conditions, as a consequence not only of the toxicity of ethanol, but also the inadequate diet of patients dependent on alcohol. This organic damage contributes to the pattern of cognitive impairment in alcoholics and is an important factor in documenting the clinical consequences of alcoholism.

In Chapter 3 we consider the problems implicit in measuring cognitive deficits and in quantifying drinking practices. Study of the neurological deficits of alcoholics is limited by our inability to determine accurately the amounts of alcohol that subjects have been exposed to and the way in which their physical condition has changed with time. This lack of experimental control means that the study of alcoholics involves primarily correlational methods, with one set of variables, individual differences in drinking history, being extremely difficult to quantify.

Part 2

In Part 2 we review research that has focused directly on damage to the nervous system. The morphological abnormalities that were identified by Wernicke, Korsakoff, and others at post-mortem have been studied more recently *in vivo* with an increasingly sophisticated range of brain imaging techniques. Advances in neuroradiology during the last two decades have greatly facilitated our understanding of the effects of alcohol on brain structure and functioning, and led to the modification of the concepts that were previously applied. Chapter 5 considers the findings from neuro-radiological studies, and Chapter 6 reviews the findings from post-mortem studies of the brains of alcohol-dependent patients. Studies of the effects of chronic alcohol abuse on the electrical activity of the brain and on cerebral blood flow have shed light on the neurophysiological changes associated with alcoholism. The final chapter in this section describes the findings of studies of evoked brain potentials, regional cerebral blood flow, and positron emission tomographic studies of brain metabolism.

Part 3

Research in which neuropsychological tests and other experimental procedures have been used to examine the acute and chronic effects of alcohol on cognition is surveyed in Part 3. Implicit in the way the chapters in this section are organised is the notion that there are progressive differences in the severity of neuropsychological deficits between social drinkers, alcoholics, and patients with Wernicke–Korsakoff syndrome. We will return to look at the validity of continuity models of cognitive deterioration at the conclusion of Chapter 10. Chapter 7 reviews studies of the acute effects of alcohol intoxication. This research is typically conducted with groups of social drinkers, who consume prescribed doses of alcohol under carefully controlled conditions. The initial objective of this field of study was to document the acute behavioural effects of alcohol. Increasingly sophisticated experimental procedures, incorporating placebo controls, have shown that ingestion of alcohol does have a measurable effect on cognition and psychomotor coordination, even at the low doses of alcohol that can be administered ethically to groups of volunteers. Perhaps the most interesting development in research with alcohol intoxicated subjects is the use of alcohol to explore the parameters of acute amnesia. The transient impairments in memory induced by alcohol intoxication can be used to determine specific effects on discrete information processing stages.

Alcohol produces acute effects on emotional, cognitive, and behavioural competence, as any social drinker can testify, but the possible long-term consequences of social drinking have more important psychosocial implications. In 1977, Parker and Noble reported the results of a study of Californian social drinkers, from which they concluded that there was a significant relationship between current intellectual performance and usual quantity of alcohol consumed during a drinking episode. They went on to establish similar results in a large community sample recruited in Detroit. Chapter 8 reviews this research, and the studies that have followed. There are numerous problems in conducting and interpreting the outcome of studies of cognition in social drinkers and there has been considerable discussion of the validity of these studies. With people who are labelled alcohol abusers or alcohol dependent, however, there is no such doubt that heavy consumption leads to dysfunction on neuropsychological tests.

Chapter 9 will focus on studies that have documented neuro-psychological impairment in alcoholics. In addition, research that examines recovery following abstinence and attempts to understand individual differences in performance will be considered. Patients with Wernicke–Korsakoff syndrome, because of their profound degree of amnesia, have been amongst the most intensely studied groups of patients with neurological disorders. Much of what is known about the effects of chronic organic amnesia comes from the study of Korsakoff patients. Chapter 10 reviews some of the clinical and cognitive disabilities of these patients.

Part 4

The final section of the book considers some of the implications of research on brain damage and its consequent neuropsychological impairments for the assessment and management of clinical cases. It looks first at studies that have investigated the relationship between cognitive deficit and treatment outcome in alcoholic patients. This research has the objective of clarifying the practical effects of neuropsychological changes on the ability to participate in therapy and to achieve long-term therapeutic goals. Chapter 12 reviews studies that have examined the management and rehabilitation of patients with alcohol-related cognitive impairment. These include studies of patients with profound impairments in information processing, such as those with Wernicke–Korsakoff syndrome, who present the clinician involved in cognitive retraining and rehabilitation with a considerable challenge.

PART I

DIAGNOSTIC AND
MEASUREMENT ISSUES

CHAPTER TWO

Adverse Effects of Alcohol Consumption

Within a total and balanced approach to alcoholism the physical element must be seen as often very important. Helping services must be organised as to cope effectively with diagnosis and treatment in the physical domain, and whatever the particular professional affiliation of the person who is working with the alcoholic, there is a need for an alertness towards possible physical pathologies.

Edwards (1987, p. 110)

On two occasions, 260 years apart, the Royal College of Physicians has submitted that the widespread consumption of alcohol represents "a great and growing evil". In the more recent publication it is claimed that "about one in five of all men admitted to medical wards has a problem related to alcohol abuse" (Royal College of Physicians, 1987, p. 1). This chapter will describe the physical health hazards associated with alcohol abuse. Prior to considering neurological disorders, we will survey the evidence associating alcohol consumption with damage to the liver and heart, and to the gastrointestinal, endocrine, and reproductive systems. In doing so, we will outline some of the metabolic disturbances caused by acute and chronic alcohol consumption, and consider the carcinogenic and teratogenic consequences of prolonged alcohol abuse. The rationale for this approach is contained in the words of Griffith Edwards, which head this chapter. The complete understanding of the neuropsychological consequences of alcoholism requires an awareness of related medical complications.

There is a substantial and wide-ranging literature on the physical damage resulting from alcohol dependence. Three basic research strategies have been used, each with some important limitations. The first strategy involves the intense clinical or laboratory study of subjects consuming certain amounts of alcohol to identify and define syndromes of impairment, and the mechanisms underlying them. In the second, an epidemiological approach is used whereby a cohort of subjects is investigated cross-sectionally or longitudinally to determine the prevalence, incidence, and risk factors for diseases in persons consuming various levels of alcohol. The third strategy is experimental and involves administering alcohol to animals to determine its effects and the mechanisms by which they occur. Throughout this chapter our objective will be to consider the following questions: "What are the major health consequences of chronic alcohol abuse?" "What is the incidence of these disorders in problem drinkers?" "What is the level of alcohol consumption at which a drinker is at increased risk for these disorders?" "What is the evidence for a causal role for alcohol in the numerous disorders associated with it?"

METABOLISM OF ALCOHOL

Research on the metabolism of alcohol is discussed in detail in many sources; we shall discuss it briefly here and recommend that the interested reader refer to Little (1991), Lieber (1982) and Sherlock (1989). Small amounts of alcohol (12–30g) are produced endogenously over a 24-hour period, probably as a result of bacterial fermentation in the gut. Enzymes for the metabolism of alcohol are also present and the capacity of this enzyme system is enhanced by drinking alcohol. Most ingested alcohol is absorbed rapidly through the walls of the stomach and the small intestine, and passes more or less directly to the liver. Less than 10% is eliminated through the kidneys or by respiration. Most of the body's enzymes capable of alcohol metabolism are located in the liver. This relative organ specificity for alcohol metabolism, and the seeming lack of feedback mechanisms to protect the metabolic state of liver cells, produces an aggravated state of imbalance in the liver during chronic alcohol consumption. Metabolism of other substances is grossly disturbed, contributing to nutritional deficiency and enhanced toxicity.

Alcohol cannot be stored in the human body in other than trace amounts. The major pathway for disposing of ingested alcohol involves the enzyme alcohol dehydrogenase (ADH), which oxidises ethanol to acetaldehyde in the liver. In a further process, acetaldehyde is reduced to acetate by acetaldehyde dehydrogenase (ALDH). A secondary pathway involves the microsomal ethanol oxidising system (MEOS). The effect of chronic alcohol ingestion is to increase the rate of degradation of alcohol, thereby increasing tolerance in the heavy drinker and paving the way for enhanced metabolic disturbance. Although tolerance is increased early in a heavy drinker's history, in later stages malnutrition and liver damage tend to offset the adaptive increase in alcohol metabolism and produce reduced tolerance.

The presence of acetaldehyde affects many tissues and inhibits a number of processes including the formation of proteins. In addition, it may enhance production of substances noxious to the liver and, in a vicious cycle, cause cellular dysfunction which in turn promotes higher acetaldehyde levels. The role of acetate is less well known, but it is thought to decrease the release of free fatty acids from the liver. We will return to further discussion of intermediary and peripheral metabolism of ethanol and its metabolites, and the effects of this, when discussing the associated health problems.

ALCOHOL AND LIVER DISEASE

It is appropriate to consider the association between alcohol and liver disease early in this chapter because it has been known for so long and has been the subject of comprehensive study (Lieber, 1973, 1975a,b, 1982; Schmidt, 1977; Sherlock, 1989; Williams & Davis, 1977). Another reason for doing so is that there is a complex interaction between liver disease, continued drinking, and dysfunction in other body organ systems, including the brain. Decreased hepatic efficiency compounds the metabolic imbalances resulting from chronic alcohol ingestion and accelerates the development of other disorders. The clinical presentation and pathogenesis of alcoholic liver disease have been the subject of a recent comprehensive review by Ishak, Zimmerman, and Ray (1991). We will not discuss it in detail here but attempt to provide an introductory overview.

Long-term abusers of alcohol usually have some degree of liver damage, ranging in severity from asymptomatic and reversible fatty liver, through hepatitis and cirrhosis, to primary liver cell carcinoma, which is usually fatal. Evidence is accruing to suggest that this spectrum of disorders may be a progressive series of stages of increasing severity. For example, fibrous precirrhotic changes are already evident in laboratory animals with simple fatty liver (Nakano & Lieber, 1982). There is other evidence that the functional metabolic abnormality that produces fatty liver is associated with cellular mitochondrial defects that have more serious implications (Lieber, 1975b). Furthermore, Galambos (1972b) showed that alcoholic hepatitis is a potential precirrhotic lesion. These issues will be discussed further when the alcoholic hepatic disorders are reviewed.

The evidence implicating alcohol as an aetiological factor in liver disease is strong. Alcoholic liver damage accounts for the vast majority of cases of cirrhosis in patients coming to autopsy (Lelbach, 1975; Martini & Bode, 1970). Changes in the availability of alcohol in times of war or prohibition are associated with shifts in the incidence of cirrhosis (Schmidt, 1977). Further, mortality from cirrhosis is associated with national per capita levels of consumption. In North American studies, alcoholic cirrhosis was one of the top five causes of mortality for people aged 25 to 64 years in the 1960s and 1970s (Lieber, 1982). Savolainen, Penttilä, and Karhunen (1992) investigated the relationship between alcohol intake and liver cirrhosis in Finland, where the per capita consumption rates doubled between 1969 and 1974. Rates of liver cirrhosis mortality rose from 4.2 to 9.7 per 100,000 between 1968 and 1988. Likewise, rates of liver cirrhosis in a Finnish autopsy series rose from 3.0% to 6.1% between 1968 and 1978, remaining at about 6.0% thereafter (Savolainen et al., 1992). In addition, the proportion of liver cirrhosis attributable to alcohol increased significantly from 23.5% in 1968 to 60.9% in 1988. Other studies have also suggested that the relationship between liver cirrhosis and alcohol abuse is strong. The mortality rate from cirrhosis has been estimated as between seven and thirteen times higher in alcoholics than in those who do not drink (Williams & Davis, 1977). Despite this, only a very small percentage of alcoholics seem to develop cirrhosis. Although it is more common in men than in women, there is evidence that liver disease progresses more rapidly in the female alcohol abuser (Morgan & Sherlock, 1977).

Alcoholic fatty liver (steatosis)

Fat accumulation in the liver occurs at some stage in most abusive drinkers. This is a clinical indication that alcohol is beginning to have adverse effects of major significance on the liver (Sherlock, 1989). The most common clinical sign is liver enlargement (hepatomegaly) in which the liver edge extends below the rib margin. Many patients do not experience any distress as a consequence, but in some there are reports of upper right quadrant abdominal pain, nausea, loss of appetite, epigastric discomfort, and bowel disturbance. The most usual accompanying signs are dilated peripheral blood vessels (known as spider naevi), reddening of the palms (erythema), tendon contractions of the hands (Dupuytren's contractures, also referred to as palmer aponeurosis), and parotid gland swelling. Laboratory tests commonly reveal abnormally large red blood cells (macrocytes), and increased levels of the serum enzymes gamma-glutamyl transferase (GGT) and aspartate aminotransferase (AST). These clinical and laboratory aspects are discussed in detail by Ishak et al. (1991).

The evidence associating fatty liver with alcohol in heavy drinkers is strong. When alcohol is ingested, ethanol becomes the preferred fuel and displaces other substrates in its intermediary metabolism. As a result, fatty acids, which are the normal fuel for hepatic cells, are not metabolised and accumulate in the liver. This accumulation is enhanced by the conversion of the excess hydrogen generated by ethanol oxidation to still more lipids (Sherlock, 1989). There is evidence, however, that hepatomegaly, the major symptom of alcoholic fatty liver, also results from impaired hepatic protein secretion and the consequent accumulation of certain proteins (Lieber, 1982). A number of studies have reported a relationship between varying levels of alcohol consumption and the risk of fatty liver. In a case control study, Coates, Halliday, Rankin, Feinman, and Fisher (1984) found that men drinking about five standard drinks (40g) per day are about six times more likely to develop fatty liver than non-drinkers and that the risk increases to about 60 times for consumers of 10 standard drinks per day (Royal College of Physicians, 1987).

Although some authors place little emphasis on the clinical relevance of fatty liver (Ishak et al., 1991; Sherlock, 1989), Lieber (1982) argued that, in association with gross distension secondary to fat and protein accumulation, fibrositic and sclerotic changes of the central venous system may, in turn, lead to necrosis and portal hypertension even at this early stage. Such findings have also been reported in animal models of chronic alcohol consumption and lend support to the assertion that alcoholic liver diseases are overlapping conditions.

Alcoholic hepatitis

Acute and chronic inflammation of the liver is a much more serious condition than alcoholic fatty liver and occurs in between 17% and 42% of heavy drinkers (ingesting more than 80g per day) after years of alcohol abuse (Sherlock, 1989). Patients with alcoholic hepatitis are generally more ill than those with fatty liver and it often leads to cirrhosis. On the other hand, there is evidence that in about half of the patients hepatitis may remain unchanged and in some it may even abate despite continued alcohol consumption (Galambos, 1972a,b). Clinical signs range from mild hepatomegaly without jaundice to fatal disease with jaundice, ascites (fluid in the abdominal cavity), gastrointestinal haemorrhage, and hepatic coma. Associated signs are bruising of the skin and poor healing of wounds, along with the other stigmata of chronic alcohol abuse described above. Laboratory tests commonly show raised serum AST and GGT and also increased serum bilirubin and alkaline phosphatase. There is usually anaemia, macrocytosis, raised white blood count, and increased clotting time. The disorder itself varies only in the intensity and frequency of the clinical signs present, the underlying hepatic changes are the same. There is ballooning and a significant disarray of hepatocytes, which are infiltrated with polymorphonuclear leucocytes. Fibrosis, steatosis, cholestasis, and necrosis are common histological findings (Lieber, 1982). Ishak et al. (1991) emphasise the significant ultrastructural changes that occur, including the development of abnormal fibrils and filaments, which have become known as Mallory bodies. In summary, the basic structure of the liver is severely damaged and its function significantly compromised. Final diagnosis is by liver biopsy which reveals the presence of the changes described above. Once the disease has progressed to the extent that clotting abnormalities are present, mortality rate is up to 60%.

Alcoholic cirrhosis

This is a serious and potentially fatal disorder that may go undetected in as many as 40% of sufferers ante-mortem. In one-third of cases dying from cirrhosis, death is due to hepatoma (primary liver cell carcinoma). Men drinking five drinks per day (40g) are twice as likely to develop cirrhosis than abstainers. Those who sustain a long term intake of 80g of alcohol per day are, according to the Royal College of Physicians (1987), about 100 times more likely to develop cirrhosis than non-drinkers. On the other hand, Sherlock (1989) suggested that, above a threshold of 40 to 50g per day (5 or 6 standard drinks), there is little change in risk. The evidence linking cirrhosis and alcohol consumption is impressive. The typical clinical signs are jaundice and hepatomegaly, although the size of the liver can vary depending on the degree of fibrosis, steatosis, and inflammation, from a relatively small shrunken and hard liver to a large organ weighing up to 4kg (Lieber, 1973, 1982; Royal College of Physicians, 1987). Associated clinical features include portal hypertension, splenomegaly (enlarged spleen), ascites, encephalopathy with tremor, gastrointestinal haemorrhage, and other abnormalities. The other stigmata of chronic alcohol abuse described above are usually present and patients are prone to spontaneous peritonitis, and, in males, enlargement of the breasts (gynaecomastia) and testicular atrophy. Laboratory tests show moderately elevated serum enzymes, variably increased bilirubin concentration, and changes in the characteristics of the blood cells (principally macrocytosis and increased clotting time). These topics are discussed in detail by Ishak et al. (1991) and Sherlock (1989).

In alcoholic cirrhosis, scar tissue distorts the normal architecture of the liver by forming bands of connective tissue, which replace the proper liver tissue (Lieber, 1982). Total blood flow is decreased and blood flow out of the liver is so restricted that portal hypertension results. Reduced blood flow impedes residual hepatic function and this is further complicated if cardiac output is impaired. Although the prognosis of alcoholic cirrhosis is poor (mean life expectancy after diagnosis is less than 3 years), the 5-year survival rate is improved by abstinence from 40% to 60% (Royal College of

Physicians, 1987). Outcome is affected by stage of disease and gender of the patient, with women surviving for a shorter period on average than men (Sherlock, 1989).

Hepatoma (primary liver cell carcinoma)

Around 10% of patients with alcoholic cirrhosis develop primary liver cell cancer and, as has been mentioned, about one-third of those dying with cirrhosis die from hepatoma (Lieber, 1982). Evidence exists that heavy drinkers who cease abuse late in life are at greater risk of hepatoma than those who continue drinking (Lee, 1966). Clinical signs include abdominal pain, resistance to diuresis, and increasing hepatomegaly; the laboratory tests of liver function usually indicate deterioration. Other findings are raised plasma levels of alphafetoprotein and abnormal blood circulation in the liver. Diagnosis, however, relies on histological proof at biopsy. Most patients with hepatoma die within 6 months (Royal College of Physicians, 1987).

Susceptibility to alcoholic liver disease

As we have already mentioned, the available evidence suggests that there may be significant gender differences in susceptibility to alcohol related liver disease (Morgan & Sherlock, 1977). Increased risk of fatty liver and cirrhosis occurs at lower levels of consumption for women (20g per day). This is not surprising as, on average, women achieve higher plasma levels from equivalent doses due to their lower total body water values. Consequently, tissue alcohol concentrations are higher, allowing the possibility of greater long-term effects. According to Sherlock (1989), the evidence suggests that women are more likely than men to progress from alcoholic hepatitis to cirrhosis even if they stop drinking. Ethnic groups are also differentially affected with respect to liver disease. For example, American Indians are severely affected, whereas American Jews are relatively spared (Lieber, 1982). Findings such as these raise questions regarding the possible role of genetic factors in the pathogenesis of alcoholic liver disease. The role of hereditary predisposition through differential association with specific histocompatibility antigens has been studied (Bailey et al., 1976), but the findings are inconsistent. Sherlock (1989) has noted that, in various nations, different histocompatibility types have been associated with increased susceptibility to alcoholic liver disease. In addition, genetic variations in the two metabolic enzyme systems (ADH and MEOS) lead to different rates of oxidation and acetaldehyde generation. Such differences may also contribute to variability in rates of alcoholic liver disease.

ALCOHOL AND HEART DISEASE

The cardiac response to an acute dose of alcohol reflects the rate and quantity of alcohol ingested, previous use of alcohol, and the physiological state of the drinker. The general effect is depression of the strength of the contraction of the heart muscle, and thereby a reduction in the volume of blood pumped. This is more marked in persons not habituated to alcohol. In alcohol-dependent patients there is a wide spectrum of abnormalities. During binges, a pattern of symptoms including arrhythmias (paroxysmal atrial fibrillation, ventricular ectopic beats, ventricular tachycardia) is commonly reported and has attracted the label "holiday heart". Individuals experiencing this syndrome often have otherwise normal cardiac function and normal sinus rhythm is restored with abstinence, without evidence of long-term damage. However, chronic drinkers with myocardial dysfunction are abnormally susceptible to these effects and place themselves at great risk during binges. The older chronic heavy drinker typically has the circulatory features of a congestive cardiomyopathy with a hypo-contractible, dilated heart; cardiomegaly is also commonly found (Lieber, 1982; Royal College of Physicians, 1987).

Alcoholic cardiomyopathy

Alcoholic cardiomyopathy was first thought to be the result of thiamine deficiency but it is now recognised that it can result from the toxic effects of alcohol consumption alone (Tofler, 1985). According to Rubin (1979), excessive consumption of alcohol is the major cause of secondary, non-ischaemic dilated cardiomyopathy in the Western world. It is thought to result from the effects of acetaldehyde, the first product of alcohol metabolism, which acts indirectly by releasing catecholamines. Acetaldehyde may also interfere with the normal synthetic and degradative pathways of catechol metabolism. As a result, the heart is exposed to high concentrations of catecholamines and other intermediate compounds such as catecholaldehydes, whose affects on the myocardium may be harmful. Lieber (1982) noted that acetaldehyde may also promote cardiomyopathy by its alteration of myocardial lipid metabolism, inhibition of mitochondrial respiration and enzyme activity, and interference with intracellular uptake and binding.

The incidence and natural history of dilated cardiomyopathy are not well known and neither is its relationship with alcohol consumption. It is thought that patients who develop alcoholic cardiomyopathy are usually over the age of 40 at the onset of the illness and have been very heavy drinkers (daily amounts of 100g, 12 standard drinks, or more) for 10 or more years. Clinical findings include anorexia, cardiac cachexia, breathlessness, and a nagging cough. The condition is sometimes described as being like a persistent upper respiratory tract infection or a flu-like illness that does not abate. There is commonly chest pain accompanied by proneness to fatigue, abdominal discomfort, swelling from oedema, and palpitations and arrhythmias. A chest X-ray usually shows cardiomegaly, a small aortic silhouette, and absence of cardiac calcification. Electrocardiograph (ECG) findings are similar to those of diffuse myocardial disease (Royal College of Physicians, 1987).

There is a high incidence of acute myocardial infarction and sudden death from alcoholic cardiomyopathy when there is increased myocardial oxygen demand such as occurs during heavy intoxication. Perivascular fibrosis prevents adequate coronary vasodilation thereby producing myocardial ischaemia (Lieber, 1982). According to the Royal College of Physicians (1987), 80% of individuals with cardiomyopathy who continue to drink are dead within three years of the diagnosis being made. In one study, total abstinence was related to long term survival in 80% of non-smoking patients (De Makis et al., 1974).

Coronary heart disease

While there is little doubt that chronic daily consumption of large amounts of alcohol (more than 10 drinks) causes severe heart disease, evidence has emerged that low to moderate regular intake may be protective against coronary heart disease. Attention has been drawn to the low rates of coronary artery disease in France, which has a high per capita consumption of alcohol. Marmot, Rose, Shirley, and Thomas (1981) provided direct evidence of this association. They conducted a longitudinal study of 1422 male civil servants aged between 40 and 64 working in the greater London area. Food and alcohol intake were measured by a self-report dietary record administered between 1967 and 1969. Ten years later, relative risk of mortality was calculated for subjects consuming various amounts of alcohol per day. There was a quadratic (U-shaped) curve of relative risk, non-drinkers and those drinking more than four drinks per day being at significantly higher risk. Of particular relevance here was the finding that relative risk of mortality from cardiovascular disease was actually lower for drinkers than for non-drinkers. Figure 2.1 shows that there was higher risk of cardiovascular mortality in non-drinkers and higher risk of non-cardiovascular mortality in those drinking more than four drinks per day. These findings were independent of confoundings such as cigarette smoking, hypertension, plasma cholesterol, and level of employment.

Several concerns were raised about these findings and the implication that the population should be advised to drink for the good of their coronary arteries. Marmot and Brunner (1991) have recently summarised the

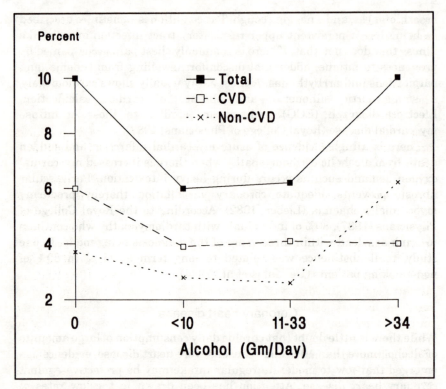

FIG. 2.1. Ten-year mortality (age-adjusted %)—all causes; cardiovascular (CVD) and non-cardiovascular (non-CVD) causes—according to daily alcohol consumption (from Alcohol and Mortality: A U-shaped Curve by Marmot M, et al. (1981), *Lancet, i,* pp. 580–582. Copyright © 1981 Lancet Inc. Reprinted with permission).

various objections. The first issue is primarily methodological: Do individuals who find that they are at risk "migrate" to the non-drinking category thereby spuriously inflating the mortality risk of non-drinkers? This migration may include those who never drank due to poor health as well as former heavy drinkers. In addition to this objection, there is the possibility that non-drinkers are an abnormal group in a society in which alcohol consumption is the norm. Yet another concern relates to the accuracy of the drinking data obtained. These objections have recently been addressed in a number of well designed epidemiological studies.

Jackson, Scragg, and Beaglehole (1991) retrospectively studied the drinking habits of all patients in Auckland, New Zealand, who had suffered myocardial infarction or had died from coronary heart disease over a 2-year period. Results indicated that the usual risk factors for coronary heart disease, such as smoking, hypertension, and low level of exercise, were operating. However, the 359 men with myocardial infarction and the 249 men who had died from coronary heart disease were more likely never to have been drinkers than their controls. In all of the "currently drinking" categories, weekly amounts of up to 56 drinks were associated with reduced risk. The small number of women drinkers precluded detailed analysis of their data.

Further evidence of the inverse relationship between alcohol consumption and the risk of coronary artery disease comes from a large prospective study of 51,519 male health professionals in the United States (Rimm et al., 1991). Care was taken to control for the effects of diet and other risk factors such as smoking and pre-existing diseases. At follow-up, 2 years after collection of data on the subjects' dietary habits of the previous 10 years, there had been 350 incident coronary events. Alcohol intake was inversely related to risk of non-fatal myocardial infarction and also to death from coronary artery disease. Exclusion of "non-drinkers" and of "reducers" did not alter these results. In another large prospective study of 123,840 subjects in which there were 1002 cardiovascular deaths, Klatsky, Armstrong, and Friedman (1990) found similar results. Although alcohol consumption was positively correlated with hypertension, cardiomyopathy, and haemorrhagic cardiovascular disease, it was found to be negatively associated with coronary artery disease. In this study, the protective effects of alcohol were present in both men and women. Similar findings have been reported by Bottetta and Garfinkle (1990) in their prospective study of 276,802 males over a 12-year period between 1959 and 1971. It is now possible to conclude that methodological issues such as group assignment biases and inadequate measurement methods cannot account for the findings. Study results are consistent despite a wide range of means of assessing alcohol intake, and specific control for the effects of heavy drinkers who move to the non-drinker category because of health problems. The empirical evidence currently available suggests that one or two drinks per day reduces the risk of coronary heart disease.

The mechanism for this protective effect has been the subject of considerable speculation. Psychological explanations have focused on the stress-relieving effects of alcohol but at a biochemical level most authors implicate the positive association of alcohol intake with high density lipoprotein (HDL) concentration. HDL is known to be positively associated with reduced risk of coronary heart disease (Ballantyne, Clark, Simpson, & Ballantyne, 1982; Miller & Miller, 1975; Stampfer et al., 1991). Jackson et al. (1991) demonstrated a significant positive correlation between alcohol consumption and HDL concentration in both men and women. This relationship, however, could explain only part of the protective effect and the authors suggested that the influence of alcohol on platelet aggregation and fibrinogen concentration might also contribute.

The evidence that having two drinks per day is associated with no cardiovascular harm and may in fact be protective against coronary heart disease has rather interesting public health implications. Marmot and Brunner (1991, p. 567) argued that a "public health recommendation that emphasised the positive effects of alcohol would be likely, however, to do more harm than good". They noted that above two drinks per day there is evidence of increased risk of biological and social harm, and that there is a strong correlation between the mean per capita consumption in a population and the prevalence of heavy drinking. The implication is clear: Anything that increases the mean level of consumption may increase the prevalence of harmful levels of intake. They concluded that the balance of harm and benefit does not encourage the recommendation that the public should drink to protect their hearts.

Blood pressure

Since the late 1970s it has generally been recognised that excessive alcohol consumption is the most common identifiable cause for the elevation of blood pressure in hypertensive patients. Almost every large population study has demonstrated an association between blood pressure and reported alcohol intake (Beevers, 1977; Klatsky, Freidman, Sieglaub, & Gérard, 1977). Laboratory studies have shown that administration of moderate doses of alcohol to normotensive subjects can elevate blood pressure for some hours (Potter, Watson, Skan, & Beevers, 1986) and this effect is exaggerated in hypertensive patients (Potter, McDonald, & Beevers, 1986). At above two or three standard drinks per day (20 to 25g) there is a steady positive relationship between alcohol intake and hypertension. Klatsky et al. (1977) reported that only about 10% of abstainers and light drinkers (more than 2.5 drinks) had raised blood pressure, whereas more than 20% of heavy drinkers were hypertensive.

Clinical studies have shown that significantly raised blood pressure is three times more common in clinic-referred alcohol abusers than it is in the general population. Subsequent abstinence lowers diastolic pressure by up to 10 mmHg (Royal College of Physicians, 1987). Raised blood pressure places some alcohol abusers at a greatly increased risk of stroke (Kannel, Wolf, Verter, & McNamara, 1970; Gill et al., 1991).

ALCOHOL AND THE DIGESTIVE TRACT

Drinking alcohol alters function at most levels of the digestive tract and chronic heavy intake is associated with many adverse effects. Continuous local irritation of the oesophagus damages the mucosa and this is thought to be the mechanism of increased risk of oesophageal cancer in chronic alcoholics. When present, oesophogeal reflux enhances the irritant effect of alcohol by exposing the digestive tract to acid, pepsin, and bile. Reduced lower sphincter pressure is also a common problem and associated peptic oesophagitis a frequent clinical finding.

Alcohol affects the rate of gastric activity and the nature of gastric secretions. Gastric activity is slowed and the gastric mucosa is altered in a number of ways including reduced production of gastric mucus, changes in mucosal blood flow, and diverse cellular changes. The consequences such as superficial ulceration and mucosal erythema are thought to result from the operation of a number of factors, but the precise mechanism of chronic gastritis in alcohol abusers is unknown.

Upper gastrointestinal bleeding in alcohol abusers

It is generally agreed that upper gastrointestinal bleeding is very common in middle-aged and older alcoholics. It is no longer thought that blood in the urine and faeces of these patients is due to peptic ulceration. Instead, several large studies employing endoscopy have now shown that haemorrhagic gastritis (due to acute gastric mucosal lesions) is the predominant cause. Rates of haemorrhagic gastritis of up to 36% have been reported in chronic alcohol abusers and there are several other sources of upper gasatrointestinal bleeding. These include permanent dilation of veins in the oesophagus, mucosal tears in the cardio-oesophageal area, duodenitis, oesophagitis, and chronic peptic ulcer (Lieber, 1982).

Effects of alcohol on the small intestine and colon

Alcohol taken chronically in large doses has both direct and indirect effects on intestinal function. These factors interact to contribute to altered intestinal function and malabsorption, as is shown in Fig. 2.2. In terms of direct effects, alcohol is absorbed rapidly from the stomach and upper small intestine where high concentrations are present for more than 60 minutes. There, it is rapidly absorbed into the blood but, in the meantime, it alters the metabolic balance of that region exerting a direct effect on cellular structure. There is some evidence (Lieber, 1982) that these changes may be reversed with abstinence.

Intestinal motility is affected. Type I—impeding waves—are diminished while Type II—propulsion waves—are enhanced. As a result, there is accelerated transport through the small intestine, an effect that may contribute to the diarrhoea present in many chronic alcohol abusers. To further exacerbate matters, intestinal absorption is affected by a number of mechanisms. Cell membrane transport is disrupted with increased fluidity and increased concentrations. There is associated malabsorption

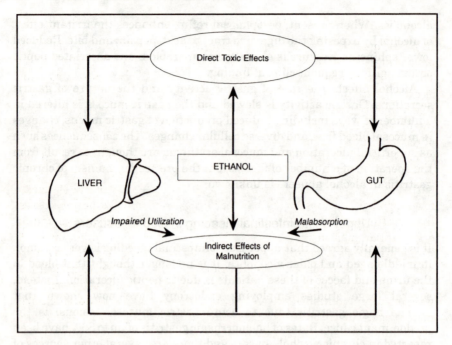

FIG. 2.2. Schematic illustration of the direct and indirect effects of alcohol on the liver and gut.

of lipids. Transport of sugar, amino acids, electrolytes, and water is inhibited, but the precise mechanisms of these changes are not completely understood. Vitamin transport and absorption are seriously affected by heavy alcohol ingestion. Thiamine, in low concentrations, is actively transported across the intestine whereas, at high concentrations, it diffuses passively. High concentrations of ethanol in the small intestine inhibit active transport but not passive diffusion. The implications of this for periodic binge drinkers who restrict their food intake are considerable. Malabsorption results from the combined effects of alcohol and the complications associated with alcoholism and the interested reader is referred to reviews by Burbige, Lewis, and Halsted (1984), and Lieber (1982), and to a recent comprehensive review by Persson (1991).

Finally, motility of the colon is altered by acute doses of alcohol and chronic alcohol abuse changes the histological and ultracellular appearances of the colon. The evidence of increased risk of colonic cancer in chronic alcohol abuse will be discussed below.

Alcoholic pancreatitis

In Western nations alcohol is an important cause in at least 50% of patients presenting with chronic pancreatitis (Royal College of Physicians, 1987). The first attack of alcoholic pancreatitis usually occurs after 10 to 20 years of heavy drinking and is more common in those over the age of 40 years. It is a condition that produces severe and constant pain poorly localised in the upper abdomen, radiating to the back. The pattern of onset is usually of recurrent attacks precipitated by heavy intake and these may occur at intervals of weeks or months. They tend to become more frequent but less severe, but this is not indicative of decreasing severity of the underlying pathophysiology. In severe attacks, which may persist for 2 to 4 weeks, fever develops within a few days. Complications include kidney abscesses, liver dysfunction, disturbances in coagulation, hypoglycaemia, spreading organ inflammation, and disturbed mental state (Benjamin, Imrie, & Blumgart, 1977). A mortality rate of up to 30% has been reported in severe attacks. As the disorder becomes more chronic, further complications emerge. These include diabetes and malabsorption, and the result is a weakened, malnourished state, the outcome of which may be death in early middle age. The chronic form may follow insidious onset with few, if any, acute inflammatory episodes to bring the disorder to medical attention.

The actual mechanisms of alcoholic pancreatitis are not well known. It is thought that repeated insults from heavy alcohol intake alter the function of the sphincter of Oddi, change metabolism within the pancreas and increase the action of pancreatic enzymes. This process has been described as overcoming the ability of the pancreas to resist autodigestion. In the terminal stage of the illness pseudocysts requiring surgical drainage may develop. The rupture of such a cyst may produce pancreatic ascites which will also require surgical intervention (Benjamin et al., 1977).

Clinical studies suggest that those who abstain from alcohol after an acute attack have a good prognosis and a survival rate of 90%. On the other hand, patients over 55 years of age with the chronic form usually experience severe complications and die within 10 years. Unfortunately, it is this group that is most resistant to treatment of their problem drinking.

ALCOHOL AND THE ENDOCRINE AND REPRODUCTIVE SYSTEMS

There is a large literature on the effects of alcohol on the endocrine system where much of the intermediary metabolism of the substance occurs (Lieber, 1982). The effects are mediated by the presence of liver damage and the nutritional status of the patient. Some of the most notable effects are on sexual functioning and the reproductive system. Alcohol, and its direct metabolite acetaldehyde, are gonadal-toxic in both laboratory animals and humans. Decreased levels of plasma testosterone have been reported following alcohol ingestion. Persistent heavy drinking can lead to long-lasting effects on the testes, ovaries, hypothalamus, and the pituitary gland (Morgan, 1982a). In male patients with alcoholic cirrhosis, hypogonadism, loss of libido, and feminisation are often reported. In women these effects are manifest as menstrual disorders, breast shrinkage, and a range of signs of defeminisation. Russell (1982) has indicated that, in women of child-bearing age, alcohol abuse produces a range of reproductive problems, with lowered fertility and increased rates of spontaneous abortion and stillbirth as part of a spectrum that includes the fetal alcohol syndrome. Little is known about the extent to which such reproductive system changes are reversible; however, Morgan (1982b) has reported increased sperm counts in previously infertile men who cease drinking.

Chronic alcohol abuse is also associated with adrenocortical activation, and physical changes resembling those of Cushing's syndrome have been reported. Plasma and urine cortisol levels are raised and the daily rhythm of secretion is lost. There is some evidence that these abnormalities are reduced by abstinence. Signs of thyroid overactivity are also often observed as is increased urinary excretion of calcium and magnesium. Hypoglycaemia is a common finding in hospitalised alcoholics and has been associated with cirrhosis. The implications for bone growth and skeletal abnormalities are quite significant. There is decreased bone mass, increased incidence of fractures, decreased bone density, rickets with bone softening and there are also metabolic and necrotic bone changes. Another common finding is that the endocrine pancreas is affected by alcohol abuse (Royal College of Physicians, 1987). Severe hypoglycaemia may follow within 6 to 36 hours of an alcoholic binge that is not accompanied by adequate food intake. Coma and death may ensue due to potentiation of insulin in conjunction with alteration of carbohydrate metabolism. The production of glycogen from sugar, which is suppressed by alcohol, cannot keep pace with peripheral glucose utilisation. This process will be potentiated when there is significant liver dysfunction due to fatty liver or cirrhosis. The presence of diabetes mellitus, which is potentiated by alcoholic pancreatitis, will compound the clinical picture. These processes are complex and interrelated and the effects of chronic alcohol abuse on the endocrine system are severe. There are many gaps in our knowledge and the incidence, risk factors, and prognosis are not well established.

ALCOHOL AND CANCER

The extent to which low and moderate consumption of alcohol places drinkers at increased risk of cancer has been a matter of some controversy. The debate has focused on the validity of the argument that social drinkers are at increased risk (Anderson, 1989). After assessing the available evidence, Turner and Anderson (1990) concluded that the positive association reported between alcohol and cancer is valid and may be dose related. They argued that the association is particularly marked for cancers of the upper digestive tract and also the upper respiratory tract. Alcohol consumption has also been implicated in the aetiology of cancers of the stomach, pancreas, large bowel, thyroid, and breast; we have already discussed hepatocellular carcinoma (hepatoma), which is associated with cirrhosis itself and is nearly always an alcohol-related disorder (International Agency for Research on Cancer, 1988). Some have claimed that the conclusion that alcoholic beverages are carcinogenic to humans is not wholly justified, particularly when applied to the vast numbers of drinkers who regularly consume small or moderate quantities. On the other hand, it may be argued that in common cancers, such as cancer of the breast, even a very slight increase in risk would be associated with a significant increase in incidence. The association between alcohol and breast cancer will be discussed later.

Several carcinogenic mechanisms of alcohol have been postulated, the first of which involves the presence of carcinogenic substances in certain alcoholic beverages. These include nitrosamines, polycyclic hydrocarbons, fusel oils, and asbestos fibres, all of which have been found in various alcoholic drinks. The bulk of this evidence comes from regions where large quantities of locally produced beverages are consumed by the population. In certain areas of France, high incidence of oesophageal cancer has been linked to locally made ciders, brandies, beer, wine, and liqueurs. Overall, the evidence linking alcohol and cancers of the upper alimentary and upper respiratory tracts indicates that alcohol exerts a co-carcinogenic effect with cigarette smoking. It has been suggested that the combined risk associated with drinking and smoking is greater that the sum of the two separate risks (Turner & Anderson, 1990).

The two most likely mechanisms of alcoholic carcinogenesis are cytotoxicity and microsomal enzyme induction (Lieber, 1982). The first of these is supported by the strong evidence linking cancer in heavy drinkers with body areas and systems in which exogenous alcohol is present in high concentrations. There is also evidence that when alcohol causes mucosal or tissue damage, such as in gastritis or cirrhosis, cancers follow. The second mechanism, the microsomal biotransformation system, is thought to be operating at sites that are not exposed to high concentrations (e.g.

breast cancer). This enzyme system promotes the conversion of many chemicals to mutagens and carcinogens, and its activity is significantly enhanced by chronic alcohol abuse. Experimental studies have found evidence of such processes in the liver, lung, intestine, and other tissues (Turner & Anderson, 1990).

It is not yet known whether alcohol is the initiator of carcinogenic effects or if it acts as a postinduction promoter. It has been argued that nutritional deficits and immune system depression, both of which are associated with chronic alcohol abuse, are the primary causes of the increased risk of a broad range of cancers in this population. A great deal is yet to be learned about the mechanisms by which alcohol exerts carcinogenic effects.

Alcohol and breast cancer

Breast cancer is a common condition, affecting more than one in ten women in the United States (Seidman, Stellman, & Mushinski, 1982). For this reason, intense efforts have been directed at determining the risk factors of this often fatal disease. Evidence for an association with alcohol is of particular interest because, unlike other cancers where there is a known risk factor, alcohol does not reach breast tissue in high concentrations. Longnecker, Berlin, Orza, and Chalmers (1988) undertook a meta-analysis of studies on alcohol consumption and breast cancer conducted up to 1987. In pooled data from case-control and cohort studies they found relative risks of 1.4 and 1.7, respectively, in those drinking more than two drinks per day. Lowenfels and Zevola (1989) analysed reports published between 1974 and 1987 dealing with alcohol and breast cancer. They reported that although the increased risk was consistent, temporally related, and dose dependent, its magnitude was slight (relative risk or odds ratio < 2). In addition, most subjects with breast cancer consumed low levels of alcohol, which raises questions about the biological plausibility of the presumed effect. They concluded that to reduce the risk further, abstinence from alcohol would need to be recommended and that the strength of the data did not justify this conclusion.

Results of two large case-control studies have added to the picture. Sneyd, Paul, Spears, and Skegg (1991) found that, for women consuming more than 14 drinks per week, the relative risk of cancer of the breast was 1.8. Former heavy drinkers were also at a slightly increased risk. Howe et al. (1991) provided further evidence of an association. When data from studies conducted in Argentina, Australia, Canada, Greece, and Italy were combined they showed that the risks were negligible for low to moderate consumers but that above five drinks per day, women were at increased risk (relative risk 1.69).

Although the relative risk of breast cancer associated with regular consumption of small amounts of alcohol can be considered modest, it is nevertheless important when one considers the number of people affected and the fact that drinking habits are modifiable. It is likely that controversy will continue to afflict public policy on this matter, as it does in other areas where market freedom and potential risk to society meet head on and where governments take significant revenue from purchase of the product in question.

ACUTE EFFECTS OF ALCOHOL ON THE NERVOUS SYSTEM

In this section and the next, the effects of alcohol on the nervous system are introduced from a largely clinical perspective. The neurological disorders attributable to alcohol abuse are:

1. Alcohol intoxication.
2. Acute alcohol-induced memory loss ("blackout").
3. Idiosyncratic (pathological) intoxication.
4. Tolerance, neuroadaptation, and alcohol dependence syndrome.
5. Alcohol withdrawal syndrome (tremor, hallucinosis, seizures, delirium tremens).
6. Alcoholic cerebellar atrophy.
7. Alcoholic polyneuropathy (peripheral neuropathy)
8. Alcohol amnesic disorder (Wernicke-Korsakoff syndrome).
9. Alcoholic dementia.
10. Hepatic encephalopathy

The focus in this section is on the acute effects of intoxication and withdrawal.

Alcohol intoxication

The acute neurological effects of alcohol begin with excitement and end with stupor or coma. There is a continuous spectrum of effects that correlate well with blood alcohol concentration. The behavioural expression of these effects is, however, modified by the rapidity of increase in blood alcohol level, history of alcohol intake, and the psychosocial setting in which consumption occurs. The genetic makeup of the individual, their culture, and the presence of other central nervous system depressants or their metabolites may also contribute. Table 2.1 presents a general description of the acute effects of exposure to various blood alcohol levels. These are averages about which there is a large degree of variation

TABLE 2.1
Effects and Blood Alcohol Level (BAL) of Specific Quantities of Alcohol
Intake (from Royal College of Physicians, 1987)

Number of standard drinks	BAL (mg/ml)	Approximate amount in beverage form	Effects
2	30	Beer—1 pint Wine—2 glasses Spirits—2 glasses	Reduced care and vigilance
5	80	Beer—2.5 pints Wine—5 glasses Spirits—5 glasses	Impaired ability to operate machinery or drive a vehicle
12	200	Beer—6 pints Wine—2 750ml bottles Spirits—12 glasses	Speech and motor impairment, double vision, memory loss, belligerence
24	400	Beer—12 pints Wine—4 750ml bottles Spirits—1 750ml bottle	Sleepiness, coma

associated with gender, body mass, setting, and drinking history. For example, frequent consumers of excessive amounts of alcohol may remain "sober" when exposed to blood alcohol levels exceeding 100mg/10ml (Buck & Harris, 1991). At this blood alcohol level, naive drinkers are severely affected.

Generally speaking, alcohol acts as a central nervous system (CNS) depressant in a way that is analogous to, but slower than, anaesthetic agents such as the barbiturates (Lishman, 1987). The excitability observed during the early phases of heavy consumption is thought to result from alcohol's depressant effects on the reticular activating system, which is known to exert inhibitory control over the cortex. Reduction of this inhibition increases excitation of the cortex.

The behavioural and emotional effects occurring during the early stages of intoxication include exhilaration, loss of restraint, decreased self-awareness, and for some, anxiety reduction. Improvements in social interaction may result, but are short-lived if rapid consumption continues, and may be followed by loquaciousness, mood swings, and emotional outbursts. At this stage, a number of cognitive and psychomotor impairments can be detected. There is a decreased sensitivity in fine discrimination, judgement is impaired, and concentration and memory are adversely affected. Complex thinking is affected first, but, as blood alcohol level increases, even simple behaviour becomes slowed and inaccurate. Peterson, Rothfleisch, Zelazo, and Pihl (1990) found impairment on a range of neuropsychological tests in student subjects administered high doses of alcohol (blood alcohol concentrations of 0.083 to 0.103), but not in subjects exposed to lower doses (0.002 to 0.044). Cognitive skills associated with the prefrontal and temporal cortex were differentially affected and the results could not be accounted for by expectancy effects. On the other hand, Laberg and Loberg (1989) found that subjects exposed to blood alcohol concentrations of 0.07 were prone to manipulations of expectancy. Furthermore, expectancy and tolerance effects interacted in a complex fashion to impair sensorimotor co-ordination. Expectations of alcohol affected the performance of severely dependent alcoholics compared to that of soft drinks whereas moderately dependent subjects showed the opposite pattern. The effect of intoxication on psychomotor and cognitive performance is complex and will be discussed in Chapter 7.

The physical effects of alcohol in the early stages of acute intoxication are less easily detected. Strength and rapidity of spinal reflexes increase, pupils are dilated and at increasing doses, nystagmus (rapid involuntary oscillation of the eyes), and diplopia (double vision) occur. Slurred speech and motor inaccuracy with loss of balance appear later in this phase. At low blood alcohol levels only some of the effects described above may be seen and, as we have mentioned, their presentation will be modified by psychosocial factors. As the level increases to 150–200mg/100ml, most of the features become apparent. By this later stage it is thought that direct toxic effects are operating on cortical neurons. There is progressive drowsiness with continued consumption and ever increasing blood alcohol concentration; this finally leads to coma. Hyporeflexia is followed by loss of the reflexes, and the pupils become constricted or terminally dilated and fixed. Respiration is depressed and blood pressure low, and body temperature is abnormally low. The significance of these effects depends largely on the frequency, severity, and setting in which intoxication occurs (Lishman, 1987).

Prior to describing the mechanisms of the CNS effects of alcohol ingestion, it is necessary to mention two aspects of intoxication with significant forensic implications. The first of these is acute loss of memory for the period of intoxication and for a variable duration following it. The second is idiosyncratic or "pathological" intoxication.

Acute alcohol-induced memory loss

Any impairment of consciousness, regardless of cause, will be associated with impairment of memory. When severe alcohol intoxication is involved, such amnesic episodes have been referred to as alcoholic "blackouts" (Goodwin, Crane, & Guze, 1969a,b). On some occasions these amnesic periods will be fragmentary, with the patient remaining unaware of the memory loss until it is reported to them. During other "blackouts" there may be associated fugue-like behaviour, the subject regaining awareness some distance from home with no memory of how they got there (Lishman, 1987). Although we have discussed "blackouts" as an acute effect of alcohol intoxication, this phenomenon usually occurs only in those who have been drinking heavily for a number of years. Jellinek (1952) linked it to the development of alcoholism and considered it to be a prodromal sign. It is generally agreed, however, that blackouts are directly associated with the severity of alcohol dependence and there is evidence that they are more likely to occur when there is a rapid rate of increase of blood alcohol concentration. In this regard, the consumption of large amounts of spirits has been associated with the disorder in clinical studies. While both psychodynamic and psychosocial explanations (i.e. repression and malingering) have been offered, the experimental evidence favours an organic cause. The considerable literature on state-dependent learning effects, and the effects of repeated intoxication on volunteers and alcoholics, provide the most convincing evidence of this. Furthermore, there is clinical evidence that persons with diffuse brain injury are more prone to both intoxication and alcohol-induced amnesia.

Idiosyncratic (pathological) intoxication

When alcohol consumption is followed by sudden uncontrollable outbursts of belligerent, combative behaviour that is unusual and out of character for that individual, the label "pathological intoxication" or something similar is applied. This is meant to indicate that the behaviour is out of proportion to both the amount of alcohol consumed and to the setting in which it occurs. Although there is little available literature on this subject, it remains of interest, clinically and forensically, because it suggests that the individual is affected beyond their control in a way that they could not reasonably have expected. In his review, Coid (1979) found little evidence to support the notion that such reactions occur after consumption of small amounts of alcohol by previously stable persons. There is some clinical evidence, however, that persons with pre-existing brain damage may react in this way and it is well known that such individuals are unduly prone to intoxication. The topic of idiosyncratic or pathological intoxication requires further research.

Mechanisms of the acute neurological effects
of alcohol

As the abnormalities of acute alcohol intoxication are reversible with no apparent structural changes occurring, they may be classified among the metabolic encephalopathies (Lishman, 1987). The abnormalities in this group are neurochemical and/or neurophysiological, and include hypoglycaemia and hepatic coma. The specific mechanisms are not well understood and several issues have been investigated. The first is whether it is alcohol or its metabolites that is responsible for the acute effects. Several lines of evidence suggest that alcohol itself is the toxin. These include the finding that very little metabolism of alcohol occurs in the brain, the rapidity with which the acute effects occur (before significant blood acetaldehyde levels are reached), the fact that acute effects occur even when alcohol metabolism is blocked, and evidence that the other metabolite—acetate—has little effect. It should, however, be noted that the effects of acetaldehyde have not been well studied. The second issue is the actual site at which alcohol acts to cause acute stimulatory effects. As the acute effects of alcohol involve disturbance of level of consciousness, it has been assumed that the areas of the brain implicated in the modulation of consciousness are involved; these are, however, not well defined. They may include the reticular activating system, the cortex, and subcortical regions, probably in some balanced interaction. Some reviewers (e.g. Lishman, 1987) have suggested that the reticular activating system is affected early, while the cerebral cortex, is involved later, at more severe levels of intoxication. There are at least two other possibilities: (1) alcohol may have a direct stimulant and then depressant effect on some brain regions; or (2) alcohol (or its derivatives) might act directly on a neurotransmitter system.

The more easily observed depressant effects have been subject to extensive research. Four possible mechanisms have been identified; (1) disturbance of normal energy metabolism; (2) changes in neuronal membrane composition; (3) alterations of ion transport; and (4) changes in neurotransmitter production and availability. There is good evidence that all membrane changes lead to decreases in normal Na^+ influx. This, in turn, decreases the action potential. Alcohol has also been shown to alter Ca^{2+} homeostasis and therefore disturb neuronal conductance and neurotransmitter release.

EFFECTS OF CHRONIC ALCOHOL CONSUMPTION ON THE NERVOUS SYSTEM

The effects of long-term alcohol consumption on the nervous system can be, somewhat arbitrarily, divided into three categories; (1) the effects of social drinking; (2) the effects of alcohol dependence; and (3) the outcome of decades of sustained alcohol abuse.

Tolerance

As we have already indicated, an early effect of regular intake of even moderate amounts of alcohol is the development of tolerance to its neurobehavioural effects. Prolonged frequent and excessive drinking permits an individual to remain relatively unaffected at blood alcohol concentrations that would be intoxicating for the naive drinker. Over time, similar doses exert reduced effects on the heavy drinker and, consequently, ever larger doses are consumed. The result is higher blood alcohol concentrations, maintained for longer periods; this increased exposure causes further damage to tissue and organs. The rate at which tolerance develops may be related to an individual's inherent tolerance, but, in the main part, appears to be determined by exposure to alcohol. Clinically, the heavy drinker manifests fewer central nervous system effects for a given blood alcohol level, and months of abstinence may be required to reverse this.

The mechanisms by which tolerance develops are not completely understood, but there are two known pathways. The first involves the increased rate at which alcohol is metabolised after prolonged exposure. That is, the induction of hepatic enzymes, as described earlier. The second mechanism involves changes in the target tissues in the receptor organ, in this case, neuroadaptation in the brain. The literature on neuroadaptive responses to chronic alcohol ingestion has recently been reviewed comprehensively by Buck and Harris (1991), who described five systems by which neural function is acutely affected by alcohol. It has been assumed that at least some of these are also operating in the development of chronic adaptation or tolerance. The research is complex but indicates that changes to various ion channels and cell membrane function are implicated. Some of the adaptive responses are thought to occur because of the actions of alcohol at the level of gene expression. Recently, Littleton (1989) has presented a neuronal hypothesis of alcohol intoxication and physical dependence that emphasises the role of inhibitory neurotransmitter system potentiation. In this model, frequent potentiation of the GABA inhibitory system results in neural adaptation that is expressed as tolerance and physical dependence.

At present, the major implication of the neuroadaptive responses referred to as tolerance is that they allow the body to be exposed to very large amounts of alcohol with drastic consequences. It is also important to mention that tolerance to other drugs may occur as a result of neuro-adaptation to alcohol. This cross-tolerance may reduce the therapeutic usefulness of a large number of other drugs (e.g. benzodiazepines, barbiturates) making their clinically safe dose range much narrower.

Dependence and withdrawal

Closely associated with the development of tolerance are the related clinical phenomena of alcohol dependence and withdrawal. The cellular adaptations resulting in tolerance to the acute effects of alcohol also result in a requirement for the presence of large amounts of alcohol for normal function. In other words, as the brain becomes increasingly adapted to the presence of large amounts of alcohol, the individual becomes dependent on exposure to alcohol to maintain neurobehavioural and emotional stability. A relative decrease in blood alcohol, and therefore brain alcohol level, produces clinically obvious withdrawal signs. In naive drinkers, individual differences are such that even after a single exposure, signs and reactions somewhat similar to a full withdrawal syndrome can be seen. These are usually hyperactivity, agitation, sleeplessness, and dysphoria. Mood during withdrawal may be extremely unpleasant and some evidence exists that there is an association between alcohol withdrawal states and homicide or suicide. Nevertheless, for most moderate drinkers, this state, which is usually referred to as a "hangover", is not severe and does not require medical attention. Its known cure is another dose of alcohol, and craving for a drink the morning after a heavy drinking session is one of a number of symptoms included in self-report measures for the assessment of the severity of drinking problems. In this approach to problem drinking, the symptoms and signs of alcohol withdrawal contribute to the "alcohol dependence syndrome" (Edwards, 1977). The major features of this syndrome are:

1. Narrowing of drinking repetoire.
2. Highly salient drink-seeking behaviour.
3. Increased tolerance to alcohol.
4. Repeated withdrawal symptoms.
5. Avoidance drinking, or drinking to relieve withdrawal.
6. Compulsion to drink.
7. Rapid reinstatement of dependence after abstinence.

These are discussed more fully in Chapter 3.

In heavy drinkers the nature and severity of the symptoms emerging during withdrawal are determined in large part by the quantity and frequency of recent drinking. The withdrawal syndrome may be severe and protracted, taking several days, and medical consultation is advisable. Perhaps the best clinical descriptions of the syndrome come from the work of Victor and Adams (1953). The symptoms are extremely unpleasant and, in the case of seizures and delirium tremens, may be life-threatening. There are four distinct symptoms of alcohol withdrawal that occur at different times after a reduction in blood alcohol level: (1) tremors (3–12 hours); (2) hallucinosis (3–12 hours); (3) seizures (12–48 hours); and (4) delirium tremens (3–4 days). Isbell et al. (1955) conducted an experimental investigation of the withdrawal syndrome in 10 subjects. Their findings have been of great assistance in understanding the time course and outcome of the symptoms. Lishman's (1987) review of the literature in the area from a clinical perspective is particularly useful.

If the alcohol intake of dependent patients is curtailed abruptly, they typically develop a withdrawal syndrome in which tremors, weakness, vomiting, hyper-reflexia, and fever occur. A smaller number will experience seizures, hallucinations (auditory and visual, occasionally tactile), and delirium tremens. The intensity of the withdrawal syndrome is related to the blood alcohol levels maintained prior to cessation. Very significant central nervous system changes correlate clinically with the severity of the withdrawal syndrome; within 20–30 hours, electroencephalographic (EEG) changes become apparent. There is diminished alpha activity followed by random spikes and occasional slow waves. Although sleep rhythms become normalised during repeated intoxication, on withdrawal of alcohol, there is rebound rapid eye movement (REM) sleep. Prior to the onset of delirium tremens, this can be almost continuous and Lishman (1987) has suggested that REM sleep may merge with wakefulness as a precursor of delerium tremens. It has also been suggested that chronic changes in neural excitability may be wrought by repeated episodes of alcohol withdrawal. Goddard, McIntyre, and Leech (1969) showed that repeated episodes of such subthreshold stimulation may lead to seizure disorders in experimental animals through a process referred to as "kindling". Lishman (1987, p. 512) has summarised the clinical relevance of such findings: "Long-term changes in neural excitability may accordingly underlie the progressive escalation of withdrawal symptoms from tremors, to seizures, and ultimately, delirium tremens".

Tremor and hallucinosis

Tremulousness is the most common withdrawal sign and it is usually associated with symptoms of weakness, irritability, and nausea. There is general alertness, craving for alcohol, and the individual is easily startled. Persistent tremor that particularly affects the upper limbs is the most easily observed sign and there is insomnia that requires sedation if the person is to sleep. About one-quarter of tremulous patients experience transitory misperceptions, including illusions and hallucinations. These are usually fleeting, occur in a clear sensorium, and last for between 1 and 4 days. Phenomena range from tinnitus (ringing in the ears), through visual flashes, to malignant and threatening verbalisations that the individual may answer back to or act upon; these may be accompanied by secondary explanatory delusions. These symptoms usually clear within a few days and although some may last for months, only a small proportion (<10%), persist as a schizophrenia-like illness. The greatest risk during this phase of withdrawal is that the patient will be injured accidentally by acting to avoid fearful internal stimuli, or that they will, in terror, commit suicide (Lishman, 1987).

Withdrawal seizures ("rum fits")

Within 12 to 48 hours of terminating a period of particularly heavy consumption, the long-term alcohol abuser may experience convulsions if appropriate prophylactic medication is not administered. Seizures occur in more than 10% of patients hospitalised for treatment of alcohol-related problems (Victor & Adams, 1953). As we have already mentioned, this usually occurs only after many years of severe alcohol abuse and it may be initiated not only by cessation of drinking but also by a relative fall in blood alcohol level. Such convulsions occur in persons without previous history, or with a tendency towards epilepsy. Although the EEG is abnormal during such seizures, it seems to return to normal afterwards. It is usual for "rum fits" to occur in bouts of one to half a dozen or so, but sometimes status epilepticus may occur. In about one-third of persons manifesting alcohol withdrawal convulsions, the syndrome will proceed to delirium tremens. It should be noted that "rum fits" are independent of the well-known tendency for individuals with epilepsy to experience seizures on the morning after an episode of heavy drinking (Lishman, 1987).

Delirium tremens

Literally a trembling and quaking delirium, this is the end stage and most severe aspect of the alcohol withdrawal syndrome. It occurs in about 5% of patients admitted for treatment of alcohol-related problems. The core symptoms are vivid hallucinations, delusions, tremor, agitation, and insomnia. Autonomic overactivity is manifested in tachycardia, sweating, and fever. Although there is seldom marked disturbance of consciousness, profound confusion is the norm. The clinical impression of sudden onset is inconsistent with the outcome of research indicating that there is a prodromal phase involving restlessness, insomnia, and fear. Initially, transient illusions and hallucinations occur in the context of retained insight but intense anxiety. As the disorder progresses, so does the severity of the mental and physical symptoms, until, eventually, it ends in prolonged sleep. Delirium tremens may last up to 3 days and only rarely recurs. It may mask a coexisting Wernicke's encephalopathy and if so, the patient may emerge with a profound amnesic disorder. Delirium tremens has a mortality rate of about 5%, usually due to cardiovascular collapse, infection, hyperthermia, or self-injury. Perhaps the most dramatic symptoms of delerium tremens are the bizarre illusions and hallucinations accompanying it. In the visual mode, these may involve animals or people, often of lilliputian dimensions, and sometimes involved in overactive and playful activities. Auditory perceptual disorders include accusatory verbalisations and, associated with the hallucinations, usually as secondary explanatory phenomena, are delusions. The associated emotional experiences consist of a paradoxical mixture of amusement and fear (Lishman, 1987). The mental phenomena are transitory and changeable, and speech may be slurred, dysphasic, and incoherent.

The pathophysiology of delirium tremens is not well known, although most authors agree that its onset is related to rapidly falling blood alcohol levels. On the other hand, the possibility that onset of the symptoms may encourage markedly reduced alcohol intake is difficult to exclude. Isbell et al. (1955) showed that the disorder can occur despite adequate nutrition. Severe liver damage is more common in alcoholic patients who develop the disorder than in those who do not. Lishman suggested that the cause is probably complex involving multiple metabolic and neurophysiological components and that a variety of different effects may combine to produce the same clinical picture in different patients.

Monitoring alcohol withdrawal

More than 20 scales have been developed to monitor and rate the severity of symptoms and signs prevalent during alcohol withdrawal (e.g. Foy, March, & Drinkwater, 1988; Gross, Lewis, & Nagarajan, 1973b; Shaw et al., 1981). Only a small number of these have adequate reliability and validity data. Their major application in research and clinical practice is in predicting when, and in what dose, tranquillising drugs should be given. This is no trivial task, as insufficient medication may not arrest the progression of the withdrawal syndrome and excessive medication will slow the process, increase the duration of hospitalisation, and delay entry into active treatment and rehabilitation programmes. Examination of the content of one these instruments provides a useful overview of the clinical effects of the alcohol withdrawal syndrome (Alcohol Withdrawal and Intoxication Scale [AWIS] items, adapted from Liskow et al., 1989, p.416):

1. eating disturbance;
2. nausea/vomiting;
3. tremors;
4. sweating;
5. sleep;
6. nightmares;
7. disorientation;
8. hallucinosis;
9. delusions;

10. quality of contact with assessor;
11. agitation;
12. temperature;
13. pulse;
14. convulsions;
15. drowsiness;
16. dysarthria;
17. ataxia;
18. nystagmus.

Liskow et al. (1989), showed that this scale had high clinical utility in measuring the course of alcohol withdrawal modified by the benzodiazepine, chlordiazepoxide. The authors concluded that the scale was valid, reliable, and sensitive enough to follow the course of their patients' clinical status. Furthermore, it was able to differentiate between the younger (21–33 years) and older (55–77 years) age groups, the latter showing more severe withdrawal effects and requiring larger doses of medication. Another scale, the Revised Clinical Institute Withdrawal Assessment for Alcohol scale (CIWA-Ar; Sullivan et al., 1989) has also been subject to considerable psychometric evaluation. It has been reduced to 10 items, thereby raising its clinical utility without sacrificing reliability or validity. The items, each assessed on an eight-point scale are: nausea and vomiting, tremor, paroxysmal sweats, anxiety, agitation, tactile disturbances, auditory disturbances, visual disturbances, headache, and orientation and clouding of sensorium.

Residual neurological disorders
in chronic alcohol abusers

Several residual neurological disorders are present in chronic alcohol abusers and persist beyond the period of detoxification and withdrawal (Charness, 1993). Their frequency in a particular study population depends largely on the setting, the subject selection procedures employed, and the diagnostic criteria applied. For example, in a recent study of 641 patients referred to an Australian neuropsychology unit for assessment of suspected alcohol-related brain damage, the frequency of disorders was as presented in Table 2.2 (Tuck & Jackson, 1991). These categories were not mutually exclusive, many patients having more than one of the disorders. In contrast, Foy, March, and Drinkwater (1988) found lower rates of seizures and Wernicke's encephalopathy (4% and 2.5% respectively) in a general hospital setting in Newcastle, Australia. Although the residual neurological disorders of chronic alcohol abuse have been well described clinically, good epidemiological data regarding them are not available.

TABLE 2.2

Incidence of Neurological Disorders in Cases
Referred for Neuropsychological Assessment

Neurological disorder	Percentage of patients
Cerebellar degeneration	38
Peripheral neuropathy	34
Seizures	14
Korsakoff's psychosis	8
Wernicke's encephalopathy	4
Dementia	4
Hepatic encephalopathy	2

From Social, neurological and cognitive disorders in
alcoholics, by R. Tuck and M. Jackson. Copyright © *The
Medical Journal of Australia*, 1991; 155: 225–229. Reprinted
with permission.

The 1970s and 1980s have seen very significant changes in the way that
the residual effects of alcohol abuse on the nervous system have been
studied. The focus of research has moved away from detection and
description of neurological disorders in alcoholics with lengthy histories of
alcohol dependence. The presence and rates of neuroradiologically defined
structural changes and neuropsychologically measured functional
impairments have become major topics of interest (Lishman, 1981).
Populations studied have included not only long-term alcohol abusers with
obvious neurological disorders, but also moderate and heavy social
drinkers. We will discuss the outcome of these investigations in Parts 2
and 3.

The best-researched neurological disorder associated with long-term
heavy alcohol abuse is the Wernicke–Korsakoff syndrome. This disorder
has been of particular interest to neuropsychologists because the Korsakoff
patient has a persistent and irreversible amnesic sydrome. The classic
features of an episode of Wernicke's encepalopathy include severe
confusion and disorientation, delerium, a staggering ataxic gait, and
oculomotor disturbances. The disturbances in eye gaze typical of the newly
admitted Wernicke patient are illustrated in Fig. 2.3. Oculomotor paralysis
and conjugate gaze disturbance respond well to vitamin treatment and are
rarely seen in Korsakoff patients.

When this acute, confused state resolves, many patients gradually
return to their premorbid level of functioning, but some are left with a
profound and dense amnesia, typically referred to as alcoholic Korsakoff's
syndrome. Korsakoff patients, although disoriented for time, are typically

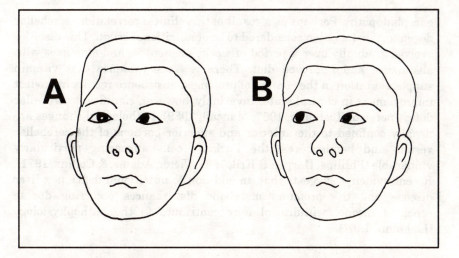

FIG. 2.3. Ocular palsy and gaze paralysis in a patient with Wernicke's encepalopathy. The patient has been instructed to look to the right. A: At time of admission. Paralysis of the right lateral rectus muscle prevents movement of the right eye. The underadduction of the left eye is a sign of gaze paralysis. B: After thiamine and glucose treatment, the signs of ophthalmoplegia have disappeared.

lucid and have no residual ocular problems. In the 1950s the link between these two disorders was recognised and Wernicke's encepalopathy came to be regarded as the acute precursor of Korsakoff's syndrome in chronically dependent alcoholics. Subsequent research has revealed a more complex relationship between chronic alcoholism, Wernicke's encephalopathy, alcoholic dementia, and Korsakoff's syndrome. This will be an issue considered in more detail when the Wernicke–Korsakoff syndrome is reviewed in Chapter 10.

In addition to the Wernicke–Korsakoff syndrome, there are several other residual neurological sequelae of nutritional deficiency in the context of severe chronic alcohol abuse: cerebellar degeneration, peripheral neuropathy, Marchiafava–Bignami disease, central pontine myelinosis, and amblyopia. Although the first two of these conditions are commonly found in chronic alcoholics, the last three conditions are rare.

Cerebellar degeneration

Chronic alcoholics often display a cerebellar syndrome comprising ataxia affecting mainly the lower limbs. This ataxia typically involves a wide-based "drunken" gait together with poor co-ordination of individual leg movements, and has usually been associated with Wernicke's encephalopathy. Perhaps as a result of this clinical correlation, cerebellar degeneration has been considered to be of nutritional origin. This disorder evolves gradually over a period of weeks or months, and stabilises with abstinence and improved diet. There is some evidence that vitamin supplementation in the context of prolonged abstinence results in modest improvement in clinical state. Invariably, however, significant cerebellar deficit persists (Lishman, 1987; Mancall, 1989). Pathological changes are usually confined to the anterior and superior portions of the cerebellar vermis and hemispheres, the Purkinje cells appearing particularly vulnerable (Phillips, Harper, & Kril, 1987; Victor, Adams, & Collins, 1971). Recent evidence suggests that, in addition to nutritional deficiency, liver disease and the profound metabolic disturbances occurring during repeated alcohol withdrawal may contribute to the pathophysiology (Lishman, 1987).

Peripheral neuropathy

This is perhaps the most frequently encountered and best known neurological disorder occurring in the context of chronic alcohol abuse (Strauss, 1935). Sensory and motor disturbances in the hands, feet, and legs are the most common features. Their distribution is usually symmetrical and their onset gradual. The disorder has been attributed to both nutritional deficiency and toxic effects of alcohol, but there is conclusive evidence for neither hypothesis (Messing & Greenberg, 1989). There is certainly strong clinical evidence that peripheral neuropathy commonly coexists with Wernicke's encephalopathy or Korsakoff's amnesic syndrome. Although the main deficiency is likely to be thiamine, as Lishman (1987) points out, neuropathy can result from deficiencies of other substances also (e.g. pyridoxine and pantothenic acid).

The clinical manifestations of this disorder range from subtle changes, such as the loss of ankle jerks, to disturbing sensory abnormalities, such as pain, burning sensations, numbness, and pins and needles. The knee and ankle reflexes may be lost and there may be muscle wasting and oedema in the same distribution as the sensory changes. Progression of alcoholic polyneuropathy can often be halted by abstinence and vitamin supplementation (Messing & Greenberg, 1989) and slow recovery can occur (Lishman, 1987).

Marchiafava–Bignami disease

This rare disease, which was first described in 1903 among Italian men, was thought to be associated mainly with the heavy consumption of wine. Now, however, it has been observed in persons drinking all kinds of alcoholic beverages. The clinical features of the disease are non-specific and include a variety of psychological symptoms such as dementia, aphasia, reduced attentiveness, and diminished ability to concentrate and to sustain mental activity. Associated signs are seizures, stupor, and coma. Motor signs are prominent and include heightened muscle tone, tremor, and paralysis (Lishman, 1987; Messing & Greenberg, 1989). The neuropathological lesions are patchy, diffuse necrotic changes and demyelination at the junction of the grey and white matter in the mid zone of the corpus callosum (Charness, 1993; Lishman, 1987). There are associated losses of neurons and myelinated fibres in the basal ganglia and cerebellum. Marchiafava–Bignami disease is usually progressive and the deficits irreversible (Messing & Greenberg, 1989), but the rate of progression is variable and remissions of symptoms have been observed (Lishman, 1987). The time course may usually be measured in months or years but death usually results from liver disease, infection, or some cause other than the neurological disorder.

Central pontine myelinosis

This disorder was first described by Adams, Victor, and Mancall (1959), who reported four cases. It presents as rapidly evolving flaccid quadriplegia with bulbar paralysis (Mancall, 1989). During the early stages, state of consciousness allows communication but the only remaining motor activity by which this may be achieved is movement of the eyelids. Later, vomiting, confusion, and coma are commonly seen (Lishman, 1987). Patients usually die within 3 weeks of onset, although Bearcroft et al. (1988) reported a case in which good functional recovery occurred. This 40-year-old patient presented after an alcoholic binge with poor nutrition in the context of many years of inadequate diet. He had a 12-day history of inability to walk or talk. There was severe spastic dysarthria, poor palatal movements, reduced gag reflex, and ataxic spastic quadriparesis; the patient was also emotionally labile.

The disorder not only occurs in the context of chronic alcoholic malnutrition but has also been observed in non-alcoholic patients with significant electrolyte imbalance. It has been suggested that there may be iatrogenic causes associated with rapid intravenous correction of fluid and electrolyte disturbances (Bearcroft et al., 1988; Mancall, 1989). The pathological lesions are essentially situated in the pyramidal tracts of the pons, and involve demyelinating processes. Characteristically, they are bilateral and symmetrical involving focal destruction of the ventral pons but in about 10% of cases they extend beyond this region (Messing & Greenberg, 1989).

Amblyopia

This is a rare disorder involving retrobulbar neuritis with optic nerve atrophy, colour blindness, and loss of acuity, that is most often found in malnourished alcoholics. In these instances, it is referred to as tobacco–alcohol amblyopia due to its clinical association with heavy smoking. While it may proceed to complete blindness, dimness of central vision is more commonly found (Lishman, 1987). The lesions responsible are thought to be mainly in the conductive pathways rather than the retinal nerve cells as in amblyopia of methyl alcohol toxicity (Mancall, 1989). The optic nerves, chiasm, and tracts are usually affected. There is usually significant improvement with the introduction of supplementary B-group vitamins, particularly thiamine and B_{12} (Lishman, 1987; Mancall, 1989). For this reason, many believe that ethyl alcohol or smoking are unlikely to play a direct toxic role in amblyopia. In a recent case report, Sivyer (1989) described significant clinical improvement in a 40-year-old patient in response to abstinence and nutritional treatment. This bricklayer was consuming 80 to 100 small bottles of beer (330ml) and smoking up to 80 cigarettes per day at the onset of the condition. His CT-scan showed evidence of cerebral shrinkage and there was no visual evoked potential on EEG testing. Improvement occurred despite the patient's continued heavy smoking.

Neurological effects of alcoholic liver disease

Although the profound effects of severe liver disease on neurological function have been known for more than 130 years, the more subtle, but more common effects of liver dysfunction on human mental performance have only been subjected to detailed study in recent years (Frierichs, 1858; Tarter et al., 1986). The hepatic encephalopathy resulting from severe liver disease has stages of both excitement and depression in which delirium and convulsions are followed by diminished consciousness and coma (Lockwood, 1989). In such cases, the neurological symptoms and jaundice associated with liver failure have closely related onset, the symptoms of nervous system dysfunction usually occurring within 8 weeks of those of liver disease. These examples of the neurological effects of severe terminal liver disease must be differentiated from the much more common and recently studied effects of chronic mild to moderate liver disease.

Preliminary findings suggested that the presence of cirrhosis was at least as important as a predictor of neuropsychological test performance as was history of drinking. Tarter et al. (1988) investigated this question by comparing the performance of alcoholics with cirrhosis, non-alcoholics with cirrhosis, and normal control subjects on a battery of 18 neuropsychological tests. Cirrhotic patients manifested a range of cognitive and visuomotor deficits, but a history of alcoholism did not contribute substantially to these impairments. In other words, the impairments observed were attributable to hepatic encephalopathy with no significant contribution of direct neurotoxic effects of alcohol.

Further evidence to support this position emerged from an interesting study by Arria, Tarter, Starzl, and Van Thiel (1991) who tested alcoholic patients before and after liver transplantation. The operative procedure involved replacement of the diseased liver with a functionally normal allograft. Alcoholic subjects and age- and sex-matched controls were tested on 16 neuropsychological measures prior to, and 1 year after the transplant surgery. The alcoholic liver transplant patients showed significant improvement on tests of psychomotor, visuopractic, and abstracting abilities, while the performance of the control subjects remained unchanged. The memory capacity of the transplant patients did not improve significantly, but the authors suggested that this may have been due to the lack of sensitivity of the tests employed.

To further examine the effect of cirrhotic liver disease on memory functioning, Arria, Tarter, Kabene, Laird, Moss, and Van Thiel (1991) administered a range of memory tests to alcoholics with and without cirrhosis, non-alcoholic cirrhotics, and healthy controls. Significant effects associated with both alcohol consumption and liver disease emerged. These results confirmed the earlier findings suggesting that neuropsychological deficits in chronic alcohol abusers may result from a combination of alcohol ingestion and liver disease.

In a recent review, Gallant and Head-Dunham (1991) concluded that non-cirrhotic liver disease was also associated with neuropsychological impairment. This impairment seems to be reversible, but significant correlation between such improvement and normalisation of liver function indices has not yet been reported.

Alcohol consumption and cerebrovascular disease

There has been considerable debate recently concerning the relationship between alcohol consumption and brain infarction due to ischaemic or haemorrhagic cerebrovascular disease. In a recent review, Hillbom and Kaste (1990) concluded that most of the evidence for this association has come from error-prone clinical studies. Results of such studies have suggested that there is an increased risk of brain infarction when more than 300g of alcohol is consumed each week (more than five standard drinks per day). In some of these studies, however, no increase in risk has been shown in regular heavy drinkers, but a binge drinking pattern has been associated with stroke. In an unpublished study of their own, Hillbom and Kaste found that consumption of more than 10 drinks above the usual intake, occurring within 24 hours of the onset of brain infarction, was a significant risk factor in patients aged between 16 and 49 years.

Several mechanisms may give rise to an increased risk. As we have mentioned, alcohol abuse is correlated positively with the development of arterial hypertension which is perhaps the most important risk factor for stroke in the middle aged. Alcohol is also known to affect clotting functions under certain circumstances and heavy drinkers are prone to deep vein thrombosis. Both of these alcohol-related changes increase the risk of brain infarction. Furthermore, cycles of heavy drinking and withdrawal cause fluctuations in platelet function, which also contribute to abnormalities in bleeding and clotting variables. The effects of alcohol abuse on the heart also place the chronic heavy drinker at increased risk of stroke. Alcoholic cardiomyopathy may give rise to emboli, and atrial fibrillation during binge drinking may dispatch thrombi to the brain. Spontaneous or trauma-induced damage to carotid and vertebral arteries has been observed in alcohol-abusing haemorrhagic stroke patients. Finally, heavy drinking is associated with habitual cigarette smoking and it is possible that the combined effect of both of these is greater than the sum of their independent contributions to risk of stroke. In concluding their review, Hillbom and Kaste (1990) suggested that, while it is highly probable that alcohol abuse and binge drinking are risk factors for stroke, all criteria for identifying a causal relationship had not yet been met.

In contrast to the above findings, the results of recent carefully controlled clinical and epidemiological studies have suggested that low doses of alcohol may exert a protective effect against occlusive brain infarction.   Table 2.3 reports the relative risks of haemorrhagic and ischaemic brain infarction associated with various levels of alcohol consumption in patients hospitalised for stroke (Gill et al., 1991; Klatsky, Armstrong, & Friedman, 1990). It should be noted that, in both studies, the alcohol consumption data was collected retrospectively by interviewing patients and their relatives. The validity and reliability of this method has been criticised, but in studies such as these there are few options available for collecting this kind of data. In general, the results of these studies suggest that moderate alcohol consumption (less than three drinks per day) is protective against stroke in comparison with abstaining from alcohol. Beyond this level, however, the risk of haemorrhagic infarction begins to increase and, above seven drinks per day, it is markedly elevated.

Recent reviews of the epidemiological evidence regarding alcohol consumption and stroke have reached similar conclusions. In a comprehensive review, Camargo (1989) concluded that, despite methodological problems, the epidemiological evidence suggested that moderate alcohol consumption reduces risk of ischaemic stroke (i.e.

TABLE 2.3
Relative Risks for Brain Infarction Associated with Various Levels of
Alcohol Consumption in Two Controlled Clinical Studies

Author	Type of stroke	Abst.	Level of alcohol consumption		
			< 20g/day	20–70g/day	> 70g/day
Gill et al. (1991)	SAH	1.00	0.70	0.50	1.30
	ICH	1.00	0.60	0.50	2.50
	CI	1.00	0.60	0.70	2.40
		Abst.	Former	<10g/day	10–20g/day	> 30g/day
Klatsky et al. (1990)	Haemorrhage	1.00	0.78	0.85	0.75	1.38
	Occlusion	1.00	0.97	0.63	0.54	0.44

Abst., Abstinent; CI, cerebral infarction; ICH, intracerebral haemorrhage; SAH, subarachnoid haemorrhage

occlusion) but increases the risk of haemorrhagic stroke (i.e. subarachnoid and intracerebral haemorrhage). The influence of possible "effect modifiers" has, according to Camargo (1989), yet to be researched adequately. In a similar vein, Gorelick (1989, p. 1609) concluded his review by stating: "The weight of evidence suggests that excess alcohol consumption is a risk factor for both ischaemic and haemorrhagic cerebrovascular disease, whereas moderate alcohol consumption may exert a protective effect similar to that proposed for coronary artery disease".

Summary of effects of alcohol on the nervous system

A wide range of neurological disorders have been attributed to the primary and secondary effects of alcohol abuse. Tolerance or neuroadaptation to the effects of regular drinking develops rapidly and, in heavy drinkers, stable neurological and emotional functioning depends upon the ingestion of alcohol. The greater the regular dose, the more severe the withdrawal symptoms when ingestion of alcohol is curtailed abruptly. Withdrawal symptoms are predictable in long-term heavy drinkers and require medical intervention in a significant proportion of cases.

Concepts applied to the residual neurological effects of alcohol abuse have changed markedly in the last decade or two. It is now recognised that heavy social drinkers may suffer partially reversible structural and functional neurological changes that might not be readily apparent (Grant, Reed, & Adams, 1987). On the other hand, light social drinkers may benefit from the reduced risk of occlusive stroke compared with abstainers.

Permanent irreversible and severe brain damage is suffered by a small, but significant proportion of chronic abusers. These are usually the heaviest drinkers, who also have episodes of nutritional deficiency. The longer and more severe the abuse pattern, the more likely such damage is to occur. The causes of such damage are probably multiple and include neurotoxic effects of alcohol; nutritional deficiency; dysfunction secondary to metabolic, cardiovascular and cerebrovascular changes; and cerebral trauma.

EFFECTS OF PRENATAL MATERNAL ALCOHOL CONSUMPTION ON OFFSPRING

In their historical review, Warner and Rosett (1975) noted that drinking during pregnancy has been known to effect the development of the fetus since the time of the early Greek physicians. Russell (1982) and other authors have drawn attention to the epidemiological significance of the London Gin Epidemic of 1765–1785, when gin prices became particularly low. Throughout this period of plentiful crops and absence of epidemic diseases, neonatal and infant mortality rates were high. Given this lengthy history, it is somewhat surprising that early reports associating alcohol ingestion with adverse pregnancy outcomes met with such controversy when published in the 1970s.

Modern recognition of the adverse effects of maternal alcohol abuse has been attributed to Ulleland (1972) and to Jones and Smith (1973), whose early studies contained descriptions of a variety of abnormalities present in children whose mothers were diagnosed alcoholics and who were thought to have been drinking heavily during pregnancy. The abnormalities now given the label fetal alcohol syndrome (FAS) and sometimes alcohol embryopathy (e.g. Majewski & Goeke, 1982) include pre- and postnatal growth retardation below the 10th percentile, neurological abnormalities including developmental delays with or without intellectual impairment, and characteristic craniofacial anomalies, such as microcephaly, deformity of the eyes and eyelids, nose and central face, poor formation of the lips, and large, low-set ears. The characteristic facial deformities are illustrated in Fig. 2.4. Associated congenital abnormalities involving the heart, kidneys, and musculoskeletal system are among other anomalies reported in FAS.

When isolated anomalies and neurobehavioural disorders occur in children of alcohol abusing mothers in the absence of the dysmorphologies and other features of the complete syndrome, the term "Fetal alcohol

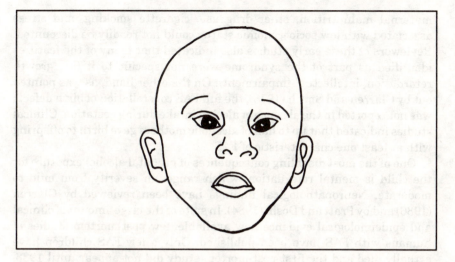

FIG. 2.4. Facial features in a boy with fetal alcohol syndrome. The most characteristic signs are the short upward-slanting palpebral (eyelid) fissures, flat midface, and the thin extended upperlip. Other features often observed are epicanthal folds, low nasal bridge, and small jaws (micrognathia). Mild hirsuitism is sometimes present at birth.

effects" (FAE) has sometimes been applied. As Sokol and Clarren (1989) have indicated, this terminology has been used somewhat inconsistently to suggest that either the defects were of mild form or that alcohol use was suspected, but not confirmed, as the teratogen involved. These authors have published guidelines for the use of terminology describing the impact of prenatal alcohol exposure on offspring. These were formulated by the Fetal Alcohol Study Group of the Research Society on Alcoholism, who recommended that the term "fetal alcohol syndrome" be applied only to those children displaying abnormalities in the three major domains: (1) growth retardation; (2) craniofacial anomalies; and (3) neurological abnormalities. In addition, they suggested that use of the term "possible fetal alcohol effects" be discontinued in favour of "Alcohol related birth defects". However, this group was unable to reach agreement on the latter recommendation and examination of the literature published since 1989 suggests that the latter term has not been widely adopted.

The early descriptions of the syndrome were followed by a proliferation of case reports. Mendelson (1978) reviewed 245 cases published world-wide in one 12-month period. Although these case reports made a significant contribution to the definition and identification of the syndrome, they did not provide information on its incidence or distribution. In addition, although the case reports could hint at aetiology and mechanisms, they could not identify alcohol as the teratogen; other possible causes such as maternal malnutrition, other drug use, cigarette smoking, and stress associated with low socioeconomic status could not readily be discounted. Reviewers of these early studies also indicated that many of the features identified as part of the syndrome were not specific to it (i.e. growth retardation, intellectual impairment). On the other hand, as was pointed out by Clarren and Smith (1978), the full FAS constellation of birth defects was not reported in the absence of alcohol intake during gestation. Clinical studies indicated that up to half of alcoholic mothers gave birth to offspring with at least one characteristic of FAS.

One of the most disabling consequences of prenatal alcohol exposure for the child is mental retardation, which ranges in severity from mild to moderate. Neuropathological findings have been reviewed by Clarren (1986) and by Pratt and Doshi (1984). In spite of the large amount of clinical and epidemiological evidence now available, few post-mortem studies of humans with FAS have been published. Only a few FAS children have actually died and the first post-mortem study did not appear until 1986. Of the 16 cases reviewed by Clarren (1986), five were stillborn and a number of others died as neonates. Although these cases were probably at the severe end of the spectrum, Clarren provided computed tomographic (CT) evidence that their brains were, in gross terms, not unlike those of FAS infants who survived. In five of the 16 cases there was evidence of severe disorganisation of the central nervous system which probably emanated from first trimester destruction of the germinal matrices that give rise to brain tissue. Abnormalities included cortical disorganisation, and agenesis of the interhemispheric commissures. Clarren noted that the white matter lesions could also have resulted from encephaloplastic processes occurring later in fetal development. A further 10 cases had more limited malformations due to impaired neural development or cellular migration. Overall, there was extreme variability in the nature and degree of brain malformation, which is consistent with the variations seen in neurological, behavioural, and intellectual deficits emerging during development. Pratt and Doshi (1984) have cautioned that some of the features of brain damage observed in FAS are similar to those seen in other syndromes not involving prenatal alcohol exposure. The point has repeatedly been made that "funny-looking kids" whose mothers may have consumed alcohol during pregnancy should not automatically receive the label "Fetal Alcohol Syndrome".

Early clinical and epidemiological studies

Initially, studies of FAS sought to elucidate the relationship between maternal prenatal alcohol consumption, and birth and developmental defects. The incidence and distribution of full and incomplete FAS were investigated, and attempts made to establish dose–response relationships and determine if there was a threshold effect. A further issue was whether a crucial gestational period for alcoholic damage existed. After a comprehensive review of this research, Russell (1982) concluded that, in general, the findings tended to favour the presence of teratogenic effects of alcohol. She noted, however, that although several research strategies had been employed, all had limitations. There is no doubt that the task of testing hypotheses in this area is a daunting one. To understand fully the current perspectives on FAS/FAE, it is useful to consider some of the early studies, their findings, and their strengths and weaknesses.

An early research strategy involved the retrospective investigation of the children of women known to be alcoholic and who were thought to have been drinking heavily during the pregnancy. In one such study, Russell (1977) examined the records of all female patients seen at an outpatient alcoholism clinic and extracted information about psychiatric diagnosis, maternal drinking history, birth of children, and paternal alcoholism. Birth weights and rates of congenital malformations were compared with those of controls matched for gender, maternal age, race, education, year, and region of birth. Rates of prematurity and intrauterine growth were compared with State averages. The cases were lighter, twice as likely to be premature, and three times as likely to suffer intrauterine growth retardation. Other studies of similar design conducted in Moscow, West Germany, Sweden, Ireland, and elsewhere in the United States produced similar results. There were a number of problems with these studies. Precise ascertainment of prenatal alcohol abuse was difficult to achieve, control groups were often inadequate, and appropriate data about the operation of other variables such as maternal smoking, were seldom included. Another strategy was to identify children with congenital anomalies and study their mothers' alcohol intake during gestation retrospectively. For example, Berkowitz, Holford, Kasl, and Kelsey (1979), quantified the maternal drinking of 225 premature (less than 37 weeks) and 313 full-term (more than 36 weeks) births. They found increased risk of prematurity when alcohol consumption was more than seven standard drinks per week. Examination of the effect of other potential risk factors was, however, revealing. Moderate alcohol intake was not as great a risk as a history of infertility, induced abortion, or being of low socioeconomic status. Such studies are subject to the same limitations as are others of retrospective design and their results must be interpreted with caution.

Data collected from large cohorts studied to determine factors important in pregnancy outcome have also been analysed retrospectively to test hypotheses about fetal alcohol effects. Although such studies tend to identify only small numbers of mothers drinking hazardously during pregnancy, and although the quantification of alcohol consumption is crude, some useful findings have emerged. For example, Sokol, Miller, and Reed (1980) found 204 women who had been identified clinically as alcoholics in a cohort of 12,127 pregnancies. The alcoholic women had a history of habitual abortion, low birth-weight babies, and fetal abnormalities. The relative risk of intrauterine growth retardation was 1.8 in smokers, 2.4 in alcoholics, and 3.9 in smoking alcoholics. Confounding factors such as differences in maternal age and marital status between the alcoholics and controls limit the validity of this study. Other studies of this kind are subject to similar criticisms.

Prospective studies of pregnancy cohorts are expensive, time consuming, and difficult to conduct. They are, however, the most satisfactory way of determining the incidence of the disorder, although the accurate and reliable measurement of amount and timing of alcohol consumption remains a problem. Two prominent examples of such studies are the Boston Pilot Study (Ouellette, Rosett, Rossman, & Weiner, 1977) and the Seattle Longitudinal Prospective Study on Alcohol and Pregnancy (Streissguth, Barr, Martin, & Herman, 1980). Results of these studies suggest that FAS is seen in about 1:1000 births and that significant FAEs are seen at a rate of 3:1000. Complete FAS was seen only in the children of very heavy drinkers, but mothers who drank more than one drink per day were at an increased risk of having developmentally retarded babies, with a range of anomalies consistent with FAEs. Since 1980, epidemiological investigations of FAS/FAE have focused on dissecting the various contributing factors that may coexist with maternal alcohol abuse. The findings are subject to a number of criticisms, but it is reasonable to conclude that they favour the effect of alcohol as a teratogen in its own right. Some studies have also assessed the effects of reducing alcohol consumption during pregnancy. For example, Halmesmaki (1988) followed 85 problem drinkers throughout their pregnancies. Twenty of the infants had complete FAS and a further 22 had some features of fetal alcohol effects. All the women received counselling to limit their drinking and 55 of them were able to reduce their consumption by at least half. Of those who continued to abuse alcohol, 89% gave birth to infants with at least one feature of FAS, compared with only 40% of those who decreased their consumption. This study contributed further to the accumulating evidence of a dose-dependent relationship between alcohol intake and FAE. In particular it added to the data reported by Ouellette et al. (1977) that heavy-drinking women who reduce their consumption are more lkely to have normal babies. Of course, it remains possible that there are other factors operating that are associated with resistance to this advice and also contribute to FAE outcome. Despite major advances in knowledge achieved by the epidemiological and clinical studies of FAS/FAE, the findings of such studies can only indicate an association between alcohol intake and fetal effects. Evidence relating to pathogenesis and pathophysiological mechanisms has emerged from the experimental study of animals (in vivo studies) and of *in vitro* embryo culture systems.

Pathogenesis and pathophysiological mechanisms of FAS/FAE

This topic has been the subject of a number of comprehensive reviews (Randall, Ekblad, & Anton, 1990; Schenker et al., 1990; Streissguth, Sampson, & Barr, 1989). In general, research has focused on the source—the teratogenic agent—and the mechanism by which the agent exerts its effects. Related issues have been whether or not there are critical periods during gestation and the threshold dose required to exert the effect.

The fact that alcohol crosses the placental barrier easily and that blood levels in the fetus and the mother are quickly equilibrated does not necessarily mean that alcohol causes its teratogenic effect directly. It is possible that the fetal effects are secondary to mechanisms such as metabolic imbalance in the mother. There are, however, two sources of evidence consistent with the view that alcohol is directly teratogenic. In non-mammalian animals, where the toxic effects can be tested independently of the mother, alcohol has been shown to be teratogenic. A similar effect has been found in mammalian in vitro embryo culture systems. This does not discount the possibility that the primary metabolite of alcohol—acetaldehyde—which is at about 50% of maternal blood concentration in the fetus, may be toxic either on its own or in combination with alcohol. This evidence that alcohol is teratogenic for the fetus independently of maternal effects raises the question of whether or not the health of the mother is also important. Significant malnutrition is frequently observed in alcoholics and can itself be a cause of fetal growth retardation. Certain key nutrients must be supplied from mother to fetus to support normal development. As we have already discussed, alcohol impairs nutrient absorption and, in heavy-drinking mothers who are already in serious metabolic imbalance, it is possibile that malnutrition during crucial periods may be an important factor in generating FAS. Data on this issue are sparse but animal studies have examined a number of important aspects of fetal malnutrition. In alcohol-ingesting pregnant laboratory animals, supply of glucose to the fetus is impaired. As glucose fuels fetal metabolism, and as low blood glucose is associated with growth retardation in clinical studies, this is a possible contributor to FAS. Fetal vitamin deficiency could also be a factor because there is diminished uptake, impaired absorption, and enhanced utilisation and excretion of water-soluble vitamins in those abusing alcohol. As yet, there is no consistent evidence about this, but it remains a possibility. The trace metal, zinc, plays an important role in the synthesis of DNA, RNA, and protein, and a number of other vital processes. Low tissue levels of zinc have been associated with impaired infant growth and malformations similar to FAS. The experimental data suggest that while zinc deficiency may be contributory, it is not a necessary factor in FAS. Preliminary evidence implicating fetal amino acid deficiency in FAS is stronger. Amino acids are the building blocks of protein and their transport across the placental barrier is impaired in alcohol-ingesting laboratory animals. It is obvious that relative deficiency of amino acids has th potential to cause several features of FAS. In general, however, the evidence implicating malnutrition in FAS is not as strong as that supporting a direct effect of alcohol plus or minus acetaldehyde.

After 15 years of intensive clinical and experimental laboratory work, the mechanisms by which alcohol exerts its teratogenic effects are still not certain. There are, however, a number of possible pathophysiological mechanisms. As growth of the fetus is dependent on normal placental transport, placental dysfunction and dysmorphology have been invoked as a possible mechanism for intrauterine growth retardation. Experimental animal studies have demonstrated both dysfunction (altered properties of placental transport) and dysmorphology (decreased weight and protein production, etc.) of the placenta in association with alcohol consumption. Placental changes could not only impair provision of nutrients to the fetus, but also cause hypoxia due to changes in blood flow. Prostaglandins are involved in the regulation of vasoconstriction and dilation. The prostaglandin balance is altered by alcohol ingestion in experimental animals and FAS neonates have been found to have higher concentrations and increased urinary excretion of certain prostaglandin derivatives. By this mechanism, umbilical and placental blood flow can be deranged leading to both hypoxia and nutritional deficiency in the fetus.

Other researchers have emphasised the particular vulnerability of the brain to the toxic effects of alcohol and its metabolite acetaldehyde. As has already been mentioned, neuropathology studies of humans with FAS have shown degrees of structural malformation and derangement that vary in severity. Pratt (1984) speculated that many of the developmental and neuro- logical abnormalities seen in FAS could be accounted for by prenatal CNS damage. Four possible mechanisms of damage have been suggested by Pratt (1984):

1. Cell death or chromosomal errors in the first month after conception, causing early spontaneous abortion.

2. Toxic effects of alcohol during the period 4 to 12 weeks after conception, causing cell loss and abnormal migration. Resulting in structural disorganisation of the brain, microcephaly, and the mental retardation associated with FAS.

3. Delays in neuronal migration leading to synaptic malformation caused by alcohol intoxication from about 2 months post-conception. Responsible for behavioural abnormalities in early childhood.

4. Suppression of hypothalamic functioning and release of growth hormone resulting from intoxication from about 1 week after conception. Causes a general growth deficit.

In his review, Michaelis (1990) also emphasised that the central nervous system is particularly vulnerable to the effects of alcohol and that, even when other teratogenic effects are barely detectable, neurological and behavioural effects are evident. Michaelis postulated a number of mechanisms, some of which we have already mentioned. In addition to the inhibition of protein synthesis, disruption of placental transport of nutrients, and changes in vascular tone and hypoxia, Michaelis suggested that alcohol ingestion causes abnormalities of calcium handling mechanisms with subsequent effects on neuronal migration and differentiation. Michaelis concluded by noting that much of the evidence is as yet weak or circumstantial, and that research in the area is becoming increasingly complex and specialised. It is not appropriate to discuss this research in greater detail in this context and interested readers are referred to the comprehensive reviews cited above.

The possibility that alcohol acts as a mutagen has been investigated following some epidemiological evidence that paternal alcohol abuse may affect the fetus (Little & Sing, 1986). Fertility is impaired in experimental animals but there is little evidence of behavioural effects in the offspring. In addition, there is no evidence of chromosomal damage in human offspring with FAS. It is possible that such damage accounts to some extent for higher rates of spontaneous abortion, which is its most likely expression in mammals.

Many as yet unanswered questions about the prenatal effects of alcohol relate to the timing, dose, and pattern of maternal consumption. Most reviewers agree that the spectrum of effects expressed in human offspring probably relate in some way to the gestational phase of alcohol exposure. The Royal College of Physicians has postulated that dysmorphologies may be the result of interference with organ formation in the embryonic stage (16–24 days) and that neurological and growth abnormalities may result from restricted development of rapidly growing tissues during the fetal stage (73–280 days). Schenker et al. (1990) suggested that, like other teratogens, the period during which the alcohol was consumed by the mother is probably critical. They speculated that while heavy consumption throughout gestation will cause the full range of abnormalities, episodic binge drinking may lead to period-specific developmental anomalies.

Schenker et al. (1990) also suggested that alcohol exposure during the first trimester will interfere with organogenesis and lead to skeletal and visceral anomalies. On the other hand, maternal drinking during the second and third trimesters will lead to abnormalities of brain growth and development causing behavioural teratological effects in the absence of overt physical defects. This is a difficult hypothesis to test in human subjects. Although mothers who drink during the first trimester, perhaps before knowing they are pregnant, may reduce their consumption, those drinking heavily during later pregnancy probably drank throughout. In addition, there may be other crucial differences between those who stop drinking and those who continue. There is, however, significant evidence to support the critical periods hypothesis from the experimental animal literature (Randall, 1987; Webster, Walsh, McEwen, & Lipson, 1983).

The critical dosage or exposure level has been much more difficult to investigate and, as yet, a minimal dose level has not been established. In discussing the relationship between dose and response, Streissguth (1977) suggested that there is a dose-related gradient of effects. In this scheme, teratogens are capable of producing death, malformations, growth disturbances, and functional disorders. Behavioural effects can be produced at doses just below the threshold for the induction of morphological abnormalities. According to this formulation, there is no safe dose or critical dose, but effects will be more severe as exposure increases depending, of course, on other factors such as the timing of exposure.

After studying cases at the severe end of the spectrum, Majewski and Goeke (1982), who prefer the term alcohol embryopathy (AE) because they believe that the craniofacial malformations by which the syndrome was identified are induced during the embryonic period, have developed a grading system. In this system, points were accrued according to the number of symptoms present, and the children were divided into three classes on this basis. Children with the mild form, AE I, had a small number of symptoms including intrauterine growth retardation, low birth weight, and microcephaly, but few if any craniofacial anomalies or internal malformations. Children in the AE II group, the moderate form, had the AE I symptoms plus mild neurological anomalies such as hypertonicity and hyperactivity, some facial anomalies, but few internal malformations. Retardation of mental development was present in nearly all of the AE II cases. The patients with AE III, the severe form, demonstrated almost all of the symptoms associated with the disorder. Of considerable relevance here, Majewski and Goeke (1982) also reported a relationship between the severity of alcoholic illness in the mother and level of AE.

Investigation of the dose–response relationships in epidemiological studies is compounded by the difficulties of collecting data about consumption, the low rate of female alcoholism, and the complex pharmacokinetics of alcohol. It is thought that women consuming more than six standard drinks per day place their offspring at very great risk, and rates as low as three drinks per day are associated with some discernible effects, such as a reduced level of intellectual functioning during preschool years. Experimental animal findings have suggested that perhaps the total amount of alcohol consumed is less important than the pattern of consumption. Smaller amounts administered in a condensed pattern appear to be more harmful than larger amounts distributed evenly. At present, no unitary level can be defined, but it is clear that large amounts (more than three drinks per day) consumed throughout gestation will, in all likelihood, harm the child. It is as yet unknown why the children of some women drinking above this level are apparently unaffected. It is currently advised that women who are pregnant or contemplating pregnancy should abstain from alcohol.

Long-term outcome of FAS and FAE

In general, the evidence suggests that there is little in the way of developmental "catch-up" demonstrated by these children in the long term. The picture is complex, however, and depends on whether one focuses on complete FAS or less severe forms, and also on the symptoms being studied. In addition, the effects of inadequate or deprived environments confound any attempt to study outcome. Despite clear evidence from animal studies that alcohol is teratogenic, it remains difficult to determine, in individual cases, the degree to which functional deficits are induced by prenatal or postnatal conditions or by some interaction of the two.

In considering long term outcome we will begin with those children diagnosed as FAS and examine the evidence regarding their later progress. Streissguth (1986) has reviewed the outcome literature prior to the mid-1980s and found general agreement between authors that FAS was associated with a wide variation in IQ scores, and that this variation correlated with degree of morphological and growth abnormality. Majewski and Goeke (1982) found that the average IQs for AE I, II, and III, were 91, 79, and 66 respectively. Although there was within-group variability, most marked in AE I, there was a strong trend for intellectual performance to covary with severity of other symptoms. Streissguth, Herman, and Smith (1978) found that average IQ for a group of 18 FAS children changed little over 12–36 months. Although there was marked variability in degree of change, this was associated with age of testing and IQ is known to be particularly unstable in very young children. In general, if the expected instability of IQs in early childhood is taken into account, the evidence does not encourage the view that there will be any significant improvement in intellectual functioning during this stage. This is particularly so for children with overt dysmorphologies who were diagnosed FAS early and whose mothers were severely alcoholic during pregnancy. One confounding factor in the measurement of intelligence in these children is the presence of hyperactivity, a common symptom of FAS. Changes in the frequency and intensity of such a behaviour disorder may account for some of the instability in measured IQ as these children mature. A particularly significant example of this was reported by Streissguth, Clarren, and Jones (1985).

Similar findings have been reported for growth as measured by weight, height, and head circumference. While there is some catch-up in stature for the least severely affected, those with complete FAS generally show little change. For example, Majewski and Goeke (1982) found no improvement in relative stature for their eldest AE III case at 9.5 years of age. This girl's height remained below the 3rd percentile for her age. On the other hand, the results of a study by Spohr and Steinhausen (1984) showed that there were significant overall improvements in physical and intellectual measures but that hyperactivity and lack of social integration persisted. Perhaps as a result of this, educational functioning showed little promise and their general conclusion was that, although there was some hope, these children were not becoming normal in middle childhood. Lack of methodological detail reported in this study makes the results difficult to compare with those of other studies.

Conry (1990) conducted neuropsychological assessments on 19 school-aged children with FAS or FAE in a rural Indian community in Canada. Such communities have been shown to have high rates of maternal alcohol abuse and correspondingly high rates of FAS (i.e. 190/1000 children, compared with international prevalence estimates ranging from 0.4 to 3.1 per 1000). After diagnosis of FAS or FAE was established, each subject was matched with a case control and all were tested on age-appropriate neuropsychological tests. There were significant differences between the alcohol affected and control subjects on all but two (reaction time and finger localisation) of the 14 separate measures. Measures of intelligence, educational performance, and motor function differentiated the FAS and control group. The FAE and control group differed only on grip strength. Conry (1990) concluded that the influence of FAE may have been masked by coexisting cultural deprivation. Overall, the results are consistent with other studies showing that, at school age, FAS continues to affect intellectual and educational performance very severely. Verbal and performance IQs in the FAS group, were 58.5 and 67.6 respectively, compared with control averages of 82.3 and 95.1 The verbal and performance IQ scores for the FAE group were 84.3 and 90.2.

The neonatal behavioural manifestations of FAS and FAE include difficulty with homeostasis, abnormal EEG, and seizure activity, effects which are possibly related to alcohol withdrawal. During infancy these children tend to be irritable, jittery, difficult to feed, and gain weight slowly. In childhood they are often described as hyperactive, distractible, and impulsive, with short attention spans. In a recent study of the long term behavioural effects of FAS and FAE, Nanson and Hiscock (1990) compared 20 children who had been subject to prenatal alcohol exposure, 20 children with attention deficit disorder (ADD), and 20 normal controls on three experimental attention-demanding tasks and various other tests. The FAS/FAE school-age children performed less well on tests of intelligence (IQ = 78), and experienced more difficulty on the tests of attention than did the ADD children. They tended to be slower and they were unable to make speed–accuracy trade-offs, but the attentional deficits and behavioural problems of the children in both groups were similar. At an observational level, the FAS/FAE and ADD groups were indistinguishable. Nanson (1992) has published data on six cases of FAS where a secondary diagnosis of autism was recorded. All six functioned in the moderately to severely mentally retarded range and were also severely autistic according to clinical and behavioural criteria.

In the longest follow-up study available to date, Streissguth (1988) compared the outcome of 58 young adults with FAS to that of 34 young adults with FAE. Although FAS certainly resulted in more severe intellectual impairment, the two groups could not be differentiated on academic or social indices of performance. The severe long-term consequences of FAE may be due in part to a host of environmental factors that remain to be identified. For example, the deleterious effects of living with an alcoholic father have been reported (Nylander, 1960) and Ervin, Little, Streissguth, and Beck (1984) have found that a seven-point IQ decrement is associated with having an alcoholic father as caregiver.

Long-term follow-up studies of children born to alcoholic mothers and who were therefore highly likely to have been exposed to alcohol prenatally, have also been reported. As a group, these children have been found to have lower IQ than matched controls at age 6 and 7 (Jones, Smith, Streissguth, & Myrianthoupolis, 1974; Streissguth, 1976). Those children with characteristics of FAS generally had the lowest levels of intellectual functioning. In children of alcoholic mothers, intellectual and neuropsychological deficits were generally more common than either low birth weight or physical malformations (50%, 15%, and 10% respectively). Particular neuropsychological deficits have been identified on timed motor tasks, and fine motor tests and it seems possible that such impairments are correlated with abnormalities in the cerebellar region found on post-mortem examination of FAS/FAE children. It should be noted, however, that language, verbal response, and visuospatial task performance are also affected. It is difficult to argue that the effects are not rather global as was shown by Conry (1990).

Mattson et al. (1992) conducted a multidisciplinary study of two teenage boys (aged 13 and 14 years) with FAS. Investigations included neuropsychological, MRI, and EEG assessments. Both subjects had intelligence quotients in the mentally deficient range and additional specific deficits in immediate memory, verbal functioning, visual motor skills, new learning and delayed recall. When compared with normal 5-year-olds they showed a similar rate of learning, but excessive intrusion errors and impaired discrimination ability. Magnetic reasonance imaging (MRI) scans showed clinical abnormalities in both cases. In subject 1, these were restricted to asymmetry of the ventricles and moderate hypoplasia of the corpus callosum. Subject 2 showed failure of development of the corpus collosum and enlargment of the ventricles that may have been secondary to the callosal abnormality. Morphometric analyses showed the FAS subjects to have smaller cranial and cerebellar vaults and increased amounts of ventricular and subarachnoid CSF. Grey matter was reduced in the caudate and thalamus. Electroencephalographic (EEG) findings were moderately abnormal with preponderance of theta activity in both cases. There were no focal abnormalities and no significant asymmetries in either case. The results reported by Mattson et al. (1992) were consistent with those of earlier studies, but extended knowledge of the affects of FAS in two important respects. First, the learning impairments of these subjects were not restricted to attentional deficits, and included abnormalities of encoding and storage. Second, the structural abnormalities of the brain extended beyond those that can be accounted for by microcephaly.

The findings of prospective studies of large cohorts of mothers who drank various amounts during pregnancy have been inconsistent with respect to the effects of prenatal alcohol consumption on growth retardation. However, recent cohort studies, have shown that prenatal alcohol consumption is negatively associated with later growth of offspring. Day et al. (1991a) reported that growth at 18 months, measured by weight, height, and head circumference, was negatively correlated with average daily volume of alcohol consumed. At three years, statistically significant effects on growth were still present and the rate of growth between birth and age 3 was slower in the prenatally exposed children (Day et al., 1991b). The risk of three or more minor physical anomalies was 1.4 in those women consuming one or more drink per day during pregnancy. Although the overall effects were statistically rather than clinically significant, they did indicate biological effects, which also manifested themselves as behavioural teratology. In contrast to the findings of the two previous studies, Greene et al. (1991) found little evidence that prenatal alcohol exposure produced effects which persist during the preschool years. It is worth noting that the inconsistent findings in this area, together with trends towards the publication of positive findings, may have overestimated the long-term physical effects of moderate levels of prenatal alcohol exposure such as would be equated with social drinking. The same cannot be said for the long-term effects of moderate prenatal alcohol consumption on neurobehavioural functions. Even when the offspring of those drinking more than about five drinks per day during pregnancy were excluded, a range of functional sequelae have been found in preschool and school-age children. Attentional deficits have been found in both naturalistic settings (Landesman-Dwyer, Ragozin, & Little, 1981) and on laboratory measures (Streissguth et al., 1984b). Although overt hyperactivity was not present in these children, thre were subtle deficits, such as lack of task persistence and slower reaction times, which coexisted with attention deficits and have significant educational implications. As Streissguth (1986) has indicated, these findings have significant support in the experimental animal literature (Abel, 1979; Clarren & Bowden, 1984; Lochry & Riley, 1980). Many animal studies have shown that prenatal exposure to moderate amounts of alcohol leads to developmental delays and learning deficits. Most reviewers now suggest that social drinking during pregnancy can cause behavioural teratology in the absence of physical dysmorphology and growth defects. In a longitudinal, prospective, population-based study of moderate prenatal alcohol exposure on 482 school-aged children, Streissguth, Barr, and Sampson (1990) showed that deleterious effects on IQ and learning can persist to age 7.5 years. Children exposed to greater than two drinks per day in midpregnancy had lower IQ scores, and prenatal binge drinking (five or more drinks on any occasion) was negatively correlated with educational achievement. The effect of prenatal consumption of one ounce of alcohol (two standard drinks per day) throughout pregnancy was to decrease IQ score at age 7.5 years by about seven IQ points on average. The authors point out that this is equivalent to shifting the whole distribution almost half a standard deviation downwards, and that such a shift would produce about a 3.5-fold increase in IQ scores less than 85. As this was essentially a normal, primarily middle-class population, these results have very significant implications.

Concluding comments

Taken together, the results of prospective studies showing the continuous nature of deficits (Streisguth, Barr, & Sampson, 1990; Streissguth, Clarren, & Jones, 1985) and the demonstration of direct teratology of alcohol in innumerable experimental animal studies indicate that the long-term FAS/FAE effects are due to prenatal intrauterine alcohol exposure. However, there remains the possibility that the postnatal environment contributes in a significant way to the expression of FAS/FAE in the long term. Spohr and Steinhausen (1984) reported improvement in clinical status and cognitive functioning over a 4-year period in 56 FAS children. On the other hand, Streissguth et al. (1985) found little change in clinical or psychometric function in eight children with FAS followed up over more than 10 years. While there is considerable evidence that the symptoms of FAS children change as they mature, in general, there is little evidence that the most severely affected children are influenced by changes in their environment during childhood. When improvement has been noted (Steinhausen, Gobel, & Nestler, 1984) this has not been related to environmental factors. As we have already mentioned, Streissguth et al. (1985) reported a 30-point IQ improvement in one child but attributed this to the child's decreased hyperactivity.

The influences of environment on less severely affected children have been examined in prospective cohort studies. Streissguth et al. (1990) reported that lower paternal education and larger numbers of young children in the household were positively associated with more adverse effects at the same level of prenatal alcohol exposure. The combined effect of these variables was to increase the risk of these children falling into the subnormal IQ range. Russell et al. (1991) employed three measures of the quality of the child-rearing environment and one of these, the Home Screening Questionnaire, differentiated between mothers who abstained and mothers who drank during pregnancy. However, measures of the child-rearing environment did not make a significant contribution to the effects of prenatal drinking on dysmorphology, growth retardation, or cognitive/neuropsychological deficits in the long-term.

In general, prospective studies of both physical and neurobehavioural variables have failed to detect a significant contribution of environmental factors to long-term outcome. It is true to say, however, that the concern has been with controlling or statistically adjusting for the effects of these variables rather than with investigating their effects. It seems likely that research with such a focus would identify environmental factors that contribute to outcome, particularly in those children who are mildly affected. One of the features of the early lives of FAS/FAE children is that they are likely to have experienced multiple caregiving arrangements. Even when removed from a potentially noxious environment, their child-rearing experiences are unlikely to be optimal. In addition, there do not appear to be any empirically validated treatment programmes, which may well be an indication that effective treatment is not readily available. Nanson and Hiscock (1990) suggested that treatment designed to ameliorate attention problems and facilitate learning in children with ADD might be of benefit to children with FAS/FAE. There is obviously a great need for research in this area. In a recent conservative estimate, Abel and Sokol (1991) have suggested that offspring with complete FAS cost $74.6 million US in incremental annual cost; three-quarters of this being the cost of providing intensive care to low birthweight children and providing institutional care for those with intellectual disabilities. Research into methods of compensating for the deficits such children acquire is an important future objective.

CHAPTER THREE

Assessment of Cognition and Drinking Practices

... we have termed alcoholism any use of alcoholic beverages that causes any damage to the individual or society or both. Vague as this statement is, it approaches an operational definition.

Jellinek (1960, p. 35)

An alcoholic is a person who drinks too much—and you don't like anyway.

(Popular saying, variously attributed)

This chapter has two major objectives. The first is to introduce some of the measures that neuropsychologists use when conducting research with persons who have alcohol-related problems. In doing so, the emphasis will be on describing those tests most commonly used; no attempt will be made to review the range of measures available for assessing neuropsychological deficits. Readers who want a more comprehensive survey are referred to Crawford, Parker, and McKinlay (1992) or Lezak (1983). The second objective is to consider some of the methodological issues involved. This includes the difficulties encountered in documenting drinking behaviour, and in recruiting and defining representative sample of subjects.

NEUROPSYCHOLOGICAL ASSESSMENT

Terry is a 52-year-old man with a 10-year history of admissions for inpatient treatment of alcohol dependence. The longest period of abstinence recorded on his file is 8 months. The son of a prominent barrister, Terry spent 5 years at high school, but left university after only a year of studying accountancy. Since then, he has held a variety of jobs, mostly as a salesperson or office worker. His marriage produced three children, but his wife left him nearly 15 years ago, after laying a complaint of assault against him to the police. Unemployed, Terry now lives by himself in a small rural community where he spends much of his time in the bar of the local hotel.

Terry was admitted to hospital on this occasion when his neighbours became concerned about his erratic behaviour and inability to care for himself. After about 10 days in hospital, his confused state has improved and Terry is able to take part in the routine of ward activities. He now has no problem with simple tests of mental functioning; he can count backwards from 100 in 7s, and recall a string of five digits. It is apparent, however, that his memory is profoundly impaired. Nursing staff report that he cannot learn people's names, becomes easily lost in unfamiliar settings, and repeatedly returns to ask questions that have already been answered just a few moments previously. The ward charge nurse considers he may have developed alcoholic Korsakoff's disease and requests a psychological assessment to determine the extent of Terry's amnesia.

In the clinical setting, patients like Terry are commonly referred for a neuropsychological evaluation. The psychologist's task is to detect and document the cognitive impairments that the patient has acquired as a consequence of alcohol abuse. In Terry's case it seems likely that there has been some brain damage and that this has resulted in some degree of amnesia. The psychologist's objective may therefore be to quantify the amount of memory loss and to determine whether there are any other significant neuropsychological deficits. In this section some of the tests and procedures that the psychologist has available to accomplish these objectives will be reviewed. Where relevant, data from Terry's assessment will be used to illustrate the output of particular neuropsychological tests and the way in which the results contribute to an understanding of his current disabilities.

Measures of intelligence

Most neuropsychological investigations involve some assessment of current intellectual functioning. Measures of intellectual abilities have been extensively used in research with social drinkers and alcoholics. In most of the studies, the measure of choice has been the Wechsler Adult Intelligence Scale (WAIS) or more recently, the WAIS-Revised (WAIS-R).

Wechsler Adult Intelligence Scale-Revised.   The WAIS, first published in 1955, became the pre-eminent individual adult intelligence scale in the decade that followed. Its successor, the WAIS-R, has come to occupy a similar central position in research and clinical practice. The WAIS-R is a multi-subtest battery, comprising six subtests designated part of the verbal scale (Information, Comprehension, Vocabulary, Arithmetic, Similarities, and Digit Span) and five performance subtests (Block Design, Digit Symbol, Picture Completion, Object Assembly, and Picture Arrangement). The verbal subtests tend to rely on verbal–education skills, using familiar formats for testing; the performance tests are somewhat more novel and place greater emphasis on psychomotor skill. Test output includes Verbal IQ (VIQ), Performance IQ (PIQ), and Full Scale IQ (FSIQ) scores with a mean of 100 and a standard deviation of 15. The subtest scores have been scaled to have a mean of 10 and a standard deviation of 3. Normative data from a sample of 1880 individuals, representative of the United States population with an age range of 16 to 74 are presented in the test manual. The WAIS-R is one of the best constructed and normed individual tests available.

The Wechsler intelligence scales will be familiar to most psychologists. Detailed discussion of the accumulated clinical and interpretive material is provided by Lezak (1983). Nevertheless, some discussion of the usefulness of the WAIS-R as a means of detecting acquired organic impairment is of relevance in considering the neuropsychology of alcoholism. An important consideration, particularly in the case of brain-damaged alcoholics, is the extent to which some degree of dementia has occurred. This is often critical not only in clinical practice but also in the constitution of samples of research subjects. It is not easy, however, to show that intellectual capacity has changed; that is, to demonstrate that a patient was once able to do better than they can now. To illustrate how a neuropsychologist might go about this, we can examine the WAIS-R results of Terry, the case described at the beginning of this section. These are detailed in Table 3.1. At the time of testing, Terry had a current Full Scale IQ of 107, which placed him in Wechsler's Average range (between 90 and 109). His Verbal IQ was in Wechsler's High Average range and his age-scaled subtest scores ranged from 7 to 15. However, these scores only provide an indication of Terry's current level of intellectual functioning. Further analysis of the test results is needed to determine if there has been any decline in his general intellectual capacity. In principle, such an analysis involves comparing his present test scores with some valid estimate of his best level of previous functioning. This is not readily achieved. Sometimes individuals have test scores available that were

TABLE 3.1
Wechsler Intelligence Scale (WAIS-R) Scores for a Patient with Suspected
Brain Impairment due to Alcohol Dependence (Terry)

Verbal subtests	Scaled scores		Performance subtests	Scaled scores
Information	11		Digit Symbol	8
Digit Span	15		Picture Completion	8
Vocabulary	12		Picture Arrangement	9
Arithmetic	9		Block Design	8
Comprehension	14		Object Assembly	7
Similarities	9			
Verbal IQ	113			
Performance IQ	96			
Full Scale IQ	107			

collected as part of their education or military induction. Usually, however, premorbid scores must be inferred indirectly. A number of attempts have been made to develop methods that estimate premorbid IQ; these are often used with brain-damaged and alcoholics, particularly in research studies. None of these methods is entirely satisfactory; they should be applied and interpreted with care.

One obvious way of inferring intellectual decline is to establish an estimate of a person's highest past intellectual capacity based on their premorbid achievements. It might reasonably be concluded, for example, that a former engineering graduate, who now has a FSIQ score of 95 after a stroke, has acquired some degree of intellectual dysfunction. In this case, past history provides a context within which present abilities may be evaluated. Unfortunately, the discrepancies between previous achievements and present incapacity are not usually so pronounced. In order to estimate premorbid IQ more systematically, attempts have been made to construct regression formulae that use basic demographic information (age, gender, occupation, and employment) to predict WAIS-R IQ scores (Barona, Reynolds, & Chastian, 1984; Eppinger, Craig, Adams, & Parsons, 1987). At best, these formulae provide estimates that should be treated with considerable caution (Sweet, Moberg, & Tovian, 1990), particularly when results from individual patients are being considered in the absence of other information about premorbid functioning. Sweet et al. (1990) do note, however, that these equations may be useful as part of the process of matching groups for neuropsychological research. Most of the demographic-based formulae are based on American samples and cannot be used readily elsewhere because of differences in the coding of occupational information and differences in the education systems. Crawford et al. (1989b) have provided regression equations for predicting WAIS IQ scores from demographic variables, for the United Kingdom. An example of the equation predicting FSIQ is given below:

Predicted FSIQ = 104.12 −4.38 (class) +0 .23 (age) + 1.36 (education) − 4.7 (sex)

If Crawford et al.'s (1989b) equations are used to estimate the premorbid IQ of our patient Terry, then his predicted WAIS Full Scale IQ is about 116, his Verbal IQ 116, and his Performance IQ estimate is about 113. Therefore, based on his demographic characteristics, using formulae established for use in the UK, Terry's estimated premorbid WAIS IQ lies in Wechsler's High Average range, and this predicted value is consistent with his current Verbal IQ from the WAIS-R. The advantages of using demographic IQ estimates are their independence from current cognitive functioning and the ease with they can be calculated without recourse to any test results. Nonetheless, demographically derived IQ estimates must be interpreted with great care. Typically they have large standard errors. For the Crawford et al. (1989b) regression equations these range from 9.08 to 10.17; thus Terry's Full Scale IQ estimate lies in a one standard error range of 107 to 125. Another problem is that Crawford et al.'s IQ estimates are based on the WAIS. In general, WAIS IQs are about seven or eight points higher than WAIS-R scores from the same individual. Thus the predicted WAIS scores will tend to be an overestimate of obtained WAIS-R scores. There is no simple way of correcting for this.

An alternative way of estimating premorbid IQ is to assume that a person's best performance on a multitask battery indicates their highest former level of intellectual functioning. This assumption is founded on the high intercorrelation of the subtests of an intelligence scale like the WAIS. Typically a brain injury impairs some functions, but not necessarily all; thus the highest scores may be indicative of preinjury capabilities.

Despite the obvious attractions of this method, in most cases drawing conclusions from subtest scatter is difficult. Interpretation of the discrepancies between subtests needs to be approached cautiously, and clinicians should guard against overinterpreting the pattern of score differences. For the WAIS-R there are 55 possible pairs of comparisons amongst the 11 subtests, and the probability of making Type II errors is substantial unless some Bonferroni-type correction to probability levels is introduced. Knight and Godfrey (1984a) and Kramer (1990) have developed tables that can be used for testing the significance of difference between subtest scores that take some account of the large number of possible comparisons. The dangers of overinterpreting subtest discrepancies are highlighted by Matarazzo and Prifitera (1989), who examined the subtest scatter of the original standardisation data, and found that the average discrepancy between the highest and lowest subtest was 6.7 points. They also reported that the magnitude of the discrepancy increased as the IQ level increased. This is an important consideration when interpreting individual score discrepancies. Subtest scores will tend to be more scattered in the middle range of IQ values than at the top or bottom end. In general, the use of a single subtest score to determine premorbid levels of IQ is a hazardous process.

A more robust method of estimating premorbid IQ from WAIS or WAIS-R scores is to combine the results from several subtests. A combination of intercorrelated subtest scores is more reliable, enhancing the prospects of a valid discrimination. One common method of achieving this is to compare VIQ and PIQ scores. It has generally been found (Knight, 1992) that Verbal subtest scores are significantly higher than Performance subtest scores in most pathological groups. Several tables have been published that facilitate the interpretation of VIQ–PIQ discrepancies in clinical practice. These tables provide estimates of the statistical likelihood of discrepancies between VIQ and PIQ occurring as a result of measurement error (reliability of the difference) and the rate at which such discrepancies occur in the normal population (abnormality of the difference). Score differences need to be substantial to attain statistical abnormality. For example, our alcoholic patient Terry produced a VIQ–PIQ discrepancy of 17 on the WAIS-R. Such a discrepancy is found in at least 10% of the normal population. A discrepancy of 27 would be needed to reach a criterion of abnormality set at 1%. It should also be emphasised that discrepancies will be limited by floor effects. As VIQ and PIQ scores tend towards the extremes of the range of IQ, the magnitude of the possible VIQ–PIQ difference will be constrained. Hence a Korsakoff patient with FSIQ scores of 85 is likely on average to have a smaller VIQ–PIQ difference than a Korsakoff patient with an IQ of 110, because a floor effect limits the possible size of the discrepancy. Thus it is not possible to compare the discrepancy between VIQ and PIQ of two patients with disparate FSIQ scores and come to any meaningful conclusions about their relative intellectual decline. The same problem arises when groups that have different average VIQ scores are compared.

Another method of aggregating WAIS-R subtest scores is to combine them on the basis of their factor loadings. A number of factor analytic studies of the correlations between subtests from the standardisation sample have been reported, with varying results. Perhaps the most plausible outcome is Waller and Waldman's (1990) three-factor solution. Factor 1, labelled Verbal Comprehension, loaded most heavily on the Information, Vocabulary, Comprehension, and Similarities subtests. The second factor, Perceptual Organization, loaded on Picture Completion, Picture Arrangement, Block Design, and Object Assembly, while Factor 3, Freedom from Distraction, loaded on Digit Span, Arithmetic, and Digit Symbol. This method of combining subtest scores to provide factorially related index scores has not been widely used in research with alcoholics.

The verbal skill least affected by any kind of diffuse brain injury, particularly the onset of a dementing process, is the ability to read aloud accurately. Capitalising on this, Nelson (1982) developed the National Adult Reading Test (NART), a test in which subjects read to the examiner a list of 50 words that have an irregular pronunciation (ache, thyme, demesne, quadruped). The number of errors in pronunciation is entered into a regression equation used to compute an estimated WAIS IQ score. The ability to read a series of increasingly difficult words is taken as an indicator of past learning achievement and thereby an indirect estimate of premorbid IQ. This estimated IQ can then be compared with a current WAIS IQ, and a discrepancy score calculated to give an estimate of intellectual decline. This procedure is especially useful in gauging premorbid IQ scores in elderly impaired patients, and has been used in research with brain damaged alcoholics, as will be seen in Chapter 10. There are some problems with this method, however, not the least of which are the large standard errors of the estimate of the regression equation (between 7 and 10). In addition, the range of possible WAIS estimates lies between 86 and 128; again, it is important to remember that the size of the IQ discrepancies will be constrained by floor and ceiling effects. The clinical utility of this procedure has been validated in several subsequent studies (Crawford et al., 1989a; Willshire, Kinsella, & Prior, 1991). Crawford et al. (1989a) have combined the original NART standardisation data with results from a cross-validation study and determined a new set of regression formulae that should normally be used in place of those presented in the NART manual.

It is now possible to end this brief introduction to the adult Wechsler intelligence scales with a review of the implications of the data in Table 3.1. The IQ scores suggest that, overall, Terry is functioning in Wechsler's Average range. Nevertheless, the pattern of subtest scores and the VIQ–PIQ discrepancy suggest that he may once have functioned at a higher level. Terry made 18 errors in pronunciation on the NART. If this score is entered into Crawford et al.'s (1989a) formulae for estimating premorbid WAIS IQ, a Full Scale IQ estimate of 113 results. Similarly, using the demographic formulae of Crawford and colleagues, a premorbid IQ estimate of 116 can be derived for Terry. Although these predictions of premorbid IQ should be compared to his present WAIS-R results with some caution, there are substantial grounds for inferring that Terry's current IQ is an under-estimate of his intellectual capacity before he became alcohol dependent.

Shipley Institute of Living Scale (SILS).   The SILS is a group or individual test of intelligence that has been used extensively in research with social drinkers. Known formerly as the Shipley–Hartford Retreat Scale for Measuring Intellectual Ability, this test was first published in 1939. The SILS is made up of two parts—a vocabulary test and an abstraction reasoning task. Subjects have 10 minutes to complete each part. The vocabulary section is a 40-item multichoice synonym test in which the subject is asked to select the best synonym from a set of five alternatives. The abstractions subtest involves completing a list made up of 20 items that requires the subject to complete a sequential pattern. Each item has the form:

hotel to stick it from or stay __

The answer is *at*. This test provides three scores: Vocabulary, Abstraction, and a Conceptual Quotient (CQ). The Conceptual Quotient is the ratio of the obtained Abstraction age-scaled score to the Abstraction score predicted by the Vocabulary score, multiplied by 100. The original objective of the SILS was to detect pathology by measuring the difference between the vocabulary and abstraction score, on the assumption that the vocabulary score would remain constant while the abstraction score would decline as a consequence of impairment. Thus a conceptual quotient of 90 or below is held to be indicative of brain injury. Interestingly, the original normative data of Shipley (1940) showed that alcoholics fell within the normal range on this test. The SILS has been found to correlate significantly with WAIS IQs; procedures for estimating WAIS IQ scores from SILS results are detailed in Paulson and Lin (1970).

Raven's Progressive Matrices (PM).   The PM is a multichoice test of reasoning ability that is intended to make few demands on the testee's verbal skills. The test can be administered in a group setting and norms are available for ages 8 to 65. Each of the 60 items on this well-known test contains an incomplete figure. The subject's task is to select the response alternative from the six to eight presented beneath that best completes the stimulus figure. Raven's PM has not found widespread use in neurological settings, with the WAIS or WAIS-R being preferred. The main problem is that the norms are relatively insensitive to subtle individual differences and the manual is not well presented. Tables are available for converting PM raw scores into WAIS IQs and percentiles (Peck, 1970).

Memory

The ability to acquire new information is particularly susceptible to any form of brain damage. As a consequence, testing of memory processes has come to occupy an important place in neuropsychology. Much of the research on cognitive functioning with alcoholics, particularly those with clinical evidence of brain damage, has involved testing their learning and memory skills. As we saw in Chapter 2, one of the endpoints of chronic alcohol abuse is the amnesia of Korsakoff's syndrome; the study of memory failure as a consequence of alcoholism has been important in the formulation of models of memory at both a cognitive and neurobiological level.

The structure of memory is often described in terms of tripartite division into sensory, primary, and secondary memory. This broad characterisation of the way information is processed, acquired, and stored is often termed the *modal* model of memory (Atkinson & Shiffrin, 1968; Baddeley, 1986). Sensory memory is best regarded as part of the process of perception and is rarely examined in neuropsychological practice. None the less, it is important to remain aware that the disruption of perceptual processes may have some impact on subsequent memory performance. Sensory deficits are a common consequence of alcohol intoxication and abuse, and the acquisition of information in circumstances where stimulus thresholds are at a low level may be disrupted by diminished sensory storage capacity.

The vast majority of research studies focusing on memory changes in neurologically impaired patients has focused on primary and secondary memory. Primary memory refers to the amount of information available in conscious awareness. One of the most venerable measures of memory is the Digit Span test, which is a traditional way of assessing primary memory. If subjects are read sequences of digits of varying length, they usually cannot recall accurately a sequence that comprises more than six or seven elements. The longest sequence of digits that can be reported completely defines the limit of the capacity of primary memory. Primary memory can be conceptualised in functional terms as a temporary working memory. As such, it communicates with the secondary memory stores that house memories on a more permanent basis. As a consequence of rehearsal and other processes, information may be passed into long-term storage. The majority of memory tests used in neuropsychological practice are measures of the rate at which information is transferred from primary to secondary memory. Although the distinction between primary and secondary memories has not been universally accepted (Melton, 1963), this division continues to play an important role in the way memory processes in amnesic patients are investigated. We will revisit this issue in Chapter 10. In the rest of this section some measures of memory that have been used in research with alcoholic clients are introduced.

Wechsler Memory Scale (WMS).   This battery of tests has come to be one of the most widely used tests of memory in neuropsychological practice. Over the past 20 years it has been the primary method of documenting memory loss in amnesic and demented patients in research practice. The

WMS has recently been extensively revised; doubtlessly the WMS-Revised (WMS-R) will come to have an equally significant role in memory testing. Some review of the WMS and its shortcomings is, however, relevant because of the extensive database that has developed using this test.

The WMS comprises seven subtests. The Information and Orientation subtests consist of a series of questions that test knowledge of public information and awareness of present circumstances. The Digit Span subtest is a measure of primary memory and attention, and the Mental Control Subtest tests the ability to produce automatic and novel sequences of letters or digits. The other three subtests are conventional clinical tests of memory loss and are vulnerable to impairments in learning. Logical Memory is an immediate recall test of two prose passages, Associate Learning assesses retention of a series of word pairs, and Visual Reproduction is a test of the ability to recall geometric designs. Subtest scores are combined to produce an age-corrected Memory Quotient (MQ), which Wechsler conceived of as being analogous to the more familiar IQ. Severity of memory deficit is often defined as the difference between IQ and MQ. The assumption here is that memory and intelligence scores are highly correlated, but memory is more vulnerable to brain damage than intellect. As a consequence, the IQ score can be used as an estimate of overall premorbid capacity against which changes in memory capacity can be measured. Until the publication of the WMS-R, MQ scores and IQ–MQ discrepancies were the most common methods of documenting memory loss in amnesic subjects for research purposes (Knight & Longmore, 1991).

There are a number of problems with the interpretation of the IQ–MQ index. The distribution of these scores is essentially unknown and the magnitude of the discrepancy necessary to indicate an "abnormal" difference is indeterminate. In addition, the size of the largest possible discrepancy is limited by the magnitude of the IQ score. Because of the large age-correction factor and the number of subtests that do not depend on functions typically impaired in amnesics (e.g. Mental Control, Digit Span), the effective floor level MQ score for a 50- to 60-year-old densely amnesic Korsakoff patient is about 65 to 70. The average MQ for most alcoholic Korsakoff patients is in the range 75 to 80. The size of the IQ–MQ difference will be largely determined by the IQ score and, where this is less than 100, the apparent severity of the memory impairment will be constrained. For this reason it is important to consider amnesic performance on the WMS not only in terms of the size of the IQ–MQ difference, which may be misleading, but also the absolute level of the MQ. Obvious problems arise when only the discrepancy score is used. For example, a patient with an IQ score of 115 and an MQ of 95, and another with an IQ of 95 and an MQ of 75, may have an equivalent degree of memory loss, but their amnesia is not likely to be equally severe.

There have been several reviews of the WMS (D'Elia, Satz, & Schretlen, 1989; Erickson & Scott, 1977; Prigatano, 1977), all of which have drawn attention to the test's various shortcomings. The normative data available in the manual are inadequate and the regression equations used to derive the MQ scores have not been cross-validated. The generally low level of intercorrelation between the subtests calls into question the meaningfulness of a unitary memory quotient based on the results from all the subtests. With the exception of Visual Reproduction, all the subtests assess verbal memory and the difficulty levels of the individual subtests vary markedly.

The WMS-R represents a considerable advance on the WMS. The normative data are more substantial, the psychometric credentials are more secure, and the range of memory skills tested more extensive. Other improvements in the revised version include the addition of new items to the Information Comprehension subtest, the elimination of the speed bonus from Mental Control, and minor changes to the Digit Span and Logical Memory subtests. Three completely new subtests have been added: Figural Memory (a test of recognition of abstract visual patterns), Visual Paired Associates, and Visual Memory Span (a visual test corresponding to the auditory Digit Span subtest). Some revisions were also made to the WMS Associate Learning subtest, renamed the Verbal Paired-Associates subtest, and to the Visual Reproduction subtest. An important development was the inclusion of a 30-minute delayed recall trial for Logical Memory, Verbal Paired-Associates, and Visual Reproduction. Scoring guidelines were revised and more detailed examples of their application provided. The output from the test takes the form of five indexes: General Memory, Attention and Concentration, Verbal Memory, Visual Memory, and Delayed Recall. Information–Orientation scores are presented separately.

Terry's results appear in Table 3.2 and can be used to illustrate how WMS-R scores are interpreted. The scores on the five major indexes have a distribution with a mean of 100 and a standard deviation of 15, comparable to Wechsler's IQ distribution. Only Terry's Attention–Concentration and Information–Orientation scores lie in the normal range. On all the explicit memory indexes, his scores are at least one standard deviation below his Attention–Concentration score and more than two standard deviations below his current WAIS-R VIQ score of 113. To determine whether these score differences are sufficiently abnormal to warrant further interpretation, a number of published tables of statistical comparisons can be consulted. For example, the analyses conducted by Mittenberg, Thompson, and Schwartz (1991) reveal that the 30-point difference between Terry's Attention–Concentration and General Memory scores is statistically abnormal, with the discrepancy lying beyond the 95%

TABLE 3.2
WMS-R Scores for an Alcoholic Client (Terry)

Measure	Score
General memory	68
Attention–concentration	98
Verbal memory	74
Visual memory	75
Delayed recall	55
Information/orientation	14

confidence limits for normal performance. A table produced by Atkinson (1991) allows a comparable comparison of WAIS-R IQ and WMS-R index scores. As an approximate guide, the average discrepancy between IQ and Index scores needed to attain statistical significance ranges from 11 to 18. The 40- to 45-point difference that Terry shows between his IQ and Memory scores is clearly significant. No normal subject in the WMS-R standardisation sample obtained a discrepancy of more than 28 points between Delayed Memory and FSIQ (Bornstein, Chelune, & Prifitera, 1989). Terry's discrepancy exceeded 50 points. There is no doubt that this psychometric evidence confirms clinical impressions that Terry has acquired a sustantial memory impairment as a consequence of his drinking history.

California Verbal Learning Test (CVLT).   This test is a measure of the ability to learn verbal material. At the present time it is the most detailed and best standardised measure of verbal learning available. The test makes use of two shopping lists, A and B. List A is administered on five occasions, followed by one trial with List B. The output from the CVLT provides measures of rate of learning, the use of learning strategies, accuracy of recall and recognition, the effects of interference, serial position effects, occurrence of perseveration, and number of intrusions in recall. The normative data available for the research edition of the CVLT come from a sample of 273 healthy subjects, ranging in age from 17 to 80. The test takes about 45 minutes to administer and evidence for the usefulness of this test in neuropsychological practice is accumulating (Delis, Kramer, Kaplan, & Ober, 1987; Delis, Freeland, Kramer, & Kaplan, 1988).

Rey Auditory Verbal Learning Test (RAVLT).   The RAVLT is similar in structure and function to the CVLT, however, the scoring and testing procedures are less detailed. A list of 15 words is administered five times with recall being tested after each trial. A second list is then administered and after recall of this list has been assessed, recall of the first list is tested again. The RAVLT does not have a published manual and normative results are scattered throughout the neuropsychological literature. A parallel form of this test has been reported, facilitating accurate retesting of brain injured subjects (Crawford, Stewart, & Moore, 1989c). The best compilation of normative information on this test is provided by Lezak (1983). The RAVLT takes about 10 to 15 minutes to administer and has been employed on occasion in research on the effect of alcohol abuse on memory.

Russell's Version of the Wechsler Memory Scale. A variation in the administration of the WMS, which involved the immediate and delayed recall of the Logical Memory and Visual Reproduction subtests, was introduced by E.W. Russell (1975; 1982). Scores on the immediate and 30-minute delayed recall trials, and a measure of percentage retained, are converted to average impairment ratings comparable to those derived from the Halstead–Reitan battery. Detailed norms have been provided by Russell (1988). This measure has enjoyed widespread use as a test of memory in clinical practice (Hightower & Anderson, 1986), however, the publication of the WMS-R may make its use less common.

Conceptual learning

Many patients who sustain brain injuries are left with evidence of a reduction in the ability to think abstractly and shift cognitive sets as demands of a task change. Failure of abstraction refers to impairments in forming new concepts, learning new rules, and generalising from specific instances. An example of a test used by clinicians to assess abstraction ability is Gorham's (1956) Proverb Test. Subjects are asked to interpret a saying such as "empty vessels make the most noise". The responses given vary in their generality. At higher levels of abstraction an answer might be "People who have the least to offer often have the most to say". A more literal and concrete interpretation might be "if you tap on the side of an empty jar it will make more noise than if it is full". Ability to generalise has been seen as part of what is meant by intelligence, and proverb interpretation items have been included in individual intelligence scales. Impairment in conceptual functioning is often seen as an inability to focus on what is relevant and a concern with the superficial aspects of a problem. Mental inflexibility is often associated with reduced abstraction ability, although as Lezak (1983) observed, they can be separated. Mental flexibility refers to the capacity to move from one mental set to another as environmental circumstances dictate. When set-shifting is affected, responding may become perseverative, that is, behaviour remains bound to a previous rule that is no longer relevant. For example, the patient asked to alternate rapidly between drawing a series of three triangles and a series of three squares may not be able to switch smoothly from one set of figures to the other, and may persist in producing triangles. The Wisconsin Card Sorting Test (WCST) is the most commonly used clinical measure for the assessment of the rate of perseverative responses.

Problems with conceptual functioning are seen in neuropsychological practice as a consequence of a range of specific and diffuse lesions and in varying degrees of severity. Reduced mental flexibility and excessive concreteness of thinking have been linked with frontal lobe injury, although failure on tests of conceptual function is not confined to patients who have frontal lobe lesions. Because frontal cortical atrophy is a frequent result of alcohol abuse, tests of conceptual functioning are often employed in neuropsychological studies of alcoholics. Two tests have predominated, the WCST and the Category Test from Halstead–Reitan Neuropsychological Test Battery (HRB). The WCST is described below and the Category Test is introduced in the next section.

The Wisconsin Card Sorting Test (WCST).   The WCST was developed initially by Berg (1948) as a means of assessing the ability to shift sets. It was based on early demonstrations that normal rhesus monkeys were able to change their response strategy on the basis of changes in reinforcement, but that monkeys with frontal lobe lesions were not. The WCST is the human analogue of a task developed in the course of the research on discrimination learning in monkeys. Subjects begin by sorting cards on the basis of a rule that the examiner conveys by means of feedback on the correctness of each sorting response. Once the subject has learned the rule to a preset accuracy criterion, the experimenter shifts, without explanation, to another. From the abrupt change in feedback, the subject must infer that the rule has changed and what the new rule is. Thus the subject's approach to the task needs to be sufficiently flexible to assimilate these rule changes.

The WCST requires subjects to sort a pack of 64 cards into four piles. The pattern printed on each card varies along three dimensions: colour (blue, red, yellow, and green), number (one to four symbols), and shape of the symbols (triangle, star, cross, and circle). The four piles into which the cards may be sorted are marked with four different stimulus cards: one red triangle, two green stars, three yellow crosses, and four blue circles. The initial rule that the examiner reinforces is colour. From the experimenter's feedback, the subject learns to ignore the other two dimensions, number and shape, as irrelevant and to sort only on the basis of matching the colour of the stimulus and response cards. Once the subject has made 10 consecutive correct responses, the experimenter changes the rule to number. Now the subject must ignore colour and shape, and sort only on the basis of the number of symbols. In all, up to six category shifts may occur before testing is terminated or the subject has sorted the pack of cards twice. Scoring is often complex and several indices are derived. These include the number of switches in category successfully achieved, the total number of errors, and the number of *perseverative* errors made. Perseveration is a behaviour sometimes seen in brain injured patients whereby they persist in using a previously correct strategy of responding despite evidence that the rules have changed and that their responses are now wrong. Perseverative errors on the WCST occur when the subject continues to sort the cards on the basis of colour, for example, after the rule has changed to shape, despite receiving feedback that the colour-based responses are wrong. Often a patient who is perseverating can appreciate that the rule has changed, but seems unable to alter their pattern of responding.

In Table 3.3 WCST results from our alcoholic amnesic patient Terry have been contrasted with data from an alcoholic client with no clinical evidence of brain impairment and scores from another patient, Isabel, who has a clinical diagnosis of alcoholic dementia. This also allows the opportunity to compare the psychometric profiles of a patient with a diagnosis of alcoholic amnesia (or Wernicke–Korsakoff syndrome), with someone who is diagnosed as having an alcoholic dementia.

TABLE 3.3
Test Scores for Three Alcoholic Patients

Measure	Alcoholic dementia (Isabel)	Alcoholic amnesia (Terry)	Unimpaired alcoholic
Age (years)	60	52	54
NART IQ estimate	115	113	105
WAIS-R			
Full scale IQ	87	107	111
Verbal IQ	90	113	109
Perforiance IQ	85	96	114
WMS-R			
Attention–concentration	95	98	96
General memory	81	68	102
Delayed memory	65	55	98
Wisconsin Card Sorting Test			
Perseverative errors	55	43	22
Categories	2	4	5

Isabel is a 60-year-old woman with a long history of alcohol dependence, who has been in institutional care for the past 4 years. Most of her time is spent sitting in the lounge of the long-stay psychiatric ward where she lives. Her self-care skills have deteriorated and staff see no prospect of her being discharged to live independently in the community. Throughout the testing sessions she is passive and uncomplaining, presenting as co-operative but apathetic. On the WAIS-R, her IQ scale scores are lower than those of Terry, although her NART premorbid WAIS IQ estimate suggests she was once functioning at a higher level. There is only a five-point discrepancy between her Verbal and Performance IQ scores; this is also characteristic of dementia, which typically causes a global decline in a wide range of abilities. On the WMS-R, Isabel's General Memory and Delayed Recall Indexes are also well below the level of performance that would be expected from a woman of her age. Her scores are not as low as those of Terry. He, however, was tested just a few weeks after detoxification and, after a period of abstinence, his performance on memory tasks can be expected to improve. Isabel performed poorly on the WCST, which is also consistent with her classification in the demented alcoholic group. Terry also made a large number of perseverative errors but managed to make four category changes.

Early research suggested that failure on the WCST was indicative of frontal lobe damage (Milner, 1963). It has been found, however, that the performance of patients with frontal lobe injury on the WCST is highly variable (Anderson, Damasio, Jones, & Tranel, 1991; Eslinger & Damasio, 1985). Anderson et al. (1991) tested 91 patients with a single focal brain lesion. On the basis of neuroradiological identification of lesion sites, subjects were divided into frontal ($n = 49$), non-frontal ($n = 24$), and frontal plus non-frontal ($n = 18$) lesion groups. They found that both the frontal and non-frontal groups showed equivalent levels of performance on the WCST and called into question the validity of characterising the WCST as a measure of frontal lobe damage. They concluded that (Anderson et al., 1991, p. 920):

Using focal structural damage within the frontal lobes document by CT and MR as the criterion, these data fail to support a consistent relationship between poor WCST performance and structural damage to the frontal lobes. It was found that although many subjects with frontal lobe damage performed poorly, a large number performed within normal limits, and many subjects with comparable damage outside of the frontal lobes failed the test. These data do not support interpretation of WCST performances alone as an indication of the presence or absence of structural damage to the frontal lobes. The WCST alone should not be used to group brain damaged subjects "Frontal" and "Non-frontal" groups for research purposes.

Halstead–Reitan Battery (HRB). Apart from the Wechsler Intelligence Scales, the HRB has probably been the most commonly used measure of neuropsychological functioning in groups of alcoholics. Although the composition of the battery varies, it typically involves administration of six tests: the Category Test, the Tactual Performance Test (TPT), the Rhythm Test, the Speech Sounds Perception Test, the Finger Tapping Test, and the Trail Making test (Eckardt & Matarrazo, 1981; Golden, Osman, Moses, & Berg, 1981; Lezak 1983; Reitan & Davison, 1974; Russell, Neuringer, & Goldstein, 1970). The HRB is an extensive battery that may take several hours to administer. It was more widely used in the United States than elsewhere.

The Category test is a measure of the efficiency of acquiring a new rule and is considered to be a measure of conceptual learning and problem-solving skills. For each of the six sets of items, subjects are instructed to uncover the relationship between each new stimulus item and a set of four response alternatives. Each time a response is made, the subjects receive feedback about whether or not their response is consistent with the underlying rule. The number of errors committed by the subject is used as a measure of conceptual learning ability. The TPT involves instructing the subject to complete a formboard while blindfolded. The task is carried out three times, first with the preferred hand, then the non-preferred hand, and finally with both hands together. The score for each trial is the time taken to complete the formboard successfully and these scores are combined to produce a measure of Total Time. Once the formboard has been completed three times it is placed out of the subject's sight and the blindfold removed. The subject is then instructed to draw the board from memory. This yields two further scores, the Memory score (the number of shapes recalled) and the Location score (the number of shapes correctly positioned on the drawing).

The Rhythm test comes from the Seashore Measures of Musical Talent and involves testing the ability to discriminate between pairs of musical beats presented on a tape recording. The Speech Sounds Perception Test requires the subject to identify, on a written multichoice form, 60 phoneme sounds also presented on a tape recording. Scores on the Finger Tapping Test are the sum of the average number of taps made during five 10-second trials; both hands are tested. The Trail Making Test (TMT) requires the testee to join together with a pencilled line first the letters of the alphabet (Trails A) distributed randomly across a sheet of paper, and second, the letters of the alphabet and the numbers 1 to 20 alternately and in correct ascending order (Trails B). The overall output from the Battery reported in many studies is the Impairment Index. This is the ratio of tests on which the subject is impaired to the total number of tests administered. Seven tests is the most usual number given; if three of the seven are failed, this gives an index of 0.42, which is usually indicative of brain damage. We will review the performance of alcohol dependent subjects on this battery in Chapter 9.

Measurement of deficits

The rationale of much of the research considered in Part 3 involves the comparison of a clinical group (such as inpatient alcoholics) with a matched control group, on one or more cognitive tests. Often, even when the same cognitive processes are tested, conflicting results emerge from studies conducted in different laboratories. Sometimes the clinical group is found to have impairments and, on other occasions, there are no statistical differences between the clinical and the control groups. Differences in the sensitivity of the measurement and statistical procedures that researchers employ provide one explanation for this inconsistency. Finding a real difference between two groups is critically dependent on the power of the test that is made of the null hypothesis. This, in turn, depends on the magnitude of the difference between the two groups (the effect size, ES), the level of significance the experimenter selects, and the reliability of the measures used (Cohen, 1977). These three factors determine the power of the statistical test that the experimenter uses and hence the chances of detecting a significant difference between groups. Cohen (1962) in a review of studies that contrasted pathological and control groups appearing in the *Journal of Abnormal Psychology* found that many researchers handicap themselves in their search for clinically significant deficits by designing experiments that result in statistical tests that are insufficiently powerful to detect real effects.

Statistical power depends in part on the significance criterion adopted. Typically the significance criterion, which is the rate of rejection of a true null hypothesis (making a Type II error), is set at the conservative levels of 0.05 or 0.01. The lower this value is, the less the power of the test to detect true differences between groups. For example, a significance criterion set at 0.001, implies a power value of 0.1 (statistical power is expressed in terms of a 0 to 1 scale; Cohen, 1962). The chances of detecting a significant difference are also determined by the magnitude of the effect size. ES can be regarded as a parameter indicating the strength of a difference between two groups varying from zero to some non-zero value. When a statistical test is not significant, this indicates that the ES value is some negligible value. The measurement of ES values has become more prominent with the use of meta-analysis, a method of combining results from a range of studies by aggregating ES values, illustrated in Chapter 9. In general, less powerful tests are needed to show the presence of larger than smaller effect sizes. For example, the effect on memory processes of

20 years of alcohol abuse is greater than the effect of 2 years of controlled social drinking. Thus the power of the test needed to detect the effects of alcohol consumption in a group of long-term alcoholics, all other things being equal, is far less than for a group of social drinkers. As the size of the significance criterion is set by convention and the magnitude of the ES is an implicit characteristic of the groups tested, the experimenter has little control over these factors. Consequently, the reliability of the measure used is perhaps the most important determinant of power, and reliability estimates are constrained to a considerable extent by sample size. As Cohen (1977, p. 7) states, "whatever else sample reliability may be dependent on, it *always* depends upon the size of the sample". Psychologists who have completed a course in psychometrics will be familiar with the Spearman–Brown formula, which is used to estimate the effect on reliability of altering the number of observations that determine a test score. The implication of this formula is that reliability *increases* as the number of items employed in a test increases. Similarly, the standard error of the mean of any set of observations *decreases* as the number of observations is increased. Sample size is one factor that can be used to enhance the prospects of detecting a real ES, which experimenters do have under their control. Further, anything that improves reliability and reduces error variance in the course of measurement, increases the power of a statistical test. In summary, an important reason for inconsistencies in findings by different groups of researchers is often differences in the power of the statistical tests and measurement procedures employed.

The chances of detecting a difference between groups also depends on the difficulty level of a particular neuropsychological test or measurement procedure. Most researchers are familiar with the idea that ceiling or floor effects operate to reduce the chance of discriminating between two groups. A test that is too difficult may be failed by both groups, and therefore not discriminate between them. For example, on a delayed free recall test both moderately and severely impaired amnesics may obtain scores that are close to zero. If the test is made easier, perhaps by reducing the delay before recall or by testing memory with a recognition procedure, then differences between moderate and severe amnesia may emerge. The relationship between difficulty level and discrimination can be illustrated with an example from Anastasi (1988). When the difficulty level of a test is about 0.5 (that is, about half the subjects pass, the other half fail), a test reaches its maximum discrimination power. In this case, with 100 subjects, 50 will pass and 50 will fail, providing a possible maximum of 2500 (50 × 50) discriminations between subjects. In contrast, a test passed by 80% or 20% of subjects makes just 80 × 20 (1600) discriminations. Thus, all other things being equal, tests with around 50% difficulty level are the most discriminating.

We have now identified two factors that are important in determining the chances of detecting a deficit in a pathological group that are controlled by the researcher: the difficulty level and reliability of the measures used. In an important article, Chapman and Chapman (1973) drew attention to the importance of these two factors, which they held determined the *discriminatory power* of any specific test used to detect deficits in pathological groups. In particular, Chapman and Chapman (1973) made explicit the fact that when any two groups are compared on more than one test, it is necessary to match these tests for discriminatory power; when no account is taken of this factor, spurious dissociations may arise. They observed (Chapman & Chapman, 1973, p. 380) that "If deficient subjects are as inferior to normal subjects on one ability as on another, but the test that is used to measure one of the abilities is more discriminating than the test of the other, a greater performance deficit will be found on the more discriminating test". Failure to match tasks for discriminatory power is responsible for many of the simple dissociations that appear in the neuropsychological literature. For example, it might be found that memory- impaired patients perform more poorly on tests of free recall than on measures of yes/no recognition. Usually, however, this is an obvious consequence of differences in the difficulty level of the two tests, and the same pattern is apparent in normal performance. To show that this difference was valid it would be necessary to construct matched tests of free recall and recognition, taking account of both difficulty level and reliability. It should also be noted that difficulty level effects cannot be removed by linear scaling techniques. Rescaling test results so that they have the same mean and standard deviation does not make them equivalent; underlying differences in difficulty level will remain. The fact that a Wechsler Intelligence or Memory subtest or index scores have scaled to have the same mean and standard deviation does not mean they are of the same difficulty levels.

Chapman and Chapman (1988) have extended their consideration of discriminatory power to the problem of comparing difference scores. They used as an example the way differences in scores are employed as indicators of cerebral asymmetry. In this case, the performance of a particular function by the left hemisphere (LH) is contrasted with the performance of the right hemisphere (RH). One way of indicating hemispheric dominance is simply to subtract the score on a LH test (A) from the score on a RH test (B) to give a laterality index of A–B. Chapman and Chapman (1988) showed that the value of A–B is constrained by the absolute values of A and B. Hence, as the sum of the two scores (A+B) tends toward its maximum or minimum values, the possible size of A–B is increasingly constrained. This means that if two groups are to be meaningfully compared on the size of their A–B index scores, their A+B scores must be equivalent. Further, the closer the average of A+B is to the midpoint of the distribution of the scores on A and B, the greater the chance of observing significant A–B discrepancies between groups. Conducting an experiment in which difference indices are compared necessitates making sure that (A+B)÷2 is in the median range and equivalent for the contrasted groups. The use of discrepancy scores (e.g. between intelligence and memory tests) is common in neuropsychology and it is important that the constraints imposed by the factors that Chapman and Chapman (1988) have identified are taken into account.

Conclusions

A number of the measures of intelligence and learning commonly used to determine if alcohol abuse causes cognitive impairment have been introduced in this chapter as a prelude to their consideration in Part 3. The measures most commonly used to detect impairments in alcoholics have been the WAIS and the Halstead–Reitan Battery. Although these tests were not originally constructed to assess brain impairment, as psychologists became involved in testing brain-damaged patients these multitask batteries came to be administered. As neuropsychology has developed, the role of testing in clinical practice has changed from an emphasis on formulating diagnostic statements, to a greater involvement in documenting deficits for the purpose of case management. More precise and valid measures of cognitive changes continue to be developed and knowledge about the validity of individual neuropsychological measures to accumulate. This has an important impact on testing hypotheses about the specific effects of alcohol on cognitive function. For example, the proposal that alcohol abuse causes discrete corticofrontal atrophy can only be tested in neuropsychological studies by tests specifically sensitive to such neurological damage. The validity of particular measures of memory is a major concern in developing theories about the nature of amnesia. The psychometric characteristics of the assessment procedures used to document cognitive deficits in neuropsychological investigations play a significant role in the usefulness of the results that emerge. As will become apparent in the next section of this chapter, similar considerations apply to the assessment of drinking behaviour.

An important theme of this brief introduction to neuropsychological assessment is the importance of considering the psychometric properties of neuropsychological measures when planning or evaluating a study of the deficits of people who drink. A prime consideration is that the measures administered and procedures used have the requisite statistic and discriminatory power to detect any decrements in performance that might occur. Important determinants of statistical power that are under the control of the experimenter are test reliability and the number of observations sampled. Chapman and Chapman (1973) have shown that the discriminatory power of individual neuropsychological tests is dependent on test difficulty and reliability. They also observed that where groups are tested on more than one measure, these measures must be matched for discriminatory power if valid conclusions about the relative magnitude of separate deficits are to be made. Spurious dissociations may emerge when task matching is not satisfactory.

In a recent extension of their discussion on discriminatory power, Chapman and Chapman have demonstrated that difference scores are constrained by the magnitude of the absolute scores on which they are based. For example, if ability to discriminate shapes is tested in blindfolded subjects using first the left and then the right hand, then performance by the left hand is typically superior because tactual discrimination proceeds more effectively in the right hemisphere (which is directly linked to the left hand) than in the left hemisphere. The difference between left and right hand discrimination might be taken as index of laterality in individual subjects. Between-group differences in laterality index scores, however, are constrained by absolute performance with both the left and right hands. Groups of 3-year-old and 10-year-old subjects may well have different average laterality index scores, but unless their average performance of the left- and right-handed discrimination task is equivalent, the laterality differences will not be meaningful. Constraints are placed on difference scores by floor and ceiling effects and it is important to be aware of this when considering other neuropsychological indices, such as VIQ–PIQ or IQ–MQ differences.

ASSESSMENT OF DRINKING PRACTICES

In addition to testing neuropsychological functions, many of the studies reviewed in Parts 2 and 3 of this book assess the drinking practices of their subjects. This is done for two basic reasons. The first is diagnostic; the researchers wish to establish that their subjects are classified appropriately, for example, as social drinkers or dependent alcohol abusers. The second objective is to document the behaviour of individual drinkers, so that individual differences in consumption can be used as an independent variable in studies of biological or psychological impairment. The adequacy of these assessments of drinking practices are often critical in establishing the utility of research procedures and in the resolution of discrepancies between studies. In what follows, some of the methods used to document drinking behaviour are described.

The *Subjects* section of most neuropsychological research reports involving alcoholics contains a more or less detailed outline of the characteristics of the clinical group tested. Typical of such a description is that provided by Ellis (1990):

> Participants in the alcoholic groups were recruited from local halfway houses. The diagnosis of alcoholism was based on information derived from the NIMH Diagnostic Interview Schedule (DIS), a structured psychiatric interview, and from the CAGE questionnaire. These data were validated by comparison with information provided by the referring facilities. The sections of the DIS devoted to alcohol use disorders render data concerning both psychosocial dysfunction or abuse, and signs of physical dependence, such as tolerance or withdrawal. Duration of illness also was assessed, thus providing an estimate of the number of years of alcoholic drinking tallied by each individual ... Subjects were accepted into the study only if they met criteria for alcohol abuse and dependence while being free of other major psychiatric diagnoses. Those subjects meeting DSM-III criteria for organic brain syndrome, multiple drug abuse, psychosis, or recent (6 months) history of manic or depressive episodes, were excluded from the study ... In addition, medical exclusion criteria included the following: history of head injury with extended loss of consciousness, neurotoxin exposure, recent use of psychotropic drugs or medications, seizures, stroke, or other neurological illness. Alcoholics were denied participation if they demonstrated clinical or psychometric signs of memory impairment suggesting Wernicke–Korsakoff disease. All alcoholics had been previously detoxified, and were abstinent for at least 30 days prior to testing.

This is a fuller description of a research alcoholic group than is provided in the majority of studies, and illustrates most of the decisions that a researcher has to make about the inclusion or exclusion of patients. Ellis begins by defining the source of the sample. Most alcoholic patients are defined in the first instance by their need for treatment or care. The alcoholic recruited for research purposes is generally undergoing detoxification or some therapy regime; thus heavy drinkers residing in the community or alcoholics barred for some reason from treatment facilities (by virtue of their personal circumstances or multiple failures in treatment programmes) are not represented. Diagnosis is often confirmed by the use of a structured interview that systematically reviews a patient's psychiatric history. One widely used measure is the Diagnostic Interview Schedule (Robins, Helzer, Croughan, & Ratliff, 1981). Complementing the interview may be standardised self-report inventories, such as the Michigan Alcoholism Screening Test (MAST). Typically data from all sources are used to formulate a diagnostic statement expressed in terms of DSM-III categories. Many studies contain a statement to the effect that "All patients included met DSM-III criteria for alcohol abuse or alcohol dependence". Often, explicit diagnostic exclusion criteria are provided. Patients who have primary drug addiction problems or who have a history of psychosis are excluded. Many neuropsychological studies of alcoholics specifically exclude patients who have neurological complications such as head injury or symptoms of Wernicke–Korsakoff syndrome. Another class of data about alcohol-related behaviour that Ellis does not report are consumption variables. As his subjects were abstinent resident outpatients, these data were of little relevance in detailing his clinical sample. In many studies, however, daily average consumption or lifetime drinking practices are reported in terms of such variables as average grams of alcohol per day, usual amount consumed per occasion, or "years of heavy drinking". Such data are almost invariably reported in studies of social drinkers.

Table 3.4 summarises the results of a survey of all studies using alcoholic subjects published in the 1990 issues of the *Journal of Studies on Alcohol* and *Alcoholism: Clinical and Experimental Research*. All studies were included, regardless of the nature of the research focus. The aim was to document how researchers formally described their alcoholic groups. Only measures that were explicitly mentioned in the *Methods* section were recorded; for example, consumption data were not recorded for a particular study unless they were reported explicitly. It is possible that such data were collected during the course of a structured interview and used to formulate diagnoses; thus the percentages reported in Table 3.4 may under-represent the use of some measures in actual practice.

It can be seen from Table 3.4 that an alcoholic is first and foremost someone located in the system for treating alcohol-related problems. Nearly half the studies stated that subjects met DSM criteria for alcohol dependence or abuse. Often the implication was that this was the only

TABLE 3.4

Percentage of Studies (*n* = 41) Reporting Particular Data Sources or Diagnostic Criteria for Groups of Alcoholics

Variable	Percentage
Description of treatment facility sampled	100
DSM-III or related criteria applied	42
Consumption data reported	39
Structured interview employed	27
Self-report inventories administered	24
Psychiatric exclusion criteria detailed	17
Primary drug addicts specifically excluded	17

psychiatric diagnosis subjects had; however, this was stated explicitly in less than 20% of studies. Again, it could be assumed that the alcoholic samples did not include primary drug users, however, multiple drug use was seldom documented or used as an exclusion criterion. Consumption variables were reported regularly and use of structured psychiatric interviews or self-report inventories such as the MAST was also common. In the remainder of this section, we will look at some of these methods of assessing drinking behaviour or specifying diagnoses in more depth.

Diagnostic criteria

Traditionally, psychiatric classification has been dominated by a categorical or typological perspective. In this view, patients with common symptoms are clustered into discrete groups with discontinuous boundaries. As we saw in Chapter 2, until recently alcoholism was regarded as a categorical disorder. An alternative view is that problem drinking can be measured on a continuous dimension, extending from mild social drinking to severe alcohol dependency. The categorical approach was implicit in the influential work of Jellinek (1946; 1960), who identified a set of distinct subgroups of persons with alcohol-related problems. One of these he termed gamma-alcoholism, and this condition was characterised by the presence of physiological dependence and tolerance. The gamma-alcoholic was the drinker with the disease of alcoholism of primarily biological aetiology; the aetiology of abusive drinking in other groups was assumed to be psychosocial in origin. This division of drinkers into those who abused alcohol and were dependent, and those who were alcohol abusers but not dependent, was incorporated into the major diagnostic classificatory systems for psychiatric disorders, the International Classification of Disease (ICD) and the DSM-III.

The rigid categorical formulations of diagnosis, whereby alcoholism or dependence was considered to be an all-or-none disease-like phenomenon, were relaxed during the 1970s. In part, this was a response to the problems involved in making decisions about the presence of dependency, and evidence that the lifetime patterns of many drinkers did not easily fit into an inflexible categorical system. The emphasis changed towards viewing alcohol dependency as a syndrome with degrees of severity (Edwards, 1977; Edwards & Gross, 1976). This is reflected in the changes made to the ICD in 1979, when the label "alcoholism" was replaced by "alcohol dependence syndrome". When the DSM-III was revised, the new DSM-III-R allowed degrees of dependence (mild, moderate, severe) and a range of cognitive, physiological and behavioural features of dependency were defined. The primary dimensions along which alcohol dependence may vary are:

1. Drinking episodes more prolonged, or amount consumed greater than intended.
2. Inability to reduce or abstain from consumption.
3. Excess time spend obtaining, consuming, or recovering from drinking.
4. Intoxication or withdrawal symptoms occur when fulfilling major role obligations (e.g. at work or home).
5. Drinking reduces involvement in important social or occupational activities.
6. Drinking continues despite recognition of social, psychological, or health-related problems.
7. Development of tolerance and a need to increase by at least 50% the amount consumed to achieve intoxication.
8. Withdrawal symptoms occur when consumption is stopped or prevented.
9. Drinking is used to relieve the effects of withdrawal.

At least three of these features must be present for the diagnosis of substance dependence to be made. A separate diagnosis—alcohol abuse—is used to describe people who have maladaptive patterns of drinking that may lead to psychosocial problems and a desire for treatment, but who do not meet the usual criteria for dependence.

The DSM criteria are frequently cited as the way in which groups of alcoholics constituted for research purposes have been diagnosed. Although the new DSM-III-R criteria for dependence are stated carefully, operationalising these features in the assessment of clinical cases in practice does require some judgement. Consistency in application across studies may be obtained in the future by greater use of self-report questionnaires that are based on the features of the dependency syndrome. The Alcohol Dependency Scale (ADS; Skinner & Allen, 1982), for example, is a questionnaire measure that contains 29 items relevant to the diagnostic category of alcohol dependence. Another example of the way in which the DSM dependence features can be operationalised in practice is provided by Grant and Harford (1990). Table 3.5, provides examples of the criteria and the way they were operationalised by Grant and Harford.

Self-report questionnaires

A number of inventories are in common use for the identification and assessment of alcohol abuse and dependence (Davidson, 1987). Initially, these questionnaires were predicated on the assumption that alcoholism was a disease, and they included a range of questions about the reasons for, and the consequences of, alcohol abuse. More recent measures have

TABLE 3.5
Operationalising DSM-III-R Dependency Criteria
(From Grant & Harford, 1990)

Criteria		Operationalisation	
1.	Alcohol use in large amounts or difficult over longer periods than intended	1a.	Once I started drinking it was difficult for me to stop before I became completely intoxicated
		1b	I sometimes kept drinking after I had promised myself not to
8.	Characteristic withdrawal symptoms	8a.	My hands shook a lot the morning after drinking
		8b.	Sometimes I have awakened during the night or early morning sweating all over because of drinking

been based on the concept of the alcohol dependency syndrome identified by the ICD and DSM. Some of the most widely used self-report scales are described below.

The Michigan Alcoholism Screening Test (MAST). Undoubtedly the best known measure of alcohol-related consequences, beliefs, and behaviours is the MAST (Selzer, 1971). This 25-item scale has been used in numerous studies to identify alcoholics and to quantify the effects of alcohol abuse. Variations of this scale have been published, including the brief MAST (Pokorny, Miller, & Kaplan, 1972). A similar scale, suitable for use with adolescents—the Rutgers Alcoholism Problem Index—has been constructed by White and Labouvie (1989). The range and style of questions can be seen in Fig. 3.1. The focus is on the patients' perception of their drinking behaviour and on the consequences that have resulted. Using a cutoff score of 5, Pokorny et al. found that the scale correctly identified 60 alcoholics and misclassified 7 of 62 non-alcoholics.

As is apparent from the items on this scale, the focus is on identifying alcoholics in terms of the traditional discrete category of the disease of alcoholism. The alcoholic is also diagnosed in the Brief MAST largely by their past involvement in treatment. The aim of the test is to distinguish alcoholics from non-alcoholics with the least possible error. The implication of the content of the items is that alcoholism is an unchanging disease state; hence the questions have no specified time context. Most are introduced by the phrase "have you ever", indicative of the notion that alcoholism "is a chronic lifetime illness" (Davidson, 1987, p. 245), and that even after a period of abstinence or controlled drinking the diagnosis remains in force. In addition, it is of note that scales such as the MAST use direct questions,

Questions	Circle correct answers	
1. Do you feel you are a normal drinker?	Yes (0)	No (2)
2. Do friends or relatives think you are a normal drinker?	Yes (0)	No (2)
3. Have you ever attended a meeting of Alcoholics Anonymous (AA)?	Yes (5)	No (0)
4. Have you ever lost friends or girlfriends/boyfriends because of drinking?	Yes (2)	No (0)
5. Have you ever gotten into trouble at work because of drinking?	Yes (2)	No (0)
6. Have you ever neglected your obligations, your family, or your work for two or more days in a row because you were drinking?	Yes (2)	No (0)
7. Have you ever had delirium tremens (DTs), severe shaking, heard voices or seen things that weren't there after heavy drinking?	Yes (2)	No (0)
8. Have you ever gone to anyone for help about your drinking?	Yes (5)	No (0)
9. Have you ever been in a hospital because of drinking?	Yes (5)	No (0)
10. Have you ever been arrested for drunk driving or driving after drinking?	Yes (2)	No (0)

FIG. 3.1. The Brief MAST.

which have a high face validity but are susceptible to faking. This issue will be considered further when we review the validity and reliability of alcoholics' self-reports.

The CAGE.   This scale has been widely used in clinical practice and in epidemiological surveys (Mayfield, McLeod, & Hall, 1974). Occasionally it has been used to verify a diagnosis of alcohol abuse, as in the Ellis (1990) study. The CAGE comprises four items (Fig. 3.2); a positive response on two items identified over 80% in a validation trial (Mayfield et al., 1974).

Severity of Alcohol Dependence Questionnaire (SADQ).   The content of the 20 items of this scale is based on the alcohol dependency syndrome identified by Edwards (1986) and others. The SADQ instructs the respondent to consider a specific month typical of their heavy drinking. There are four items assessing five features of the dependency syndrome (physical withdrawal effects, affective signs of withdrawal, withdrawal relief drinking, quantity and frequency of consumption, and rapidity of reinstatement of withdrawal symptoms after abstinence). Thus, not all the

1.	Have you ever felt that you should *cut down* on your drinking?
2.	Have people *annoyed* you by criticising your drinking?
3.	Have you ever felt *bad* or *guilty* about your drinking?
4.	Have you ever had a drink first thing in the morning to steady your nerves or get rid of a hangover (an eyeopener)?

FIG. 3.2. The CAGE questionnaire.

features of alcohol dependence are addressed. There are some preliminary norms for this measure and evidence of high test–retest reliability (Stockwell et al., 1979; Stockwell, Murphy, & Hodgson, 1983).

Short-form Alcohol Dependence Data Questionnaire (SADD). This 15-item questionnaire is also derived from the Edwards and Gross conceptualisation of the alcohol dependency syndrome (Raistrick, Dunbar, & Davidson, 1983). Respondents are asked to think about their most recent drinking habits and to answer each question using a four-point frequency scale. A selection of items from the scale are presented in Fig. 3.3. In contrast to scales such as the MAST, the emphasis is on the present and the items assess a wide range of cognitive, behavioural, and physiological effects of alcoholism. The SADD is highly correlated with the SADQ and there is evidence for a good level of reliability (Jorge & Masur, 1985).

Alcohol Dependence Scale (ADS). This scale is a refinement of the Alcohol Dependence Scale of the Alcohol Uses Inventory (Horn, Wanberg, & Forster, 1974). The 29 questions come from four domains of alcohol dependence: loss of behavioural control, obsessive drinking style, psychoperceptual withdrawal, and psychophysical withdrawal (Skinner & Allen, 1982). Test development was based on results from 225 patients in treatment at the Toronto Clinical Institute of the Alcoholic Addiction

1.	Do you find difficulty in getting the thought of drink out of your mind?
5.	Do you drink for the effect of alcohol without caring what the drink is?
8.	Do you know that you won't be able to stop drinking once you start?
11.	The morning after a heavy drinking session do you wake up with a definite shakiness of your hands?
15.	Do you go drinking and next day find you have forgotten what happened the night before?

FIG. 3.3. Sample questions from the Short-form Alcohol Dependency Data Questionnaire.

Research Foundation. The initial version of the scale was found to have a high degree of internal consistency (alpha = 0.92) and to correlate highly with the MAST ($r = 0.69$). Although the items of the initial scale assessed a broad range of the features of alcohol dependence, no items were included that were relevant to the development of tolerance or reinstatement after abstinence (Skinner & Allen, 1982). A revised version of the scale with four new items relating to these areas has been prepared. Concurrent validity has been confirmed in a study by Kivlahan, Sher, and Donovan (1989), and Ross, Gavin, and Skinner (1990) identified a cutoff score of 8–9 for the detection of alcohol dependence as identified by the DSM-III.

Consumption-related variables

Assessment of alcoholic clients in clinical practice typically involves obtaining a description of their current drinking practices in terms of amount of alcohol consumed. Although definitions of alcohol dependence are not linked to quantities, amount consumed is often employed as an index of severity of alcohol abuse in empirical studies. The assessment of drinking patterns, however, is complicated by the sheer variety of individual drinking behaviours and available beverages. There are correspondingly numerous methods of quantifying the amount consumed.

One common method of quantifying consumption is to compute an average (daily, weekly, or monthly) volume statistic based on responses to questions about frequency of drinking and usual amount consumed. Typical of the kind of questions asked to derive a unidimensional volume estimate are those displayed in Fig. 3.4. Total volume consumed each month can be computed by multiplying the number of occasions by the modal quantity for each occasion, and summing over the three beverage types. However, simple estimates of volume ignore important variations in patterns of consumption. For example, there is no way of discriminating between a low, but regular level of consumption and heavy binge drinking on the basis of a volume estimate. Heavy episodic use may result in the user seeking treatment or being subject to more severe psychosocial and physical effects than the moderate regular drinker.

As a consequence, many questionnaires also ask about maximum quantity consumed on any one occasion. In their influential report on *American Drinking Practices*, Cahalan, Cisin, and Crossley (1969) used a quantity–frequency–variability index, where variability was determined as a combination of modal and greatest quantities consumed. The measures that Cahalan and colleagues used have formed the basis for the collection of consumption data in several studies of cognition in social drinkers.

Another instance of a consumption statistic that takes some account of maximum quantity consumed is the annual absolute alcohol index (AAAI)

1. Over the past month how often have you had any of the following types of alcohol:				
	not at all	1 or less per week	2–3 × per week	4–5 × per week	6–7 × per week
Beer	0	1	2	3	4
Wine	0	1	2	3	4
Spirits	0	1	2	3	4

2. Over the past month, on average, how much of each drink have you consumed at any one time:					
Pints of beer	0	1–2	3–4	5–6	6–7	8 or more
Glass of wine	0	1–2	3–4	5–6	7–10	11–14	15 or more
Measure of spirits		1–2	3–4	5–6	7–10	11–14	15 or more

FIG. 3.4. Sample quantity–frequency consumption questionnaire.

of Khavari and colleagues. This index is based on responses to the 12-item Khavari Alcohol Test (Mercer & Khavari, 1990). From this test, four consumption statistics are derived: Usual frequency of drinking (FU), Usual amount consumed per occasion (VU), maximum amount consumed per occasion (VM), and frequency of consumption of maximum amount (FM). Respondents are asked to reports amounts in terms of number of 10oz glasses/cans beer, 4oz glasses of wine, and 1.5oz measures of spirits. For each beverage annual volume (VA) is computed, using the following formula:

$$VA = (FU - FM) VU + (FM \times VM)$$

From this, an estimate of annual absolute alcohol intake is derived by incorporating estimates of amount of alcohol in each drink (e.g. beer contains about 4.5% alcohol by volume):

$$AAAI = VA \text{ (beer)} \times 0.045 + VA \text{ (wine)} \times 0.15 + VA \text{ (spirits)} \times 0.45$$

The Khavari AAAI calculation involves subjects estimating their consumption in terms of number of "standard" drinks. Asking how many drinks are consumed per occasion on the basis of a standard drink is a method sometimes employed in consumption surveys (Miller, Heather, & Hall, 1991). For example, Webb, Redman, Sanson-Fisher, and Gibberd (1990) investigated consumption amongst people involved in the wine industry in the Hunter Valley of New South Wales. They defined the standard (Australian) drink as 285ml beer, 30ml of spirits, 120ml of table wine, and 60ml of fortified wine. They assessed consumption with a quantity question ("On a day when you drink alcohol, how much do you usually have?") and a frequency question ("How often do you drink alcohol on average?"). The data were then aggregated to produce an estimate of the number of standard drinks per week. As the beverage quantities in each drink do not contain an equal amount of alcohol by volume, the aggregate measure cannot be converted to a volume of alcohol statistic. Quantifying consumption in terms of a "standard drink" has been a common practice. However, there has been considerable variation in the amount of alcohol regarded as standard, making comparisons across studies difficult (Turner, 1990).

Another method of collecting consumption information is by use of a retrospective diary. For example, Redman et al. (1987) administered a 14-day diary that subjects used to record their daily consumption in terms of number of standard drinks. A more complex procedure is the Time-Line Follow-Back interview used in the treatment and clinical evaluation of problem drinkers by Mark and Linda Sobell and colleagues (Sobell, Maisto, Sobell, & Cooper, 1979). This technique is used to assess consumption over a year-long period. Patients are presented with a 12-month calendar and, for each day, they are asked to recall their drinking behaviour. This is done by helping the patient to identify temporal anchor points that mark significant dates within the year, such as birthdays, holidays, or major sporting events. Personal events, such as hospitalisations, illnesses, or employment activities are also used. The respondent is encouraged to use these anchors to recollect their pattern of drinking around the time of the event. They are also asked to describe their habitual pattern of drinking and to locate periods of abstinence. Sobell et al. observed that, over the course of several studies, it was unusual for subjects to report highly variable drinking patterns. This technique has been found to be highly reliable (Sobell et al., 1979), and there is also evidence of the procedure's validity. For example, when O'Farrell et al. (1984) categorised their Time-Line data into days of abstinence, light-drinking (3oz or less of alcohol), heavy-drinking (3+ oz of alcohol), hospital, treatment, and prison confinement, correlations between results from spouse and patient were greater than 0.85 for all categories except light- and heavy-drinking days. Although the Time-Line Follow-Back method has been used successfully in the clinic, the painstaking nature of the task means that it is unlikely to be used routinely in neuropsychological research, particularly in large studies of social drinkers, who tend to have variable drinking patterns.

Many studies of alcohol-dependent subjects report summary statistics describing the pattern of consumption in their sample, usually as part of the evidence of the validity of their diagnostic statements. For example, Keshavarzian, Polepalle, Iber, and Durkin (1990, p. 561) stated that: "All alcoholics had a history of drinking at least 150gm of ethanol daily for the 3 months before admission and had no period of sobriety exceeding 6 months during the past 5 years". Researchers often provide information on the average length of the period of alcohol abuse in their subjects and estimates of lifetime consumption totals are sometimes reported. In most cases, these data do not have a critical bearing on the nature of the procedures that are used or the results that emerge. In studies of social drinkers, however, because the analyses used involve correlating estimates of consumption with cognitive test scores, the psychometric credentials of the consumption measures are critical. If these are unreliable or invalid, then the correlations are likely to be seriously attenuated and the chances of finding significant effects reduced. In the next section, the trustworthiness of alcoholics self-report is examined.

Dependability of drinkers' verbal self-report

As has already been observed, the predominant means of obtaining data from drinkers and alcoholics about their consumption and the effects of drinking are based on self-report. Quantification of consumption practices, for example, relies on subjects being able and willing to recall their drinking behaviour over an extended period of time. They also need to be capable of making judgements about their typical or usual patterns of consumption, which requires the ability to abstract a general formulation from a complex series of specific events. There are various opinions about the dependability of the verbal self-reports of alcohol abusers. Many clinicians are frankly sceptical of much of the information that alcoholics provide about themselves. In contrast, "there is a general perception within the alcohol research community that verbal self-report procedures are reliable and valid under most circumstances for the purpose of obtaining research data" (Babor, Stephens, & Marlatt, 1987).

Untrustworthiness has been imputed to the self-report data of alcohol abusers for a variety of reasons. Many people with alcohol-related problems do not accept the role of alcohol in their lives and often deny that their drinking behaviour represents a hazard to themselves or their families. In the process of denial, the personal and psychosocial consequences of alcohol abuse may be minimised, leading to a possible deliberate underestimate of consumption and its effects. In addition, the client under treatment may perceive the need to distort reports of drinking practices because of the demands of the therapeutic environment. For example, patients in research studies are often described as being abstinent for a specific period of time. This is not easy to ensure. In practice, clients in treatment have strong disincentives to admitting episodes of alcohol abuse during or after treatment. In addition to motivated or unconscious denial, the ability of alcohol-dependent subjects to report accurately may be impeded by the acute effects of intoxication, the effects of permanent cognitive impairment, or some combination of both factors. Even under the most favourable circumstances, it can be difficult for anyone who has been intoxicated to remember with precision how much they consumed. Finally, the context of the research may be ambiguous for the dependent subject and this may have a bearing on their responses. For instance, inpatient alcoholics may be uncertain about the status of the research, the security and confidentiality of their data, and the relationship between their performance on the tests and their ongoing management or access to hospital privileges.

Despite these potential sources of error, self-report is often the only way of assessing some aspects of drinkers' experiences of alcohol use. It is therefore important to have some empirical evidence of the validity and reliability of self-report, and to investigate methods of making these data more dependable.

Reliability

The test-retest reliability of self-reported consumption in the recent past, and the consequences of alcohol abuse have been investigated in a number of studies. Babor et al. (1987) in their survey found that reliability estimates typically exceeded 0.75 for both inpatient and outpatient alcoholic samples. However, "Skidrow" alcoholics tend to provide less reliable reports. Annis (1979) tested a group of chronic alcoholics admitted to a detoxification centre on two occasions separately by 2 to 6 months. Percentage agreement figures for some of the data they collected are detailed in Table 3.6. As far as consumption practices were concerned, their frequency estimates tended to be more stable than their reports of amount consumed. These consumption retest statistics may, however, reflect genuine changes in habit as well as unreliability of report. On the whole, college students and adolescents have been shown to provide reliable estimates of frequency (Sobell et al., 1986) and quantity (Needle, McCubbin, Lorence, & Hochhauser, 1983).

Reports of drinking behaviour several years previously are less reliable. Simpura and Poikolainen (1983) found that 67 non-alcoholic men, reinterviewed 18 years after participation in a drinking survey, over-estimated their past consumption by an average of 76%. Sobell et al. (1988) investigated the accuracy of current reports of drinking behaviour 8 years previously. Subjects were asked on two occasions, separated by 2 to 3 weeks, to provide estimates of their consumption during a specific year (1976). The

TABLE 3.6

Percentage Agreement of Selected Information Given by Skidrow
Alcoholics on Two Occasions (From Table1, Annis, 1979)

Variables	Percentage agreement
Age	93
Number of children	85
Marital status	71
In the past year, months of:	
outpatient treatment	75
residential treatment	50
time in prison	58
Usual frequency of drinking	85
Usual daily consumption	56

results are presented in Table 3.7. These reliability estimates were in the
moderate to high range, although precise quantity estimates tended to be
less reliable than the frequency data. Czarnecki, Russell, Cooper, and
Salter (1990) found that original and retrospective reports of consumption
5 years earlier were highly and significantly correlated for the most
frequently consumed beverages, beer, and spirits.

TABLE 3.7

Current Reliability of Reports of Drinking Patterns 8 Years Previously

Variable	Reliability
Days any alcohol consumed (Frequency; F)	0.81
Total number of drinks (Quantity: Q)	0.66
Drinks/drinking days (Q–F)	0.67
Greatest number of standard drinks on any single day	0.65
Days 1–4 standard drinks	0.53
Days > 4 standard drinks	0.52
Days 1–6 standard drinks	0.73
Days > 6 standard drinks	0.70
Longest consecutive abstinent period	0.88

Reprinted with permission from *Journal of Studies on Alcohol, 49*, 225–232, The reliability
of alcohol abusers' self-reports of drinking and life-events that occurred in the distant past,
by Sobell et al., 1988. Copyright © 1988, Alcohol Research Documentation Inc.

Validity

Although alcoholics may report on their consumption patterns with a reasonable degree of consistency, self-reported and actual drinking practices may not agree. The extent to which verbal self-report of alcohol use can be corroborated by data from other sources has been examined in several studies. There are three major ways of concurrently validating alcohol users self-report: Use of collateral informants (spouses or friends), checking data against official records, and collecting physiological measures such as blood alcohol levels (BALs). Of these three options, collateral informant methods have been most commonly used. The validity of alcoholics' self-reports is of considerable importance, particularly in determining the outcome and value of various therapies. Results from validity studies have been variable and indeed excited some controversy (Maisto & O'Farrell, 1985; Watson, 1985). Evidence of a moderate to high degree validity was provided by Maisto, Sobell, and Sobell (1979). They obtained consumption data from 52 outpatient alcoholics and compared their estimates with those of collateral informants, mostly spouses. Overall, correlations were highest for subjects who had been either mostly drunk or mostly abstinent over the period assessed. Although there was no systematic difference in the number of days abstinent, the patients reported fewer drunk days and more limited drinking, days in prison, and days in hospital than did the collaterals. The number of days collaterals were in contact with patients did not predict the magnitude of the subject–collateral differences.

In another study of the relationship between alcoholics' and collaterals' reports of drinking behaviour, Watson et al. (1984) compared self-reports from 100 male inpatients and information from collaterals (friends or relatives) on drinking over an 18-month post-treatment follow-up period. They used a 5-point rating scale: 1 = no drinking since last contact; 2 = has complete control of drinking; 3 = controls drinking most of the time; 4 = has control over drinking less than half the time; and 5 = does not have control over drinking. The patients tended to rate themselves as having more control than they were perceived as having by their collaterals. Correlations ranged from a modest 0.57 to 0.76. These results were less encouraging than those of Sobell and colleagues (1979). However, in reviewing this study, Maisto and O'Farrell (1985) raised a number of methodological issues and, in particular, drew attention to the adequacy of the 5-point rating scale that Watson et al. had used. They observed (Maisto & O'Farrell, 1985, p. 449) that " ... the authors used a 5-point nominal scale, with referents lacking behavioural specificity, to measure subjects' drinking behaviour. Besides the relative insensitivity of such measurement procedures, it is also likely that whatever data are obtained will not be reliable and, therefore, not valid". In response to these criticisms, Watson (1985) clarified many of these issues, however, the reliability of the scale remained indeterminate. It is possible that the low correlations reflect patient–collateral disagreements over the precise meaning of such anchoring statements as "has complete control over drinking" and the consequent unreliability of the ratings.

Overall, studies that have examined the validity of alcoholics' self-report using correlations between collateral and self-ratings have provided encouraging evidence for some measures of consumption in follow-up studies. Validity tends to be lowest with individual cases where drinking is variable; data are also dependent upon the informant having sufficient knowledge about the target subject's drinking behaviour to make accurate judgements. Not all drinkers have available a reliable informant and it may be that those who do are unrepresentative of alcoholics in general. Data from official records, and alcoholics' self-reports of such information as number of arrests, days of treatment, and days in prison, tend to be in reasonable agreement. For example, Sobell and Sobell (1978) reported that the agreement between records and self-report for voluntary outpatients was between 78% and 93% for number of hospitalisations, and 92% and 100% for arrests. Figures were comparable for coerced outpatients and voluntary inpatients. Finally, there have been studies which show good correlations between level of self-reported consumption over a drinking session and BAL readings (Babor et al., 1987; Meier, Brigham, & Handel, 1987).

Although much of the data reviewed in this section comes from studies with alcoholic clients, accuracy of reporting consumption is equally important in research with social drinkers. Of relevance to the determination of the validity of consumption data from social drinkers is a study by Lemmens, Knibbe, and Tan (1988), which involved a sample of 399 Dutch subjects from a general population survey. They compared recall of weekly consumption in an interview setting with results from a 14-day consumption diary. The diary method resulted in higher estimates (over 20%) than the weekly recall data (12.4 glasses on average per week versus 10.1 glasses for the interview recall data). Regardless of the method, however, the ranking of individuals was described as stable, which is critical for the validity of correlational data. Webb et al. (1990) compared the retrospective diary method with general quantity and frequency questions and also found that the diary method produced higher consumption figures. Similar results were reported by Werch (1990), who found that the correlations between daily measures of alcohol consumption and Quantity/Frequency questions (using a monthly time frame) was 0.86. These results suggest, in summary, that Quantity–Frequency and diary methods produce linearly related estimates of consumption, although estimates from diary methods tend to be consistently higher. This systematic bias will not affect correlations between consumption rate and cognitive variables, but classification of subjects in terms of high, moderate, or low consumption social drinking, may be influenced by the data collection method used.

Conclusions

Inaccuracies in determining the consumption levels of individual subjects are typically not fatal to most neuropsychological studies of drinkers; however, measurement error and low validity serve to reduce the likelihood of quantifying the association between levels of consumption and cognitive or psychological changes. This is especially true of research with social drinkers. Quantifying consumption retrospectively is not an easy task, even for social drinkers with a completely intact and predictable lifestyle. For alcoholics, there are a host of physiological and psychological factors that make remembering drinking behaviour a difficult feat. A number of variables have been shown to influence the reliability and validity of self-report and have important implications for planning methods of documenting drinking practices. These include framing questions and response alternatives with clear instructions and useful examples. The quality and clarity of questions in both written and interview surveys is of considerable importance. It is also apparent that using diary methods with clear reference to individual drinking episodes produces higher estimates of consumption that general Quantity–Frequency questions in social drinkers. Different ways of estimating Quantity and Frequency statistics based on questions aimed at determining usual drinking practices tend to be highly correlated, even if levels of estimates vary. It is also important to make the context and purpose of the data collection clear to subjects, particularly to alcoholics under treatment. Confusion of the roles of experimental subject and patient under treatment is likely to undermine validity. Ensuring confidentiality is also likely to enhance the meaningfulness of self-report. Bias and inaccuracy in interview surveys can be reduced by the use of structured interviews and the careful training of interviewers. Finally, it is important that the consumption levels of alcohol abusers in neuropsychological studies are assessed at times when they are in a stable physical state. Whenever possible, the validity of self-report data should be checked against the records of treatment agencies and the information of collaterals and discrepancies and misunderstandings clarified and resolved.

RESEARCH SAMPLE CHARACTERISTICS

The constitution of samples of drinkers for experimental study presents a number of problems, and variations in the way in which subjects are selected contribute to the inconsistencies in results reported by different research groups. The impact of many of these factors will be examined in more depth in later chapters; at this time, however, some of the significant factors involved will be introduced.

Many of the differences in research samples emanate from the absence in definitions of terms like 'alcohol abuse' or 'social drinking' of explicit reference to the amount of alcohol consumed. For example, the definitions of alcoholism that have emerged in clinical practice, for good reason, describe the disorder in terms of its psychosocial impact and make no reference to quantity. Thus, within any group of clients being treated for alcohol abuse problems there will be a wide range of drinking practices and medical consequences. In addition, we have already seen that the methods used to establish drinking practices and to define alcoholism for the purpose of research studies vary considerably. Differences in the precise criteria used in experimental studies are likely to lead to differences in the samples recruited and tested.

The absence of a definitive consumption level for the diagnosis of alcohol abuse has an impact on the recruitment of subjects for community or college samples of social drinkers. It is probable that any randomly constituted group of social drinkers will contain a significant percentage of people at risk for a diagnosis of alcoholism. Such people may not have been treated for problem drinking, although they may receive therapy in the future. If their self-report is valid, they may exceed some arbitrary weekly limit of consumption and thereby be excluded. If not, they may bias conclusions about the detrimental effects of social drinking practices. Social drinking samples also differ in their possible membership from one study to the next. Samples vary from predominantly middle-class and middle-aged men, to factory workers, with different drinking norms and practices. Social drinking samples also differ in their average age, level of affective disorder, and gender balance.

Samples of alcoholics similarly vary in their demographic and clinical characteristics. Subject factors likely to influence scores on neuropsychological tests include age, sex, race, education, level of physical impairment (e.g. presence of cardiac, gastric, hepatic, and neurological complications), as well as duration and pattern of consumption. Another factor that may be significant is a family history of alcoholism. An important determinant of the make-up of a particular sample is the nature of the treatment centre(s) from which they are recruited. Treatment facilities vary considerably in their explicit admission criteria. There are also unstated biases in the selection of clients for therapy that may include repeated treatment failure, age, level of neurological impairment, and clinical estimates of the clients' readiness for therapy (O'Leary, Speltz, Donovan, & Walker, 1979b). This means that those patients who are available for testing may be unrepresentative of the population of alcohol abusers, many of whom may be refused admission to treatment programmes or are discharged after their medical problems have been treated and detoxification is complete. Those patients who remain in therapy and are tested late in an 8- or 12-week programme may also be atypical of alcoholics in general. For similar reasons, follow-up studies of the effect of prolonged abstinence can be particularly difficult to execute. Alcoholic patients are often hard to find after discharge, and when they are located, their abstinence, or lack of it, is hard to determine and quantify accurately. Thus any group of patients tested after discharge, or even late in the course of a treatment programme, may be biased or unrepresentative.

Another factor that may bias the constitution of groups for study is the use of volunteers. Strohmetz, Alterman, and Walter (1990) compared the alcohol drinking practices of subjects who either agreed or disagreed to volunteer for a treatment study. From a sample of 91 patients who completed an intake interview process that determined their recent drinking habits, Stohmetz et al. obtained full consent for participation in a treatment trial from 25 patients, partial consent from 31 others, and a refusal to volunteer from the remaining 38 patients. They found that the full consent volunteers reported higher numbers of days on which alcohol was drunk and days drunk to intoxication than the other two groups. Overall, there was a positive relationship between self-reported severity of their alcohol abuse problem and degree of research participation. There is evidence, however, that the reverse is true of neuropsychological research. Nixon, Parsons, Schaeffer, and Hale (1988) investigated the cognitive impairments in subjects who were selected versus unselected and who agreed or declined to participate. All subjects had routinely received the SILS, Beck Depression Inventory, State-Trait Anxiety Inventory, and a hyperkinesis-minimal brain dysfunction checklist, prior to being approached about possible involvement in the study. The researchers' selection criteria involved eliminating subjects with a SILS vocabulary age below 12–7 or who had not completed an 8th grade education. Nixon et al. found that alcoholics who were eligible to participate, but declined, performed less well than those who either agreed to participate or were ineligible, on SILS Abstraction scale. These effects were independent of levels of affect, SILS–Vocabulary, and the neurological symptoms checklist scores. These results suggest that the use of volunteers may lead to an underestimate of the severity of neuropsychological impairment.

PART 2

ALCOHOL AND
THE NERVOUS SYSTEM

CHAPTER FOUR

Neuroradiological Studies

It is a good morning exercise for a research scientist to discard a pet hypothesis every day before breakfast. It keeps him young.

Lorenz (1966, p. 8)

The purpose of this chapter is to provide an introductory overview of research in radiological brain imaging of alcohol users. The references provided will allow the interested reader to locate sources for further study. The emphasis is on the findings of neuroradiology studies of long-term alcoholics and social drinkers; however, the findings of brain imaging studies of more severe neurological disorders like Wernicke–Korsakoff syndrome will also be discussed.

EARLY RADIOLOGICAL STUDIES

Prior to the 1970s, *in vivo* studies of structural brain abnormalities in alcoholics were conducted using the technique pneumoencephalography (PEG; also known as air encephalography). PEG permits the radiological study of the intracranial spaces, notably the ventricular system. Because ordinary X-rays do not differentiate clearly between brain substance and the cerebrospinal fluid (CSF) occupying the ventricular system, a lumbar puncture is performed and about 25ml of air injected as a contrast medium. A small amount of cerebrospinal fluid is drained to maintain stable fluid pressure. The subject can then be rotated in various planes to enable the air to rise through the fluid to the area of interest. This allows standard X-rays to depict endocranial spaces that would otherwise appear indistinguishable from cerebral tissue.

In most of the early studies using PEG, alcoholics showed evidence of cerebral abnormalities (Haug, 1968). However, a number of clinical and methodological problems associated with PEG made interpretation of such findings difficult. The radiographic images derived clearly depicted changes to the ventricular system, but showed only vague structural abnormalities of the cerebral cortex. In addition, because PEG requires the painful procedures of lumbar puncture and CSF drainage, which frequently caused headache, for practical and ethical reasons study samples were frequently restricted. Most often these consisted of highly selected groups of alcoholic patients with obvious, or strongly suspected, brain damage (Brewer & Perrett, 1971).

The advent of X-ray computerised axial tomography imaging (CT scanning) techniques facilitated the study of larger and more representative groups of alcoholics. It also permitted easier access to large populations of social drinkers. Briefly, CT scanning utilises the tendency for X-rays to penetrate different tissue types to differing degrees. Computer programmes are employed to construct a visual image of the organ in question, on the basis of the pattern of X-ray penetration. Figure 4.1a, b, & c shows scans of three different brains (taken from the levels depicted in Fig. 4.1d).

A number of dimensions of brain structure are commonly measured by CT scanning. They are listed here and some are depicted in Fig. 4.2:

1. Inspection of the width of sulci and fissures in a number of brain regions.
2. Linear assessment of maximum width of the ventricles at various points.
3. Calculation of ventricle/brain indices reflecting the ratio of the area of the ventricles at a particular level, to the area of cerebral hemisphere at that same level (see Fig. 4.2).
4. Computer-assisted estimation of the volume of the cerebrospinal fluid-filled spaces. This is achieved by demarcating boundaries of areas of interest and conducting volumetric projections based on the area visible in each of a series of brain "slices" (Longmore, Knight, Menkes, & Hope, 1988).
5. More recently, computer programmes have also been developed to assess brain absorption density in specific regions of interest (Baldy et al., 1986).

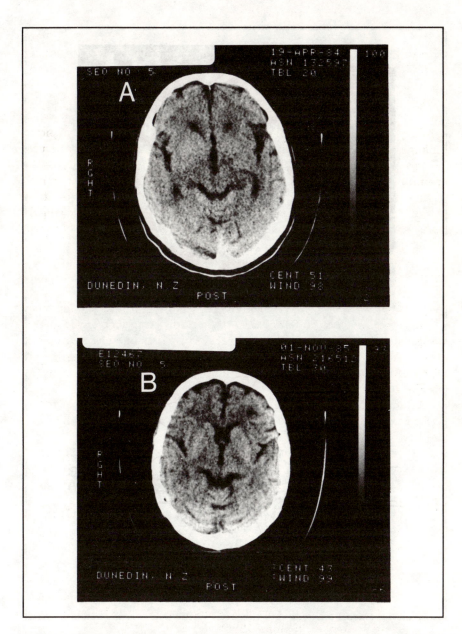

FIG. 4.1 (a and b). CT-scan images and aspects of their assessment. A: CT-scan of healthy 68-year-old male. B: CT-scan of a 62-year-old male with Korsakoff's syndrome. Anatomical features often employed in the assessment of scans are: (i) width of the Interhemispheric fissure; (ii) width of the cortical sulci (usually from the more superior cuts of the dorsal convexity); and (iii) width of the lateral sulcus (Sylvian fissure).

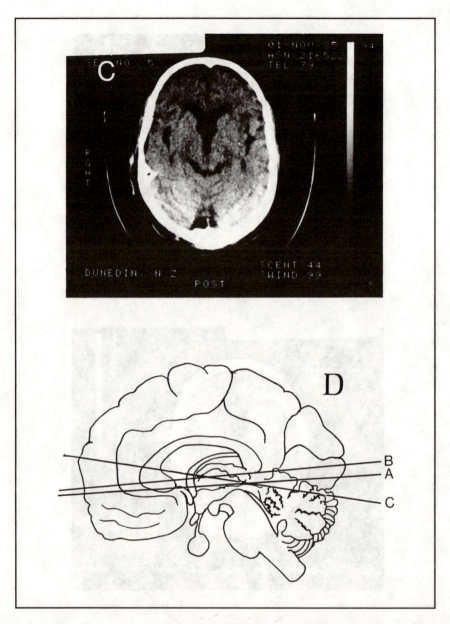

FIG. 4.1 (c and d). CT-scan images and aspects of their assessment. C: CT-scan of 69-year-old male with non-amnesic frontal atrophy. D: The levels at which each of the scans were taken. Anatomical features often employed in the assessment of scans are: (i) width of the Interhemispheric fissure; (ii) width of the cortical sulci (usually from the more superior cuts of the dorsal convexity); and (iii) width of the lateral sulcus (Sylvian fissure).

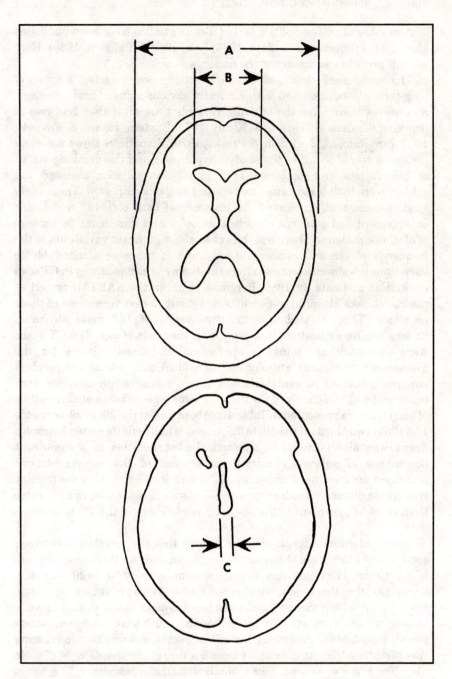

FIG. 4.2. Linear measures of ventricular dimensions. The ratio B : A provides the anterior horn index of dilation of the lateral ventricles. C is the third ventricle width.

A number of reviews of the early CT-scan studies have been published (Jernigan, Pfefferbaum, & Zatz, 1986; Ron, 1983; Wilkinson, 1985). Here we will provide a summary of the findings.

The usual methodology of the early studies was to select a group of long-term alcoholics, often with clinically obvious signs of brain damage, and assess their CT-scans at some variable time after they had ceased drinking (Carlen, Wilkinson, & Kiraly, 1976; Epstein, Pisani, & Fawcett, 1977; Fox, Ramsey, Huckman, & Proske, 1976). Sometimes those assessing the scans were "blind" to the study's hypotheses and the drinking status of the subjects, and sometimes appropriate controls were assessed, but seldom were both blind raters and control subjects employed. These early studies consistently reported the presence of both cerebral ventricular enlargement and evidence of cortical atrophy in a significant percentage of alcoholic patients. There was, however, also significant variability in the frequency of cerebral abnormalities. Some of this was attributable to variations in subject selection criteria and some to inconsistency in CT-scan evaluation methods. In 1980, Bergman et al., in the KARTAD project at the Karolinska Hospital in Stockholm, set out to overcome some of these problems. They divided a consecutive series of 148 male alcoholics undergoing detoxification, into groups on the basis of age. The CT scans were evaluated according to operationally defined criteria for the assessment of cortical atrophy (sulcal width) and subcortical cerebral changes (reflected in ventricular dilatation measured by anterior horn index and width of the third ventricle). Percentages of brain abnormalities of each type are presented in Table 4.1. About half of the 20- to 29-year-olds and about two-thirds of the 50- to 59-year-olds had definite cortical atrophy. There was also evidence of subcortical abnormalities in a significant percentage of subjects. Thirty-three percent of the sample showed increased anterior horn index and 53% had increased third ventricular transverse diameter. Both of these types of subcortical changes were more than twice as prevalent in the 50- to 59-year-olds as in the 20- to 29-year-olds.

Of considerable interest was the finding that the correlation between cortical and subcortical changes was significant only for those over 40 years of age. Cortical changes were already present in many 20- to 29-year-olds, suggesting that these occur within the first 5 to 6 years of abusive drinking. Ventricular enlargement tended to be less frequent in the younger group, becoming more common with age, although in such a cross-sectional study it was impossible to determine the role of duration of drinking in creating this picture. Although this study tested a representative sample of male alcholics, there were a number of methodological weaknesses. There was no control group, making it likely that those rating the CT scans were probably aware of the drinking status of the subjects. This is a particular

TABLE 4.1
Frequency of Computed-tomography Abnormalities of Alcoholics and
Controls (from Bergman et al., 1980)

	Alcoholics %	Controls %
Anterior horn index > 0.31		
20–29 years	15	3
30–39 years	20	3
40–49 years	41	8
50–59 years	37	19
60–65 years	67	23
Third ventricle > 6mm		
20–29 years	31	9
30–39 years	42	3
40–49 years	58	8
50–59 years	67	19
60–65 years	66	23
Cortical changes		
20–29 years	46	5
30–39 years	62	5
40–49 years	56	13
50–59 years	67	27
60–65 years	89	31

problem when one considers that, although they are defined operationally, the CT-scan assessment criteria require a degree of subjective judgement in their application. In addition, 18% of these patients had a previous admission for head trauma.

Lishman, Ron, and Acker (1980) addressed these problems in a study conducted at the Maudsley Hospital in London. They also assessed consecutive male admissions ($n = 100$), but they excluded patients when there was obvious mental impairment or reason to suspect brain damage, such as a severe head injury or history of drug abuse. A healthy non-alcoholic control group was also assessed and CT-scan raters were "blind" to the drinking status of each subject. High rates of agreement were achieved between raters on the four operationally defined CT-scan indices. There were highly significant differences on all measures of brain atrophy. On average, the alcoholic patients had ventricles half as large again as those of the control subjects. In Fig. 4.3, the percentage of alcoholics with normal (Grade 0) or abnormal widening of the sulci or Sylvian fissure are illustrated. There was a clear relationship between age and brain changes, and the greater apparent damage in the older subjects could not be accounted for simply by differences in self-reported duration of drinking. There were also some interesting relationships between drinking variables and brain morphology. Lishman et al. (1980) reported that the greater the

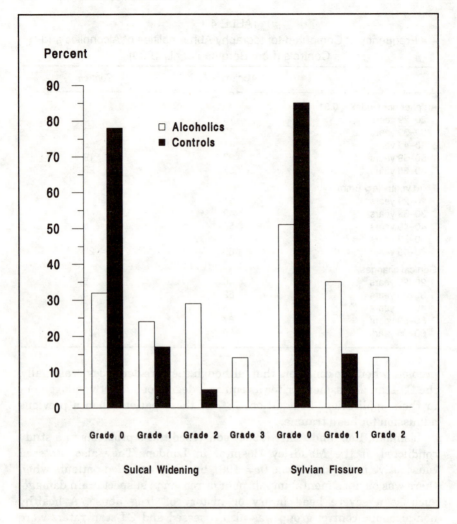

FIG. 4.3. CT-scan findings of alcoholics and controls. Alcoholic patients had a significantly greater incidence of abnormal sulcal widening (on the left) and abnormal widening of the Sylvian fissure (on the right).

duration of abstinence prior to the CT-scan and the greater the number of weeks abstinent in the previous year, the less pathological the CT-scan appeared.

In addition, when 23 patients were scanned again, an average of 1 year after the initial assessment, cortical and subcortical appearances had improved in some of the nine "abstainers" whereas there was no improvement in the scans of the 14 continuing abusers. These findings were consistent with earlier evidence of reversibility reported by Carlen et al. (1978) who suggested that alcohol-related brain changes seen on CT scan may be reversible. They have advocated application of terms like "reversible brain shrinkage" and "volume reduction" because these avoid the connotation of permanent cell loss conveyed by the phrase "cerebral atrophy". Application of such terms should also be a reminder that these CT-scan studies primarily assessed cerebrospinal fluid volume. This is a very indirect way of measuring brain morphology and tells little about the nature of the brain as an organic whole. This point will be discussed further below when the degree of structural normalisation, its time course and possible mechanisms are considered.

Conclusions

The general conclusions of the early CT-scan studies were that cerebral abnormalities involving both cortical and subcortical structure occur in a large proportion of chronic alcoholics, and that these changes begin within the first 5 years of abusive drinking. Partial normalisation of brain structure was shown to occur with abstinence, but this was more common in younger subjects, took some months to run its course, and was far from complete in all alcohol abusers. Due to the many methodological problems associated with the longitudinal study of alcohol abusers (Goldman, 1983), findings relating to aetiology, time course, and recovery required careful interpretation. For example, selection of subjects for inclusion in studies of reversal of atrophic changes during abstinence is biased by the common phenomenon of rapid relapse after treatment.

Perhaps the most important contribution of these studies was the questions that their results posed for earlier conceptions of cerebral impairment in alcoholism. The traditional view had been that brain damage was a rare complication of alcoholism, which most often occurred as the Wernicke–Korsakoff syndrome in the context of nutritional deficiency. The early radiological evidence findings were consistent with the view that chronic alcoholics also sustained demonstrable brain lesions.

STUDIES OF SOCIAL DRINKERS

Consistent demonstration of high rates of morphological brain abnormalities in alcoholics raised a very important public health issue. What was the lower limit of routine alcohol consumption leading to such changes? An attempt to answer this question was initiated by Cala and colleagues (Cala et al., 1983; Cala, Jones, Mastaglia, & Wiley, 1978). Working in Western Australia, they studied 39 social drinkers, who consumed less than 120g/day. The 24 men drank 69g per day on average (about eight standard drinks), while the 15 women drank 31g per day on average (about four standard drinks). There was considerable variation in the amount consumed and some of the subjects were drinking at levels usually associated with alcohol dependence. Evidence of cerebral atrophy was detected in 31 of their subjects. The subjects with abnormalities had a markedly higher average daily consumption (62g) than the eight subjects with normal CT-scans (24g). In all, 11 subjects took part in follow-up studies after between 3 and 12 months' abstinence—there was a reduction of apparent atrophy, reflected in increases in the density of both grey and white matter, not just in a reduction of CSF volume.

From a public health perspective, the very high rate of abnormality detected by Cala et al. (1983) was greeted with some dismay. However, in other quarters doubts were raised about the methodology employed in their study. Of particular concern was the relatively small sample size and failure to ensure that the CT-scan ratings were "blind". The findings from Cala et al.'s study were challenged by results from a large comprehensive investigation by Bergman (1985) who reported CT-scan results on 387 subjects (of whom 200 were women) selected randomly from the Stockholm community. Careful assessment showed that their average daily alcohol consumption during the last 6 months was about two drinks (women 1.75; men 2.33), much lower than the mean intake of Cala et al.'s social drinkers. Rates of CT-scan assessed brain abnormalities were much lower and the correlations between drinking pattern and brain appearance were generally weak, even for the heaviest drinkers. There was, however, a significant correlation between the mens' consumption in the previous week and measures of both sulcal widening and third ventricle enlargement. On the other hand, there was no significant relationship between tests of perception and cognition and alcohol consumption. On the basis of this study Bergman (1985, p. 275) concluded that "… it seems premature to make any definitive or precise statements about safe alcohol intake and the risk of brain damage in social drinkers from the general population".

In a later study, Mutzell and Tibblin (1989) conducted ᥟT-scans on a random, age-stratified sample of 195 men, also from Stockholm. Subjects were distributed across five age ranges (from 20–29 to 60–65). They were further grouped according to their alcohol consumption and whether or not they reported symptoms of alcohol dependence syndrome. There was evidence of significant cerebral atrophy in as many as one-third of the subjects who both drank more than 33g of alcohol per day and had one of three dependence symptoms (either loss of control over drinking, morning drinking, or blackouts). Another important finding was that cerebral abnormalities were more common in those subjects who also used prescription medications known to cause liver toxicity as a side-effect.

Mutzell and Tibblin (1989) concluded that above 33g per day (about four standard drinks), increasing alcohol consumption was associated with accelerated shrinkage of the brain, the frontal lobes being affected first, and that the process was exacerbated by concurrent use of prescribed liver toxic drugs.

It is reasonable to conclude that there is evidence that regular consumption of in excess of three standard drinks per day is associated with "brain shrinkage" in about one-third of cases. Although the precise relationship between consumption and brain damage in this group is unknown, it seems clear now that there is a continuum of cerebral abnormality that includes the relatively young, heavy social drinker at one end and the older chronic alcoholic at the other. It has subsequently been suggested that the severe end of this continuum should also include the Wernicke–Korsakoff syndrome (Bowden, 1990; Jacobson & Lishman, 1990).

FUNCTIONAL SIGNIFICANCE OF CT-SCAN ABNORMALITIES

The nature of CT-scan assessed cerebral atrophy in alcoholics has been relatively consistent across studies, but the correlation between these apparent abnormalities and impaired performance on neuropsychological tests known to be sensitive to damage resulting from alcoholism has been less impressive. Since the early PEG studies (Brewer & Perrett, 1971; Ferrer et al., 1969) psychometric tests have been employed alongside radiographic imaging to assess cognitive and perceptual deficits. In general, the results have been disappointing, only modest correlations being reported. Initially, this was attributed to the insensitivity and lack of specificity of the morphological measures, poor selection of psychometric measures, or both. However, the continued failure to find such correlations, despite refinement of methods of measurement and analysis, has led to a search for alternative explanations, which will be discussed below. First, however, it is useful to review some of the relevant findings. Wilkinson and Carlen (1980), working at the Addiction Research Foundation in Toronto, Canada, examined the performance of 72 hospitalised, detoxified alcoholics on tests of intelligence, memory, and neuropsychological functioning (Halstead–Reitan battery). These patients had also been CT-scanned to detect cerebral changes. After conducting multiple regression analyses, the authors concluded (Wilkinson & Carlen, 1980, pp. 695–696) that summary measures from the extensive testing added "... surprisingly little in the prediction of brain morphology, to simply having a knowledge of the subject's age". Similarly, Bergman et al. (1980) also reported that significant correlations between the brain structural abnormalities of their alcoholic subjects and psychometric test performance all but disappeared after the influence of age was partialled out.

Lishman et al. (1980) included tests of cognitive functions in their controlled CT-scan study. They were forced to make statistical corrections between the control and experimental groups due to differences in estimated premorbid functioning. Despite exclusion of subjects with clinically obvious cognitive impairment, the alcoholic group showed a range of significant deficits. Although some relationships between cerebral atrophy and cognitive impairment were present, the predicted systematic relationships failed to emerge from the statistical analyses. In a further investigation, Acker, Ron, Lishman, and Shaw (1984) found that differences in premorbid intelligence accounted for much more of the variance in psychological performance than did any of the CT-scan measures. Lishman and colleagues (Lishman, Jacobson & Acker, 1987, p. 11) have since concluded that "... the conventional scan measures employed are relatively coarse indicators of morphological change. They may have been inappropriately chosen to reveal correlations with psychological performance".

Recognising the multifactorial nature of the relationship between alcohol ingestion and brain damage (Grant, 1987; Parsons, 1986), Pfefferbaum, Rosenbloom, Crusan, and Jernigan (1988) took a different approach to the problem. Rather than trying to control for, or exclude the effects of, extraneous variables, they incorporated such variables in their investigation. They examined the effects of age, lifetime alcohol consumption, nutritional state, and cerebral atrophy as measured by cerebrospinal fluid volume, on cognitive test performance. They excluded patients with severe liver disease, brain damage of other causes, and mental illness. Their 37 alcoholics voluntarily seeking treatment were compared with 57 healthy, non-alcoholic, community controls. The alcoholics had more cerebrospinal fluid and less brain tissue than the controls. Sulcal widening was evident across the age range, whereas ventricular enlargement was frequent only in older subjects. There was a significant relationship between inferior nutritional status and ventricular enlargement. There was also evidence of a modest dose effect in the correlation between life-time alcohol consumption and cerebral atrophy. The pattern that emerged suggested that the cortex was least resistant, showing effects in younger subjects. Ventricular enlargement appeared in older subjects and was exacerbated by nutritional deficiency. This finding was consistent with the reported effects of liver-toxic drugs in the community sample studied by Mutzell and Tibblin (1989).

Of greatest significance for the present discussion was Pfefferbaum et al.'s (1988) report of only modest correlations (0.06 to 0.47) between CT-scan measures and neuropsychological test performance. Even after adjustments were made in neuropsychological test scores to correct for premorbid intellectual differences using VIQ scores, structure–function relationships were not impressive. Only four of the twelve correlations were significant, three involving ventricular dimensions and one involving sulcal appearance. Pfefferbaum et al. (1988) argued that significant relationships may have been suppressed by statistical correction for premorbid differences in cognitive ability, and also by the selection procedures employed in the study. They also agreed with Lishman and his colleagues (Lishman et al., 1980; 1987), who argued that relationships with function may not be detected because of the lack of regional specificity of the CT-scan measures. As will be discussed below, there are other reasons for the paucity of correlation as well.

In one of the few longitudinal CT-scan studies of the relationship between alcohol consumption, brain morphology and cognitive function, Muuronen, Bergman, Hindmarsh, and Telakivi (1989) re-examined the alcoholics first studied by Bergman et al. (1980). At follow-up, 5 years after initial testing, 37 patients aged less than 50 years were retested. The 16 patients who had abstained or become minimal consumers showed significant reduction in cortical atrophy and third ventricular enlargement. However, the degree of improvement did not constitute complete recovery, atrophy still being significantly more frequent in the alcoholics than in the controls (56% versus 8%). A similar pattern emerged from the cognitive test results. When change scores were calculated, decreasing width of the third ventricle during long-term abstinence was associated with improvement in cognitive functioning. Muuronen et al. (1989) questioned the clinical relevance of cortical measures and emphasised the continuum of cognitive impairment associated with periventricular cerebral abnormalities. This continuum ranged from the cognitive impairment relatively common in the advanced stages of alcoholism, to the severe neurological deficits of the much less common Wernicke–Korsakoff syndrome.

CT-SCANS IN KORSAKOFF'S SYNDROME

Several studies of structural brain changes in alcoholic Korsakoff's syndrome patients have utilised CT scanning. In single case studies, McDowell and Le Blanc (1984) and Mensing, Hoogland, and Slooff (1984) showed midline diencephalic abnormalities. Wilkinson and Carlen (1980) had earlier reported sulcal widening and ventricular enlargement that was negatively correlated with intelligence test performance in 25 alcoholic Korsakoff's syndrome patients.

The disposition of structural abnormalities and their correlation with memory impairments and other cognitive deficits in Korsakoff's patients has been of great significance for theories of amnesia. Of particular interest is the degree to which Korsakoff's syndrome patients have CT evidence of widespread cortical atrophy in addition to diencephalic abnormalities. Jacobson and Lishman (1990) reported the results of a comprehensive study of the relationship between clinical variables and CT structural changes in 25 male Korsakoff subjects. The Korsakoff patients had wider third ventricles and larger lateral ventricles than abstinent non-Korsakoff chronic alcohol abusers. These groups also differed in width of interhemispheric fissures, but sulcal and Sylvian fissure widths did not differ significantly. The authors concluded that, in addition to diencephalic changes, many Korsakoff patients also have widespread cerebral changes. This finding was consistent with a dual pathology in Korsakoff's syndrome: diencephalic lesions consequent on thiamine deficiency and cortical damage secondary to neurotoxicity of alcohol.

In an earlier study, Shimamura, Jernigan, and Squire (1988) utilised computer analysis of tissue density and fluid volume CT scan measures to correlate brain changes and memobehavioural deficits in seven patients with Korsakoff's syndrome. As expected, the Korsakoff subjects showed lower density values in the thalamic region and greater fluid volume in the area of the third ventricle than chronic alcoholic controls. These two groups did not differ on measures of cortical atrophy in frontal sulcal and peri-Sylvian areas. Both showed significant abnormalities compared with non-alcoholic controls. The correlations between the structural brain changes and neurobehavioural performance of the Korsakoff's subjects were of considerable interest. Memory test performance was correlated with low density values in the thalamus and with high fluid values in the region of the frontal sulci. The implications of these findings were twofold: (1) they were consistent with other studies showing widespread cerebral changes in Korsakoff subjects; and (2) they indicated that memory impairment in these subjects is related to both diencephalic and frontal changes. The significance of these findings for theories of amnesia will be discussed further in Chapter 10.

METHODOLOGICAL WEAKNESSES OF THE CT-SCAN STUDIES

There are many potential methodological pitfalls associated with the research described above. These include the validity and reliability of CT-scan assessment as a means of determining the organic state of the brain, accuracy of reports of amount and pattern of alcohol consumption, appropriateness of subject selection criteria, and testing of appropriate comparison and control subjects. There is also the matter of comparability of images derived from different models of scanner. The quality of images from later generation machines is significantly better, and cross-study comparison is made difficult by this. In this section we will discuss briefly how failure to consider such issues has cast doubt on the validity of some of the findings reported in the literature.

Ron (1987) reviewed almost 10 years of research on the brain morphology and cognitive performance of alcoholics conducted at the Maudsley Hospital in London by Lishman and colleagues. She concluded that there is strong evidence of cerebral and cognitive changes in a large proportion of male subjects. These are age-related and partly reversible. She also concluded that there may be two types of lesions in different locations: (1) affecting the external cortical zones; and (2) affecting the central areas of the brain. Ron suggested that these changes are also observed in women, but at that time their frequency and severity had yet to be reliably determined. Data since published suggest that women may show equivalent CT abnormalities after much briefer drinking histories than their male counterparts (Jacobson, 1986). In a recent study, Mann, Batra, Günther, and Schroth (1992) compared the CT-scans of 51 male and 14 female subjects at admission for alcohol detoxification and again 6 weeks after controlled abstinence. They were careful to exclude patients with clinically obvious neurological complications of alcohol abuse and other causes of organic brain damage. The gender groups were carefully matched for age, liver function test results, indices of nutritional status, and average daily consumption (after correction for body weight differences). The men had significantly longer histories of drinking than the women (9.2 years versus 3.8 years). CT-scans were assessed on multiple linear measures by raters "blind" to the group or timing of the scan. There were no sex differences in rates of brain shrinkage or re-expansion.

Bergman (1987) has provided a summary of the KARTAD project findings. His conclusions were largely consistent with those of Ron (1987). He also identified two syndromes of impairment: (1) an early, more acute and less permanent cortical process; and (2) a later, more insidious and longer-lasting series of abnormalities affecting the central parts of the brain. Bergman (1987) went further, stating that the early, cortical changes are not related to neuropsychological test performance. He claimed that changes associated with dilatation of the central ventricular system are significantly related to cognitive deficits, particularly in older patients with dilated third ventricles. This is consistent with the findings of Shimamura et al. (1988) and Jacobson and Lishman (1990).

There are, however, several reasons to be cautious in accepting these interpretations of the study findings. Not least of these is the question of the causal role of alcohol in the CT-scan findings. Attempts to demonstrate significant relationships between drinking history variables and radiographic indices of brain damage have, in general, yielded disappointing results. While Pfefferbaum et al. (1988) found some evidence for a dose–effect relationship, no such relationship was found in another comprehensive study of the hypothesis (Melgaard, Danielsen, Sorenson, & Ahlgren, 1986). Wilkinson (1987) has suggested that symptoms of alcohol dependence may be more closely correlated with brain structural abnormalities than are putative measures of lifetime consumption. The latter may be affected by unreliable memory, while the dependence symptoms may actually reflect the processes causing damage. There is some evidence to support this view from the recent community study by Mutzell and Tibblin (1989) described earlier. Either method of assessing pattern of consumption will be prone to the biases associated with retrospective self-report. Although most of the studies have used standardised drinking interview schedules, few have employed collateral interviews. In the absence of such methods of determining drinking pattern, it may be argued that neither rate of consumption nor presence and duration of periods of abstinence has been established.

Bergman (1987) has suggested another reason for the existence of only modest dose–response relationships. This view is that the model upon which they are based is not valid in this context. He has advocated the application of a threshold and genetic vulnerability model. This formulation would consider the combination of genetic vulnerability and neurotoxicity occurring only beyond a certain threshold dose. To our knowledge, such a model is yet to be tested.

Another cause for concern is the consistently poor correlation between CT-scan measures of brain morpholgical change and functional impairment on tests of perception and cognition that are known to be sensitive to the effects of alcohol abuse. Many explanations have been offered for this including poor choice of tests, subject selection biases, and the multifaceted nature of the relationship between alcohol abuse and brain damage. These factors may all make a contribution, but there are features of CT-scan assessment itself which may contribute to the low correlations. Among others, Lishman (1987) has drawn attention to the essentially coarse nature of the indices employed in assessing morphological change. Such indices have generally been linear, and have taken cerebrospinal fluid volume to indicate change. As a result, they lack regional specificity and it may be unreasonable to expect a correlation between such indices and measures of psychological performance.

Wilkinson (1987) drew attention to a number issues in the interpretation of CT-scan results. He employed the analogy attributed to Jacoby (quoted in Bird, 1982, p. 112) who, in a thesis on this topic, described the use of linear cerebrospinal fluid parameters in determining brain morphology as the equivalent of "… assessing the size of a doughnut by measuring the hole in the middle. Not only are assumptions made about the size of the doughnut, but also about the consistency of the dough". Here, Wilkinson (1987) highlighted the degree to which such techniques are indirect measures of the organic state of the brain. When one also notes that assessment of the scan plates themselves requires a degree of psychological judgement (but see also Jernigan et al., 1986; Pfefferbaum et al., 1988), it appears that, in most studies, indices of brain change are indirect measures derived from an indirect assessment. As a result, it would be unreasonable to expect extensive correlations with psychological measures. Lishman et al. (1987) argued that recently developed CT-scan derived tissue density measures provide much more direct indices of brain morphology. Such techniques allow examination of neuroanatomically defined regions thereby permitting the testing of more specific hypotheses about the relationship between brain morphology and neuropsychological functioning. For example, they allow tissue density changes in the thalamic region to be correlated with performance on neuropsychological tests assessing memory (Shimamura, Janowsky, & Squire, 1990).

The issues discussed above raise doubts about the validity of some of the conclusions reached by Ron (1987) and by Bergman (1987) regarding differential regional sensitivity to the neurotoxic effects of alcohol. As Wilkinson (1987) suggested, there is no strong reason to believe that linear measures of cerebrospinal fluid volume are equally sensitive to both distributed (i.e. sulcal widening) and to local (i.e. ventricular) changes. If distributed changes are less visible, then any conclusions about the differential local vulnerability of cortical versus central brain regions may simply reflect measurement artefact. For example, while reversibilty of brain changes is most noticeable in the cortex, it also occurs in central regions and this is confirmed by increases in density in the thalamus and caudate.

The research we have reviewed here has been referred to appropriately (Lishman et al. 1987, p. 11) as "This difficult chapter in the CT story ..." . Following a great deal of early enthusiasm, reflected in the widespread, and sometimes premature publication of CT-scan study findings, it now appears that many early assumptions have made current interpretation of the data from those studies more difficult.

RECENT ADVANCES

The advantages of the application of CT-scan density measurement in the study of alcohol-related brain damage have already been mentioned. A further advance has been the use of magnetic resonance imaging (MRI) in the study of brain morphology in alcoholism. Also known as nuclear magnetic resonance (NMR) scan, the MRI costs much more than CT-scan but has the dual advantages of providing clearer images and avoiding the risks of ionising radiation. MRI scans yield high-contrast images allowing clear demarcation of cortical and subcortical grey matter from adjacent white matter and the ventricular system. The images are obtained by placing the patient in a static magnetic field that aligns the magnetic moments of tissue hydrogen nuclei. Bursts of radio frequency pulses are applied, which shift the orientation of the nuclei, changing their energy state. When the pulse ends, they return to their normal, lower energy state. The energy changes are recorded and analysed by computer and the distribution of hydrogen nuclei is used to construct a visual image of the tissue. Various scanning sequences are suited to different visual imaging purposes. In addition to providing an improved visual image (Fig. 4.4), MRI scanning reduces the impact of several of the methodological limitations associated with CT-scan indices. Establishing the test–retest reliability of CT-scan indices has been impeded by safety concerns associated with the repeated administration of the small doses of ionising radiation administered in this technique. As a result, studies employing adequate control groups and repeated measures have been infrequent. This issue is quite crucial because the small section width (5–10mm) is well within the margin of error in matching head alignment on repeated scans. In addition, the absolute change in ventricular and sulcal size is very small thereby increasing the overall effect of error in measurement. Another advantage of MRI over CT-scan is in the ability of the advanced technique to provide information about the organic state of the brain. For example, MRI-scanning can provide an estimate of tissue water content. This has considerable relevance because the reversible brain shrinkage in chronic alcoholism has been attributed to dehydration.

As occurred with early brain imaging studies, the MRI research began with uncontrolled studies of small groups of chronic, alcohol dependent subjects. For example, Schroth et al. (1988) showed that there was significant reduction in brain abnormalities in nine alcoholics during 5 weeks of abstinence. There were significant reductions in total cerebrospinal fluid volume, ventricular volume, and in the size of the subarachnoid spaces. Zipursky, Lim, and Pfefferbaum (1989) reported a controlled study of 10 male alcoholic patients and 10 matched non-alcoholic community controls. They found a reduction of ventricular size in all of the 10 alcoholics studied during a 28-day treatment programme. At the time of the first scan, the alcoholics had significantly larger ventricles than the controls, however, at follow-up ventricular size was equivalent.

Chick et al. (1989) examined the relationship between special MRI indices of cerebral atrophy, hydration levels, and cognitive performance (measured by a computerised sorting test). They measured a parameter called T_1 relaxation time, thought to be an index of the state of water in the tissue. In 69 detoxified alcoholic subjects, scanned after 14 days of

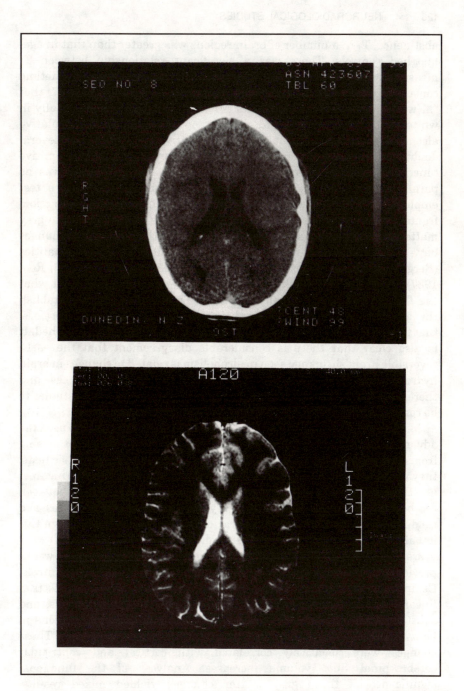

FIG. 4.4. Comparisons of a CT-scan (upper) and MRI-scan (lower) of the same patient at the same level.

abstinence, T_1 in a number of brain regions was greater than that in age-matched controls. There was a significant relationship between T_1 measurements and both cognitive impairment and estimated total lifetime consumption. Despite the authors' claim (Chick et al., 1989, p. 517) that "... we believe we have shown that MRI T_1 measurements, especially in white matter, are elevated in alcoholics proportionate to their cumulative alcohol intake and and to the degree of (cognitive) impairment ..." several doubts remain. Although there were improvements in cognitive functioning in 15 subjects during 6 months abstinence, there was no parallel amelioration of T_1 measures. Also, while the cognitive test employed was considered by the authors to reflect frontal lobe dysfunction, frontal T_1 abnormalities in the alcoholic subjects were confined to grey matter. Other researchers have argued consistently that cortical changes have less clinical relevance than subcortical white matter abnormalities (Bergman, 1987; Harper, Kril, & Holloway, 1985; Lishman, 1987; Ron, 1987). In addition, Zipursky et al. (1989) have raised doubts about what the T_1 MRI parameter actually measures. They were unable to establish the stability of such measures in their study. It would appear, therefore, that the test–retest reliability of this measure has yet to be established. It is also clear that there is considerable disagreement that the early, reversible brain shrinkage seen in alcoholism is related to changes in brain hydration. Schroth et al. (1988) concluded that this was not the case and there is corroborating evidence for this conclusion from autopsy studies to be considered in Chapter 5.

In a detailed, carefully conducted study, Jernigan et al. (1991a) used the advantages of MRI scanning to address some of the ambiguities arising from the CT studies. In combination with a battery of psychometric tests, they used MRI scanning of grey-matter changes in alcoholics. Jernigan et al. (1991a) conducted a detailed evaluation of the relationship between cerebrospinal fluid increases and grey and white matter changes and conducted correlations between various MRI indices and cognitive impairments. The subjects were 28 middle-aged alcoholics (49.5, SD = 9.9 years) admitted for treatment having undergone detoxification 4–5 weeks previously. They were compared with 36 matched non-alcoholic controls. Comprehensive exclusion criteria were employed to rule out the effects of linear, metabolic, vascular, neurological and psychiatric disorders, and substance abuse. Results showed significant grey matter reductions in both cortical and subcortical regions in the alcoholic subjects. These changes were negatively correlated with cortical and ventricular cerebrospinal fluid volume increases. Analyses of the functional significance of these grey matter changes yielded mixed results. Cerebrospinal fluid indices were significantly correlated with some neuropsychological test results indicating that volume loss in the periventricular area is associated with cognitive impairment in these subjects. The authors agreed that, for a variety of reasons, it may be unrealistic to expect high correlations between specific regional measures and neuropsychological test scores. For example, as was discussed in relation to CT-scan indices, various MRI measures probably have differential sensitivity, accuracy, and reliability. Furthermore, behavioural measures probably tap the concerted functioning of multiple brain system.

Magnetic reasonance image scanning has also been employed to examine the relationship between alcohol consumption, age, and brain tissue loss. Pfefferbaum et al. (1992) applied an age regression model to semiautomated computer-derived MRI scans of alcoholic men aged 26–63 obtained after about 4 weeks of detoxification. Controls were 43 non-alcoholic males aged 23–70 years. Exclusion criteria were similar to those employed by Jernigan et al (1991a) and scan raters were "blind" to subject identity, age, and group membership. Results showed that alcoholic drinking was associated with deficits in both cortical grey and white matter and increase in cerebrospinal fluid volume in both cortical and subcortical regions. Adverse effects of alcohol consumption appeared to be interactive with age such that there was an accelerating effect of alcohol with increasing age. Tissue loss was not correlated significantly with lifetime alcohol exposure, which led the authors to suggest that the aged brain may be particularly susceptible to the adverse effects of alcohol.

The first reported application of MRI scanning to the study of Korsakoff's syndrome was that of Christie et al. (1988). Fourteen subjects aged between 54 and 67 were selected on the basis of clinical, electrophysiological, haematological, and biochemical criteria. Psychometric assessment was confined to Luria's Neuropsychological Investigation (LNI). Korsakoff's syndrome subjects had increased T_1 values in both grey and white matter in frontal and parietal regions. The Korsakoff group also showed significant cortical atrophy and a number of these patients had gross pathological changes reflecting infarctions. Some significant correlations between structural integrity and functional psychological performance emerged. T_1 values in the left body of the caudate nucleus were negatively correlated with expressive speech, writing and reading, and logical thinking assessed on the LNI. Only logical memory was significantly correlated with cortical atrophy score; again in the predicted direction. The emergence of such a small number of significant correlations from such a large pool is disappointing and difficult to interpret.

More recently, Jernigan, Schafer, Butters, and Cermak (1991b) compared cerebrospinal fluid increases and grey matter decreases in eight alcoholic Korsakoff patients and 12 age-matched non-amnesic alcoholics. Both groups showed more cerebrospinal fluid and less grey matter than non-alcoholic control subjects, but the changes were more marked in the Korsakoff subjects. These patients had unusually large volume losses in the anterior diencephalon, mesial temporal, and orbitofrontal regions. In other words, patterns of loss were similar, but there was disproportionate diencephalic, mesial temporal, and orbitofrontal loss in the Korsakoff subjects.

CONCLUSIONS

It is reasonable to conclude that CT-scan studies have changed the way alcoholic brain damage has been conceptualised. As Lishman (1987) has observed, there is now a growing appreciation of how commonly brain morphological changes occur in alcohol-abusing subjects. In addition, it is now accepted that the brain abnormalities are diffuse. Current formulations encompass the traditional descriptions of Wernicke–Korsakoff syndrome within a continuum of severity of brain abnormalities ranging from those associated with heavy social drinking to those of chronic severe alcoholism. Despite the reservations mentioned, CT study findings have clearly demonstrated a high incidence of cortical shrinkage and ventricular dilatation in large and unselected populations of alcohol abusers. While there are problems with the reliability of repeated CT-scan measures, it is clear that there is some reduction in degree of abnormality of brain structure during abstinence.

Attempts to demonstrate the functional significance of CT assessed changes by neuropsychological testing, have been largely disappointing. Given the indirect, relatively coarse nature of the CT indices employed, the modest array of correlations derived is probably all that could reasonably be expected. The use of anatomically specific density measures may yield greater correlations. It is promising that specific density measures and specific cognitive tests have been significantly correlated in alcoholic Korsakoff subjects (Shimamura et al. 1988). While most of the studies have been conducted on male subjects, the data available on female subjects are suggestive of cross-gender consistency (Bergman, 1987). Despite the fact that the studies described above were carried out in a number of different countries, we agree with Wilkinson (1987) that there is remarkable international congruence in the CT-scans of alcoholics.

Magnetic resonance imaging has provided new opportunities for the *in vivo* study of alcoholic brain damage. The new imaging techniques have higher resolution and are safer for repeated measures. They also allow the derivation of indices of organic brain state. Several lessons have been learned from what Lishman described as "the difficult chapter in the CT story". Recent findings have contributed greatly to knowledge about region- and structure-specific brain changes and the interactive effects of ageing and alcohol abuse. These findings have been highly consistent with recent neuropathological evidence that long term alcohol abuse is associated with widespread cerebral damage. Problems of differential sensitivity and reliability of various MRI indices await solution, but the detail and quality of recent research is very encouraging. The functional significance of many of the observed structural changes remains unclear. The implications of neuroradiological abnormalities for the clinical management of individual patients has received scant attention in the literature.

CHAPTER FIVE

Neuropathological Research

I have very poor and unhappy brains for drinking: I could well wish courtesy would invest some other custom of entertainment.
Shakespeare (1622/1975, *Othello*, Act II, iii, lines 1144–1145).

The first substantial reports of post-mortem brain lesions in alcoholics have been attributed to Wernicke and Korsakoff (Victor et al., 1971). The Polish neurologist, Karl Wernicke (1881/1973) described the presence of pathological lesions in three cases of acute confusional state with impaired consciousness, ataxia, and ophthalmoplegia. Two of these cases were alcoholics, the other had persistent vomiting leading to malnutrition. In each case, the pathology involved small punctate, haemorrhagic lesions of the grey matter, which occurred symmetrically around the third and fourth ventricles and extended into the brain stem (in the region of the ocular motor nuclei). Wernicke noted that the onset of the clinical disorder was acute, that the syndrome was progressive, and that the patient died within approximately 2 weeks. Although other authors soon added abnormalities of the thalamus and the mammillary bodies to the pathological lesion complex, this, and the associated clinical features, have remained essentially as Wernicke's initial descriptions.

In 1887, the Russian physician Sergei Sergeyevich Korsakoff published the first of a number of papers describing a chronic amnesic and confabulatory disorder (Victor & Yakovlev, 1955). He related the presence of these symptoms to disorders of polyneuropathy in general and to chronic alcoholism in particular. Korsakoff noted that these symptoms also occurred in conjunction with conditions such as persistent vomiting and other disorders of food absorption and metabolism. He reported a series of cases in which peripheral neuritis and severe amnesia were observed in non-alcoholics and was moved to speculate that the aetiology of the symptoms might not be due to the toxic effects of alcohol: "Perhaps further researches will show that this disease is not only a disease of the nervous system ... and one most probably depending on the development in the organism of some noxious substance disturbing the nutrition of all the tissues, but chiefly the nervous system" (Victor & Yakovlev, 1955, p. 406). He was less specific than Wernicke had been about the location of the pathological lesions responsible for the clinical symptoms, but attributed the mental changes in his cases to the widespread cortical lesions he observed post-mortem. According to Lishman (1981), it was not until the publication of Gamper's post-mortem findings in 1928 that the cortical basis of the clinical features of Korsakoff's syndrome was seriously challenged. These findings suggested that the essential lesion lay in the region of the walls of the third ventricle and involved the mammillary bodies. Although this site was similar to that identified by Wernicke, the connection between the two syndromes was not widely accepted at that time.

In subsequent articles and research reports, acceptance of a dual pathology of Korsakoff's syndrome began to appear. In time, a cortical basis of Korsakoff's syndrome yielded to the primacy of a diencephalic pathology. An important contribution to this formulation was identification of dietary deficiency as an aetiological factor in Wernicke's encephalopathy during the 1930s. This research culminated in the demonstration that thiamine could reduce the symptoms of Wernicke's encephalopathy (Jolliffe, Wortis, & Fein, 1941) and ameliorate the severity of memory impairments that followed it (Bowman, Goodhart, & Jolliffe, 1939). Further confirmation of the role of malnutrition was reported by De Wardener and Lennox (1947) who described 52 cases of Wernicke's encephalopathy in prisoners of war in Singapore. These subjects responded rapidly and positively to the administration of thiamine, implying that the aetiology of Wernicke–Korsakoff syndrome in alcoholics might be malnutrition rather than neurotoxicity. Later, an article by Malamud and Skillicorn (1956) drew attention to the essential overlap in neuropathology of the two syndromes. Perhaps because of the severe or irreversible memory impairment associated with it, the Wernicke–Korsakoff syndrome maintained a dominant position in conceptualisations of alcoholic brain damage until the last 20 years or so.

THE NEUROPATHOLOGY OF KORSAKOFF'S SYNDROME

Once the association between the two syndromes had been established, neuropathological research focused on the identification of the crucial lesion. In an influential report, Victor et al. (1971) described the outcome of a series of post -mortem studies on the brains of 82 Wernicke–Korsakoff patients, whose diagnosis had been confirmed clinically prior to death. They observed that the topography of the lesions was symmetrical and consistently located in the thalamus, hypothalamus, midbrain, pons, and medulla, and, less frequently, in the fornix and cerebellum. They then went on to consider which were the crucial lesions for the development of amnesia. They noted that memory failure was highly correlated with lesions in the mammillary bodies, the dorsomedial nucleus of the thalamus, and the medial region of the pulvinar nucleus of the thalamus. There was extensive atrophy of the dorsomedial nucleus of the thalamus in 38 of the 43 brains in which the thalamus was examined. In the five brains without such atrophy, amnesia had not been long-lasting. In a number of the amnesic cases, there were also lesions to the mammillary bodies; however, in the five non-amnesic cases there was damage to the mammillary bodies. This suggested that damage to the mammillary bodies alone could occur without memory failure. They were unable to separate the effects of damage to the dorsomedial nucleus from damage to the pulvinar because the amnesic cases had lesions in both nuclei. Although convolutional atrophy of the cerebral cortex was observed in a quarter of the cases, the predominant clinical feature of the Korsakoff syndrome patients—their profound amnesia—was attributed to the diencephalic lesions.

Many other similar findings were reported, but all of these studies had a common clinical weakness; they failed to provide detailed and convincing clinical evidence of the neuropsychological functioning of their subjects prior to death. Two more recent studies have addressed this problem. In the first of these, Mair, Warrington, and Weiskrantz (1979) studied the post-mortem brains of two amnesic Korsakoff patients who had previously been subjected to longitudinal neuropsychological assessments. They reported the presence of macroscopic and histological abnormalities of the mammillary bodies. Damage to the thalamus was restricted to a band of gliosis that overlapped the medial dorsal nucleus and extended anteriorly to it next to the wall of the third ventricle. One of their patients, E.A., had shown signs of some intellectual deterioration prior to his demise while the other, H.J., had shown no IQ decrease. Only E.A. showed histological evidence of more widespread cell loss beyond the mammillary bodies. The implication of the Mair et al. (1979) findings was that the necessary and sufficient lesion for Korsakoff's syndrome was midline diencephalic damage to the mammillary bodies and perhaps also to small regions of the thalamus.

In the second of the two more recent neuropathology studies, Mayes, Meudell, Mann, and Pickering (1988) reported data that were similar to those of Mair et al. (1979). The major damage was to the medial nuclei of the mammillary bodies, but they also found a bilateral band of gliosis adjacent to the third ventricle but not extending to the dorsomedial nucleus. One of their cases, B.C., who had less severe amnesia, but a wider range of cognitive deficits, showed more widespread damage involving the frontal and parietal lobes of the cerebral cortex. Their other case, J.N., who had more severe but circumscribed amnesia, had no visible cortical atrophy. Reduced neuron counts in the basal forebrain, which Butters (1985) had argued might contribute to the memory deficits of Korsakoff patients, were not present in either of Mayes et al. cases.

The results of these neuropathological studies suggested that the critical lesions causing memory failure were localised to the thalamus and mammillary bodies. This view relegated the early pathologists' findings of widespread cortical pathology, particularly of frontal regions, to secondary importance in the neuropsychology of Korsakoff's syndrome. Support for the primacy of diencephalic lesions in the expression of cognitive impairments has been inadvertently reinforced by experimental neuropsychologists, who tend to select only Korsakoff syndrome patients with circumscribed amnesia. At this stage it is important to bear in mind that the neuropathological studies of Wernicke–Korsakoff patients have generally shown that they have extensive lesions beyond the diencephalon, and that severe amnesia is not the only significant clinical manifestation of the syndrome.

Figure 5.1 shows the main diencephalic structures implicated in the memory failure of Korsakoff patients. Mayes et al. (1988) have concluded that the pattern of neuropathological results available suggests three possible neuropathological explanations for the severe amnesia in Korsakoff patients. The first is that the amnesia results from thalamic lesions in the vicinity of the dorsomedial nucleus. The second is that the mammillary body atrophy is entirely responsible. A third possibility is that both the mammillary body and thalamic lesions are necessary to produce severe amnesia. This latter notion is consistent with Mishkin's (Aggleton & Mishkin, 1983) dual circuit model of the neuroanatomical basis of memory. This model is represented in Fig. 5.2. Based on studies of the effects of lesions in macaque monkeys, this model suggests that there are two circuits involved in acquiring new learning. The first connects the amygdala with the dorsomedial thalamic nuleus, the second proceeds from the hippocampus to the anterior thalamus by way of the mammillary

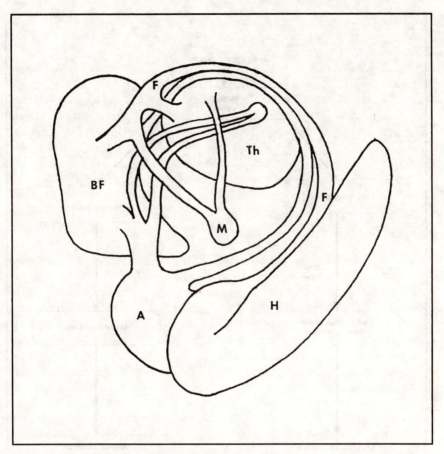

FIG. 5.1. Diencephalic and connected strucutres implicated in theories of amnesia.
M, the mammillary body; Th, thalamus; F, fornix; BF, basal forebrain region;
A, Amygdaloid complex; H, hippocampal formation.

bodies. Both circuits pass to the prefrontal lobes and are connected to the
cortex. It is apparent from Fig. 5.2, that, if the Korsakoff patient sustained
lesions in both mammillary bodies and fibre tracts connected to the
dorsomedial nucleus, both circuits would be severed. Mishkin, studying
learning in monkeys, has found that where only one circuit is lesioned, mild
and variable memory loss occurs; complete bilateral destruction of both
circuits is necessary to produce severe failure of new learning. Although
this model has many attractive features and is largely consistent with the
human amnesic literature, the issue of the critical lesions necessary to
produce the amnesia of Wernicke–Korsakoff syndrome remains to be
resolved completely.

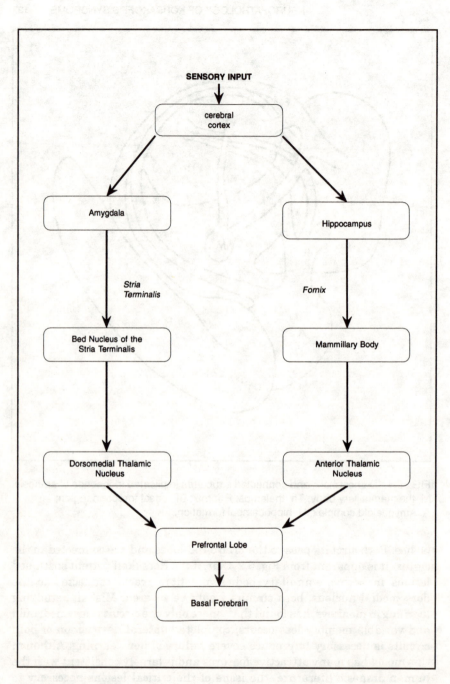

SENSORY INPUT

cerebral
cortex

Amygdala

Hippocampus

Stria
Terminalis

Fornix

Bed Nucleus of the
Stria Terminalis

Mammillary Body

Dorsomedial Thalamic
Nucleus

Anterior Thalamic
Nucleus

Prefrontal Lobe

Basal Forebrain

FIG. 5.2. Schematic representation of Mishkin's dual circuit model of neuroanatomy of memory.

BRAIN LESIONS IN ALCOHOLISM

One reason why the Wernicke–Korsakoff syndrome came to dominate the interest of early neuropathologists was that the study of non-amnesic alcoholics produced inconsistent and somewhat disappointing findings. Lishman (1981, p. 8) commented that: "The pathologists, frankly, disappoint us. There is no consensus or consistency in their observations. Some report cortical atrophy but many do not. Some find neuronal degeneration and loss, patchy and diffuse, whereas others declare the cerebral hemispheres essentially normal". Neubuerger (1957, p. 1) had earlier noted that cortical changes reported in chronic alcoholics coming to post-mortem were "rather monotonous and non-specific". The likely clinical effects of such ill-defined pathological lesions were difficult to understand, especially in contrast to the striking relationships between the clinical and pathological features of the Wernicke–Korsakoff complex. What is more, because the cortical changes were so inconsistent, being present in by no means all alcoholic brains studied, compelling brain-behaviour relationships could not be postulated. Neuropsychologists and cognitive psychologists were therefore much less interested in such lesions.

After the second World War, some pathologists began reporting that Wernicke–Korsakoff lesions were becoming less common in cases available for post-mortem study. For example, in a study of 42 brains, Wernicke–Korsakoff lesions were found to be rare, and cortical lesions were ill-defined and not consistently present (Neubuerger, 1957) . Neuberger (1957, p. 2) reported that: "The most impressive changes were found in the cerebellar cortex", and attributed the reduced incidence of Wernicke–Korsakoff lesions to increased public awareness of the importance of vitamins and more adequate treatment of the acute Wernicke syndrome. Although Neubuerger concluded that cerebellar involvement was a prevailing feature of alcoholic brain damage, other authors were less convinced of the relevance of these findings. Lynch (1960, p. 350) observed that: "It is apparent to all that cerebellar lesions, no matter how severe, are insufficient to account for the protean impairment of cerebral function so commonly seen in alcoholics". Lynch also suggested that a reason for the relative neglect of cortical changes was that they were difficult to detect compared with lesions in periventricular and cerebellar territories. He claimed that, with careful examination, such lesions could be detected, and reported gross and microscopic cortical changes in all 11 of the chronic alcoholic brains in his sample. In an early application of an information processing model Lynch (1960, p. 350) commented: "If we take the simplest view of the nervous system, viz. that of a multi-million unit electronic computer, activator, and integrator, it is obvious that the loss of some 15%

to 50% of its 'transistors' will lead to detectable impairment in many ranges of its functional endeavours".

Additional evidence that direct damage to the brain occurs as a consequence of chronic alcoholism had already been hinted at in the concentration camp data reported by De Wardener and Lennox (1947). In contrast to alcoholic Wernicke–Korsakoff patients, the nutritionally depleted prisoners usually showed recovery of amnesic deficits after treatment with thiamine. The implication that has been drawn from this was that the classic alcoholic Korsakoff's syndrome state required additional lesions. Indeed, Freund (1973) suggested that permanent memory disorder seemed to follow thiamine deficiency accompanied by alcohol abuse much more commonly than as a consequence of nutritional deficiency alone. It is paradoxical to assume that development of the Wernicke–Korsakoff syndrome is protective against coexisting neurotoxic effects of alcohol on the cortex. More recent studies of the neuropathology of chronic alcoholism have provided evidence to confirm this.

LATER STUDIES OF THE NEUROPATHOLOGY OF CHRONIC ALCOHOLISM

Perhaps the strongest advocate of the presence of cortical damage in alcohol abusers has been Courville (1955). In his influential book he strongly expressed the opinion that widespread cerebral atrophy was a common element of alcoholic neuropathology. He reported that cortical lesions were present consistently and described alcoholism as the most common cause of brain shrinkage in the fifth and sixth decades of life. Results of pneumoencephalographic studies tended to support these findings and the CT-scan studies that followed indicated that a revision of the traditional view of alcoholic neuropathology was necessary (see Chapter 4).

During the 20 years since the publication of Courville's work, many post-mortem studies showing that chronic alcoholics may have widespread pathological brain changes have been reported. It is now well accepted that brain changes in alcoholism are far more widespread than those responsible for the Wernicke–Korsakoff syndrome and that they may occur independently of the effects of nutritional disorder (Lishman et al., 1987). Macroscopic changes identified have included diffuse cerebral atrophy, ventricular dilatation, and meningeal thickening. At the microscopic level, findings include cortical cell loss and demyelination. As in the neuroradiology literature reviewed in Chapter 4, earlier studies tended to be afflicted by methodological weaknesses, which cast doubt on the conclusions reached. Problems with post-mortem diagnosis of alcoholism often meant that samples were biased towards very severe chronic alcoholism. Conclusions were usually based on the authors' subjective examination of a small number of single cases. Adequate control or comparison data were seldom available. In addition, methods for identifying cortical changes were poorly developed and perhaps this is one of the reasons why early studies of these changes produced such discordant findings. There are many problems inherent in defining loss of cortical tissue and in determining ante mortem drinking behaviour. Recent advances in neuropathological methods have overcome some, but not all, of these problems.

Studies of brain weight and cerebral atrophy

The major contributors in this area have been Harper, and his colleagues at the Department of Neuropathology at Royal Perth Hospital, Australia. Early work included studies on the incidence of the Wernicke Korsakoff complex (Harper, 1983) and on the post-mortem weights of the brains of chronic alcoholics (Harper & Blumberg, 1982). Harper and Kril (1985) reported the results of a study of brain atrophy in 25 chronic alcoholic patients who they compared with 44 matched controls. They used measurements of both brain and intracerebral volume to calculate a parameter termed the pericerebral space (PICS, shown in Fig. 5.3). This is the space inside the skull not occupied by the cerebrum. Selection criteria were based on retrospective reports by relatives and on medical notes. Cases were excluded if there was evidence of a positive neurological history, apart from Wernicke's encephalopathy or epilepsy. Ten of the 25 alcoholic brains had evidence of Wernicke's encephalopathy and the results from these cases were analysed separately. Differences between the PICS values of the control and alcoholic groups were significant, and exclusion of patients with epilepsy did not alter the results. There was also a tendency for PICS values to correlate with blind subjective assessments of cortical atrophy, ventricular dilatation and atrophy of the cerebellar vermi. Finally, PICS values were higher in cases with coexisting Wernicke's encephalopathy, and highest in the 40% who also had evidence of liver disease. However, the authors maintained that this result could not be accounted for by the presence of hepatic encephalopathy.

These findings were consistent with the results of brain weight studies in alcoholics conducted by both Harper's group (Harper & Blumberg, 1982) and by Torvik, Lindboe, and Rodge (1982) in Norway. However, it was apparent in each of these studies that there was wide variation in degree of atrophy. In only 32% of cases in the Harper and Blumberg's study were the PICS values statistically abnormal. This was at odds with the much higher incidence of cerebral shrinkage demonstrated in the neuroradiology studies. Schroth et al. (1988) have suggested that this discrepancy may

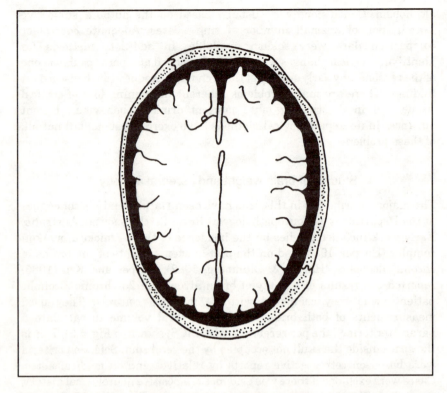

FIG. 5.3. Schematic representation of the pericerebral space (PICS), the area in black, a measure of the space between skull and brain, used as an index of atrophy.

result from rapid regression of alcohol-induced brain shrinkage during the early stages of abstinence. They pointed out that alcohol consumption is frequently restricted or discontinued at some variable time prior to death. Whether this is due to the fatal condition itself, or to a period of hospitalisation, its effect will be that the dynamic course of regression detected in radiology studies will not be apparent at post-mortem examination. As some of the normalisation of brain appearance occurs within a few weeks, it may already have run its course prior to death. Consequently, lower rates of gross, macroscopic brain abnormality would be expected at post-mortem than are observed in CT-scan studies.

Regional distribution and basis of cerebral atrophy

The regional distribution of atrophic changes has been a topic of great interest as has been the extent to which cerebral atrophy reflects loss of neurons or a reversible degeneration of myelin and axons. Many of the

CT-scan studies have been interpreted as showing atrophy of the cerebral cortex with presumed death of neurons. However, it has been argued that this mechanism would be incompatible with the significant reversibility of abnormalities that has been observed during abstinence. It has been suggested that reversible atrophy and partial recovery of cognitive impairment are more compatible with degeneration of myelin and axons. Initial studies focused on the distribution of atrophic changes. Harper et al. (1985) examined changes in grey and white matter in the brains of chronic alcoholics compared with controls. They reported that while there was a diffuse reduction in white matter, there was no corresponding reduction in grey matter volume. In another study, de la Monte (1988) reported the presence of cortical, subcortical, and ventricular differences between the brains of chronic alcoholics and the brains of age-matched patients who had suffered non-alcohol-related liver disease. Although brain weights were not significantly different, there were significant differences in cross-sectional area at five standardised coronal slices. The alcoholic brains also had a greater degree of ventricular enlargement. The percentage atrophy in the alcoholic brains was between 1.5 and 7 times greater in cerebral white matter than in corresponding slices of cortical grey matter.

Interpretation of such findings has been circumspect. As Harper et al. (1985) observed, these results do not necessarily mean that cortical neuronal counts in the brains of chronic alcoholics are normal. Although white matter loss may result from cell death, equivalent neuronal death in cortical grey matter may be compensated for by proliferation of glial cells and the presence of cortical neuronal loss may be disguised by this. In a study designed to establish the numbers of neurons present in various brain regions, Harper, Kril, and Daly (1987) conducted objective, quantitative comparisons of alcoholic and age-matched control brains. There was a significant decrease of 22% in the number of neurons in the superior frontal cortices of the alcoholics. There was no parallel loss of neurons from the motor cortex, a finding which suggested that the neuronal loss may have been selective. Harper and Kril (1989) further investigated this hypothesis by testing whether or not the changes were specific to the size and/or layer of the neurons. They reported the selective loss of large neurons from the superior frontal cortex, this loss being greater for those with coexisting Wernicke's encephalopathy or cirrhosis of the liver. There was much less difference between alcoholic and non-alcoholic brains when the large neurons from the motor cortex were examined. The difference only reached statistical significance in brains from those who also had Wernicke's encephalopathy. Harper and Kril (1989) found no difference in the number of small neurons in the superior frontal cortex but in the region of the motor cortex, brains from alcoholics with cirrhotic livers tended to have greater numbers of small neurones. The authors hypothesised that this could result from shrinkage of large neurons in the motor cortex thereby shifting them into the category of small neurons. There were no differences in rates of loss from upper, middle, or lower lamina.

The average extent of neuronal loss reported by Harper and Kril (1989) was impressive: 52% for chronic alcoholic; 55% and 57% respectively for alcoholics with Wernicke's encephalopathy and cirrhotic liver. They pointed out that it is the same class of large neurons that is particularly susceptible to the effects of ageing and Alzheimer's disease, but did not imply that this indicates a common mechanism. They did, however, speculate (Harper & Kril, 1989, pp. 87–88) that: "One unifying hypothesis to explain the changes described is a retraction of the dendritic arbour which leads to a progressive shrinkage of the neuronal soma proceeding to neuronal death". This hypothesis awaits further investigation. As yet, the neuropathological mechanism remains unknown.

Cerebellar atrophy

There has long been interest in the presence of abnormalities of the cerebellum in alcoholics. Attention has been drawn to lesions in this region by the clinical syndrome of gait ataxia frequently observed in chronic alcoholics. Both post-mortem and radiological studies have shown reduced size of cerebellar lobes. Post-mortem findings reported by Victor et al. (1971) suggested an association between clinical evidence of ataxia and lesions in some cerebellar regions. However, such findings have been reported inconsistently and it has been unclear whether shrinkage was due to nerve cell loss, or to some other, reversible cause.

Phillips et al. (1987) conducted a quantitative histological study of the cerebellar vermis in 10 male alcoholic brains and eight matched controls. There were no significant differences in the cerebellar weights or total cross-sectional areas of the cerebellar vermis. Histological area measurements were taken from three of the 10 lobes of the cerebellum. Lobe IV in the alcoholic group showed significant reduction in total histological area and also significant reduction in molecular/granular area ratio (due to decrease in the area of the molecular level). The trend was the same for the other two lobes assessed (VII and X) but differences between alcoholic and control groups did not reach significance. In lobes VII and X, the molecular layer showed the greatest reduction.

Although there was great variability in Purkinje cell counts in all of the lobes in both groups, there was a marginally significant difference between groups. Overall, the alcoholics had lower cell counts. In three lobes (I, III, and IX) the differences reached statistical significance. Patients with lesions characteristic of Wernicke's encephalopathy had lower Purkinje cell counts than those with only alcoholic cerebellar degeneration. Although it is usual to see a reduction in Purkinje cell counts with age, the fact that the control group in this study was on average 10% older rendered this a conservative comparison.

Alcohol encephalopathy without changes in histology

The findings described above raise important questions about the causes and mechanisms of the progressive cognitive changes observed in long-term alcohol abusers. Perhaps the most significant issue is the extent to which these deficits result from the direct effects of alcohol toxicity or from the many other potential contributors to brain impairment (e.g. nutritional disorder, hepatic damage, head trauma, and other brain diseases). Freund and Ballinger (1988a) hypothesised that long-term exposure to alcohol has a direct neurotoxic effect that, in conjunction with genetic and environmental factors, causes an "alcohol encephalopathy". This results from the effects of alcohol on neural receptors in certain brain regions. Such effects may precede the development of specific histological changes and can occur in the absence of gross cerebral atrophy. In other words, Freund and Ballinger postulated that the progressive cognitive changes that are clinically evident long before severe dementia, result from the toxic effects of alcohol on neural receptors independent of the influence of Wernicke–Korsakoff syndrome, hepatic damage, and other incidental causes of brain damage or disease.

Freund and Ballinger (1988a) tested this hypothesis directly at autopsy and employed methods that allowed them to either exclude or control for the influence of extraneous variables. They obtained the brains of 30 alcoholic and 49 control subjects aged over 18 years (mean ages 59.8 and 63.1 respectively) who had died in hospital without coma or localising brain disease such as tumour or stroke. Diagnosis of alcoholism was by hospital records and relatives' retrospective reports. Subjects were assigned to the alcohol abuse group if they had consumed a daily average of greater than 80g of alcohol on average for 10 years. Tissue samples were removed from the left frontal poles and the left superior temporal gyri of these brains and examined for both histological and chemical changes. There were no differences between the groups in cortical atrophy, dilatation of the lateral ventricles, or in brain weights. After exclusion of the effects of other diseases and conditions, there was a significant difference between groups in the density of cholinergic muscarinic receptors in the frontal cortex but not in the temporal cortex. There was no difference in the efficiency of remaining receptors. Freund and Ballinger (1988a) concluded that these results supported the hypothesis regarding the direct toxic effects of alcohol on neural transmission and suggested that this was a mechanism for the progressive deleterious effects on cognition and intellect observed clinically. In three other studies employing essentially similar methodology, Freund and Ballinger (1988b; 1989a,b) have demonstrated alcohol-abuse-related loss of benzodiazepine receptors in the frontal cortex and loss of muscarinic cholinergic receptors in the temporal cortex and the putamen (a large basal ganglial structure concerned with co-ordination of motor movements).

Although these studies were conducted with great care, it should be noted that the researchers did not appear to be blind to hypotheses or the origins of samples tested when assessing changes. In addition, two important assumptions about the degree of cognitive deterioration of their subjects were made. The first was that as the subjects were not institutionalised, none had reached what the authors refer to as end stage dementia. The second was that because other subjects of similar age and drinking history would be expected to have cognitive deficits, their subjects would also. In other words, the presence of mild to moderate cognitive deterioration was assumed on the basis of demographic and retrospective clinical data. Cognitive impairment was not demonstrated. Although it is obvious that provision of convincing data on either point would require overcoming considerable practical problems, the absence of neuropsychological information does have some implications for the validity of these findings.

The full extent of alterations in brain receptors attributable to alcohol abuse is yet to be determined and the clinical significance of these changes remains unclear. However, there are two reasons why these findings are important for our understanding of the neuropsychology of alcohol abuse: (1) they provide compelling evidence that long-term alcohol abuse can have a direct neurotoxic effect on the brain; and (2) they indicate that this effect can precede specific morphological and significant clinical indications of damage. These findings provide a possible mechanism for the progressive cognitive and intellectual impairments associated with chronic alcohol abuse. A mechanism that, prior to the studies of Freund and Ballinger, may have been overlooked.

NEUROPATHOLOGY OF MODERATE ALCOHOL CONSUMPTION

Of great importance as a public health issue is the effect of social drinking on brain structure. In the CT-scan studies of such populations discussed in Chapter 4, there was evidence of atrophic brain changes in persons drinking more than of 30g of alcohol per day. Harper, Kril, and Daly (1988) studied the brains of moderate drinkers who consumed between 20g and

80g per day on average. This range of consumption includes persons whose average daily drinking is almost certainly risk-free and also those whose level of consumption is damaging. This is a very wide range and it may be for this reason that the 14 brains of moderate drinkers did not differ significantly from the brains of control drinkers whose average daily consumption was less than 20g. Not surprisingly, there was some evidence that moderate drinkers may occupy an intermediate position on a continuum of damage. In a consistent trend, the moderate drinkers showed loss of cerebral tissue, reduced brain weight, increased ventricular volume, and increased space between brain and skull. The mean cerebellar weights did not differ, however. It is not yet possible to determine safe amounts of "social" alcohol consumption on the basis of neuropathology studies.

CONCLUSIONS

During the century or more since the early work of Wernicke and Korsakoff, there have been great changes in the way alcoholic brain damage has been conceptualised. Initially, a separate pathology for each syndrome was postulated. With the implication of nutritional deficiency and observation of the beneficial effects of thiamine, identification of the clinical relationship between the two syndromes emerged. Understanding of the shared pathological basis of the two clinical entities soon followed. Throughout the period 1930–1980, pathologists seemed generally uninterested in the widespread cortical changes in alcoholics and concentrated instead on pathological lesions with specific locations and related clinical features (e.g. Wernicke–Korsakoff syndrome, cerebellar ataxia). This focus resulted in part from the difficulty of identifying and delimiting damage to the cerebral cortex. The dominant conceptualisation of alcoholic brain damage prior to the neuropsychological and neuroradiological studies of the 1970s and 1980s accorded Wernicke–Korsakoff syndrome pre-eminence. It was thought that, in general, those who escaped the effects of the damage wrought by nutritional deficiency incurred no significant pathological change. Several research findings have demanded a reformulation of this model.

First, with regard to the clinical symptoms of Korsakoff's syndrome, it has become increasingly clear that the deficits range along a continuum from specific impairment of memory on the one hand, to global cognitive impairment on the other. Cutting (1978), and later Lishman (1981), have drawn attention to this continuum by discussing the true nature of alcoholic "dementia". Cutting (1978) related the specificity of impairment to rate of onset and degree of recovery after correction of thiamine deficiency. In his retrospective survey of cases admitted to the Maudsley Hospital, those with acute onset tended to have less global impairment and responded better to thiamine while those with insidious onset showed little response, remaining severely globally impaired. Observations of this sort have prompted authors such as Bowden (1990) to question the practice of separating some of the cognitive impairments related to chronic alcohol abuse into Wernicke–Korsakoff syndrome. He has produced compelling arguments that such a nosological separation is unwarranted and unhelpful.

Second, neuropathological findings have contributed to recent doubts about the distinction between Wernicke–Korsakoff syndrome and other forms of alcoholic brain damage. Harper, Giles, and Finlay-Jones (1986) and Torvik, Lindboe, and Rodge (1982) reported in separate studies that the majority of cases showing Wernicke lesions at autopsy had not received the diagnosis during life. In many cases there was an appearance of the chronic or inactive lesions, which had earlier led Harper (1983) to conclude that many patients suffered repeated subclinical episodes of Wernicke's encephalopathy. It seems plausible that such lesions, although not identified as Wernicke's encephalopathy at the time, may produce the pattern of insidious onset of severe irreversible impairment described by Cutting (1978).

Third, the autopsy findings reported by Mair et al. (1979) and Mayes et al. (1988) fell within the continuum of impairment identified by Cutting (1978) and Lishman (1981). In each study, one of the two cases showed lesions that were widespread throughout cortical and subcortical regions, certainly not confined to the diencephalon. On reflection, it now seems somewhat surprising that the focus on a specific locus of brain damage in chronic alcoholism endured for so long. Korsakoff had himself described cortical abnormalities. Courville (1955) and Lynch (1960) argued strongly for the presence of significant cortical damage. Results of recent neuropathology studies have supported their assertions. As techniques for identifying macroscopic and microscopic abnormalities have improved, the widespread nature of alcoholic brain damage has been recognised. It is now well accepted that Wernicke–Korsakoff lesions coexist with other changes in a continuum of damage to brain structure. Neural receptors mediating cognition are also affected in ways that, although as yet ill-defined, may prove to be an early stage of the pathological changes induced by chronic alcohol abuse.

Neuropathological researchers face a number of methodological challenges in their attempts to relate structural abnormalities to cognitive dysfunction. Some of these are highly technical and relate to the difficulty of fixing different types of tissue prior to examination. Other issues are more straightforward. Understandably, subject numbers tend to be small. For this, and other reasons, it is important that more information be made available about the clinical presentation of each case. Retrospective studies do not allow relationships between neuropathological lesions and behavioural changes to be identified. Assumptions about the likely cognitive deficits can be misleading. The need to make such assumptions suggests that there is a lack of communication between disciplines in the area. Only a collaborative prospective study collecting detailed clinical, neuropsychological, and neuropathological data will provide valid information about the neuropathological basis of the behavioural deficits of chronic alcohol abusers.

CHAPTER SIX

Neurophysiological Research

If a large dose of alcohol is taken at one sitting, i.e. within two to four hours, the symptoms referable to the nervous system are such as are commonly spoken of as drunkenness or intoxication, and the stages of exhilaration followed by brain failure and collapse occur in more or less rapid sequence.

Horsley & Sturge (1911, p. 67)

Too much of a good thing is wonderful.

Mae West (Weintraub, 1967, p. 12)

In this chapter, the findings of studies aimed at detecting physiological or functional changes in the living human brain are surveyed. We will begin by examining the findings of electrophysiology studies that have employed electroencephalography (EEG), computer-assisted EEG tomography, and evoked brain potentials. Later in the chapter, we consider studies that have utilised cerebral blood flow and conclude by discussing findings derived from positron emission tomography (PET).

ELECTROENCEPHALOGRAPHY STUDIES

The development of the electroencephalogram enabled the study of functional, electrophysiological states of the brain by recording from non-invasive scalp electrodes. EEG rhythms are classified by their frequencies into four components according to convention. These are (Lishman, 1987):

1. delta, less than 4Hz;
2. theta, 4-7Hz;
3. alpha, 8-13Hz;
4. beta, in excess of 13Hz.

There are normal ranges for the proportion of each wave form recorded from various electrodes either at rest or during a range of stimulus presentations or activities. For example, in a relaxed state with eyes closed there is normally a well-developed alpha rhythm, which attenuates when the eyes open, and reappears when they close again (Lishman, 1987). Engagement in mental activity, such as problem solving, also attenuates the alpha rhythm. Other wave forms are associated with particular mental states. Delta activity is usually only seen during sleep, and theta activity during drowsiness. Figure 6.1 shows samples of electrical activity recorded during various states of arousal.

Marked deviations from these normal EEG patterns occur when brain dysfunction or damage is present. These changes take the form of reduced

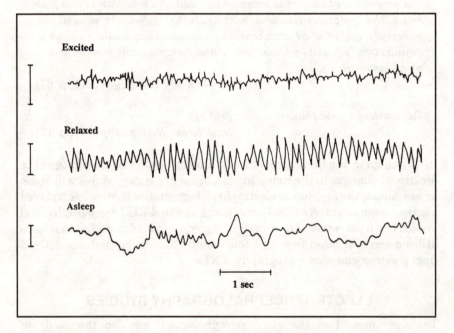

FIG. 6.1. Electroencephalographic records during excitement, relaxation, and varying degrees of sleep.

alpha, or the presence of "spikes", "sharp waves", "slow waves", or combinations of these components. Abnormalities such as these are often diagnostic of epilepsy and, in uncertain cases, a range of "activating" procedures, including hyperventilation and photic stimulation, may be used to induce brain hyperexcitability and elicit the abnormalities. Recording of the EEG during sleep and under the influence of certain drugs is another clinical method of eliciting abnormalities. Deep electrode placement is sometimes employed to enhance the diagnostic utility of the EEG.

Certain limitations are associated with the EEG as a clinical diagnostic tool; these also apply to research data derived from it. As many as 15% of asymptomatic patients have abnormal EEG readings and the proportion of abnormal recordings is even higher among populations with functional psychiatric disorders. Furthermore, the absence of an abnormal EEG record does not guarantee the absence of neuropathology. The accuracy of localisation of the site of the abnormality is variable and the EEG record may be affected by a range of factors unrelated to neuropathology such as blood sugar level (Lishman, 1987). Despite these limitations, application of the EEG to the study of alcohol abuse has made a significant contribution to our understanding. Access to an ongoing record of the neuroelectrical activity of the brain has enabled exploration of the relationships between alcohol ingestion, subjective states, behavioural changes, and electrical activity. EEG studies of the effects of alcohol can be divided into four topics: (1) the effects of acute administration of alcohol; (2) changes associated with chronic experimental administration of alcohol; (3) the effects of chronic alcohol abuse; and (4) EEG concomitants of tolerance and abrupt withdrawal.

Acute administration of alcohol

In general, the effects of acute alcohol ingestion on EEG rhythms parallel changes in the affective state and level of arousal of the subject. All vary as a function of both dosage and the rate of increase in blood alcohol level (BAL) over time. Begleiter and Platz (1972) reviewed the early literature and reached several conclusions. The percentage of alpha time is increased, as is the abundance of alpha. There is increased synchronisation of the EEG pattern, greater stability of component wave forms with less dispersion, and slowing in the dominant alpha frequency. EEG changes appear slight even in the presence of marked changes in mood and behaviour. There are, however, discrepancies between the results of studies employing similar methods. Although Engel, Webb, and Ferris (1945) found close correspondence between clinical ratings of degree of intoxication, consciousness and awareness, and the amount of slowing of waves, Davis et al. (1941) had earlier reported a significant latency in the development of peak EEG changes, which were not reached until BAL began dropping. Five hours after drinking, EEG changes were still near their maximum, despite subjects appearing to have regained sobriety.

The observation that EEG records showing fast normal and abnormally fast initial values become more normalised during intoxication, encouraged Begleiter and Platz (1972) to speculate on the relationship between predrinking EEG differences and the aetiology of alcoholism. They advanced the hypothesis that the alcoholic may drink to "normalise" predrink EEG states. They cited Holmberg and Martens (1955), who showed that maximum slowing lagged behind peak BAL by only 6 minutes in alcoholics compared with 45 minutes for a non-alcoholic control group. As we shall see below, this has been a recurrent theme in the findings of electrophysiology studies of alcohol abusers.

Chronic experimental administration of alcohol

In a particularly interesting study, Wikler, Pescor, Fraser, and Isbell (1956) maintained three subjects on BALs of more than 200mg% for long periods of between 48 and 55 days. At first, previously normal EEG records became slowed diffusely during intoxication; this persisted to a milder degree throughout the experimental drinking phase. There was an increased percentage of slow (theta) wave activity (4–6Hz), an increase in the percentage of alpha wave activity recorded at occipital sites, and a slowing of mean alpha frequency. After the development of tolerance, a reduction in BAL was associated with a partial return of EEG records to normal values. During abrupt withdrawal, more significant changes in the EEG were observed. After 12 hours, when the BAL had dropped from 200 to 30–40mg%, the EEG resembled the initial record, but after 15–20 hours, when BAL approached zero, moderately high voltage, rhythmic slow waves and associated reduction in percentage of alpha appeared. Lasting throughout the first 2 days of the withdrawal, and corresponding to periods of marked anxiety and tremor, random spikes and paroxysmal bursts of slow wave, high voltage activity appeared. There were also transient dysrhythmias of mild degree. Similar results were reported by Isbell et al. (1955) who kept 10 subjects continuously intoxicated for between 6 and 12 weeks and then subjected them to abrupt withdrawal. Sixteen to 33 hours after cessation of alcohol ingestion, the EEG records of those subjects with more severe withdrawal effects showed reduced alpha, random spikes, and slow waves. This is about the stage that withdrawal convulsions ("rum fits") are sometimes seen in chronic alcoholics. Authors of both studies found that the apparently hyperexcitable brain state associated with alcohol withdrawal returned to normal within 3 months and that EEGs recorded at other times in such subjects are usually within normal limits. The clinical implication of these findings was that problem drinkers without pre-existing EEG abnormalities may develop epileptiform electrophysiological activity during abrupt alcohol withdrawal.

Chronic alcohol abuse

The findings that have emerged from the study of abstinent chronic alcoholic patients have been much less consistent and subject to numerous sources of error. These include lack of standard definitions, and large variations in subject selection criteria, study methodologies, and recording techniques and apparatus. Assembling control groups matched on important extraneous variables present in chronic alcohol abusers (e.g. history of head trauma, hepatic disease) has been a challenge that has seldom been adequately met. Longitudinal methodologies are required to differentiate between those abnormalities that are concomitants of withdrawal and those that are residual effects of abuse. However, most studies are of a cross-sectional design, partly because of the chronic relapsing nature of the disorder. Finally, medications administered during the withdrawal period may themselves modify the EEG records, but it is ethically difficult to standardise treatments for heterogeneous clinical samples.

In general, it can be concluded that definite and severe EEG abnormalities occur only in chronic alcoholics with clinically obvious signs of neurological deterioration. In those studies where percentage of alpha time and characteristics of the alpha rhythm have been shown to differ between non-deteriorated alcohol abusers and normals (e.g. Bennett, Doi, & Mowery, 1956; Davis et al., 1941), it has not been possible to demonstrate that this was independent of the withdrawal process. One trend to emerge from this research, however, was that severity of EEG abnormalities tended to be correlated with the severity and advancing stage of the alcohol problem.

Clinical relevance of EEG study findings

Despite the limitations of the EEG studies mentioned above, two quite interesting sets of findings have emerged. The first relates to motivation to drink excessively and was implied by the finding that the "prealcoholic" has a chronically "irritable" CNS state characterised by poor alpha and chronic anxiety. For such an individual, alcohol intoxication would "normalise" the alpha, quell the CNS discomfort and thereby, in combination with the hyperexcitability of withdrawal, provide continuous and dual motivation to drink. Perhaps the more important findings to emerge from the early EEG studies were those relating to gross electrophysiological abnormalities present during abrupt withdrawal. The discovery that abnormal, paroxysmal EEG records accompanied withdrawal or sharp drop in BAL in otherwise neurologically normal subjects, had significant implications for the medical treatment of the alcohol withdrawal syndrome. The prophylactic use of CNS depressant medications has become much more widespread as a result.

The major criticisms of the EEG as a research method relate to its largely subjective interpretation and the time required to conduct evaluations of the records obtained. Recent developments arising from the application of modern computer technology may return the EEG to prominence in human alcohol research. We will examine these advances below.

BRAIN EVOKED RESPONSES

Although providing voluminous information regarding the general electrophysiological state of the brain, EEG rhythms are extremely complex and difficult to associate with psychological concepts. Part of the problem is that although they are relatively constant with respect to time, EEG rhythms fluctuate greatly and in an irregular manner, across the brain as a whole. The extraction of intrinsic components such as alpha rhythm allows intense study, but this has been conducted in isolation from both the background activity and from responses evoked by sensory stimuli. In reality, there exists a reciprocal interaction in which the intrinsic rhythms of excitability modify the amplitude and latency of responses to signals in the efferent channel which, in turn, modulate the amplitude, phase, and frequency of the intrinsic rhythms (Porjesz & Begleiter, 1983). The application of computer technology has facilitated the development of new methods for extracting signals from the background noise of the EEG. In particular, electrophysiological responses evoked by sensory input at the level of peripheral sense organs, sensory nerves, and higher points on the sensory pathways have been studied. Stimuli in all sensory modalities have been employed, including visual, auditory, and somatosensory modes. Stimulation has taken the form of flashes of light, clicks, electrical current, distinctive odours and other methods. All have the common property that they can be controlled from an external source and therefore time-referenced. Electrophysiological responses can then be divided into background noise, and foreground signal. As the signal is non-random, summation of repeated time-locked responses will reveal the evoked brain response while the intrinsic background noise will average to zero. The signal derived from such a process has become known as an evoked potential (EP), or an event-related potential (ERP). Recordings of ERPs provide knowledge of complex aspects of brain function because they permit observations of electrophysiological changes while the subject is engaged in cognitive processes. The functional integrity of different anatomical systems (e.g. cortical and subcortical) may be tested by these methods. It is believed that evoked potential methods are capable of identifying changes that are more subtle and dynamic than the static and rather gross changes detectable by CT-scan. EP and ERP methods have been applied to the study of both acute and chronic alcohol effects. Examples of average evoked responses to auditory and visual stimuli are shown in Fig. 6.2.

Evoked potentials and acute alcohol ingestion

The findings of the earliest EP studies raised interesting questions about the nature and sites of the effects of acute and chronic alcohol ingestion. Subjects who were studied after alcohol intoxication showed reduced amplitudes in their auditory EPs, reduced amplitudes in somatosensory EPs, and decreased amplitudes of both visual and somatosensory late EPs. Such findings appeared to support the conclusion that alcohol ingestion significantly reduced the amplitude of the late components of EPs.

During the last two decades, very significant advances have been made in the study of evoked brain potentials. The development of new techniques for recording from a variety of sites during sensory and cognitive challenges has contributed greatly to knowledge of the nature and regional

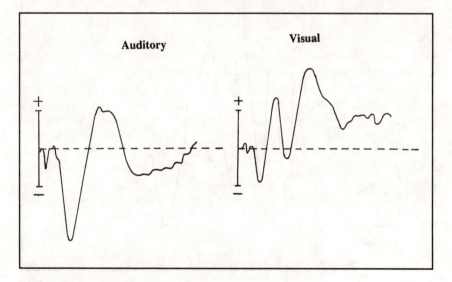

FIG. 6.2. Averaged auditory and visual evoked response waves.

distribution of acute and chronic alcohol effects. Studies have included healthy and chronic alcohol-abusing subjects and participants have been studied during acute alcohol ingestion, during alcohol withdrawal, and after a significant period of abstinence. The non-drinking sons of chronic alcoholic fathers have also been studied. Methods of study have included brain stem potentials (BSPs, non-invasive scalp electrode measures of subcortical brain function), sensory evoked potentials (EPs evoked by presentation of stimuli in any sensory mode), and event-related potentials (ERPs, the early and late positive and negative electrophysiological responses to simple and complex cognitive challenges to the brain).

The auditory BSP is particularly well suited to the study of acute effects of alcohol because it allows measurement of seven discrete time-locked positive deflections indicating the neuroelectrical activity occurring at different levels in the auditory pathway. Figure 6.3 shows the seven peaks occurring over time in the normal auditory BSP. Peaks I–III are thought to represent activity in the auditory nerve, cochlear nuclei, and superior olivary nucleus of the medulla. Peaks IV–VI are thought to tap activity at the nuclei of the lateral lemniscus, inferior colliculi, and medial geniculate bodies. The meaning of peak VII is less well known. Latency to each peak,

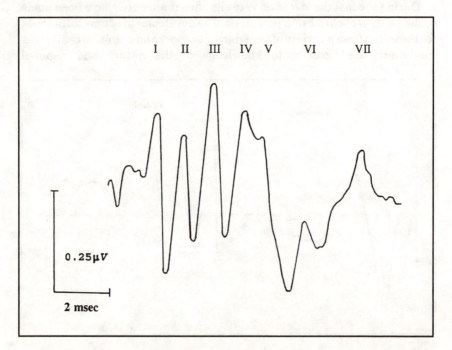

FIG. 6.3. Representation of the auditory brainstem response to a click. Numerals I to VII label the response peaks.

as well as latency of each peak with respect to peak I (central conduction time), is used to determine the presence of pathology from the level of the receptor organ to the brain (Begleiter & Platz, 1972; Porjesz & Begleiter, 1987; but see also Williams, 1987).

The findings of BSP studies during acute alcohol ingestion have been quite consistent. Squires, Chu, and Starr (1978) followed up their earlier work with animals by demonstrating normal latency to peak I, but abnormally delayed latency to peaks IV–VII in healthy alcohol-ingesting subjects. The latency delays were found to parallel clinical signs of intoxication more closely than did BALs. This work was replicated in Japan (Fukui et al., 1981) where subjects with the "flushing" response to alcohol showed larger shifts in latencies of peaks III, V, and VII than non-flushers despite the same BALs. The implication of this finding is that evoked BSPs are sensitive to individual neurophysiological differences in the way that alcohol affects the CNS.

Sensory evoked potentials recorded from various scalp electrodes are able to detect early (P1, a positive deflection occurring about 100ms after stimulus onset) and later (N1, P2, and P3; negative and positive deflections occurring at 100, 200, and 300ms after stimulus onset, respectively) components representing cortical electrophysiological responses. Figure 6.4 shows an example of N1, P2, N2, and P3 recorded during cognitive tasks. In general, early components (less than 100ms) are resistant to the depressant effects of alcohol on the CNS no matter which of the sensory modalities is stimulated. There is significant amplitude depression in late component EPs and this is marked over association areas rather than primary processing areas. For example, for visual EPs occipital electrode sites record less depression than central electrodes thought to be monitoring association areas. Porjesz and Begleiter (1983) suggested that while all brain areas will ultimately be affected by very high doses of alcohol, polysynaptic association areas are affected differentially at low to moderately high doses. There is also some evidence to suggest that visual EP amplitudes recorded from central sites are slower to recover than those recorded from occipital sites (Porjesz & Begleiter, 1975).

Amplitude depression of evoked potentials is related to dose, BAL, and time course of BAL increase. There are no significant effects at low doses (0.4–0.8g/kg and BALS of 30–60mg%), while at high doses (more than 1.2g/kg and BALs in excess of 90mg%), amplitudes are decreased significantly (Porjesz & Begleiter, 1983; 1987). There are large individual differences in time to peak BAL after a single dose, in magnitude of peak EP amplitude, and in time after ingestion that this is reached. These individual differences are probably due to drinking history, age, constitution, nutrition, and placebo. As we shall see later, they may also be due to genetic factors.

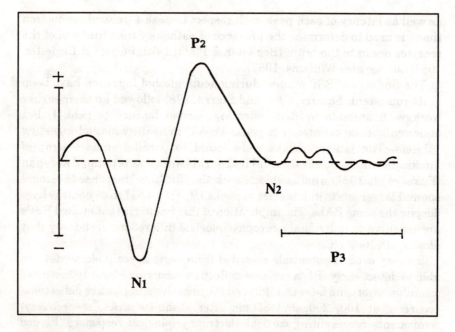

FIG. 6.4. Components of the auditory evoked response potential recorded during a cognitive task.

Sensory evoked potentials are recorded during relatively passive attentional states that may vary a great deal. Also, as alcohol may affect attention itself, EPs recorded under these conditions may reflect this artifact rather than the cognitive processing elements of interest. Furthermore, attentional manipulations themselves affect EP responses so that passive attentional tasks can only be considered to at best reflect an interaction between the affects of alcohol and attention. Recently, EP research has attempted to separate the effects of alcohol and attention on late evoked potentials by involving subjects in cognitive processing and recording the associated event related potentials from cortical regions by way of strategically placed scalp electrodes (Krein et al., 1987). A variety of tasks have been employed including visual and auditory target selection tasks and memory retrieval paradigms. A great deal of research effort has been expended developing tasks that can reliably elicit late ERPs. The ERP component that has been the subject of the most attention has been the late P3 (or P300) peak. This is a large positive deflection that occurs approximately 300–500ms after the onset of the stimulus. The P300 component is elicited only under certain conditions of motivational significance to the subject. Manipulations for achieving this include task relevance, unpredictability, infrequency, and motivation (to gain reward or avoid punishment). The P300 amplitude is normally maximal over parietal areas and is bilaterally symmetrical with identical distribution regardless of stimulus. Most researchers assessing P300 as a dependent variable consider that cognitive functions are being directly tapped in this paradigm.

Drinking has been shown to depress the amplitude of the P300 component and/or to delay its latency in target selection paradigms in a number of studies (Pfefferbaum, Horvath, Roth, & Kopell, 1979; Porjesz & Begleiter, 1983, 1987). The conclusion that has been drawn from these findings was that when accurate task-relevant detection is required, alcohol ingestion may slow the processing time. There has, however, been significant variability, results appearing to be task-dependent and idiosyncratic responses being prevalent. This has made generalisation of the results and derivation of their psychological meaning difficult. Williams (1987) has suggested that P300 has no simple cognitive or psychological correlate and that functions as diverse as uncertainty reduction, memory scanning, orienting, salience, reward value, updating recent memory, and an attentional resource with limited capacity have been associated with it. In this regard, it should be noted that Begleiter, Porjesz, Chou, and Aunon (1983) reported that P300 is enhanced to stimuli to which financial reward is attached. We will return to the difficulties in interpreting the meaning of ERP findings later.

Evoked brain potentials in chronic alcohol abusers

The effects of chronic alcohol abuse are much easier to study in animals than in humans. In animals, prolonged alcohol ingestion produces decrements in EP voltage and delays in BSP latencies. Tolerance is associated with reductions in the alcohol-related abnormalities while abrupt removal produces CNS hyperexcitability with associated increases in EP amplitudes and shortened BSP latencies. This CNS excitability persists for at least 3 weeks (Porjesz & Begleiter, 1983; 1987). The results of studies of chronic alcohol consumption in human subjects parallel those of the animal literature (Begleiter, Porjesz, & Yerre-Grubstein, 1974; Wagman, Allen, Funderbuck, & Upright, 1978). Such studies are, however, prone to error from a number of sources. For example, during detoxification, medications are usually employed to ameliorate emotional and physical symptoms such as tremor, acute anxiety and seizures. In addition, the drug Antabuse (disulfiram), which is often prescribed to chronic alcohol abusers during abstinence, is itself known to increase visual EP amplitude (Coger et al., 1976). There are also significant subject selection biases that are difficult to control. The type of carefully controlled longitudinal study necessary to identify the effects of chronic intoxication and withdrawal on the EPs of chronic alcohol abusers has not, to our knowledge, been conducted.

Nevertheless, a considerable amount is known about the EP abnormalities of hospitalised chronic alcohol abusers who have been abstinent for at least 3 weeks. Begleiter, Porjesz, and Chou (1981) reported delayed auditory BSP latencies and slow central conduction velocities of peaks II–V in alcoholics abstinent for 1 month. Porjesz and Begleiter (1983, 1987) have suggested that these abnormalities may reflect the process of demyelination of auditory pathways begining at the level of the pontine formation. Pojesz and Begleiter (1987) have provided evidence that BSP aberrations are related more closely to nutritional deficits, a well- known cause of demyelination, than to duration of drinking history itself. Marked BSP abnormalities were more prevalent in a subgroup of subjects with less than 8 years of heavy drinking but with evidence of malnutrition than in a subgroup with more than 20 years of heavy drinking without evidence of dietary insufficiency. On the other hand, Williams (1987) has indicated that, while the BSP abnormalities constitute an important finding that adds to the CT-scan literature identifying mainly cortical changes, it may be due to a number of causes other than demyelination. These other causes include, synaptic changes, neuronal loss in the brain stem, or lowered brain temperature. Williams (1987) argued that the BSP changes in Squires et al.'s (1978) intoxicated healthy subjects and Begleiter and colleagues' chronic alcoholics may reflect a similar process: that of alcohol-induced hypothermia. He suggested that the brain hypoexcitability occurring about 1 month after withdrawal may induce a similar reduction in brain temperature as alcohol induction itself. If this were true, then the BSP abnormalities of chronic alcoholics probably reflect an interaction of both temperature-dependent and temperature-independent effects (Williams, 1987). For this, and other methodological reasons, validation of the demyelination hypothesis awaits futher research.

Late event-related electrophysiological activity has also been studied in chronic alcoholics. As in most of the areas already discussed, credit for the most comprehensive research on this topic must go to Begleiter's group (see Begleiter & Platz, 1972; Porjesz & Begleiter, 1983, 1987, for reviews). After 1 month or more of abstinence, chronic alcoholic subjects show abnormally reduced late component (N1–P2) but not early component (P1) amplitudes. The N1 component is normally enhanced to all stimuli in the relevant mode and decreased to stimuli in the irrelevant modality. Reduced N1–P2 amplitudes have been taken to indicate that abstinent chronic alcoholics have impaired sensory filtering, as they do not differentiate electrophysiologically between relevant and irrelevant stimulus channels or modalities. In a particularly interesting study, Porjesz, Begleiter, and Garozzo (1980) required abstinent chronic alcoholics in a visual evoked potential paradigm to differentiate between relevant and irrelevant inputs and to probability-match stimuli in terms of frequency of occurrence. This design required the subjects to change sets, because stimuli relevant in one block were no longer relevant in the next and vice versa. Results showed that N1–P2 late component amplitudes were significantly depressed in the alcoholics and that P300 was also depressed or absent over parietal areas where it is usually maximal. Porjesz and Begleiter (1983; 1987) have interpreted these findings as suggesting that their alcoholic subjects failed to differentiate between relevant and irrelevant inputs. In other words, there was, in these subjects, an underlying brain dysfunction that impaired sensory filtering and probability matching processes.

Others have advanced alternative explanations. For example, Williams (1987) has suggested that chronic alcoholics who have been abstinent for 1 month may be characterised by low grade depression and boredom. He noted that Begleiter's own work (Begleiter et al., 1983) showed that motivational factors in the form of financial rewards enhance P300 amplitudes. In essence, Williams has suggested that the abnormalities observed may be due to low arousal and low motivation rather than cognitive deficits due to brain dysfunction. Another study by Begleiter's group goes some way to countering this argument. Begleiter, Porjesz, and Tenner (1980) divided a sample of abstinent chronic alcoholics into two groups: (1) those with CT-scans suggestive of a high degree of cortical atrophy (positive CT); and (2) those with no significant cortical atrophy (negative CT). Both groups had lower P300 amplitudes to target stimuli than did healthy controls; however, the P300 amplitude in the positive CT group was significantly lower (or absent), than that in the negative CT group. Although both alcoholic groups showed a similar P300 morphology regardless of the task relevance of the stimulus category, the amplitude of this component was clearly related to degree of structural brain change.

A large number of studies of late components of ERPs have been conducted, including complex reaction-time tasks. The N2 and P300 ERP differences that have emerged suggest that abstinent chronic alcoholics have difficulty evaluating the potential significance of a stimulus because they maintain the same ERP characteristics regardless of the task requirements. They also tend to take more time to make easy discriminations relative to controls than to make difficult discriminations. Their P300 latencies are similar for both easy and difficult tasks and they appear to adopt a strategy of speed over accuracy in complex reaction-time tasks (Porjesz & Begleiter, 1983, 1987; Williams, 1987). In information processing terminology, the increased N2 latency suggests that the response template is relatively inaccessible and the low P300 voltage suggests that the match/mismatch process is impaired.

It is somewhat disconcerting to find that comprehensive studies of late component ERPs in chronic alcoholic subjects conducted by other researchers have yielded different results (Pfefferbaum et al., 1979; 1980). Although Begleiter and colleagues found generally normal latencies and decreased amplitudes in their alcoholic subjects, Pfefferbaum and colleagues found increased latencies and normal amplitudes. In discussing this apparent discrepancy, Porjesz and Beglieter (1983) proffered a number of possible explanations. There were marked differences in mean ages and durations of abstinence of the subjects studied. Begleiter's subjects' average age was 36.1 compared to Pfefferbaum's 50.1, and the mean durations of abstinence were 60 and 21 days respectively. It seems possible that Pfefferbaum's subjects were significantly more deteriorated and it is known that age *per se* affects ERP latency, but not usually its amplitude (Williams, 1987). There were also differences in the methods employed to both elicit and record the ERPs. Furthermore, there is now some doubt that the two studies were measuring the same electrophysiological events, as it has now been claimed that there is both more than one N2 (Renault, Ragot, Lesevre, & Redmond, 1982; Ritter et al., 1984) and many P300s (see Williams, 1987). Although helping to clarify the reasons for the discrepancies in results, these observations significantly complicate interpretation of study findings. It now appears that there is little standardisation of methods between research laboratories and that slightly different methods yield very different results. Thus, psychologists without specialist knowledge of the techniques employed in this field are at serious risk of misinterpreting study findings. This hyperspecialisation places this field of human neurophysiology at great risk of becoming remote from the clinical setting and readers to whom its findings would be of great value.

Recovery of ERPs with long term abstinence

The research reported above was conducted on hospitalised chronic alcoholics who had been abstinent for less than 2 months. Subsequently, the ERPs of patients abstinent for longer periods have been studied. Such studies are complicated by the presence of prolonged withdrawal phenomena (Grant, 1987) and self-exclusion by relapse, not to mention the concurrent use of other prescribed and non-prescribed medications. The two medications most commonly prescribed to abstinent chronic alcoholics—chlordiazepoxide and disulfiram—both affect the electrophysiological activity of the CNS. As we have already mentioned, a longitudinal methodology is necessary to separate completely the effects of concomitant withdrawal phenomena from long-term brain dysfunction.

Between 1 and 3 months after cessation of drinking, there appears to be some improvement in the ERPs of chronic alcoholics, but the recordings do not reach normal. Brain stem potentials and pattern evoked potentials show decreases in latencies and in conduction times and their morphology is improved, but neural transmission velocities are still slower. Late ERPs show improved morphology and better signal to noise ratio but only some N1–P2 and P3 amplitudes improve while most do not. There appears to be more recovery in younger subjects, but the reason for this is far from clear (Porjesz & Begleiter, 1983). At this early stage it is still unclear whether these are long-term abnormalities or concomitants of prolonged withdrawal. Porjesz and Begleiter (1987) have discussed their findings regarding recovery of EP latency, amplitude, and morphology in hospitalised chronic alcoholics abstinent for at least 4 months. They found evidence of improvement of BSP waveforms, shortening of latencies, and improved conduction time, but the wave peaks were still later, on average, than in control subjects. In contrast to the improvements in electrophysiological functions recorded from the brain stem, ERPs recorded from the cortex did not appear to recover with long term abstinence. ERP wave forms and voltages were the same at 4 months as they were at 3 weeks. In a few patients, abstinent for 3 years, these abnormalities were still present.

The current state of research into recovery of short latency EPs and long latency ERPs with abstinence should be considered preliminary and, as we have emphasised, prone to several sources of error. In general, subjects comprising the chronic alcoholic groups have been hospitalised for treatment and are therefore a biased sample. We have already mentioned the fact that the treatments themselves may confound the results. The valid study of recovery of function with abstinence requires that the subjects who complete the study and those who drop out through relapse are in similar proportion with regard to extraneous variables directly related to performance on the dependent variable. Differential relapse rates, with regard to age and severity of abuse, bias the sample and raise significant questions about the degree to which the results are representative. Older subjects, who may be more likely to relapse rapidly, may have more severe abuse problems and other physical complications. Williams (1987) has reviewed literature showing that chronological age is associated with increased central conduction time, increased P1–N2 latencies, slower conduction velocity in somatosensory EPs, and larger peak latencies for P300. There is also evidence of a trend for age and alcohol to interact to increase P1–N2 latencies.

Quite apart from concerns about their internal validity, it is not yet clear what the EP and ERP recovery findings mean. Concerns have been raised about both the internal consistency and the validity of EP and ERP measures. Recent research by Parsons and his colleagues has addressed these issues. Parsons, Sinha, and Williams (1990) studied the relationship between several ERP measures and non-concurrently measured neuropsychological test performance in sober middle-aged male and female alcoholics and matched non-alcoholic controls. Results supported the hypothesis that both neuropsychological and ERP abnormalities would be present in the alcoholic patients, but there were many interactions between the independent variables studied. The male subjects showed significant abnormalities on both types of measure and these were more marked in subjects with a positive family history of alcoholism. However, despite the fact that the female alcoholics showed inferior performance on the neuropsychological tests, they showed no significant family history or alcoholism related to ERP abnormalities. These results suggest that the relationship between ERP and neuropsychological test performance in male alcoholic subjects may be due to some abnormality not present in the females. Another possibility was that menstrual cycle fluctuations in ERP performance may have masked differences between female alcoholic and control groups. Adequate explanation of this inconsistent finding awaits further research.

In a later publication, Sinha, Bernardy, and Parsons (1992) reported results of a study of the long-term stability of ERP measures in 71 alcoholics and 44 control subjects. The authors argued that their results reflected good long term stability. For example, over an average of 14 months, correlations for N1, N2, and P3 amplitudes in visual and auditory target conditions ranged between 0.47 and 0.68. The test–retest correlations for ERP latencies were somewhat less impressive, ranging from 0.23 to 0.48. In all but one of the 28 comparisons, the correlations in the alcoholic group were as high as those in the control group. These results lend support to the usefulness of ERP measures as a clinical research tool. However, a number of other problems with EP and ERP studies of abstinent alcoholics must be acknowledged here. There is insufficient evidence to differentiate between long term effects and the concomitants of prolonged withdrawal, such as CNS hypoexcitability. The observation that BSPs show some recovery while ERP morphologies, particularly decreased P300 amplitudes, remain aberrant, may simply reflect different recovery rates. On the other hand, the recent evidence indicating differential recovery functions for BSPs and ERPs (Porjesz & Begleiter, 1987), the presence of interesting individual differences in electrophysiological responses to challenge doses of alcohol (Elmasion et al., 1982; Pollock et al., 1983, 1988), and pre-drinking abnormalities in the ERPs of sons of alcoholic fathers (Begleiter, Porjesz, Bihari, & Kissin, 1984; Pollock, Teasdale, Gabrielli, & Knop, 1986), have provoked speculation that some alcoholics may have premorbid neurophysiological abnormalities. This has been the subject of interesting recent research.

ELECTROPHYSIOLOGICAL STUDIES OF THE SONS OF MALE ALCOHOLICS

The biological sons of male alcoholics are at higher risk of developing chronic alcohol dependence even before they take a drink (Bohman, Sigvardsson, & Cloninger, 1981; Cloninger, Bohman, & Sigvardsson, 1981; Goodwin et al., 1973). The findings of these and other studies (see Cloninger, 1983) have suggested the existence of two genetically distinct forms of alcohol abuse. The first is distributed equally across genders and emerges only in certain environments, while the second, and much smaller category, is highly heritable from father to son. In this second type, mothers and daughters are seldom affected (Williams, 1987). This is consistent with the findings of animal studies of the genetics of alcohol abuse that have shown differential heritability of predispositions to drink alcohol and genetic differences in neurophysiological responses to challenge doses. Such findings raise the intriguing question of whether electrophysiological responses might have use as biological markers for alcoholism. Results of recent studies suggest that this may indeed be the case. Begleiter, Porjesz, Bihari, and Kissin (1984) found that in a reaction-time task, P300 amplitudes were lower in both easy and difficult conditions in the young sons (aged 7–13 years) of alcoholic fathers. Begleiter, Porjesz, and Bihari (1987) then examined another group of boys meeting similar criteria and found that there were no BSP abnormalities. This pattern mirrored the results of studies of ERPs and BSPs in long-term abstinent chronic alcohol abusers. The implication was clearly that the non-recovery of ERP abnormalities with abstinence may be due to their being abnormal premorbidly. That is, the P300 abnormalities may be antecedents rather than consequences of alcohol abuse. Further evidence has emerged recently to support this view. Male college students with a family history of alcohol abuse manifested different P300 components in their ERPs to a challenge dose of alcohol and to placebo than did matched controls (Elmasion et al., 1982). Pollock et al. (1983; 1986; 1988) have reported EEG and EP differences between groups considered at high and low risk for the development of alcoholism on the basis of their family history. Finally, as we noted above, Fukui et al. (1981) have shown that subjects inheriting the facial "flushing" response to alcohol are more susceptible to BSP delays during consumption than those without this characteristic.

Although the results of these studies converge (Freedman & Nagamoto, 1988), the nature of the relationship between electrophysiological differences and alcohol abuse remains unclear. Findings reported subsequently suggest that it may not be alcoholism *per se* that is reflected in the ERP aberrations but some concomitant personality disorder. Branchey, Buydens-Branchey, and Lieber (1988) divided alcoholics into subgroups and found that the lowest P3 amplitudes occurred in those with aggressive tendencies. These subjects, with disorders of mood and aggression control, had lifelong histories of aggressive behaviour and incarceration for crimes involving physical violence. The tendency of this group to antisocial behaviour and a high genetic loading for alcoholism allow them to be classified as type 2 alcoholics. Branchey et al. (1988) were unable to rule out the possibility that the P300 deficits could be associated with some psychopathological conditions that coexist with alcohol abuse rather than with alcoholism *per se*.

EFFECTS OF ALCOHOL ON CEREBRAL BLOOD FLOW

Brain metabolic processes place demands on oxygen and glucose. When these demands are changed by neural dysfunction or destruction, the changes are reflected in adaptations in the flow of blood within the brain. The coupling between cerebral blood flow and metabolism makes regional cerebral blood flow (rCBF) an indicator of the integrity of neuronal function. Methods of studying changes in rCBF in cerebrovascular and other disorders have been applied to investigations of the effects of alcohol on the functional state of the brain. Most of this research has been conducted by Berglund and colleagues in Sweden. Research into the effects of alcohol on rCBF has been reviewed by Berglund (1981), Risberg and Berglund (1987), and Shaw (1987).

Initially, the methods of study were quite invasive and restricted the sampling techniques and research designs that could be applied. Kety and Schmidt (1948) had subjects inhale N_2O and then took serial blood samples from an artery and the jugular sinus. Lassen and Ingvar (1961) injected 95Kr or 133Xe into the internal corotid artery and then recorded arrival and clearance of tracers from scalp detectors. The most recent, and least invasive, technique involves the inhalation or intravenous administration of Xe and recording from scalp electrodes (Mallet & Veall, 1963). There have been few studies of alcoholics, so the available evidence is limited. Early research investigated the effects on rCBF of alcohol intoxication in healthy subjects. Battey, Heyman, and Patterson (1953) reported no change at low doses while at high doses there is an increase in CBF but a decrease in cerebral metabolic rate of oxygen ($CMRO_2$). The paradoxical dissociation between the CBF and metabolic indices raised the important issue that higher doses of alcohol may uncouple their linkage. We will return to this issue later. Newlin, Golden, Quaife, and Graber (1982) also reported a grey-matter increase in rCBF in all brain regions with the exception of the frontal parts of the left hemisphere. The paucity of studies in this area makes it difficult to draw conclusions with any confidence.

Regional cerebral blood flow during
alcohol withdrawal

The study of rCBF during alcohol withdrawal was assisted by the development of the non-invasive Xe133 inhalation method, as it allowed repeated measurement across time. Berglund and Risberg (1981) studied rCBF of 12 alcoholics aged 27–60 years during 13 periods of alcohol withdrawal over the course of 30 days. During one period, two of their subjects developed alcoholic hallucinosis. Medications used to manage withdrawal symptoms were chlormethiazole 2–6 g (n = 10), and dixyrazine 75mg (n = 3). Ratings of withdrawal symptoms were made about 1 hour before the rCBF measurement. Results showed that CBF was decreased during the first 2 days compared with levels 1 week after withdrawal. On the third day some patients had returned to normal and on the fourth day most values were in the lower part of the normal range. There was a significant correlation between the magnitude of the flow rate decrease and duration of the previous drinking period (r = 0.70, P < 0.01) and a significant correlation between one of the withdrawal symptoms (confusion) and flow decrease (r = 0.62, P < 0.05). The clinical correlates of rCBF during early withdrawal were associated with disturbances of arousal (i.e. clouding of consciousness).

Perhaps the most interesting finding of this study was the distribution of rCBF in two cases who experienced withdrawal hallucinosis. One 45-year-old patient who had been drinking 750ml of alcohol per day for 3 weeks heard his brother and sister singing religious hymns in the background throughout CBF measurement. The rCBF over the Sylvian fissure of the left hemisphere was approximately 15% above hemispheric averages. Twenty minutes after injection of haloperidol (an antipsychotic medication), the hallucinations faded and there was a contemporaneous decrease in rCBF to about 5% above average. Similarly, a patient with visual hallucinations showed rCBF values 75% and 40% above average in the occipitoparietal regions of the left and right hemispheres respectively. Berglund and Risberg (1981) concluded that the increases recorded during hallucinations reflected cortical activity and were similar to rCBF increases seen in normal subjects during activation by sensory and cognitive challenges. The small subject numbers, absence of control data, and the possibility of alcoholic relapse during the phase of the study conducted while the subjects were outpatients all serve to limit confidence in these findings.

Some of these limitations were addressed in a more recent study on rCBF during the early stages of abstinence also conducted by Berglund and colleagues (Berglund et al., 1987). In this study, 22 alcoholics (19 male, three female) ranging in age from 34 to 61 years, were subjected to rCBF assessments under both resting and cognitive activation conditions at intervals of 1, 3, 5, and 7 weeks after ceasing alcohol consumption. The Xe inhalation method was employed and 16 detectors were placed on each hemisphere. Psychometric tests and rating scales to assess low vitality and emotional deficiencies were administered concurrently with rCBF measures. Twenty two male control patients who were closely matched for age (range 34–63 years) had their rCBF measured on one occasion only. The mean rCBF was lower in the alcoholics at all measurement phases than the control mean. There was a significant interaction, however, between the effects of age and alcohol withdrawal. Although younger alcoholics (< 45 years) did not differ significantly from their controls, older alcoholics did. The older subjects also showed significant increases in rCBF between weeks 1 and 7 while the younger subjects remained unchanged. Normally, there is a right–left asymmetry in the resting CBF that is larger in the superior and orbital frontal regions. In the older alcoholic patients studied by Berglund et al. (1987), this asymmetry was reduced compared with the controls, the difference being most marked after 1 week of abstinence. There was other evidence that the right hemisphere might be more susceptible to the effects of alcohol. The alcoholics showed significantly lower flow in the superior regions of the frontal lobe of the right hemisphere. The finding that CBF changes are more marked in frontal regions is consistent with the findings of neuroradiology, neuropathology, and neuropsychology studies. However, no convincing explanation of the hemispheric asymmetry reported here by Berglund et al. (1987) has yet emerged. It was of some interest that increases in mean rCBF from the first to the seventh week were related to increased vitality ($r = 0.41$, $P < 0.05$) and improved mood ($r = .58$, $P < 0.01$).

On the basis of these two studies, it might be concluded that CBF is decreased during early withdrawal and that it normalises quickly in young alcoholics but takes longer in older patients. However, there are a number of reasons to believe that this conclusion might be premature. The size of the sample and the biases present in their selection (e.g. hospitalised patients known to remain abstinent during treatment), the inadequacy of control group procedures, and lack of background knowledge about the interaction of ageing, alcohol abuse, and CBF changes, all limit the generalisability of these results. The administration of medications for treatment of withdrawal symptoms may also have modified CBF changes during the early phases of abstinence. Risberg and Berglund (1987, pp. 67–68) stated that: "Further research in this area is needed, with minimal and carefully controlled administration of drugs, and if possible some control of the alcohol consumption during the preceding drinking episode".

Cerebral blood flow changes in chronic alcohol abusers

Berglund and Ingvar (1976) reported rCBF data collected from 60 alcoholics who had been admitted voluntarily for psychiatric treatment. Their mean age was 45.2 years (range, 21–65) and their histories of excessive alcohol use ranged from 5 to 40 years. They met two of three criteria of alcohol dependence: craving, blackouts, or physical withdrawal symptoms. Seven of the subjects met the authors criteria for Korsakoff's psychosis. Subjects were receiving a variety of medications for the amelioration of withdrawal symptoms, including tranquillisers, anticonvulsants, disulfiram, and antidepressants, and because the method employed was invasive and discomfiting, chloral hydrate was administered the evening prior to the rCBF studies. One hour before the studies, phenobarbital and atropine were given. The rCBF was calculated from data obtained from arrangements of eight or 32 detectors. Results were compared with those from seven healthy non-alcoholic controls with a mean age of 31 years. Four other reference groups included healthy young and healthy old subjects, 20 schizophrenic patients, and 50 patients with presenile dementia.

The first major finding to emerge was that rCBF was abnormally low in 53 of the 60 subjects and that it fell with increasing age. Decreases in rCBF were greatest in inferior frontal and anterior temporal regions. The anterior temporal changes seen in the oldest group of alcoholic subjects were similar to those seen in the presenile dementia group who had selective memory impairment. In addition to grey matter CBF changes, there were also changes in white matter flow in all alcoholic age groups. The authors had some difficulty interpreting the higher rCBF rates found in their seven Korsakoff's psychosis patients but speculated (Berglund & Ingvar, 1976, p. 595) that this finding "may imply some abnormality of the normal regulation of the cerebrovascular resistance".

Although the authors attributed the rCBF changes observed in this study to the prolonged effects of alcohol, this conclusion was based on comparison with data collected under very different conditions. For example, most of the comparisons were made with data from other studies in which the patients were not on pharmacological withdrawal regimens. Furthermore, Shaw (1987) has argued that, although alcohol is theoretically capable of accelerating the normal changes of ageing, the aetiology and mechanisms of this effect are unclear. As Shaw (1987) suggested, coexisting hypertension and arteriovascular changes rather than alcohol abuse may account for the age-related effects observed.

In a summary of the research on rCBF changes in chronic alcohol abusers, Risberg and Berglund (1987) concluded that, while most 30 to 40- year-old alcoholics have relatively normal cortical rCBF, excessive drinking after age 45–50 years is likely to produce progressively abnormal flows. Their opinion is that normal age-related flow reductions are accelerated by alcohol abuse. Regions most affected seem to be frontal, but sometimes also anterior temporal cortical areas. In addition, white matter reductions associated with abnormal liver function have been reported (Johannesson, Berglund, & Ingvar, 1982). Risberg and Berglund (1987) interpreted the available evidence on CBF during withdrawal as indicating rapid normalisation of flow during the first week. This process is completed much earlier in young subjects but continues throughout at least 7 weeks in older subjects (older than 45 years). Normalisation of CBF is correlated with improvements in vitality and energy in the older group.

There are a number of reasons in addition to those already mentioned above, why the conclusions reached by Risberg and Berglund (1987) should be treated with caution. Shaw (1987) drew attention to the inadequacy of control groups employed. Specifically, he noted the need to exclude social drinkers due to the possible presence of subclinical measureable effects on CBF in this group. Furthermore, sampling techniques employed to date have been inadequate. Studies conducted have been subject to selection bias, survivor effects, and their generalisability has therefore been limited. The possibility that CBF abnormalities in some alcoholics might be antecedents of alcohol abuse rather than consequences has not been examined.

There are also limitations associated with the methods themselves. As we have already seen, early studies involved carotid puncture to determine CBF for the brain as a whole. Despite its limitations, this method allowed simultaneous measurement of cerebral metabolic rate for oxygen ($CMRO_2$). The restrictions on the use of such an invasive technique encouraged the development of the Xe inhalation, scalp callimator method that yielded similar results without the risks or discomfort. However, the data required to conduct correlations between CBF and $CMRO_2$ were not available with this method. This is important because the link between CBF and $CMRO_2$ may be uncoupled by both acute and chronic alcohol consumption. Such an uncoupling, which would make the results of CBF studies uninterpretable, may also result from coexisting hypertension and cerebrovascular disease, both of which are more common in older alcoholics. Shaw (1987) has also argued that alcohol's vasodilating or vasoconstricting effects might give rise to significant artifacts. The validity of rCBF as an index of brain metabolic activity and therefore as an indication of functional state of the brain is in some doubt in the studies discussed above. The advent of positron emission tomography (PET) scanning as a method of assessing brain metabolism has relegated some of these issues to academic interest, because it provides a direct measure of cerebral metabolism.

PET SCAN AND ALCOHOL CONSUMPTION

PET scanning represents a major advance in the cross-sectional assessment of brain function but is restricted in its availability due to the necessity for a cyclotron to be on hand for the manufacture of short-lived radioactive isotopes employed in the procedure. In PET scanning, compounds labelled with short-lived isotopes are injected or inhaled until they reach a certain level in the target tissues. Uptake of the labelled substance by the tissue creates instability resulting from the excess of protons over neutrons and forces a discharge of positrons (positively charged electrons). Stability is thereby regained and, in the meantime, an index of the uptake of the isotope-labelled compounds in the target tissue is provided. PET scanning involves the quantification and localisation of the projected emission of photons associated with positron annihilation in the tissue. The application of complex mathematical procedures and computer-generated algorithms, similar to those employed in CT scanning, yields a visual image of the uptake of the isotope-labelled compound in the target tissue. Different physiological processes can be studied by varying the isotope employed. For example, regional cerebral blood flow and oxygen utilisation may be assessed by administering oxygen-15 by inhalation, and injection of fluorine-18 incorporated into 2-deoxy-d-glucose (18-FDG) allows the measurement of local glucose metabolism. As we have mentioned above, metabolic processes have been taken as indices of the functional state of the brain. PET allows their direct assessment and therefore constitutes a major advance over the measurment of rCBF as an indirect estimate (Duara et al., 1984; Phelps et al., 1979).

To date, PET scanning has been applied to the study of a range of cerebral disorders with considerable success (Benson et al., 1983; Farkas et al., 1982; Friedland, Budinger, Koss, & Ober, 1985; Kuhl, Metter, & Riege, 1984; Metter et al., 1982). Lishman (1987, p. 125) has written enthusiastically about such scanning techniques:

> Special promise attaches to further possibilities of examining the brain in the resting state and during responses to defined tasks. Other molecules can be labelled, such as amino acids, fatty acids, sugars and drugs, similarly compounds with high affinity for receptor sites. A considerable variety of active metabolic processes should thus become accessible to study, including protein synthesis and the correlates of response to drugs. Accurate mapping of receptor sites could yield particularly valuable information.

The application of PET scanning to the study of the effects of alcohol on the brain is a recent development and the number of studies available for review is small. All of the studies to be discussed here examined either regional cerebral glucose utilisation rate (CMRglu) or regional cerebral blood flow (rCBF). The initial applications of PET to the study of alcohol effects examined chronic alcoholics with and without overt neurological evidence of organic brain syndromes. Prior to reviewing the findings of those studies we will examine the use of PET to study rCBF and rCMRglu during acute administration of alcohol to healthy volunteer subjects.

Volkow et al. (1988) studied the effect of acute alcohol intoxication on rCBF measured with PET, and reported decreased flow in the cerebellum and increased flow in the right parietal and prefrontal cortex. These findings were, however, inconsistent with other reports of rCBF during intoxication. Matthew and Wilson (1986) had earlier reported increased rCBF in the frontal cortex only, while Newlin, Golden, Quaife, and Graber (1982) had reported increased CBF in grey matter in all areas other than the left frontal region. When considered in the context of the concerns raised by Shaw (1987) about the possible uncoupling of CBF and metabolism at higher BALs, the inconsistency of these results is discouraging.

Subsequently, deWit, Metz, Wagner, and Cooper (1990) used PET to study regional CMRglu after placebo, 0.5g/kg, and 0.8g/kg of alcohol in eight healthy, male, paid volunteers aged between 21 and 29 years. The effects of alcohol and placebo on subjective and behavioural reponses were measured both during the PET scan and separately, in a naturalistic setting. Behavioural responses included assessment of preference for alcohol versus placebo, and subjective responses were assessed by administration of the Drug Effects Questionnaire (DEQ) and the Profile of Mood States (POMS). During PET scanning, subjects were required to undertake a visuomotor task designed to minimise intersubject variability and control effects such as drowsiness, day-dreaming, or restlessness. PET scans were analysed with respect to 14 bilateral regions of interest (ROIs): frontal, parietal, temporal, and occipital areas of the cortex, basal ganglia, thalamus, and cerebellum. Whole brain CMRglu tended to decrease after alcohol and this change was more marked and consistent after the higher dose. Although all regions were affected, the decrease was particularly marked in both left and right frontal cortical areas. This finding was consistent with the EEG changes reported by Lukas et al. (1989)—increased alpha activity and associated euphoria after alcohol ingestion. Furthermore, it has been shown that increased alpha activity is related to decreased cerebral metabolism (Metz, Yasillo, & Cooper, 1987). Despite the consistency in subjective effects across both the naturalistic and PET scan settings, correlations between subjective effects and metabolism were, on the whole, inconsistent and difficult to interpret. The authors concluded that, while alcohol produced generally uniform effects on CMRglu across brain regions, subjective effects were much more variable and largely unrelated. Larger and more heterogeneous samples will be required for the results of such investigations to justify their expense.

PET studies of the effects of chronic alcohol abuse

Samson et al. (1986) studied six patients (four males and two females) aged between 30 and 60 years who had been admitted to the psychiatric department of a public hospital due to chronic alcohol dependence. These patients had no evidence of other psychiatric, neurological, or physical disease, and had never suffered from head trauma sufficient to induce unconsciousness. Nor had they had seizures, hepatic cirrhosis or insufficiency, or drug abuse histories. In other words, they were a highly selected group, chosen for their lack of serious complications, and not representative of the wider population of chronic alcohol abusers. PET studies of CMRglu were carried out using the FDG method sometime between the end of first week and the end of the first month after admission. Examination was conducted in resting state when the subjects had been free from medication for at least 24 hours. Thirty regional CMRglu values were calculated from 42 original circular ROIs and results were compared with scans obtained from six age-matched, non-alcoholic control subjects. Results showed that, although regional CMRglu values were slightly lower in alcoholics than in controls, the differences never reached statistical significance. It is noteworthy, however, that for CMRglu in the upper mediofrontal region, the difference of 17% approached significance ($P < 0.07$). This finding is consistent with reports from neuropsychological, neuroradiological, and neuropathological studies of neurologically normal chronic alcoholics. In subcortical regions and in the cerebellum, the CMRglu values of the alcoholics did not differ from those of the controls. One plausible reason for failure to find significant differences was that, although highly selected, the alcoholic group was in many ways quite heterogeneous. They differed greatly in age, education, duration of alcohol abuse, and socioeconomic status.

Sachs, Russell, Christman, and Cook (1987) obtained PET scans from 10 chronic alcoholic males in order to study their CMRglu. These subjects had been drinking for an average of 18 years, and eight of the 10 had positive family history of alcoholism. They were scanned in a resting state between 8 and 45 days after ceasing drinking. Forty-four ROIs were delineated from CT-scans obtained previously. The control subjects were an age matched group of 25 males. Absolute global CMRglu was significantly higher for the control subjects and there were fewer interregional correlations in the alcoholic group. When a procedure designed to activate the right hemisphere was administered (presentation of non-verbal auditory stimuli), the expected increase in glucose utilisation did not occur in the alcoholic group.

In reviewing these two studies, Eckardt, Rohrbaugh, Rio, and Martin (1990) concluded that localised CMRglu at rest is not dramatically affected by chronic alcohol abuse and that, quantitatively, the effects are subtle compared with the changes identified by neuropsychological, neuroradiological, and neuropathological studies. They proposed that insufficient is yet known about the relationship between glucose metabolism and brain function to regard even subtle changes as behaviourally insignificant. Eckardt et al. (1990) also suggested that CMRglu might be less indicative of the functional state of the brain when PET scanning is conducted in resting state than when it is recorded during the performance of cognitive tasks.

Perhaps the most positive results reported in this area to date have come from a study by Wik et al. (1988) which was not considered in Eckardt et al.'s (1990) review. Wik et al. (1988) assessed resting state PET in nine male subjects between the ages of 36 and 58 years, who met DSM-III criteria for alcohol dependence and had been free from alcohol and other drugs for between 4 and 56 weeks. The durations of their drinking histories ranged from 9 to 29 years. These subjects were compared with 12 healthy male controls ranging in age from 21 to 68 years, but whose mean age was only 38 years. To avoid error induced by inclusion of inactive CSF spaces, these researchers first delineated ROIs in each individual by CT scanning. The results showed lower mean rCMRglu in alcoholics compared with controls in more than half of the 19 ROIs, after PET data were subjected to covariance analysis with age as the covariate. Subcortical regions appeared less affected than the neocortex where frontal, temporal, and parietal regions showed the most marked differences. Correlations between age and CMRglu ranged between −0.14 and −0.78 in the control subjects and were significant in nine of the 14 ROIs studied, whereas none of the age by PET correlations in the alcoholic subjects was significant. The significant negative correlation between age and PET in the control subjects in this study was in contrast with the findings of Duara et al. (1984) who failed to find such a relationship when subjects were carefully selected to exclude the effects of ill health. Wik et al. (1988) also conducted such screening and concluded that the likely reason for the absence of such an association in their own alcoholic subjects was the narrower age range of that group.

The findings of the Wik et al. (1988) study are largely consistent with the CBF, neuropsychology, neuroradiology, and neuropathology studies in that chronic alcohol abuse was associated with fairly widespread brain changes. It is probable that the contrast between the positive findings of this study and the less striking differences reported by Samson et al. (1986) and Sachs et al. (1987) can be attributed to exclusion criteria employed in the latter studies. These criteria excluded patients with many of the common sequelae of alcohol abuse such as head trauma and significant physical illness.

PET studies of alcohol-induced
neurological disorders

As we have seen above, PET study of CMRglu has been applied successfully to a range of neurological disorder. Martin et al., in an unpublished report cited in Eckardt et al. (1990), studied 10 detoxified male patients aged 66 years who had clinically obvious neurological signs of organic brain syndrome and compared their PET scans with those of seven age-matched normal volunteer control subjects. The patients were carefully screened to exclude other causes of dementia and effects of active cardiovascular, renal, endocrine, hepatic, or psychiatric disorders. Overall grey and white matter CMRglu did not differ significantly between the groups, but the regional patterns in utilisation were different in the alcoholics. The results suggested a functional disruption of right-sided and frontal brain regions and a possible hyperactivity of cerebellar cortical connections.

The results from the study by Martin et al. differ in a number of ways from those of an earlier study by Kessler et al. (1984), who compared PET assessed CMRglu, using the FDG method, in six Korsakoff patients and eight age-matched normal controls. PET scanning was conducted at rest in a darkened room and CMRglu was measured in 46 ROIs on four planes. The mean glucose metabolic rate was significantly lower in the Korsakoff subjects and the absolute rates of regional metabolism for the Korsakoff group as a whole were decreased in numerous cortical areas, the basal ganglia, and the thalamus. There were two distinct patterns: (1) in two subjects metabolism was relatively low in anterior frontal and dorsomedial parietal regions but relatively high in basal ganglia and thalamic regions; (2) almost the opposite pattern was found in three other Korsakoff patients—the anterior frontal cortex being relatively high in CMRglu and the basal ganglia and thalamus being relatively low. Like the first group, the second group also showed relatively low dorsomedial parietal metabolism. This regional dissociation in patterns of CMRglu seems to give some support to the possible distinction between Korsakoff patients with and without concurrent dementia.

The use of PET to assess the chronic effects of excessive alcohol consumption on brain function has significant promise. For this promise to be realised considerably more attention will need to be paid to issues of subject selection. Better description of neuropsychological deficits would assist in correlating structure and function and engagement of subjects in cognitive tasks during PET scanning will further elucidate these intriguing relationships.

CONCLUSIONS

Neurophysiological studies have contributed significantly to our understanding of acute and chronic effects of alcohol on brain function. Acute doses of alcohol increase the amount of alpha rhythm and generally synchronise the wave forms but, during intoxication, the changes are slight given the marked changes in mood and behaviour that occur. Abnormally fast waves tend to change more than normal waves leading to speculation that dependent drinkers may be self-medicating. During acute alcohol ingestion, brain evoked potentials are also changed. Auditory brain stem potentials show abnormally delayed latency and although early event related potentials seem resistant, late ERPs show significantly reduced amplitudes related to the size of the dose and the time course of ingestion. The results to date have been marked by significant individual differences and it has been suggested that some of these may be associated with genetic predisposition to dependent drinking. Despite the consistency of these findings, discerning their meaning has been hampered by the fact that the psychological significance of the tasks used to elicit responses remains unclear. Regional CBF and PET studies of cerebral function are recent additions to this field and insufficient data is as yet available to reach conclusions. The fact that alcohol may induce vasodilation and vasoconstriction raises some doubts about the validity of CBF studies of acute alcohol ingestion.

Perhaps the most significant contribution from electroencephalographic studies has been in the understanding of the severe functional disturbances associated with abrupt alcohol withdrawal. About 15 hours after abrupt withdrawal, the EEG in previously tolerant individuals shows high voltage changes with reduced alpha. These are followed by random spikes and bursts of slow wave, high voltage activity, and transient dysrhythmias. These phenomena, which are associated with seizures, occur in individuals with otherwise normal EEG. Concurrently, CBF is decreased for about 2 days, returning to normal within about a week for younger alcoholics (less than 45 years), while normalisation continues for up to 7 weeks for older subjects.

Chronic alcohol abuse is associated with severe EEG abnormalities only when there is clinically obvious neurological deterioration. However, increased BSP conduction times and decreased evoked potential amplitudes occur commonly in chronically dependent drinkers. Abstinence appears to herald a reversal in BSP abnormalities but not in certain EP changes, notably the reduced amplitude of the late potential, P300. In conjunction with the discovery of similar P300 abnormalities and idiosyncratic EP responses to challenge doses of alcohol in sons of alcoholic fathers, this has led to speculation that these abnormalities might have utility as a biological marker for alcoholism.

PET studies of the effects of chronic alcohol abuse on CMRglu have yielded somewhat inconsistent findings and this has probably been due to small subject numbers and selection procedures reflecting differing research objectives. When alcoholic subjects with severe physical and neurological sequelae of chronic abuse have been excluded, abnormalities reported have been subtle. Nevertheless, this method of assessing effects of alcohol on brain function has great promise.

PART 3

NEUROPSYCHOLOGICAL RESEARCH

CHAPTER SEVEN

Alcohol Intoxication

When the strength of wine has become too great and has gained control over the mind, every lurking evil comes forth from its hiding-place.
Seneca, *Epistle LXXXIII* (1920, p. 271)

If you can lie on the floor without holding on, then you're not drunk.
Popular saying, variously attributed

The human body can metabolise the equivalent of about an ounce of whisky in an hour without noticeable effect. Beyond that, emotional, behavioural, and cognitive changes occur that become increasingly evident as the amount of alcohol consumed increases.

As the blood alcohol level (BAL) rises in the range of 20 to 80mg of ethanol per 100ml of blood, there is a gradual decline in the efficiency of psychomotor co-ordination, signs of disinhibition, and an enhanced sense of emotional well-being. The nature of the effects depends on age, gender, bodyweight, and prior experience with alcohol. The majority of studies on the effects of intoxication use dosages in the range of 80 to 100mg/10ml. Ingestion of about 1g of ethanol per kg of bodyweight will result in BAL levels that rise to about 90–120mg/100ml of blood (or 90–120mg%). The legal limit for driving in many countries is set at between 50–100mg%. When BAL exceeds 100mg%, the proportion of subjects recognised as intoxicated increases. At 100mg%, about one-third of subjects who are intolerant of alcohol have some minor speech abnormalities, disturbances of gait, and appear flushed. With a rising BAL of between 100–200mg%, the intolerant drinker appears increasingly ataxic and displays deteriorating social judgement and sudden changes in mood. Driving ability is affected and co-ordination is poor. At about 130–150mg%, most drinkers appear intoxicated to the observer. The behavioural and emotional effects become more pronounced in the range 200–299mg/%. The intoxicated subject has a marked ataxia, poor co-ordination, and deteriorated social judgement; nausea and vomiting may occur. By the time 300mg% is reached, loss of memory for the drinking episode is likely and anaesthesia is present. When levels exceeding 400 to 500mg% are reached, respiratory failure, coma, and death may ensue.

Some of the earliest research on the effects of small doses of alcohol on intellectual and memory skills were conducted by Emil Kraepelin in the early years of this century (Jellinek & McFarland, 1940). Many of his findings have been confirmed by more carefully controlled trials completed during the last 20 years. For example, it was Kraepelin who first observed that a small quantity of alcohol might initially improve simple reaction time, but only for the first few trials; with the passage of time responding became slower. He also observed that the ability to memorise new material was impeded, and that even automatically executed tasks, such as reading aloud, were reduced in accuracy by the ingestion of as little as one ounce of alcohol. Similarly, William McDougall in the first volume of the *British Journal of Psychology* (1904), reported that vigilance was impaired by alcohol (but improved by the consumption of two breakfast cups of tea). In their substantial review of the early research, Jellinek and McFarland (1940) observed that the experimental study of intoxicated subjects had demonstrated that small doses of alcohol depressed a wide range of neuropsychological functions. They noted that reaction time and concentration were impaired and that there was evidence of an "impairment of volition in continuous tasks" (p. 363). They noted that practice on specific tasks reduced the effects of intoxication and that alcohol had more effect on complex psychological functions than on those that were relatively simple. They also concluded that much of the research was difficult to interpret because no account had been taken of a range of methodological confounds. These included the experience that subjects had with alcohol, the time since their last meal, and the response of subjects to the expected effects of drinking.

In this chapter, research into the acute effects of alcohol on cognition are reviewed. Before doing so, however, some of the major methodological issues involved in separating drug effects from expectancy effects are discussed.

BALANCED-PLACEBO DESIGNS

Early research on the effects of alcohol on cognition and behaviour assumed that it was the pharmacological properties of alcohol that produced alterations in performance. Horsley and Sturge (1911, p. 69) described the basic experimental method as beginning "... by giving the brain, when unstimulated, some exceedingly simple task to perform, and then making it repeat this task after a dose of alcohol has been administered. The activity of the brain can be estimated ... by measuring the relative times it takes some small task allotted to it, under these two conditions respectively ...". It soon became apparent, however, that some behavioural changes could be elicited simply by convincing subjects they had consumed alcohol. Studies of alcohol-related beliefs have demonstrated that drinkers have consistent and well-differentiated expectations about the consequences of drinking (Brown, Christiansen, & Goldman, 1987; Leigh, 1989) and that these expectancies can affect some behaviours as powerfully as actual consumption (Abrams & Wilson, 1979; Marlatt & Rosenhow, 1980). Therefore, in order to study the pharmacological effects of alcohol, it is necessary to employ a placebo condition to control for expectancy effects.

The balanced-placebo design is one of the primary methods used to separate psychological expectancy effects from the pharmacological effects of alcohol. The basic 2×2 factorial design is illustrated in Fig. 7.1. In the context of this design, the expectancy effect can be tested by comparing conditions A and C with B and D. The main effect resulting from the pharmacological consequences of alcohol can be tested by contrasting conditions A and B, with C and D. Variations on this basic design often involve the use of more than one dosage level of alcohol (Williams, Goldman, & Williams, 1981).

An important part of the valid testing of the power of expectancy effects in alcohol research is convincing subjects that they have in fact consumed alcohol. This is not easy to do given that alcohol produces familiar changes

| | | Expectancy | |
		Told Alcohol	Told Placebo
	Given Alcohol	A	B
Alcohol Administration	Given Placebo	C	D

FIG. 7.1. The balanced placebo design.

in bodily sensation and has characteristic odours and tastes. The latter need to be disguised carefully and the experimenters must not be in a position to give any clues to the subject about which condition they are in. Some of the procedures involved in creating a valid placebo condition are:

1. Subjects are requested to gargle with a non-alcoholic mouthwash, ostensibly to enhance the accuracy of the breathalyser readings, but in fact to reduce taste acuity. Prior to serving the drinks, a slice of lemon is rubbed around the rim of the glass then squeezed into the liquid; this also serves to reduce any taste cues.

2. An apparently unopened vodka bottle is prominently displayed, which the experimenter opens and uses to mix the drinks in front of the subject. In reality, the vodka has been preopened and the seal broken in a way that can only be detected on close inspection. The vodka bottle may contain either vodka and tonic or just tonic. Vodka and tonic are usually mixed together in a ratio of one part vodka to five parts of tonic; mixed in this proportion, the vodka cannot be detected.

3. A similar procedure is used with the tonic bottles. They may contain either vodka and tonic or just tonic. Shaking the tonic bottle immediately before the subjects arrive causes the liquid to fizz on opening, adding the impression that the tonic bottle has not been opened previously.

4. Subjects often participate in an apparently random process of selecting whether they will be in the alcohol or placebo expectancy conditions. This procedure is manipulated by the experimenter, however, so that the outcome agrees with the subject's predetermined condition.

5. After the alcohol or placebo drinks have been given, the subjects are breathalysed, and readings shown to the subjects that are congruent with their expectations. Where necessary, as for example in the expect-alcohol–receive-placebo condition (Condition C in Fig. 7.1), the readings are faked.

Another important part of the experimental procedure is the use of a double-blind method of drug administration; it is important that the experimenter who interacts with the subject does not know what condition the subject is in, thus preventing any subtle influence on the subject's behaviour. Prior to the experiment, one experimenter mixes the drinks, while the other, blind to the experimental condition (but, of necessity, not to the expectancy condition), serves the drinks and collects the data.

Other procedural precautions are necessary. Experimental sessions should be scheduled for about the same time each day and the consumption of the alcohol should extend over approximately the same period of time. Both these factors can affect absorbtion rate. It is necessary to leave a 30- to 40-minute period after consumption to allow the alcohol to reach its maximal effect and to take breathalyser readings to confirm this. Subjects must be instructed not to take any alcohol or non-prescription drugs 24 hours prior to the experiment and, before the experimental session, a breathalyser reading taken to confirm they have been abstinent. Subjects also need to be weighed and the correct dosage of alcohol determined.

Do placebo deceptions work? Most experimenters check the success of their placebo manipulations by asking subjects at the end of their experiment whether they have received alcohol or not, and to estimate how much they have drunk or how intoxicated they feel. This kind of postexperimental debriefing typically reveals a high level of deception in the placebo conditions. In addition, strong expectancy effects have been found for a number of behaviours, which also implies that placebo manipulations are successful. However, Knight, Barbaree, and Boland (1986), have proposed that the usual debriefing process is potentially confounded by experimenter demand effects. Thus, when asked whether they were in the alcohol or placebo conditions, subjects may be influenced by a desire to please the researcher by confirming that the expectancy manipulation has been successful. As the same experimenter usually conducts both the experiment and the debriefing, it is not unlikely that the social demands of the experimenter–subject relationship may prevail, leading to an inaccurate report on the success of any deception.

Knight et al. (1986) tested the hypothesis that expectancy effects are determined in part by the experimenter demands in an ingenious way. They conducted a conventional balanced-placebo study and at the end of the experimental session they carried out a typical manipulation check with each of the subjects. They then simulated a computer malfunction during which data files were apparently irretrievably lost in the subject's presence. After being told about all the procedures the experimenter had used to deceive them, the subjects were asked to do their best to help the experimenter to determine exactly which condition they had been in. Following the first manipulation check, only three of the 24 deceived subjects reported correctly which beverage they had received. Thus the placebo manipulation was apparently successful. After the simulated data-file loss, however, 16 of the 24 subjects correctly nominated beverages other than the one they had been led to expect. As might be expected, correct detection was particularly evident in the told-placebo–received-alcohol condition. The deception was far more complete in the told-alcohol–received-placebo manipulation. Those subjects who correctly detected the alcohol in the placebo drink reported that they did so primarily on the basis of changes in bodily sensations.

The adequacy of the methodology of this study has been debated (Collins & Searles, 1988; Knight, Barbaree, & Boland, 1988). It is possible that the placebo manipulation was not as powerful as it might have been, for example, the drinks were not prepared in front of the subjects. In addition, the dosage level of 0.79ml/kg was somewhat higher than the level where successful deception has been most consistently reported, around 0.50ml/kg, although this is still lower than the 1.0ml/kg level used in most cognitive experiments. Nevertheless, this study does illustrate the problems of convincing subjects who have received alcohol that they are drinking a placebo and the lengths to which subjects will go to oblige the experimenter.

Is the full balanced-placebo design necessary in experiments with intoxicated subjects given that it is obviously time-consuming and difficult to do so successfully? To answer this, Hull and Bond (1986) conducted a meta-analytic review of studies investigating information processing and alcohol intoxication. They found that the average size of the effect on cognition where alcohol had been consumed was consistently large, whereas expectancy had a homogeneous and small effect. They also noted the difficulties of successfully deceiving subjects who are told they are receiving alcohol, but in fact receive placebo, and the way in which this can influence the subjects' behaviour. Williams, Goldman, and Williams (1981), for example, found that subjects in the congruent told-drug–receive-drug and the told-placebo–receive-placebo conditions out-performed subjects in the deception conditions. They proposed that this was in part a consequence of the confusion created by the lack of concordance between expectations and actual sensations after drinking. Hull and Bond (1986) concluded that the use of the full 2 × 2 balanced-placebo design is not necessary to determine the effect of alcohol on cognition, given the consistent pattern of results in the past. Use of a receive-placebo–told-alcohol condition is, however, warranted under most circumstances.

ACUTE ALCOHOL AMNESIA

Nearly two-thirds of alcoholics report experiencing frequent "blackouts" or periods of amnesia induced by excessive drinking. Although memory impairment can be induced with small doses of alcohol in chronic alcoholics, a blackout typically involves severe intoxication. On the basis of an interview survey of 100 alcoholics, Goodwin (1971, p. 1665) identified two types of blackout:

> One type has a definite beginning, terminates with a feeling of "lost time" and apprehension, and is seldom followed by a return of memory. Subjects also reported a second kind of memory loss in which events had been forgotten but there was no realization of this until the event was later recalled spontaneously or brought to the person's attention. In the latter type, eventual recall, however hazy, was the rule. Some subjects reported that subsequent drinking seemed to facilitate recall.

Like normal controls, alcoholics who consume doses of alcohol under experimental conditions typically reveal difficulties in learning new information, that is, an anterograde amnesia (Goodwin, 1977). The finding that alcohol intoxication disrupts memory and learning in both alcoholic and non-alcoholic subjects has been demonstrated in numerous studies, many of which will be reviewed in what follows. However, that alcohol produces learning deficits *per se* is of little significance. What is of importance is what the nature of this impairment can tell us about the way human memory functions.

State-dependent learning

The final sentence in the quotation from Goodwin (1971) in the preceding section alludes to an aspect of memory failure sometimes observed in clinical practice. Chronic alcoholics sometimes report that they hide bottles of alcohol in places they are unable to remember when they are sober next day. In a later drunken state, however, the memory returns, and they find their hidden drink. This experience is the essence of state dependent learning: Information learned in one drug state is best recalled when in the same state.

The experimental study of state-dependent learning involves teaching subjects some new information either while alcohol (or some other drug) is influencing the CNS or after a placebo has been administered (Lowe, 1982). Retention of the newly acquired information is subsequently tested either in the drug or the placebo state. The experimental design employed for testing state-dependent learning effects is a 2 × 2 factorial model, illustrated in Table 7.1, where the two drug states at the time of learning are crossed with the same two drug states at the time of retrieval. From this Table it can be seen that, if state-dependent learning occurs, retention in the alcohol–alcohol condition will be superior to that in the alcohol–placebo condition. Similarly, retention in the placebo–placebo

TABLE 7.1
The 2 x 2 Design Used to Evaluate State-dependent Learning (SDL)

Learning state	Retrieval state	Condition	Effects on performance
Alcohol (A)	Alcohol	AA	No SDL effect; effects on both learning and retention
Alcohol	Placebo (P)	AP	SDL effect; effect on retention
Placebo	Alcohol	PA	SDL effect; effect on retention
Placebo	Placebo	PP	No effects

condition will be superior to that in the placebo–alcohol condition. Results from such experiments are complicated, however, by the disruptive effect alcohol has on learning or retention. Consequently there are both state-dependent learning and deficit effects to be accounted for; for this reason, performance in the two control conditions will not be equivalent.

The occurrence of state-dependent learning effects has been confirmed in a number of studies using dosage levels of alcohol in the range 0.70ml/kg to 1ml/kg (Eich, Weingartner, Stillman, & Gillin, 1975; Goodwin et al., 1969c; Storm & Caird, 1967; Tarter, 1970; Weingartner & Faillace, 1971). To illustrate the effect, the pattern of scores from a rote learning task used by Goodwin et al. (1969c) are set out in Table 7.2. In this Table it is evident that state-dependent learning has occurred: Retention in the AA (alcohol–alcohol) condition is significantly better than in the AP (alcohol–placebo) condition. In a way that seems counterintuitive, administration of the drug actually facilitates recall where learning has taken place in the same drug state. In passing, it is of note that some researchers prefer to use the phrase state-dependent *retrieval* to describe this effect (Eich, 1977), because it is the congruence of drug states at both learning and retrieval that enhances recall.

In Table 7.2 it is also apparent that alcohol caused a learning or acquisition dysfunction. The number of errors in the AA and AP conditions are greater than in the PP and PA conditions. Of interest is the finding that retention in the PA condition is better than in the AP condition, suggesting better transfer of learning from the placebo than the alcohol study conditions. However, this asymmetrical expression of state dependent learning is complicated by the learning deficit effect, and the appropriate adjustment for this in the standard 2×2 factorial design is problematic (Swanson & Kinsbourne, 1979). Nevertheless, the state-dependent learning effect has been found to be robust and to occur in a wide variety

TABLE 7.2
Errors to Criterion on a Rote Learning Task
(from Goodwin et al., 1969c)

	Errors	
Condition	Acquisition	Retention
PP	12.05	13.75
PA	12.29	15.10
AP	20.56	24.55
AA	16.96	16.45

of learning tasks. The occurrence of memory impairment during intoxication at low levels of alcohol dosage has similarly been demonstrated in a range of experimental investigations.

Memory impairment

Studies of state-dependent learning have consistently demonstrated that alcohol affects memory in non-alcoholic subjects. This has been confirmed in several studies (Parker et al., 1974; Peterson et al., 1990; Storm & Caird, 1967) and in research that has used balanced-placebo designs (Miller et al., 1978). Overall, expectancy effects have been found to be small or non-significant. The effect of alcohol on standard list-learning tasks is more pronounced as intoxication increases than when it declines (Jones, 1973; Jones & Vega, 1972). Jones (1973) investigated the effects of alcohol on the free recall of 12-item word lists with a dosage of 1.32ml ethanol/kg of body weight. Subjects were tested when their blood alcohol level reached 0.09% on the ascending limb of the blood alcohol curve and again at 0.09% when on the descending limb, having reached a maximum level of 0.11%. They found that immediate free recall of word list items was impaired by alcohol intoxication and that this effect was greater on the ascending limb. Jones and Jones (1977) suggest that in view of possible differences in memory performance at different stages of intoxication, ascending and descending alcohol levels are a factor that should be taken into account when planning studies.

Several studies have attempted to determine whether the memory deficits resulting from intoxication are the consequence of consolidation or retrieval failures. This is an issue that will also be considered in later chapters when we review the memory deficits seen in alcoholic and amnesic patients. Consolidation refers to the ability to register and store input; retrieval involves the accurate accessing of this acquired information. Early evidence in favour of a consolidation hypothesis was advanced by Jones and Jones (1977), who examined the serial position curves from Jones (1973). In the study of human memory, differences in the pattern of serial position effects have frequently been used to distinguish between short- and long-term memory stores. In a typical word-list learning experiment using free recall to test acquisition, unimpaired subjects recall the words at the end of the list (recency effect) and the beginning of the list (primacy effect) better than the words in the middle portion of the list, resulting in a bow-shaped serial position curve. Words from the end of the list may be regarded as being stored in short-term memory (STM) and thus a normal recency effect may be taken as evidence that STM is unimpaired. Words at the beginning of the list, however, are assumed to have been consolidated and stored in long-term memory (LTM). The distinction between STM (a limited capacity memory store from which memory traces either pass to LTM or are lost some 30 seconds or so after rehearsal ends) and LTM (a storage system with unlimited capacity from which material can be retrieved as required), was influential in the 1960s and 1970s and underpinned much of the work with acute and chronic amnesic subjects reviewed in Chapters 9 and 10.

Jones and Jones (1977) found a normal recency effect in their intoxicated subjects, indicating that alcohol did not influence STM. However, the number of words recalled from the early part of the list was reduced, which they interpreted as evidence of consolidation failure. They proposed that words available in STM were not being normally consolidated in the LTM store. They also contended that if alcohol caused a primary retrieval deficit, then a decrement should have been observed over the entire curve, and not just for the earliest items. Perhaps more significantly, Jones and Jones also found that words learned *before* alcohol was ingested, but tested *after* subjects were intoxicated, were recalled as often as in the placebo condition, thus indicating that retrieval mechanisms are not degraded by alcohol in a uniform manner. As we have already seen in the results from Goodwin et al. (1969c) and other similar studies, recall in placebo–alcohol conditions is often equivalent to recall in placebo–alcohol conditions, and certainly superior to performance in alcohol–placebo conditions. Jones and Jones interpreted this effect (and their data) as indicative of a consolidation failure. It is of interest that similar serial position curves have been found for amnesic patients by Baddeley and Warrington (1970), who argued that the integrity of STM performance was evidence of unimpaired encoding and input and normal consolidation. Consolidation and retrieval are terms used in different ways and difficult to disentangle. The serial position data from the Jones' experiment are perhaps best interpreted as showing that both consolidation and retrieval from STM are unimpaired by alcohol intoxication but that either retrieval or consolidation processes are impaired in LTM. However, the normal recall of subjects in the "no alcohol during learning but alcohol during recall" condition, does argue for a LTM retrieval deficit in intoxicated subjects.

Birnbaum and Parker (1977) investigated the retrieval–consolidation distinction further. They found that when they made retrieval demands of the memory tests as effortless as possible, intoxicated subjects still performed worse than placebo-treated subjects. Birnbaum, Parker, Hartley, and Noble (1978) similarly found that using category cues to aid recall of word list items did not bring the intoxicated subjects' performance up to normal levels. Birnbaum et al. (1978) tested the consolidation deficit hypothesis further by having 48 subjects learn word lists while sober, and then testing them a week later while either intoxicated (1ml/kg) or sober. They found, somewhat to their surprise, that the sober and alcohol groups performed equally well on all the recall tests. They concluded that consolidation/storage deficits were more significant in alcohol-induced amnesia than retrieval failure.

The failure of their intoxicated subjects to acquire information normally was further explored by Hartley, Birnbaum, and Parker (1978), using Craik and Lockhart's (1972) levels-of-processing approach. This conceptualisation of learning is based on the finding that words processed to a level where their semantic meaning is addressed, are remembered better than words where only the acoustic or physical properties of words are accessed. Hartley et al. (1978) proposed that the failure of consolidation they had observed in their intoxicated subjects might result from a failure to encode stimulus words to an adequate depth. They reasoned that, if this was the case, and if they could ensure that their intoxicated subjects encoded stimuli to a sufficient depth, then the alcohol-induced amnesia might disappear. Their experimental procedure contrasted phonemic processing with semantic processing in an incidental learning paradigm. In the phonemic condition orienting task, words were displayed to the subject, who was asked to respond yes or no as quickly as possible to the question "Does this word contain an r sound?" In the semantic condition, the orienting task required the subject to answer the question "Is this a living thing?" following exposure of the stimulus word.

They found that their orienting tasks worked successfully for both alcohol- and placebo-treated subjects; for both groups semantic encoding produced better recall than phonemic. Also of interest was the finding that performance was not impaired by alcohol on the orienting tasks; error rates and reaction times were equivalent for both groups. Despite this, the performance of the intoxicated subjects did not reach normal levels in any of three experiments. Similar results were reported subsequently by Williams and Rundle (1984) and Maylor, Rabbitt, and Kingstone (1987). The notion that the consolidation deficit of alcohol-intoxicated subjects might be explained by a failure to encode new input to a sufficient depth has been generally found to be untenable.

In a further attempt to explain why alcohol induced consolidation failure, Birnbaum, Johnson, Hartley and Taylor (1980, p. 293) investigated the possible role of "*elaboration*, the type of thinking in which prior information is activated in order to integrate incoming information in light of what is already known". To do this, they made use of a series of sentences that were somewhat ambiguous without a context. One example was the sentence "the notes went sour when the seam split". This base sentence makes little sense without the context word "bagpipes". Recall of sentences with the context words added has been found to be superior to the situation where only the base sentences are presented. Birnbaum et al. (1980) suggested that intoxicated subjects may have difficulty with spontaneously elaborating stimuli during learning, and that they might be able to compensate for this if they were provided with a relevant semantic context by the experimenter. Over a series of three experiments, it was found that the intoxicated group's mean performance when an elaborative context was provided was *differentially* improved relative to the placebo group.

This result suggested that intoxicated subjects may be defective in their ability to produce appropriate elaborative strategies unaided. Hashtroudi, Parker, DeLisi, and Wyatt (1983) investigated this in a further study in which type of elaboration (nil, precise, imprecise, or self-generated) was compared in independent groups of sober and intoxicated subjects. The learning material comprised base sentences containing target words (italicised in the examples that follow) each of the form: "The *short* man put up the tent" or "the *old* man bought the paint". Subjects in the no elaboration condition were simply instructed to learn the base sentences. In the precise elaboration condition, the sentences were lengthened in a way that highlighted the target word, for example "The old man bought the paint to colour his cane". In contrast, in the imprecise condition, the sentences were extended without any elaboration of the target word: "The old man bought the paint that was on the top shelf". In the self-generated condition, subjects were asked to complete each of the base sentences in a meaningful way; subsequently their responses were rated as precise or imprecise by two independent blind raters. Recall of the target words was tested by presenting the base sentences with the word "blank" in the place of the designated target. The proportions of target words recalled in each of the conditions are presented in Table 7.3.

Overall, the pattern of results in Table 7.3 shows that the alcohol subjects could not make sufficiently effective use of elaborators to produce a normal performance under any of the elaboration conditions. Further,

TABLE 7.3
Proportion of Target Words Recalled in Various Elaboration Conditions

	State	
Type of elaborators	Sober	Intoxicated
Self-generated elaborators		
precise	0.89	0.54
imprecise	0.63	0.47
Experimenter-provided elaborators		
no elaborators (base)	0.57	0.31
precise	0.78	0.28
imprecise	0.38	0.19

From Hashtroudi et al. (1983), reprinted with permission.

although the precision of the elaborator did facilitate recall in the sober subjects, there was no such effect in the alcohol-intoxicated subjects. It was also apparent that experimenter-provided elaborators did not enhance the performance of intoxicated subjects (although they did improve the recall of the sober subjects). Finally, although fewer precise elaborators were self-generated by the intoxicated subjects, the quality of the self-generated elaborators was similar for both the sober and intoxicated subjects. This latter finding is of note, as it suggests that intoxication does not prevent subjects from producing effective elaborations. Hashtroudi et al. (1983) suggest that the primary deficit of memory under conditions of intoxication is a dysfunction in semantic processing that leads to a failure to integrate newly acquired input with pre-existing schema, despite these schema being normally activated by this incoming information. Failure of elaboration/integration is a similar to Warrington and Wieskrantz's (1982) explanation for the occurrence of organic amnesia.

In the comparison of retrieval failure with consolidation failure as explanations for alcohol-induced memory loss, consolidation failure has generally been regarded as the primary cause of intoxication impairments. One significant exception to the proposition that alcohol has little effect on retrieval, is the outcome of a study by Nelson, McSpadden, Fromme, and Marlatt (1986) into the effects of alcohol on metamemory. Metamemory is the awareness of one's memory; the ability to know what you can or cannot recall on demand. The procedure that Nelson et al. used involved subjects answering a series of general knowledge questions (e.g. "What is the capital of Australia?") until 12 errors had occurred. After each answer, subjects in the balanced-placebo design experiment rated their confidence in the accuracy of their answer. For each of the 12 incorrectly answered questions, subjects were then asked to make judgements about how likely they would be to recognise the answer. Both absolute and relative ratings were obtained. The absolute ratings were made on a six-point scale (6 = certain I would recognise the answer, to 1 = certain I would not recognise the answer). The index used to assess integrity of metamemory was the correlation between the confidence rating and actual performance on the subsequent recognition task. Nelson et al. (1986) found that there were no expectancy effects on either memory or metamemory performance. Of particular note was the finding that the intoxicated subjects performed more poorly on the recall part of the metamemory task. They were able to answer correctly significantly fewer of the general knowledge questions. However, alcohol intoxication had no influence on the measures of metamemory nor were the alcohol-dosed subjects less accurate in their ratings of the correctness of their responses to the general knowledge questions. The only significant effect therefore was that recall of general knowledge information, acquired while subjects were (presumably) sober prior to the experimental sessions, was impaired. This finding suggested that retrieval failure might provide the basis for impairments on remote memory tests.

In contrast to the research showing that alcohol impairs memory, there are also some studies that show that alcohol can have a positive effect on memory (e.g. Parker et al., 1980b; 1981). The basic method used in this research involves instructing subjects to undertake some new learning and, when this is complete, administering a dose of alcohol; the resultant improvement in recall relative to a placebo has been termed the retrograde facilitation effect. Lamberty, Beckwith, and Petros (1990) tested this effect with word and prose learning tasks; both learning situations known to be inhibited by pretrial doses of alcohol (Petros et al., 1985). Subjects listened to either a list of words or a prose passage that they were instructed they would later be asked to recall. They then either consumed alcohol (1mg/kg) or a placebo. When they returned next day they were tested for their memory of the words or prose passage they had heard on the previous day. It was found that for the prose passages, but not the word lists, the alcohol-treated subjects showed a better level of recall than the placebo group. Parker and Weingartner (1984) have made two suggestions for this unexpected facilitation effect. One is that alcohol acts to suppress incoming information that might interfere with new learning. The other is that alcohol has an unknown biological enhancement effect on learning by boosting the biochemical processes involved in consolidation. The facilitation effect works best when there are strong pre-existing conceptual links between the elements in the material to be learned (as with prose passages) or where the stimuli are novel.

The finding that alcohol inhibits learning when administered prior to a learning session, but facilitates it immediately after, is intriguing. As Lamberty et al. (1990) noted, most substances that interfere with learning, unlike ethanol, do so both before and after the study session. Most of these substances also bind to specific neural receptors, again unlike alcohol. This suggests that the differential effect that alcohol may have is by virtue of its ability to effect both mood and cognition. Another explanation of this facilitatory effect may be that learning is "reinforced" or made more salient by the mood-enhancing properties of alcohol.

Finally, it is of note that there are a number of memory-related tasks that alcohol intoxication does not disrupt. We have already seen that metamemory is not influenced by drinking alcohol. Hashtroudi et al. (1984) found that although free recall of items from a word list was severely impaired by alcohol, learning using Warrington and Weiskrantz's (1970) partial information technique was not. This cueing procedure requires subjects to recognise words that have been degraded by a filtering process so that 50%, 65%, or 80% of the area has been obscured. At the 80% level, the words cannot be recognised without prior learning; they become more readable at each successive level. Hashtroudi et al. found that the ability to learn to identify the degraded stimuli was normal in alcohol intoxicated subjects, at least at dose levels of 1ml/kg body weight.

Another task, which is commonly unimpaired in amnesia is priming for well-learned semantic associations. It is well-established that even densely amnesic patients are able to make use of the conceptual associations between words (e.g. gold–silver) in learning tasks, in a completely normal fashion. This aspect of their semantic memory is unaffected by the lesions causing amnesia. The same preservation of lexical priming effects has been observed in alcohol-intoxicated subjects by Nilsson, Backman, and Karlsson (1989), who found that, in both a priming and a cued recall testing using highly associated word pairs, acute alcohol amnesia did not influence performance. Similar results were reported by Lister et al. (1991). Another aspect of memory that has been tested is detection of frequency of occurrence of events. It has been proposed that encoding of frequency is an automatic process (Hasher & Zacks, 1984) and therefore impervious to the effects of alcohol. However, Birnbaum, Taylor, Johnson, and Raye (1987) found that judgements of frequency of presentation and self-generation of words were influenced significantly by alcohol. The frequency of occurrence of events tended to be underestimated by intoxicated subjects and the authors attributed this to impairments in processing at the initial input/registration stage.

Most of the research cited above employed student volunteers and was conducted in the laboratory, with the primary aim of using alcohol to elucidate the operation of memory processes. However, the effects of alcohol on memory are of more than academic interest. It is often the case that witnesses to or participants in crime have been consuming alcohol, and the effect this has on the reliability of their testimony is a matter of considerable importance. Yuille and Tollestrup (1990) conducted a study in which eye witness memory to a laboratory-simulated theft enactment was tested. Subjects observed the crime either while under the influence of moderate amounts of alcohol (1.32ml/kg) or having consumed a placebo. All subjects were interviewed when sober 1 week after the event; half were also interviewed immediately after the crime. At the end of the second interview subjects were given photographs from which they selected pictures of the perpetrator of the crime. The results are presented in Table 7.4.

The control subjects comprised both placebo and non-drug subjects, so no expectancy effects were detected. The total number of details recalled in the eye witness account and the proportion of these that were accurate are presented for the alcohol-treated and control subjects. Overall, the alcohol subjects produced significantly less information at each interview.

TABLE 7.4

Mean Number and Proportion Correct of Recalled Details as a Function of
Interview and Alcohol

	Immediate recall		Delayed recall		Delayed recall only	
Condition	Total	Accuracy	Total	Accuracy	Total	Accuracy
Alcohol	80.04	0.908	90.38	0.883	72.32	0.874
n	22		22		25	
SD	20.49	0.045	20.11	0.058	21.70	0.036
Control	97.47	0.925	109.74	0.913	85.82	0.909
n	31		35		37	
SD	25.86	0.034	40.70	0.049	22.02	0.035

From Yuille & Tollestrup (1990), reprinted with permission.

There were also significant differences in accuracy, although as is apparent
in the Table, these were small in absolute terms. One striking effect is the
way in which delayed recall after immediate recall at the time of the event
produced a significantly better performance than the delayed recall only
condition—this was true for both the intoxicated and sober eye witnesses.
These results provide evidence that intoxicated witnesses of crime recall
less than sober ones, whether interviewed at the time they observed the
event, or later, when sober. However, Yuille and Tollestrup (1990, p. 272)
urge appropriate caution:

> Given the artificial nature of the event in this study, any generalizations to
> "real-world" settings are tenuous. The strong retrieval practice effect
> suggests that police may wish to consider interviewing witnesses as soon as
> possible after an event, even if (in fact, especially if) they are under the
> influence of alcohol. Even under the influence of the drug, an immediate
> interview appears to preserve both amount and accuracy of recall. This
> tentative recommendation is restricted to moderate levels of consumption
> of alcohol, similar to that used in this study.

Summary

The consumption of alcohol has some interesting, and in some cases
unexpected, effects on learning and memory, at least in the range of the
dosages commonly used in laboratory settings. One robust effect is the
superiority of recall when the testing is conducted on the subjects who are
in the same intoxicated state as they were during the learning phase—the
so-called state-dependent learning effect. It is also apparent that learning
is disrupted by alcohol consumption in both non-alcoholic (Goodwin et al.,
1969c) and alcoholic (Lisman, 1974; Parker et al., 1974) volunteers. The

acute amnesia produced cannot be explained by expectancy effects, and the effect of alcohol on non-alcoholic subjects produces decrements in performance similar in magnitude to those seen in ageing subjects (Craik, 1977; Hashtroudi, Parker, Luis, & Reisen, 1989). Studies in which alcohol is administered either before the learning episode or before the testing session suggest that the initial learning stages of memory consolidation are more affected by intoxication than is retrieval, although the exact mechanism producing this dysfunction is unknown. One exception to this finding is that unprompted recall of general information is impaired by intoxication; assuming general knowledge is usually acquired by most people in a sober state, this implicates a retrieval deficit in some instances of amnesia (Nelson et al. 1986). Another finding of interest is that if learning is followed immediately by ingestion of alcohol, then later testing will show that recall has been facilitated, relative to a placebo condition. Finally, some attention has more recently been given to the effects of alcohol on eye witness recall of the events associated with a crime (Yuille & Tollestrup, 1990). In this context also, the accuracy of recall was reduced in intoxicated subjects.

INFORMATION PROCESSING AND MOTOR DYSFUNCTION

Numerous studies have attested to the fact that alcohol consumption increases the likelihood that errors will be made in man–machine interactions. It has been repeatedly shown that driving, flying, and operating machinery become more dangerous when alcohol is involved. For example, drinking and driving has been identified as one of the principal reasons for driving fatalities and non-fatal collisions (Waller, 1972). These findings suggest that alcohol has a deleterious effect on information processing and related psychomotor tasks. This proposal has been studied in numerous laboratory investigations employing experimental procedures designed to measure the cognitive and motor operations involved in complex skilled performance such as driving (Mitchell, 1985).

Early research suggested that simple psychomotor functions were less impaired than more complex, and that new rather than familiar skills were more likely to be disrupted by intoxication (Jellineck & McFarland, 1940). Most studies of reaction time (RT) following alcohol consumption have recorded some decrement (Maylor et al., 1987; Moskowitz & Burns, 1971, 1973; Moskowitz & Roth, 1971; Tharp et al., 1974), but this finding is not universal (Peterson et al., 1990; Shillito, King & Cameron, 1974; Vuchinich & Sobell, 1978). In a number of early studies, Moskowitz and colleagues found that RT was increased by alcohol ingestion. For example, Moskowitz and Burns (1973) found that response latencies in naming digits that were visually displayed were impaired by alcohol. They also found that the degree of impairment was consistent for alcohol and placebo subjects as the number of stimulus alternatives increased, implicating response mechanisms as being the source of reduced processing speed. Moskowitz and Murray (1976) found that backward masking was affected by alcohol— the rate of transmitting input from sensory storage to STM was slowed by quite low doses of alcohol.

Tarter, Jones, Simpson and Vega (1971) similarly found that alcohol disrupted performance on simple, two- and three-choice RT. They administered a series of tasks to 26 medical students using a counterbalanced cross-over design. This design allowed the effects of practice to be observed, and Tarter et al. found that prior exposure to tasks significantly enhanced resistance to alcohol. Although RT was affected by alcohol in the first session, in the second only on the three-choice RT task did the alcohol and placebo groups differ. This confirmed the earlier observations of Jellineck and McFarland (1940, p. 348) that "within a task of given complexity, familiarity with the task tends to lower the effects of alcohol".

The information handling processes disrupted by alcohol were studied in depth by Tharp et al. (1974), who designed a series of memory scanning experiments based on Sternberg's (1966) additive model of information processing. Tharp et al. found that manipulations designed to make stimulus encoding more difficult did not differentially affect subjects who had consumed alcohol. However, in other experiments alcohol was found to have an effect on response selection and organisation. For example, when the number of equally-possible response alternatives was increased, RT in the alcohol condition increased at a faster rate than in the placebo condition; that is, there was a strong interaction between drug condition and response uncertainty.

In one experiment where alcohol had little effect on RT, the response latencies were collected during the course of a divided attention task. Vuchinich and Sobell (1978) conducted a balanced-placebo study in which subjects performed a pursuit rotor task with their dominant hand while completing a three-choice RT task with their non-dominant hand. They found that tracking performance was significantly impaired by alcohol in the context of this divided attention task. This confirms findings from other studies that showed that even at low blood alcohol levels, divided attention tasks are particularly sensitive to the effects of intoxication (Hamilton & Copeman, 1970; Moskowitz, Burns, & Williams, 1985). However, alcohol did not affect response latencies, although the number of errors committed by the intoxicated group did increase. Interestingly, there was an expectancy effect for the errors, suggesting that RT accuracy may not be solely due to alcohol, but can be influenced by expectations.

A study by Gustafson (1986) is also of interest in understanding the effects of alcohol on RT. He found that a moderate dose of alcohol had little effect on simple auditory RT, but that if the task was maintained, with constant experimenter demand to succeed, then an alcohol effect emerged after about 10 minutes. Finally, in several other studies of processing speed in complex cognitive tasks, alcohol has been found to cause decrements. Maylor et al. (1987) found that categorisation of words either on the basis of physical or semantic properties was disrupted by alcohol. In a similar type of matching task, Haut, Beckwith, Petros, and Russell (1989) found that physical, lexical, and semantic decisions were slowed in a group of undergraduates who received 1ml/kg body weight doses of ethanol. Gustafson and Kallmen (1990) found that alcohol intoxication increased the length of time to complete a Stroop test.

Another aspect of psychomotor performance that has been assessed is whether subjects develop an acute tolerance to alcohol. For example, Lukas et al. (1989) found that performance on the Digit Symbol Substitution Test, a measure similar to the Digit Symbol Subtest of the WAIS-R, that subjects were impaired on the ascending limb of the blood alcohol curve, but not the descending limb. After a single dose equivalent to 0.5ml/kg body weight, subjects either developed a tolerance to alcohol or were able to compensate as a result of practice on the task. In contrast, body sway was abnormal during the peak and descending limbs of the alcohol curve, and an abnormal sway remained discernible 3 hours after consumption. Kaplan et al. (1985) tested performance in an interesting experiment in which they kept the subjects' blood-alcohol levels at a constant 80–100mg/dl over a period of 6 hours. On a manual tracking task, in which subjects were instructed to keep a cross in the centre of a simulated "road" made from a randomly moving set of parallel lines, alcohol impaired performance over the total period of time. No acute tolerance developed. Word recall, however, was impaired immediately, and did improve over the 6-hour period.

Fisk and Scerbo (1987) have proposed that the effects of alcohol on psychomotor performance can be explained by the distinction between automatic and control processing. Automatic processing of information is developed as a consequence of long-term consistent practice, and when this has been achieved, information can be handled in parallel, is not limited by the capacity of STM, and requires almost no conscious effort. However, control processing, is under an individual's conscious direction, and proceeds in a serial and effortful way. In many tasks, there is a transition from control to automatic processing. A child's reading, for example, is slow and effortful at first, with individual letters being deciphered and little of the meaning implicit in the text being comprehended. As the skill develops, letters are read automatically and comprehension is high. Experimental work with subjects who are intoxicated suggests that those tasks that are most resistant to the effects of alcohol are those that have been overlearned and where processing is close to automatic. Thus, in a divided attention task, where subjects are required to vary consciously the allocation of processing resources between two tasks, the consequences of intoxication become particularly apparent. The effect of alcohol intoxication is determined by the degree of automaticity of processing required by the skills being tested.

Summary

Data from psychomotor performance tasks have generally shown that alcohol affects performance. The more complex the task is, the more likely there are to be alcohol effects. On relatively simple tasks like finger tapping speed (Lukas et al., 1989) and simple RT, alcohol effects are less likely to be evident, especially at relatively low doses. It is also possible that expectancy manipulations have a more pronounced effect where alcohol effects are weakest, as in Vuchinich and Sobell's (1978) RT procedure and Williams et al.'s (1981) letter cancellation task. Prior practice on the task seems to produce some resistance to the effects of alcohol (Tarter et al., 1971) and, on very practised tasks, where processing is automatic, performance may remain normal after low to moderate doses of alcohol. Some of the failures to find effects of alcohol on RT can also be attributed to the low dose used; an alcohol effect has been seen more consistently at doses around 1ml/kg body weight. The findings of Gustafson (1986) that alcohol effected simple RT after a prolonged series of trials suggests that subjects may be able to compensate for processing impairments initially, but are unable to sustain this over time.

CONCLUSIONS

For the neuropsychologist there are a number of issues raised by a consideration of the research on the acute effects of alcohol on cognition. One is the way in which behaviour changes as a consequence of social expectancies. Studies of intoxicated patients have repeatedly demonstrated the way in which personal beliefs about alcohol-related effects influence social and interpersonal behaviour. For this reason it is necessary to use placebo treatments to separate the pharmacological effects of alcohol from the expectancy effects. It is worth noting for routine neuropsychological testing of impaired alcoholics that such testing takes place in a social context in which the person being tested may consciously, or without awareness, perform in a way that confirms their own beliefs or those of the psychologist that they are or are not brain-damaged.

Experimental study of intoxicated subjects has also increased our understanding of how the memory system works. The phenomenon of state-dependent learning, a laboratory-based effect that confirms anecdotal evidence that learning and recalling in the same drug-induced state is superior to that in different states, is an example of the way context supports retrieval. The fact that alcohol effects can be induced either during the learning or the retrieval session of a memory procedure has allowed study of the resistance of consolidation and retrieval processes to disruption. This research suggests that retrieval during an intoxicated state may be normal provided learning was undertaken in a sober state. Evidence from the studies of Birnbaum, Parker, and colleagues suggests that the administration of alcohol causes a primary consolidation deficit, possibly by disrupting the normal process of elaborating new input by reference to pre-existing schemas. Also of interest is the finding that some memory-related skills are not affected by acute alcohol amnesia, and we will see later that these same skills are also unaffected in chronic organic amnesia.

There have also been numerous studies of psychomotor performance under conditions of intoxication. It is apparent that complex vigilance and divided-attention tasks are impaired by modest doses of alcohol, well below the legal limit for driving in most countries. The less familiar a task is, and the more it requires deliberate and conscious control, the more likely it is that normal functioning will be disrupted. Voluntary motor movements of the kind employed in manual tracking are impaired consistently by alcohol, and acute tolerance to alcohol does not develop in this situation. Studies of the cognitive aspects of such tasks suggest that response-selection or execution are most affected. Few studies of the effects of alcohol on reasoning and abstracting processes have been attempted, however. Tarter et al. (1971, p. 316), who used the Shipley–Hartford scale, concluded that after alcohol consumption "conceptual and abstracting processes were disrupted, but no general decline in verbal intellectual ability was noted" Peterson et al. (1990) reported that alcohol affected performances on the Porteus Mazes and a word fluency test, but not on the WAIS Vocabulary, Information, or Digit Symbol subtests. There was also no effect on the total error score on the Wisconsin Card Sorting Test.

Finally, there are two other findings in the literature of note. The first is the possibility that subjects who have a family history of alcoholism may be more severely impaired on cognitive tasks than subjects who do not. O'Malley and Maisto (1985) found that subjects with a positive family history of alcoholism completed a grooved peg-board task more slowly than subjects with a negative background. The behavioural, social, and cognitive effects of intoxication on the children of alcoholics, who are at a high risk for becoming problem drinkers themselves, is an area of emerging interest.

The second is that alcohol may impair women more than men at comparable dosage levels (Jones & Jones, 1977) on memory tasks, and the stage in the menstrual cycle may be an important factor (Jones & Jones, 1976). These findings may have significance for the understanding of the relationship between hormonal factors and the effects of ethanol; in addition gender and menstrual phase are factors that need to be accounted for in experimental research (Lukas et al., 1989).

CHAPTER EIGHT

Cognition in Social Drinkers

For wine is the most beneficial of beverages, the pleasantest of medicines, and the least cloying of appetizing things, provided that there is a happy combination of it with occasion as well as with water.

Plutarch (*Moralia*, 1928, p.265)

Mrs Cherry Owen: *Remember last night? In you reeled my boy, as drunk as a deacon with a big wet bucket and a fish frail full of stout and you looked at me and you said, "God has come home!" you said, and then over the bucket you went, sprawling and brawling, and the floor was all flagons and eels.*

Dylan Thomas (*Under Milkwood*, 1954, p. 31)

For the large number of people who consume on average no more than one or two drinks a day, drinking is seen as a harmless and pleasurable activity. Indeed, some medical authorities regard the light consumption of alcohol as being positively beneficial, as small doses increase high density lipoproteins, a protective factor in the incidence of coronary heart disease (LaPorte, Cresanta, & Kuller, 1982).

There is, however, no doubt that the pathological use of alcohol results in neurological damage and impairments in cognition. What, then, is a "safe" level of consumption? Underlying this question is the assumption that there is a link between consumption level and neuropsychological impairment. This view, made explicit by Ryback (1971), suggests that the profound deficits seen in patients with Korsakoff's disease, grade into the lesser changes in functioning seen in chronic alcoholics and uncontrolled problem drinkers. Implicit in Ryback's continuity hypothesis is the assumption that at some level of social drinking, detectable levels of impairment will become apparent. As Parsons (1986, p. 102) has observed, if this is the case, then "At a practical level, such findings would have profound implications of a socioeconomic, medical, legal, and humanistic nature".

In this chapter we review the series of studies that have examined the possibility that low levels of alcohol use may, over a period of time, cause subtle but measurable alterations in cognitive performance. This work was initiated by the publication of a comprehensive study by Parker and Noble (1977) and followed by a number of attempts to replicate and extend these early findings. We will survey this literature in a largely chronological sequence, building towards an explanation for the findings that have emerged and an account of the obstacles to the conduct of this kind of neuropsychological investigation.

EARLY STUDIES

In a well-executed study that was to excite considerable attention, Parker and Noble (1977) reported findings suggestive of an association between the amount of alcohol consumed by social drinkers and performance on neuropsychological tests. They were motivated to undertake this study in part by the findings from their research with intoxicated subjects that we considered in Chapter 7: "In view of the number of studies reporting significant decrements in memory and other cognitive processes in non-alcoholics under moderate levels of intoxication, it seems reasonable to suspect some carry-over effects of alcohol on the intellectual capacities of sober social drinkers as well as sober alcoholics" (Parker & Noble, 1977, p. 1225).

The first stage of their study involved sending questionnaires asking about drinking practices, health, and related factors to a random sample of 450 men in suburban California. They received 211 replies, and eventually tested 102 men who agreed to participate and met a variety of health-related criteria. The sample had an average age of 43 and the majority were employed in high-level occupations. A total of 94% were married and 53% had postgraduate qualifications. By selecting such a homogeneous middle-class group of volunteers, the authors hoped to eliminate the potentially confounding effects of social class, personal stability, gender, and nutrition. The tests administered to the subjects were the Shipley Institute of Living Scale (SILS), the Wisconsin Card Sorting Test (WCST), the Halstead Category Test, and a 30-item multitrial free-recall test of memory. These first three measures were reviewed in Chapter 3. In order to assess the drinking behaviour of their subjects, Parker and Noble (1977) administered a drinking history questionnaire, which allowed them to compute a number of consumption indices and to divide their sample into heavy (36%), light–moderate (55%), and infrequent–abstainer (9%) groups using the Cahalan Quantity–Frequency–Variability index (Cahalan et al., 1969). They quantified self-reported drinking behaviour in terms of an average weighted quantity per occasion (QPO) index, current annual frequency of drinking, and lifetime consumption (QPO × frequency per annum at the current rate, corrected for periods of lighter and heavier consumption). In their sample, the average QPO was 42 ± 23ml of absolute alcohol, current frequency was 204 ± 222 occasions annually, and average lifetime consumption was 294 ± 447 litres of alcohol.

The key results of this study are presented in Table 8.1. The results of the study were presented entirely in terms of a correlational analysis—no group means were reported. Lifetime consumption and current frequency of drinking were not found to be correlated with cognitive performance and

TABLE 8.1

Age-partialled Correlations between Cognitive Tests and Current Quantity of Drinking per Occasion (Parker & Noble, 1977)

Test	Total sample (n = 102)	Non-heavy drinkers (n = 65)	Heavy drinkers (n = 37)
Shipley Institute of Living Scale (SILS)	−0.18*	0.12	−0.41**
vocabulary	−0.30**	−0.02	−0.28*
abstraction	−0.28**	−0.02	−0.26
conceptual quotient			
Category test			
total errors	0.19*	0.23*	0.42**
WCST			
trials to criterion	0.27**	0.13	0.29*
perseverative errors	0.09	−0.05	0.23
other errors	0.43**	0.14	0.23
Free recall			
memory	−0.09	0.10	−0.30*
rate of learning	−0.09	−0.01	−0.51**

WCST, Wisconsin Card Sorting Test.
*P = < 0.05; **P = < 0.01.

these findings have not been included. As is apparent in Table 8.1, when the effects of age are partialled out, there were some significant correlations between cognitive test performance and QPO, which were more marked for the 37 heavy drinkers than for those in the abstainer to moderate consumption categories. There were no significant differences between the heavy and non-heavy drinkers on any of the demographic variables.

This study was followed by a further report based on the findings from the same sample (Parker & Noble, 1980) in which the relationship between ageing, alcohol consumption, and cognitive performance was examined. They found that on the SILS and Category Test, age and consumption were significantly but independently predictive of test scores. There was interaction between these variables. However, on the WCST the interaction was significant, with subjects who were older showing more evidence of impairment than those who were younger.

This initial investigation provided some relatively consistent evidence that QPO was predictive of poorer performance on several intellectual and learning tasks. However, some problems with this study were soon expressed (Hill, 1983; Parsons, 1986). Hill drew attention to the way the analysis was primarily correlational, and observed that no group means or between-group comparisons were presented. Thus there was no method of determining the magnitude and clinical significance of any deficits that might be present in the heavy social drinking group. Parsons (1986) commented on the large number of correlations that were computed without any control for the possibility of Type 1 errors. Parker and Noble (1977) reported three sets of 45 correlations; only nine of the 45 for the total sample were significant. It was also noted that no check was made using a breathalyser to ascertain that the subjects had been abstinent prior to the testing session, and Hill suggested that a lengthy period of abstinence should be used to ensure that cognitive scores were not influenced by a recent heavy drinking episode. Another point of note, evident in Table 8.1, is the significant correlation between SILS vocabulary scores and QPO for the heavy drinker sample. Vocabulary tests are typically resistant to the effects of acquired neurological impairment and it is hard to explain why a synonym vocabulary scale might be affected by social drinking.

In the discussion of their findings, Parker and Noble made it clear that there were several possible explanations for their results. One proposal, which they favoured, was that alcohol caused a decline in cognitive performance, even at the relatively moderate intake levels of the average social drinker. Alternatively, it could be that poorer cognitive functioning leads to reports of greater consumption; thus people with lesser intellectual skills choose to drink more. The other possible explanation was that some third variable, highly correlated with both QPO and cognitive functioning, was responsible for the significant correlations. For example, Parsons (1986) proposed that some personality factor or lifestyle circumstance such as "life-stress" might cause both heavier drinking and a decline in cognitive performance

Parker and Noble's (1977) study was soon followed by several published reports of attempts to extend these findings. The first of these was an investigation of 45 male college students conducted by Parker and colleagues (Parker, Birnbaum, Boyd, & Noble, 1980a), who used the SILS and the same drinking indices as Parker and Noble (1977). The average age of their subjects was 22, and they had an average QPO of 54 ± 20ml and a frequency of consumption of between two and three sessions per week. Once again, frequency was not predictive of SILS performance. However, significant and negative correlations were found between QPO and Vocabulary ($r = -0.39$), Abstraction ($r = -0.41$), and Conceptual Quotient ($r = 0.38$). Multiple regression analysis confirmed that the amount of alcohol consumed per occasion was independently (and significantly) predictive of SILS scores. The authors made the point that the performance of their subjects on the SILS did not fall into the clinically impaired range: their average Conceptual Quotient was normal. Nevertheless, these results suggested that, even in a young adult sample, social drinking had a perceptible effect on cognition. Parker et al. (1980a) also postulated that the third variable that may cause the significant correlations could be a "genetic predisposition" that results in both poorer cognitive performance and the propensity to drink more heavily.

In a study of the effects of intoxication on memory in a group of women, Jones and Jones (1980) provided some independent support for Parker and her group's findings. They administered the verbal memory task described in Chapter 7, in which immediate recall was tested after each of six 12-item lists, and short-term recall after all six lists had been presented. A total of 32 women participated and were divided into two groups of 16 on the basis of their age (21 to 30, and 37 to 55). Each of these groups was further subdivided into equal groups of light or moderate social drinkers. The memory test was administered before and after alcohol intoxication. On the baseline testing, it was found that there was a difference between light and moderate drinkers on the short-term memory test, but no differences due to age. In addition, the moderate and older drinkers were more impaired by the effects of alcohol intoxication that either the light or younger drinkers on the short-term memory test. They concluded that social drinking may lead to short-term memory impairment and to a greater susceptibility to the effects of acute intoxication in women.

An important independent attempt to replicate the Parker and Noble results was published by MacVane, Butters, Montgomery, and Farber (1982). In this study, a sample of 102 male social drinkers in Boston, aged between 30 and 60 (mean age 44 ± 9 years), was recruited from a variety of sources including the police, employment agencies, and respondents to a newspaper advertisement. They excluded subjects who reported either an alcohol consumption greater than 58 litres per annum, or that drinking was having a significant impact on their family life, marriage, or work; 86% of their sample were employed. All subjects were paid $25 each to participate and were asked to abstain from drinking for 24 hours before the session. Three tests were administered: (1) the WCST; (2) the Digit Symbol subtest of the WAIS; and (3) the Peterson–Brown distractor procedure for the assessment of short-term memory. The latter task involved administering 20 trials, with five stimulus words being presented on each occasion. After the words had been exposed, the subjects were required to count aloud backwards from a randomly determined three-digit number for either 15 or 30 seconds. This procedure has been used extensively in the study of amnesics, and will be encountered again in Chapter 10. The total number of words recalled after the distractor-filled delay period was taken as a measure of capacity of short-term memory. The significant associations that emerged between the drinking variables and the cognitive tests are presented for the total sample (T), heavy drinkers (H), and slight-moderate drinkers (L) in Table 8.2.

TABLE 8.2

Significant Associations Between Variables for the Total Sample (n=106), Heavy Drinkers (n=58) and Light-moderate Drinkers (n=48)
(From MacVane et al., 1982)

Test	Current Frequency	Current QPO	Current Maximum QPO	Highest Annual Consumption	Lifetime Consumption
Peterson–Brown					
15 seconds	–	T*	–	H**, T**	–
30 seconds	–	T*, H*, L*	–	H**, T*	H*
Digit Symbol	T**	–	–	–	–
WCST					
total errors	–	L*	–	–	–
trials to criterion	–	L*	–	–	–
perseverative ratio	–	H*	H*	H*	–

H, significant correlation, heavy drinkers; L, significant correlation, light–moderate sample; QPO, quantity per occasion; T, significant correlation, total sample; WCST, Wisconsin Card Sorting Test.
$*P = < 0.05$; $**P = < 0.01$.

The correlations were adjusted for age and vocabulary scores. Five measures of drinking practices were derived: (1) current frequency of drinking; (2) current modal quantity per occasion (QPO); (3) current maximum QPO; (4) heaviest annual consumption; and (5) lifetime consumption. The mean current modal QPO of the total sample was 55 ± 40ml of alcohol, with the light–moderate drinkers averaging 28.2 ± 12.7ml and the heavy drinkers 78.1 ± 40.6ml per occasion. For the total sample, five of the 30 possible correlations were significant; for the heavy drinkers, eight of the 30 correlations were significant; and for the light–moderate drinkers, three correlations were significant. Details of the pattern of correlational results can be seen in Table 8.2.

MacVane et al. (1982) also compared their groups of light–moderate and heavy drinkers on the cognitive tests that they administered. The only significant difference to emerge was on WAIS Vocabulary scale. In general, the pattern of results in Table 8.2 supported Parker and Noble's earlier findings. There were low but significant negative correlations between consumption and cognitive performance. Modal QPO, an index similar to Parker and Noble's average QPO, was found to be most commonly related to test performance, but associations also emerged with frequency and lifetime consumption. There were more significant correlations for the heavy than for the light–moderate subgroup, again reminiscent of Parker and Noble's results. MacVane et al. concluded by noting that the results may have been biased by the inadvertent inclusion of some alcoholic subjects or by the possibility that some of their subjects' reports of abstinence prior to testing may have been false.

Two commentaries on MacVane and colleagues' study appeared in the same volume of the *Journal of Studies on Alcohol*. Parker (1982) saw the MacVane study as providing an important and independent replication of the early studies completed by her group in California. She also made it explicit that she did not regard the findings from the studies reported so far as indicating that social drinking resulted in brain damage, but rather as causing subtle and reversible decrements in performance, similar to those associated with ageing. Parker (1982, p. 172) concluded by outlining what she termed the "carryover" model of alcohol effects in social drinkers:

> According to this model, acute doses of alcohol produce perturbations in the central nervous system, which does not return to normal as soon as alcohol leaves the blood stream. That the drinking variable associated with reduced cognitive performance is amount of alcohol consumed per drinking occasion suggests that level of intoxication is important rather than simply total alcohol consumption.

Parsons and Fabian (1982) in their discussion of the MacVane et al. (1982) study took a more critical look at the findings. Although they acknowledged that the study made a valuable contribution and was methodologically sound, they drew attention to some of the inconsistencies between the results of this study and the earlier Parker and Noble (1977) investigation. In particular, Parsons and Fabian noted that, on the one measure that the two studies had in common—the WCST—the outcome of correlational analyses was not consistent (see Tables 8.1 and 8.2). This may be attributable in part to the use of different methods of administering this test (Parker, Parker, & Harford, 1991). They also presented some data from their own investigation of 81 college students (male and female), 54 women in the community, and 78 alcoholic women. These three groups of subjects completed the SILS and the Cahalan et al. (1969) Drinking Practices Questionnaire. Using the results from the questionnaire, Parker and Fabian computed current frequency of consumption, current average quantity of alcohol consumed per occasion, and modal QPO for their subjects, and subdivided their groups into heavy–moderate and light–infrequent drinkers. Few significant correlations emerged. For the three initial groups, only the modal QPO and the abstraction scores of the community women were significantly correlated. When the groups were divided into heavy and light consumers, there were significant correlations between modal QPO and the vocabulary and abstraction scores for the college students in the "heavy" drinking group. No other age- and education-adjusted partial correlations were significant. In view of the inconsistencies between studies and the lack of between-group mean differences, Parsons and Fabian argued that it would be premature to regard social drinking as a public health hazard.

There is another problem in the interpretation of results that show significant correlations in one group but not the other; a restricted range of values on some variables for one group may attenuate the size of the correlations for that group relative to those in another group with a greater range. Consider, for example, the comparisons of heavy and light drinkers in the MacVane et al. (1982) study. The current modal QPO standard deviation for the heavy group was 40.6ml, over three times that of the light-moderate group, 12.7ml. The total group QPO standard deviation was about 40ml. The low standard deviation for the light–moderate drinkers suggests some restriction in the range of the QPO variable and provides a statistical explanation for the absence of significant correlations for this particular subgroup. Restricted range problems may account, therefore, for Parsons and Fabian's (1982, p. 180) conclusion that there seemed "to be a trend in all studies for the heavy drinkers to have more significant and higher correlations between the drinking variables and cognitive performance than the light–moderate group".

A year later, Parker, Parker, Brody, and Schoenberg (1983) reported a sophisticated and substantial replication of the original Parker and Noble study. They selected a representative sample of 481 men and 544 women in metropolitan Detroit, and obtained from them SILS scores and information about their drinking practices using the Cahalan et al. questionnaire. The average QPO for the men was 46.7ml per occasion and women 35.9ml per occasion. The data were subjected to a multiple regression analysis and it was found that, for males, there was a significant relationship between QPO and abstraction score, when the effects of frequency of consumption, age, education, race, and vocabulary score were partialled out. Frequency of drinking occasions was not related to cognitive functioning. This result did not extend to the total sample of women. However, when a subgroup of 213 women who reported drinking alcohol once a week or more was identified (with an average QPO of 50.3ml), a regression analysis again identified QPO as an independent predictor of SILS scores. The magnitude of these associations was not affected by any of the adjustments made for the subjects' body weights. Parker et al. (1983) concluded that there was a significant linear relationship between alcohol consumption and cognition and reiterated their carryover model as an explanation for these results.

In a report that re-examined data from Parker et al. (1983) and Parker and Noble (1977), Parker, Parker, Brody, and Schoenberg (1982) presented estimates of the magnitude of changes in cognition due to age and alcohol consumption in their male subjects. They showed that, in both samples, age and QPO were significantly and negatively predictive of abstraction performance on the SILS (Table 8.3). The age coefficient of −0.20 can be interpreted as meaning that in both samples there was an average drop of 0.20 in the abstraction score for each additional year of age. Similarly, for the Californian male sample, each additional ounce of alcohol consumed per occasion resulted in an average decrease of 1.57 points in the abstraction score. Parker et al. (1982) compared this decrease to the effects of ageing, observing that, in this study, an increment in the amount of

TABLE 8.3
Unstandardised Regression Coefficients
(Adapted from Parker et al., 1982)

	California study (Parker & Noble, 1977)	Detroit study (Parker et al., 1983)
Age	−0.20**	−0.20**
QPO	−1.57	−0.94*

*$P < 0.05$; **$P < 0.01$.

alcohol consumed per occasion was associated with an average decrease in abstraction performance equal to 2.4 years of age. They suggested, therefore, that the social use of alcohol had effects that could be characterised as resembling premature ageing.

In a study of male ($n = 40$) and female ($n = 52$) college students, Hannon et al. (1983) obtained results that were also supportive of the findings reported by Parker and her co-workers. They administered the SILS, the WCST, the Digit Symbol subtest of the WAIS, the Trail Making Test (TMT), and the Tactual Performance Test (from the Halstead–Reitan battery), and correlated scores on these tests with self-reported lifetime consumption, current frequency, and average QPO estimates for males and females separately. In Table 4 of their report, a total of 72 partial correlations are presented, of which just nine are significant ($P < 0.05$). Of these, three were significant, but in the direction opposite to that predicted; for example, higher current frequency was predictive of better performance on the abstraction scale of the SILS for men. Hannon et al. (1983) could find no explanation for this. Of the significant partial correlations, for women QPO predicted WCST scores, and lifetime consumption predicted Digit Symbol results. For men, QPO predicted abstraction scores and Conceptual Quotients, lifetime consumption predicted WCST scores, and current frequency predicted reduced TMT scores. Again, there was qualified support for Parker and Noble's findings, but much inconsistency, particularly between the male and female subjects. Hannon et al. (1983) also included a seven-point rating of current life stress in their questionnaire. They found a significant relationship for men only between stress ratings and abstraction scores ($r = -0.33$), Conceptual Quotient ($r = -0.32$), and Digit Symbol ($r = 0.36$). Echoing Parsons and Fabian's earlier suggestion, they proposed that stress had some impact on the performance of men, and that this might become more apparent if a more elaborate method of assessing life stress were used.

In a study of 93 female social drinkers, again similar in procedure to Parker and Noble (1977), Birnbaum, Taylor, and Parker (1983) attempted to study the effects on cognition of reversing drinking behaviour. This represented an attempt to test their carryover model of the effects of social drinking. The main drinking variable they assessed was QPO (27.12ml for their sample) and the tests they administered included the WCST, Digit Symbol, SILS, a test of word recall, and the Profile of Mood States (POMS). The POMS is a 65-item adjective checklist, with eight subscales—Tension, Depression, Anger, Vigour, Confusion, and Fatigue. At the initial testing, QPO predicted Digit Symbol scores, but was not related to any of the SILS scales. In the second phase of the study, all subjects who reported consuming more than three drinks per week were asked to participate in a further trial in which they might be asked to abstain from alcohol for a period of weeks. A total of 29 agreed, and 18 subjects were assigned to the abstain condition, 11 to the maintain current drinking condition. After a 6-week period, 14 of the abstainers (who had reduced their average consumption from 33.6 to 21.3ml of alcohol per occasion) were compared with 11 in the maintaining group. Changed alcohol intake had no effect on any of the cognitive test scores. However, there were some changes on the POMS scale. The abstainers showed a significant reduction in anger and depression, while the maintain group showed an increase in depression. The two groups were not well matched for depression at the time of initial testing, however, and the small number of subjects involved in the reversibility trial precluded drawing any strong conclusions.

Overall, the replication studies that appeared before 1984 provided limited and inconsistent support for Parker and Noble's (1977) results. The most consistent findings came from the work of Parker and colleagues (Parker et al., 1980a; 1982; 1983) and concerned the relationship between SILS scores and quantity consumed per occasion. In Table 8.4, the correlations between QPO and SILS in studies where these are reported are presented. An optimistic view of the findings up to this time was presented by Hannon et al. (1983, p. 197), who concluded that their study supported previous findings:

> ... of decreased cognitive performance associated with both increased quantity of alcohol consumed per occasion and life-time consumption, accounting for 8–10% of the variance between various measures in men and 8–27% in women. It is impressive that both men and women subjects who are young and bright, and have a drinking history of only a few years should show this effect.

TABLE 8.4
Partial Correlations Between QPO and SILS Scores
for Total Samples in Four Studies

	Parker & Noble (1977)	Parker et al. (1980)	Parsons & Fabian (1982)	Hannon et al. (1983)	
Subjects	Community, male	College, male	College students	College, female	College, male
SILS					
Vocabulary	−0.18*	−0.39**	0.02	0.15	0.02
Abstraction	−0.30**	−0.41**	−0.16	−0.03	−0.26
CQ	−0.28**	−0.38**	−0.21	−0.12	−0.32*

*$P < 0.05$; **$P < 0.01$.

However, Parsons (1986, p. 110) expressed a more restrained enthusiasm for the findings of the studies he reviewed: "The overall conclusion is that although occasional relationships are found between self-reported drinking variables and performance on certain cognitive–perceptual tests, there are no stable and reproducible specific relationships".

REPLICATIONS AND EXTENSIONS

A number of studies have been published since 1984 that have attempted to clarify the inconsistent findings emerging from the initial studies. In an important study, reviewed in Chapter 5, Bergman (1985) correlated measures of alcohol consumption, cognitive functioning, and CT-scan indices in a random sample of 387 Swedish subjects. The average maximum QPO of his male subjects was 41.13ml, and of female subjects, 30.2ml. Despite having a large sample and a broad range of neuropsychological measures, there were no significant correlations with the QPO measures. There was, however, a negative correlation of significance, for those male subjects with a high alcohol intake in the week preceding testing, between cognitive test scores and CT-derived measures of brain impairment. These findings were also seen in a sample of male heavy drinkers (average maximum QPO = 147 ± 23ml), but not in a group of female heavy drinkers (average maximum QPO = 88.2 ± 60.6ml). In neither of these heavy consumption groups was there any evidence of an association between neuropsychological test scores and QPO.

Hannon et al. (1987) reported a replication of their earlier study (Hannon et al., 1983), that included a reversibility condition. A total of 170 students (103 women), with an average age of 20.8, participated in two testing sessions. At the first, they were administered a battery of tests that included the SILS, the WCST, the Digit Symbol subtest of the WAIS-R, and Raven's Advanced Progressive Matrices, and at the second, the Vocabulary, Block Design and Digit Symbol subtests of the WAIS-R and the Category Test. The drinking variables assessed were current annual frequency, average current QPO, and total lifetime consumption. At the end of the first session, subjects were randomly assigned to either an abstain ($n = 84$) or maintain ($n = 86$) condition.

The results of this study typified the findings that had appeared in the literature to that time. Correlations between neuropsychological test scores and drinking variables at the time of Session 1 were computed separately for males and females, resulting in 48 coefficients. Of these, 10 were significant but only six in the predicted direction. For the women, SILS vocabulary and QPO, and lifetime consumption and the SILS scores were significantly correlated. For the men, there were significant correlations in the opposite to predicted direction between QPO and the abstraction ($r = 0.38$) and Conceptual Quotient ($r = 0.39$) scores. Lifetime consumption was negatively correlated with SILS abstraction and Conceptual Quotient scores. Hannon et al. (1983) observed, however, that no correlations significant in their earlier study were significant in the present study. The reversibility phase produced equally unhelpful findings. Although the abstain group reduced their consumption markedly, there were no significant differences between the maintain and abstain groups on any of the neuropsychological tests. The only exception was the WAIS-R vocabulary scores, where the maintain group women scored more highly than their abstain counterparts. This result is unlikely to be of any consequence. Overall, the findings of this study emphasised what the authors referred to as the "elusive and variable" quality of the outcomes of such investigations; in particular, the reversibility condition provided no evidence that cognition is influenced by social drinking.

Two other studies also produced negative findings (Jones-Saumty & Zeiner 1985; Page & Cleveland, 1987). Jones-Saumty and Zeiner administered the SILS to a sample of social drinkers with an average age of about 20. No significant correlations between QPO and other indices of drinking behaviour, and SILS scores were found. Page and Cleveland included a social drinking sample in their comparison study of alcoholics, abstinent alcoholics, and non-drinkers. Although there was evidence on the neuropsychological tests of impairments in the alcoholic group, no differences between social drinkers and non-drinkers were found. In a similar study, comparing abstinent alcoholics with social drinkers and lifetime abstainers, Emmerson, Dustman, Heil, and Shearer (1988) found no significant differences between non-drinkers and social drinkers, and no correlations between consumption variables and any of the neuropsychological tests they employed.

In a study by Bowden, Walton, and Walsh (1988), a test of Parker and colleagues' carryover model was made. Bowden et al. hypothesised that the test performance of social drinkers would be best predicted by some combination of time since last drinking episode and amount consumed. They used a multiple regression analysis to determine the independent effects of recent consumption (days elapsed, most recent quantity, and days × quantity), age, and education on the WCST, SILS, and Paced Auditory Serial Addition Test (PASAT) scores. The PASAT is a measure of concentration and attention in which subjects are instructed to add mentally strings of digits presented on an audiotape at rates of 1.2 and 2.0 digits per second. The subjects add each pair of digits and give the answers aloud. Bowden et al. found that although age and education were predictive of SILS scores, recent consumption was not. The highest associations were between days elapsed since most recent episode and both SILS vocabulary

(7% of the variance) and abstraction scores (8% of the variance). The importance of these associations is tempered by the absence of any correlations with the WCST and PASAT, both measures that are particularly sensitive to neurological damage and the fact that the Vocabulary scale, which was significantly predicted by recent consumption, is especially insensitive to acquired organic impairment. This suggested to the authors that the results might best be explained by the effect of some third variable, such as innate intellectual capacity, on both the SILS scores and consumption.

Finally, in one of the most careful studies of the early effects of regular social drinking on cognition, Bates and Tracy (1990) attempted to establish whether neuropsychological impairments could be detected in young social drinkers. Their report was based on data from the Rutgers Health and Human Development Project, a longitudinal study of alcohol and drug abuse in adolescents and young adults. These independent samples were tested at ages 18, 21, and 24. In addition, selected samples of subjects were compared: abstainers (n = 84); infrequent users (n = 52); intensive alcohol-only users (n = 42); and intensive alcohol and marijuana users (n = 32). A variety of self-reported consumption measures were collected, including QPO, frequency, and recent episode estimates; the neuropsychological tests administered included the SILS, TMT, and the Digit Symbol, Vocabulary, and Digit Span subtests of the WAIS-R. The results of a series of group comparisons and hierarchical multiple regression analyses were largely fruitless. Bates and Tracy (1990) concluded that when age and sex effects were allowed for, measures of alcohol use did not contribute to the variance in the score on neuropsychological test in any substantial way. In working- and middle-class youth no evidence for the deleterious effects of alcohol use was uncovered.

In a report that describes a reanalysis of their Detroit data, Parker et al. (1991) proposed that failure to consistently replicate the findings of Parker and Noble (1977) and Parker et al. (1983) might be explained by differences in subject groups' drinking practices across studies. They proposed that an important determinant of cognitive decline might be *frequency* of drinking and that measures like QPO may only be associated with cognition when the frequency of consumption reaches a sufficiently high level. That is, "the effects of quantity of alcohol consumed may be conditional upon the frequency of alcohol use" (Parker et al., 1991, p.367).

In their reanalysis of the data from Parker et al. (1983), Parker et al. (1991) selected a group of 360 lighter-drinking men who had an average QPO of 30ml/occasion—the same as the average for the total sample of women. In this sample of males, neither quantity of frequency of alcohol consumed per occasion was related to SILS abstraction scores. Thus the findings for the total female and low consumption male groups were comparable. There was, however, a significant interaction for the low consumption male group between frequency and usual QPO, suggesting that in men who drink amounts comparable to women, correlations between quantity and cognition are dependent on frequency. They strengthened this conclusion by computing the average reported quantity and frequency for samples from those studies where significant correlations had been found, and those where they had not. For samples yielding a non-significant finding, the average frequency of drinking per week was 2.0 ± 2.1 and the average QPO was 35 ± 19.8ml. For samples with significant correlations, the average frequency was 3.4 ± 2.7 and the QPO was 47 ± 24.5. The implication of these results is that variations in the average amount consumed from one study to another determined the magnitude of the quantity–cognition correlations. This may be because a certain average level of intoxication or consumption in a population is needed before cognitive dysfunction is detectable. An alternative explanation is that samples with lower average consumption levels have a lesser range of values on consumption indices and that this serves to attenuate the magnitude of correlations. Parker et al. (1991) also found that when a measure of psychological distress was incorporated in the regression analyses, it explained little of the variance in SILS scores from their Detroit subjects. In those samples where QPO predicted SILS, psychological distress was not correlated with cognitive functioning. Thus they found no support for the suggestion of Parker and Noble (1977) and Parsons (1986) that if measures of stress of affect were to be included in regression analyses along with QPO, the predictive power of the quantity measures would be diminished.

CONCLUSIONS

In our literature survey we have traced the history of attempts to determine whether social drinking causes discernible reductions in performance on neuropsychological tests. If the damaging effects of moderate alcohol consumption could be established then neuropsychologists would have an obligation to alert the community to this potential health hazard. The fact that prolonged alcohol abuse certainly causes neurological lesions, as well as damage to other physical systems, provides a strong motivation for the determination of safe lower limits of consumption. However, after over 15 years of studies with social drinkers, the evidence remains inconclusive, inconsistent, and open to a variety of explanations. No cause for concern has been established from the results of neuropsychological testing.

The most compelling evidence for an association between social drinking and changes in cognition comes from Parker and colleagues' two studies with large samples of middle-aged men (Parker & Noble, 1977; Parker et al., 1983, 1991). These large and, no doubt, expensive studies have not been replicated by other groups and much of the research that has followed has employed younger and predominantly student samples. An exception are the Swedish CT-scan studies that were reviewed in Chapter 5 (Bergman, 1985; Mutzell & Tibblin, 1989). In these reports, evidence for some cerebral abnormalities in heavy social drinkers, predicted by the most recent episode measures, were reported. However, no relationship between cognitive performance and either CT indices or consumption variables emerged. It is important to emphasise that Parker and colleagues have not claimed that social drinking causes irreversible neurological damage or even changes in cognitive capacity that are of clinical significance. Indeed, there is no evidence that, when abstainers and social drinkers are compared, significant deficits are seen; all the evidence available comes from the association within groups of social drinkers between QPO and cognitive performance.

The explanation that Parker and her group favoured in accounting for their results was the "carryover" hypothesis, which states that alcohol causes a transient reduction in cognitive efficiency reflected in reduced scores on neuropsychological tests. This view provides only a limited and short-term role for alcohol in producing changes in mental activity, but is more consistent with their findings than an unqualified "social drinking causes brain changes" explanation. A prediction of the carryover hypothesis is that abstinence or reduced intake will reverse any cognitive reductions that occur. However, to date reversibility studies have not provided confirmatory evidence (Hannon et al., 1983). Similarly, studies focusing on the effects of the most recent drinking episode have not supported the carry-over hypothesis (Bowden, Walton, & Walsh, 1988). Other explanations of the correlational findings are also feasible; such results may be the product of pre-existing lower intellectual aptitude in subjects with higher QPO drinking behaviour or, alternatively, some third variable may be responsible for both level of cognition and consumption behaviour in groups of social drinkers. Some indirect evidence for explanations other than an alcohol causes cognitive changes view comes from a consideration of the validity of the SILS as a measure of acquired organic impairment.

Bowden (1987) drew attention to the concurrence of associations between QPO and both the vocabulary and the abstraction scales of the SILS, which is evident in a number of studies (see Table 8.4). On the face of it, this is an unlikely result. Vocabulary scores draw on memories acquired over a long period of time, particularly during the course of education. The ability to access semantic knowledge is typically well-preserved, even in the early stages of dementing disorders such as Alzheimer's disease. Indeed, the SILS Conceptual Quotient is predicated on the assumption that vocabulary scores are resistant to change and provide a reference point against which scores on the abstraction scale, presumably more susceptible to neuropsychiatric deficits, can be compared. Vocabulary test scores are often used as estimates of premorbid intellectual functioning in the process of neuropsychological assessment, because they are most likely to be preserved following brain lesions. As we saw in Chapter 7, studies of intoxicated subjects have produced no evidence that vocabulary scores are affected by alcohol, and SILS scores are not depressed in alcoholics (Jones & Parsons, 1971; Tarter & Jones, 1971) or Korsakoff patients (Malerstein & Belden, 1968). Lezak (1983, p. 574) concluded that "most research studies report that it fails to discriminate between organic patients and normal control subjects, as well as between different categories of neuropsychiatric patients ...". In sum, there is no evidence that the SILS is particularly sensitive to the kind of acquired neuropsychiatric changes that have been postulated to occur in social drinking. Many neuropsychological tests that are far more successful in discriminating between deficit and no-deficit in a range of neurological disorders, such as learning and memory tests or the WCST, have produced even less consistent evidence of cognitive changes in social drinkers.

Given that tests of intellectual capacity and vocabulary scales particularly, are relatively insensitive to subtle acquired impairments, then it seems more likely that the QPO–SILS correlations can be attributed to pre-existing individual differences between light and heavy consumers. Whether cognition causes individual differences in drinking behaviour, that is, brighter people decide to drink less per session, is a moot point, but it is possible that intellectual performance determines social and employment circumstances, which might in turn influence patterns of consumption. Such a possibility is at least as likely as an alcohol causative hypothesis. It is of interest that the only variable that discriminated between heavy and slight social drinkers in the MacVane et al. (1982) study was the WAIS-R vocabulary score.

Replications of Parker and colleagues' studies have provided either negligible or inconsistent confirmation of their initial findings. Bowden (1987) reviewed Parker's studies and seven others that reported correlations between QPO estimates and a variety of test scores. From the set of 95 correlations detailed in these studies, Bowden calculated that the median amount of variance explained was 1.4%. Only 20 of the correlations were both significant and in the predicted direction. Other measures of consumption produced even more inconsistent and irreproducible findings. Bowden (1987, p. 408) concluded that:

An examination of the evidence on social drinking illustrates that no data are presented for the position that moderate alcohol consumption harms mentation which is not open to other interpretations. Even if the evidence is accepted on face value, the proportion of explained variance is vanishingly small. As such it appears that the hypothesised effect has no practical importance.

Despite this discouraging conclusion to what has been a sustained research effort over a considerable period of time, there remains good reason for continued attention to this area of investigation. Drinking disrupts CNS functioning temporarily in mildly intoxicated subjects and pathological drinking causes physical damage and neuropsychological deficits. It is possible that even if social drinking is risk free for the majority of social drinkers, it may constitute some degree of risk for some people, for example, persons with other neurological conditions, members of particular social groups, individuals with a family history of alcoholism, or people who combine drinking with the use of other recreational or prescribed drugs. However, future research will need to take account of the limitations exposed in the experimental procedures used to date. One problem is the difficulty and expense of obtaining large and representative samples of subjects other than college students. Large samples are needed if all possible factors, such as gender, race, and family history of alcoholism are to be accounted for. It is also important to pay attention to the statistical problems inherent in conducting correlational studies. The reporting of large matrices of correlations with a cavalier disregard for the possibility of Type 1 errors characterises much research in this area. Hannon et al.'s (1983) study, where 48 correlations were reported, 10 of which were significant (four in a direction opposite to that hypothesised), is unfortunately typical. It is difficult to place much weight on the remaining six significant results. Multiple regression procedures that allow independent estimates of the predictive value of consumption variables (Bates & Tracy, 1990) are to be preferred. The discussion of results in the literature also tends to ignore the possibility that the correlations have been attenuated by the restriction of range of the variables assessed.

Finally, it is of note that most consumption measures depend on the subjects' self-report and, as we saw in Chapter 3, this may be distorted by a variety of factors including perceptions of experimenter demands, failures or distortions of memory, and degree of confidentiality. Although there is evidence for the reliability and validity of such measures, retrospective reports are likely to be most reliable where the elapsed time between the behaviour and the report is minimised. This may explain why life-time consumption estimates are less predictive of cognition that QPO. Detailed use of estimates of the most recent drinking episode, following

Bowden et al. (1988), may also be of value in future research. It would also be interesting to study samples of drinkers repeatedly tested on some cognitive test where alcohol consumption was recorded at the time of testing, using some variant of time series analysis. Finally, and perhaps most importantly, considerable care needs to be taken in the selection of the neuropsychological measures used to test for acquired changes in cognition. Such tests need to have minimal practice effects and adequate sensitivity to detect subtle changes in performance, as well as established credentials for the detection of neurological impairments.

CHAPTER NINE

Cognitive Impairment in Alcoholics

Alcoholism is a disorder of great destructive power. Depending on how one defines alcoholism, it will afflict, at some time in their lives, between 3 and 10 percent of all Americans. In the United States alcoholism is involved in a quarter of all admissions to general hospitals, and it plays a major role in the four most common causes of death in males aged 20 to 40: suicide, accidents, homicide and cirrhosis of the liver. The damage it causes falls not only on alcoholics themselves but on their families and friends as well—and this damage touches one American family out of three.

Vaillant (1983, p.1)

Reviews of the literature on the neuropsychological performance of detoxified alcoholics almost invariably begin by acknowledging that there are cognitive impairments to be found (Kleinknecht & Goldstein, 1972; Parsons, 1987; Parsons & Farr, 1981). Since the early 1980s, attention has turned from establishing that deficits occur to the design of studies that answer new questions. Does a period of abstinence lead to a return to normal cognitive functioning? What are the predictors of brain damage in alcoholics? What does the pattern of neuropsychological test performance by alcoholics tell us about the changes in the functioning of the brain caused by alcohol abuse? We will consider each of these questions as this chapter progresses. First, however, we begin with a survey of studies that have compared alcoholics' performance with that of normals.

NEUROPSYCHOLOGICAL DEFICITS

Intelligence

There have been a number of studies in which the results on standardised intelligence scales have been reported for groups of alcoholics. The most commonly used measures have been the Wechsler intelligence scales, the SILS (which featured extensively in the study of social drinkers in Chapter 8), and Raven's Progressive Matrices. We discussed these tests in Chapter 3. The findings from these studies have not been consistent. For example, in two large studies (Butters, Cermak, Montgomery, & Adinolfi, 1977; Grant, Adams, & Reed, 1979) no differences between alcoholics and controls emerged on the WAIS, with the exception of a significant Digit Symbol subtest score difference in the Butters et al. (1977) study. However, other studies have reported large and significant differences (Blusewicz, Schenkenberg, Dustman, & Beck, 1977b; Fitzhugh, Fitzhugh, & Reitan, 1965; Franceschi et al., 1984). Undoubtedly differences in outcome are largely attributable to differences in subject selection. However, since relevant subject variables are not reported in many studies, attempting to reconcile discrepancies is often difficult and unrewarding.

Table 9.1 summarises those studies in which IQ scores have been reported. Only those studies where comparisons have been made between an alcoholic and a control sample are included. For each of the studies in Table 9.1 an effect size (ES) has been computed for each of the individual scales used. The ES gives a standardised estimate of the differences between the mean scale scores for the two groups. Computation of effect sizes has been popularised by the widespread use of meta-analysis, a statistical technique used to quantify and aggregate research outcomes as part of the review of a particular research area. In this case, we have computed each ES by subtracting the mean scores of the two samples and dividing the result by the standard deviation of the control group. This means that each ES is expressed in terms of the standard deviation of the unit normal curve, that is, an ES of 1 represents a distance between the two groups equivalent to a one standard deviation shift of the alcoholic group mean from the control group mean. No control standard deviation was reported for a number of studies. As the standard deviation of the test based on the data from the standardisation sample was likely to be an overestimate for smaller and more homogeneous samples, we computed the average standard deviation for the control groups from all the studies using that particular scale and used this in making the ES estimate. In studies where more than one alcoholic group was tested (e.g. Grant et al., 1979), the results were compared separately with the control group. Where more than one control group was used, the group with the least evidence of neurological damage and closest in age to the alcoholic group was used.

TABLE 9.1
Intelligence Scale Score Effect Sizes for Alcoholic and Comparison Samples

Study	Sample	n	Age	Usage duration (years)	Abstinence (days)	Test scale	Effect size	Study effect size
Acker et al. (1984)	AC	100	43.40	9.40	34.50	Wechsler Verbal	0.56	0.57
	NC	50	42.10	–	–	Wechsler Performance	0.57	
Becker & Jaffe, (1984)	AC	44	44.10	–	–	SILS-Verbal	–0.72	–0.38
	NC	10	39.00	–	–	SILS-Abstract	–0.05	
Blusewicz et al. (1977)	AC	20	33.00	13.30	37.00	Wechsler Verbal	0.82	1.06
	NC	20	31.00	–	–	Wechsler Performance	1.31	
Eckhardt et al. (1978)	AC	91	42.20	15.90	1–7	SILS-Verbal	0.52	0.34
	NC	32	40.60	–	–	SILS-Abstract	0.29	
	AC	20	45.60	16.20	14–31	SILS-Verbal	0.46	
						SILS-Abstract	0.10	
Ellis (1990)	YA	11	25.47	7+	–	Wechsler Verbal	0.02	1.56
	OA	11	48+	–	–		1.00	
	YN	11	25–47	7+	–		1.92	
	ON	11	48+	–	–		3.30	
Fabian et al. (1981) (study 1)	AC	37	41.00	6.30	27.40	SILS-Verbal	0.28	0.49
	NC	73	41.50	–	–	SILS-Abstract	0.71	
Fabian & Parsons (1983)	AC	–	42.15	6.38	29.90	SILS-Abstract	0.69	0.60
	NC	–	42.34	–	–	SILS-Abstract	0.40	
	AC	–	42.27	9.86	48.50			
Franceschi et al. (1984)	AC	50	42.00	–	–	Ravens Matrices	1.35	1.35
	NC	20	41.00	–	–			

(continued)

TABLE 9.1
Intelligence Scale Score Effect Sizes for Alcoholic and Comparison Samples

Study	Sample	n	Age	Usage duration (years)	Abstinence (days)	Test scale	Effect size	Study effect size
Grant et al. (1979)	AC	43	36.80	6.10	21.00	Wechsler Verbal	-0.09	-0.07
	NC	40	37.00	–	–	Wechsler Performance	0.10	
	AC	39	37.40	9.00	540.00	Wechsler Verbal	-0.41	
						Wechsler Performance	0.12	
Grant et al. (1984)	AC	71	41.50	13.80	2.00	Wechsler Verbal	0.06	0.13
	NC	68	42.20	–	–	Wechsler Performance	0.11	
	AC	65	42.60	15.00	3.7 years	Wechsler Verbal	-0.24	
						Wechsler Performance	-0.06	
Gudeman et al. (1977)	AC	41	42.00	9.59	21.37	Wechsler Verbal	0.47	0.83
	NC	41	44.30			Wechsler Performance	1.20	
Long & McLachlen (1974)	AC	22	44.60	8.91	11.41	Wechsler Verbal	-0.01	0.44
	NC	22	49.00	–	–	Wechsler Performance	0.90	
Miller & Orr (1980)	AC	36	46.60	12.70	31.60	Wechsler Verbal	0.58	0.20
	NC	21	36.00	–	–	Wechsler Performance	0.98	
Mohs et al. (1979)	AC	13	47.00	12.50	49.30	Wechsler Verbal	0.22	0.28
	NC	13	42.00	–	–	Wechsler Performance	0.79	
Silberstein & Parsons (1981)	AC	25	–	6–7	30.00	SILS-Abstract	0.57	0.57
	NC	25	–	–				
Smith et al. (1973)	AC	26	43.00	–	–	Wechsler Verbal	0.58	1.30
	NC	26	40.00	–	–	Wechsler Performance	2.03	

(continued)

TABLE 9.1
Intelligence Scale Score Effect Sizes for Alcoholic and Comparison Samples

Study	Sample	n	Age	Usage duration (years)	Abstinence (days)	Test scale	Effect size	Study effect size
Smith & Smith (1977)	AC	20	–	5+	–	Wechsler Verbal	1.35	1.43
	NC	20	–	–	–	Wechsler Performance	2.26	
	AC	20	–	5+	–	Wechsler Verbal	0.87	
						Wechsler Performance	1.26	
Tarquini & Masullo (1981)	AC	28	–	16.40	21+	Ravens PM	0.39	0.39
	NC	83	–	–				
Workman-Daniels & Hesselbrock (1987)	AC		42.15	6.38	29.90	SILS-Abstract	0.69	0.60
	NC		42.34	–	–	SILS-Abstract	0.40	
	AC		42.27	9.86	48.50			

AC, alcoholic group; NC, normal controls; OA, old alcoholic; ON, old normal; YA, young alcoholic; YN, young normal; SILS, Shipley Institute of Living Scale.

229

Finally, it will be noted that ES values have been calculated only for independent IQ scales, that is, in the case of the WAIS, only for PIQ and VIQ, and not for FSIQ (which is the sum of both the other two scales).

The 19 studies listed in Table 9.1 involved the testing of a total of 833 alcoholics and 761 controls. The mean of the average age of the alcoholic samples was 41.53 years (SD = 4.68), their average drinking duration was 10.87 years (SD = 3.73), and the average length of abstinence prior to testing was 27.25 days (SD = 11.94). The latter average excludes the abstinence duration of the long-term abstinent community samples of Grant et al. (1979; 1984). As is apparent in Table 9.1, the range of ESs is substantial, extending from negative values (where the alcoholic group outperformed the controls) to over three standard deviations in magnitude. The overall trends in the data are more explicit in Table 9.2, where the average ES values are reported. The average of the total of 45 ES values was 0.65, and the average of the mean study ES was 0.63. This latter value represents a 0.63 standard deviation shift in the alcoholic group's mean from the control group's mean. Another way of expressing this difference is that the average non-alcoholic control performed better than 74% of the alcoholics (that is, the control group mean lies on the 74th percentile of the alcoholic group distribution of scores). It is also apparent in Table 9.2 that scores on verbal tests produce smaller ES values than scores on non-verbal tests. The average ES for the Wechsler Verbal Scale is 0.65, meaning that 75% of controls scored more highly than alcoholics on this scale. This is in contrast to the ES of 0.90 for the Performance Scale, which indicates that some 81% of controls performed better than the alcoholics. These results illustrate a marked decrement on IQ tests, on average, for alcoholics.

A more detailed analysis of IQ performance is presented in Table 9.3. Here, results from eight controlled studies in which Wechsler subtest scores were reported have been collated (Blusewicz et al., 1977b; Gudeman, Craine, Golden & McLaughlin, 1977; Holland & Watson, 1980; Loberg, 1977 [cited in Parsons & Farr, 1981]; Long & McLachlen 1974; Miller &

TABLE 9.2
Average Effect Sizes for Intelligence Scales

Effect size	n	Mean	SD
Overall	45	0.65	0.73
Study	19	0.63	0.53
Verbal tests	22	0.57	0.84
Non-verbal tests	23	0.74	0.63
Wechsler Verbal	18	0.65	0.88
Wechsler Performance	14	0.90	0.71

TABLE 9.3
Average WAIS Subtest Scores

Subtest	Alcoholic (n = 399) Mean	Controls (n = 328) Mean	Effect size	Rank effect size
Information	11.19	11.62	0.14	2
Comprehension	11.11	12.03	0.31	6
Arithmetic	10.73	11.31	0.19	4
Similarities	11.26	11.76	0.17	3
Digit Span	9.43	10.29	0.29	5
Vocabulary	11.42	11.63	0.07	1
Digit Symbol	7.70	9.66	0.65	10
Picture Completion	10.29	11.24	0.32	7
Block Design	9.13	11.23	0.70	11
Picture Arrangement	8.91	10.32	0.47	8
Object Assembly	9.06	10.99	0.64	9

Orr, 1980; O'Leary et al., 1979b; Smith & Smith, 1977). These results come from nine alcoholic samples and eight groups of controls.

In Table 9.3 the average Wechsler subtest scores from each study, weighted for the number of subjects used in each sample, have been aggregated to produce mean subtest scores for the alcoholic and non-alcoholic groups. The differences between means have also been computed and, for comparison purposes, converted to ES estimates using a constant control standard deviation of 3 (the SD of the standardisation sample for the WAIS subtests). The ranks of the ES values have also been included in Table 9.3. Four subtests emerge as having substantial ES values: Picture Arrangement, Object Assembly, Digit Symbol, and Block Design. These are the same four subtests identified by Parsons and Farr (1981) as being most consistently found to produce significant between-group differences. Indeed, there is a correlation of 0.93 between the ES scores and the Parsons and Farr percent significant figures. Also of note is the substantial correlation of 0.89 between the mean subtest scores for the control and alcoholic subjects. This suggests that the pattern of WAIS subtest scores may not be exclusive to alcoholism, but may reflect the general sensitivity of individual subtests to impairment. The control groups for alcoholics probably differ in education and social background from the test standardisation sample and this may explain why their WAIS subtest scores tend to have the same pattern as that of the alcoholics. Other groups with neurological damage have a similar WAIS profile. For example, persons with multiple sclerosis tend to have their lowest average scores on the same four subtests as have been identified for alcoholics (Knight, 1992). Parkinson's disease groups also tend to have their lowest scores on Picture Arrangement, Object Assembly and Digit Symbol (Knight, Godfrey, & Shelton, 1988). Thus the pattern of WAIS subtest scores may say less about the specific effects of alcohol abuse and more about the discriminatory power of individual WAIS subtests.

Halstead–Reitan Battery (HRB)

Apart from the Wechsler Intelligence scales, the Halstead–Reitan Battery has been the most widely used measure of neuropsychological function in groups of alcoholics. Table 9.4 presents a summary of descriptions of the HRB subtests, described more fully in Chapter 3, and the range of deficit scores suggested by Golden et al. (1981). The performance of alcoholics on the HRB has been reviewed elsewhere (Parsons & Farr, 1981; Parsons & Leber, 1981) and no relevant additional group comparison studies have been published since the date of those reviews. Table 9.5 lists summary data from a review of some 20 studies reporting comparisons between alcoholics and controls compiled by Parsons and Leber (1981). These data take the form of the percentage of studies reporting significant impairments in alcoholics on each individual test. It is clear from these results that the Category Test is the measure most sensitive to impairments caused by alcohol abuse, followed by the total time taken to complete the Tactual Performance Test (TPT), Trails B, and the TPT Location score. TPT memory, Finger Tapping, and the Rhythm test resulted in impairments in less than half of the studies. To illustrate the performance of brain damaged patients on the HRB, relative to that of alcoholics, results from a study by Miller and Orr (1980) are presented as part of Table 9.5. In this study, 36 alcoholics with an average age of 46.6 were compared with a group of 21 psychiatric inpatients with primary neurotic or personality disorder diagnoses, and 30 patients with well-documented neurological damage. There were no significant differences between the alcoholic and brain damaged patients, but the psychiatric and alcoholic group comparisons differed significantly on most tests. Comparing the Miller and Orr (1980) data with the abnormal ranges of scores in Table 9.4, it can be seen that the alcoholics were impaired on the Category Test, TPT, Rhythm Test, Speech Sounds Perception, Finger Tapping, Trails B, and the Impairment Index.

Are alcoholics impaired on the HRB? Parsons and Farr concluded that the answer was a qualified "Yes". They noted (Parsons & Farr, 1981, p. 323) that:

TABLE 9.4
Halstead–Reitan Battery

Test	Functions tested	Abnormal ranges
Category Test	Conceptual learning, problem solving	51–208 errors
Speech-Sounds Perception	Phoneme discrimination; matching sounds and written symbols	8–60 errors
Rhythm Test	Attention, concentration, rhythmic relationships	6–30 errors
Tactual Performance	Spatial identification and memory, tactile discrimination; manual dexterity	
total time		17–30 minutes
location		0–4 correct
memory		0–4 correct
Trails A	Visual search, planning and motor skills	40+ seconds
Trails B		92+ seconds
Impairment index		0.5–1.0

Ranges of deficit scores from Golden et al. (1981).

TABLE 9.5
Alcoholics' Performance of the Halstead–Reitan Battery

		Miller & Orr (1980)		
Test	Studies showing an impairment (%)*	Alcoholic (n = 36) Mean	Psychiatric (n = 21) Mean	Brain damaged (n = 30) Mean
Category Test	89	90.0**	51.5	93.7
TPT-Time	84	22.9**	14.2	24.3
TPT-Memory	32	6.8	8.1	4.9
TPT-Location	63	2.4**	4.2	1.7
Rhythm Test	44	6.5**	3.6	7.8
Speech Sounds	62	9.4**	6.1	12.3
Finger Tapping	29	38.1**	50.0	37.8
Trails B	80	150.0**	80.1	183.1
Impairment Index	90	0.69**	0.31	0.83

*From Parsons and Leber (1981); ** significant difference between psychiatric patients and alcoholic group.

While 13 of 15 studies (87%) indicate that the Impairment Index is significantly higher in alcoholics than in controls, only in 7 of the 13 studies (54%) is the Impairment Index for the alcoholics in the impaired range (0.5 and above) ... Age, education and general intelligence all play a role in the overall level of impairment as reflected in the Impairment Index of the HRB.

They found significant correlations of 0.62 between age and Impairment Index scores from the studies they reviewed, −0.67 between the Impairment Index and education level, and −0.60 between the Impairment Index and WAIS VIQ. As with the results from the intelligence tests, it appears that some alcoholics show impairments, often of quite a severe degree, but others show no sign of brain damage at all.

In our analyses of the literature thus far in this chapter, we have seen that, on the Wechsler intelligence scales and the HRB, some subtests are more sensitive to impairment than others. Capitalising on this, Reitan, in an unpublished seminar in 1973, suggested the computation of a Brain–Age Quotient (BAQ) as an index of the cognitive effects of ageing. The BAQ is the average of the T-scores of the Block Design and Digit Symbol from the WAIS, and the TPT-Time, TPT-Location, Category Test, and Trail Making Test scores from the HRB. Those subtests identified by Reitan as being sensitive to ageing, however, are also those most sensitive to almost any kind of brain lesion. The BAQ has been computed for several samples of alcoholics. Shau and O'Leary (1977) found significant differences on the BAQ for 38 male alcoholics compared to controls. Similar findings have been reported for women (Hochla, Fabian, & Parsons, 1982). Noonberg, Goldstein, and Page (1985) found significant differences in BAQ at four age ranges from (30 to 60 years) between alcoholics and controls matched for VIQ scores. These results show that the most sensitive tests from the HRB and WAIS, used together, can provide a good degree of discrimination between alcoholic and non-alcoholic groups.

Memory

The measurement of memory impairments has come to occupy a significant place in the neuropsychological study of alcoholics (Oscar-Berman & Ellis, 1987). In part this is due to the sensitivity of memory and learning processes to CNS damage. In addition, as will become more apparent in Chapter 10, much of the work that has been done on the investigation of the relationship between the deficits caused by alcoholism and irreversible changes seen in Korsakoff's syndrome has relied very much on contrasting performance on memory tasks. In this section, however, the focus will be on determining the pattern of memory impairments in alcoholics.

The Wechsler Memory Scale has been used extensively to study memory failure in patients with neurological damage. As we saw in Chapter 3, the WMS is a multitask measure that produces a Memory Quotient (MQ), which Wechsler intended to be analogous to the IQ score. Early studies with the WMS suggested that memory loss was not a significant characteristic of alcoholics. Parsons and Prigatano (1977) compared two small groups of alcoholics with and without head injury, with a sample of normal controls and found no significant effects due to head injury. When the full group of 20 alcoholics were contrasted with the controls, MQ did not differ significantly, although differences on the paired-associate learning subtest did emerge. Butters et al. (1977) similarly found no between-group differences on the MQ. In some later studies, significant group differences have been reported, although these are not large in magnitude (Table 9.6). Failure to find large MQ differences in performance between alcoholics and controls is not especially surprising given that many of the subtests (e.g. Information, Orientation, Mental Control, Digit Span) are not usually failed even by profoundly amnesic Korsakoff patients. These tests are combined in the WMS with a number of memory tests that are not particularly demanding of memory capacity and thus not necessarily sensitive to the kinds of changes wrought by alcohol abuse.

The Russell version of the WMS (Russell, 1988), is a more exacting test of memory that incorporates a delayed recall component into the measurement process. Subjects are administered the Logical Memory and the Visual Reproduction subtests of the WMS, tested immediately, and then tested again after a 30-minute delay. On this more sensitive measure, deficits have been consistently reported (Table 9.7). For example, Nixon, Kujawski, Parsons and Yohman (1987) tested a group of 60 alcoholics abstinent for at least 21 days, and a group of normals matched for age and SILS Vocabulary scores. They found consistent impairments on all the subscores from the Russell memory scale.

TABLE 9.6
WMS Performance by Alcoholic Subjects and Controls

| Study | Mean MQ values | | |
	Alcoholics	Controls	P
Gudeman et al. (1977)	122	133.2	< 0.013
Butters et al. (1977)	106,105	108.0	ns
Miller & Orr (1980)	93.8	107.0	< 0.023
Parsons & Priganto (1977)	104.2	110.0	ns

MQ, memory quotient.

TABLE 9.7

Russell Version of the WMS and Memory for Design Test Scores

Study	Outcome
Russell WMS Version	
De Obaldia & Parsons (1984)	Delay recall, semantic memory, primary alcoholics < controls. Secondary alcoholics = controls. Figural A < C
Hightower & Anderson (1986)	A < C on immediate figural and verbal, and delayed verbal
Nixon et al. (1987)	A < C on all measures
Acker et al. (1984)	A < C verbal immediate and delayed
Memory for Designs	
Blusewicz et al. (1977)	YA < YC
Brandt, et al. (1983)	A = C
Fabian & Parsons (1983)	Short-term abstinent < controls
Grant et al. (1979)	A = C
Leber et al. (1981)	A < C at 3 weeks; A = C at 11 weeks
Riege et al. (1984)	A = C
Yohman et al. (1985)	A < C

A, alcoholic; C, controls; YA, young alcoholics; YC, young controls.

The WMS has been revised extensively, and, in the manual of the WMS-R (Wechsler, 1987) results for a group of 62 alcoholics are presented for each of the five index scores (each of which has a mean score of 100, and a standard deviation of 15) and the Information-Orientation questions. Overall, the alcoholics were found to differ significantly from a matched sample of normals. When each of the indexes were compared individually, the alcoholics had decrements on the General Memory (*M=92), Attention and Concentration (M=97), Visual Memory (M=89.4), and Delayed Recall (M=93.9) indexes. On the Verbal Memory index (M=99.8) and the Information-Orientation questions, no group differences were observed. As will be seen when the studies of recovery of function in alcoholism reported by Goldman and his colleagues are presented later in this chapter, alcoholics are often more impaired in their learning of non-verbal material than verbal. Overall, as is apparent from the magnitude of the index scores reported in the WMS-R manual, the size of the impairments typically found in alcoholics, although significant, is not especially large.

Alcoholics have been found to have deficits, although not invariably, on tests that measure ability to reproduce geometric designs after brief 10-second delays, such as the Benton Visual Retention Test and the Memory-For-Designs Test (Graham & Kendall, 1960) (see Table 9.7). Leber,

---

*M = mean

TABLE 9.8
Performance by Alcoholic Groups on Verbal List and Paired-Associate
Learning Tests

Study	Outcome
Verbal List Learning	
Riege et al. (1984)	A < C
Tarquini & Masullo (1981)	A < C
Query & Berger (1980)	A with neurological damage < C
Weingartner et al. (1971)	A < C
Paired-Associate Learning	
Becker et al. (1983b)	Face–name A < C
Brandt et al. (1983)	Symbol–digit A < C
Ellenberg et al. (1980)	Verbal and visuospatial, A < C at 5 days;
	A = C at 25 days
Fabian et al. (1984)	Verbal A = C; Visuospatial: male A < C,
	female A = C
Kapur & Butters (1977)	Symbol–digit A < C
Leber et al. (1981)	Verbal A = C; Visuospatial A < C at 3
	weeks but A = C at 11 weeks
Ryan & Butters (1980b)	Symbol–digit OA < OC; Verbal A < C
Yohman et al. (1985)	Verbal A < C; Visuospatial A < C
Bowden (1988)	Symbol–digit YA = YC
Yohman & Parsons (1985)	Verbal A = C

A, alcoholic; C, control; OA, old alcoholic; OC, old control; YA, young alcoholic; YC, young control.

Jenkins, and Parsons (1981) found that deficits at 3 weeks had disappeared by 11 weeks. On verbal list learning measures (Table 9.8), alcoholics have typically been found to be impaired when the number of stimuli to be remembered is large enough to test the limits of their capabilities. For example, Riege, Tomaszewski, Lanto, and Metter (1984) and Tarquini and Masullo (1981) found deficits in list learning in groups of alcoholics who were able to perform non-verbal immediate memory tests normally. The Rey Auditory Verbal Learning Test has been found to be sensitive to memory deficits in two studies (Query & Berger, 1980; Tarquini & Masullo, 1981). Alcoholics have generally been found to be impaired on paired-associate learning tasks (Table 9.8), although again there are contradictions in the literature (Yohman & Parsons, 1985). Where deficits have been found, they are more common on tests using non-verbal than verbal stimuli (Kapur & Butters, 1977; Leber et al., 1981) and in older rather than younger alcoholics (Cermak & Peck, 1982; Ryan & Butters, 1980b).

Another research focus has been on short-term memory (STM). Short-term memory is a term used to describe a proposed memory process that retains information for brief periods of about 30 seconds. Rate of decay from STM has been calculated in numerous neurological studies and will be a focus in the next chapter. One method of estimating decay from STM is the Brown–Peterson distractor technique. In this procedure subjects are given material to remember, for example, a trial of three words, and then asked to recall the words 0, 9, 18, 30, or 60 seconds later. During the delay period, subjects complete an interpolated distraction task that is designed to prevent rehearsal of stimulus items. A typical distractor task involves having the subject count backwards in 3s from a randomly determined three-digit number. The slope of the line relating amount recalled to length of delay is an index of STM functioning. There is evidence (Table 9.9) that alcoholics do have deficits in STM relative to healthy controls. These deficits seem to lie in a position intermediate to the impairments of patients with Korsakoff syndrome and normal controls (Cermak & Ryback, 1976). Another measure of STM is the Digit Span subtest of the WAIS, which is typically normal in alcoholics (see Table 9.3). However, this measure tends to be relatively insensitive to STM deficits even in patients with Alzheimer's disease, who display marked STM impairments on other tests (Knight, 1992).

At the other end of the scale, remote memory tests may uncover evidence of retrograde amnesia in alcoholics, but only on subtests assessing knowledge of public events in the more recent decades. Remote memory tests are systematic measures of the subjects' general knowledge of events that have occurred over the period of their adult life. Each item should comprise a test of knowledge that is specific to one particular decade. "Who was Victor Richardson?" is an item that assesses knowledge of famous people from the decade of the 1930s. "Who was Christine Keeler?" is a

TABLE 9.9
Short-term Memory

Study	Task	Outcome
Brandt et al. (1983)	Peterson–Brown	A < C
Cermak & Ryback (1976)	Peterson–Brown	OA = KS at initial testing and 7 days later. YA > KS and OA > KS at 1 month
Mohs et al. (1978)	Memory scanning Digit span	A < C A = C
Ryan et al. (1980)	Peterson–Brown	A < C, 1.6 months' and 21.2 months' abstinence
Ryan & Butters (1980b)	Peterson–Brown	A < C regardless of age

A, alcoholic; C, control; KS, Korsakoff syndrome; OA, old alcoholic; OC, old control; YA, young alcoholic; YC, young control.

question that tests memory of a well-known person who came to prominence in the 1960s. Construction of a psychometrically sound test of remote memory is a complex undertaking, as items have to be chosen that are decade-specific, and subtests for each decade constructed that are of equivalent difficulty. Albert and colleagues have investigated remote memory in a variety of neurologically impaired patient groups using recall and recognition tests of famous people, events, and faces, Albert, Butters, and Brandt (1980) found that the only evidence of deficits in the remote memory of alcoholics occurred for the most difficult items and for the most recent decades. This may suggest that alcoholics, possibly because of their lifestyle, tend not to learn new information from TV or other media as their alcohol abuse becomes more severe. Alternatively, it may be an indication that one characteristic of cognitive decline in alcoholism is a gradual impairment in retrospective recall. This issue will be considered further in the next chapter.

Finally, Bowden (1988) found that if measures of new learning are sufficiently sensitive, impairments may be found even in carefully selected groups of young alcoholics. He tested a group of male alcoholics with an average age of 26.7 years and a drinking history of 4 years. This group was much younger and had a considerably shorter duration of problem drinking than the groups of alcoholics that are typically tested. He administered the Austin Maze test, which is a modified stylus maze procedure, with an array of 10 × 10 push-button switches. The subjects' task is to pick their way through this array pushing the correct sequence of switches. If the subject selects the correct switch, a green light comes on; red lights signal errors. Bowden found that the rate at which alcoholics learned the maze pathway over 10 trials was significantly slower than the controls. This occurred even though they performed normally on the digit-symbol paired-associate learning test, a measure particularly sensitive to impairments in alcoholics. Overall, these findings suggested that evidence of memory impairment is not confined to groups of alcoholics over the age of 40, and that deficits in learning and cognition may be observed at an early stage in the course of the disorder if sensitive measures of learning are employed.

Conclusions

We are now in a position to confirm the conclusion advanced by others (Kleinknecht & Goldstein, 1972; Parsons, 1987) who have reviewed this research: Alcoholics do show observable deficits in cognition. Deficits are not found universally in groups of alcoholics and there are many inconsistencies. The problems in resolving such discrepancies are significant. Differences in test sensitivity and subject selection (Parsons & Farr, 1981) make for confounds across studies that are not readily disentangled. In this initial section we have focused on intellectual, memory, and HRB impairments. Many other tasks have been used with samples of alcoholics and we will encounter these as we look at research dedicated to defining the underlying pattern of neuropsychological deficits more precisely. None of this research alters our conclusion that prolonged alcohol abuse causes measurable deficits in cognition.

In the studies that we have reviewed so far, it must be acknowledged that there is little of exceptional interest in the neuropsychological performance of chronic alcoholics. On tests that are usually sensitive to impairments of various kinds, including those resulting from organic brain damage, alcoholics tend to show mild to moderate impairments. Thus, on the WAIS, for example, impairments are seen on the same Performance Scale subtests as reveal deficits in other groups. Collating results from the HRB provides a similar picture. On memory tests, the more sensitive a measure is, the more likely it is that alcoholic groups will show a decline relative to matched normal controls. On average, it is apparent that severity of deficit is greatest in older samples, although some signs of dysfunction can be detected even in the youngest samples. This initial review of the literature does not encourage the view that there is a form of cognitive impairment specific to alcoholism; the results of alcohol abuse seem generalised and diffuse. We will examine challenges to this viewpoint later in this chapter.

One additional factor that may contribute to the cognitive dysfunction apparent on neuropsychological tests is motivation. It is possible that as a consequence of brain impairment, or the concurrent psychological manifestations of the disorder, alcoholics do try as hard in testing situations as unimpaired controls. Some evidence for this comes from Cynn (1992). She found that a group of young male alcoholics, despite showing no deficits on the WCST, persisted in their problem-solving deficits for significantly shorter periods than the controls. A failure in persistence may underlie some intellectual deficits seen in alcoholics.

There is also evidence that alcoholics themselves perceive that there have been changes in their cognitive functioning (Parsons, 1987; Shelton & Parsons, 1987). In a study described by Parsons (1987), a group of 99 alcoholics were administered the Neuropsychological Impairment Scale (NIS; O'Donnell & Reynolds, 1983). This self-report measure, with 50 items that describe a range of neurological symptoms, instructs subjects to rate the severity of each impairment on a four-point scale. On seven of the subscales of the NIS, including the Global Measure of Impairment index, alcoholics reported more symptoms than the normative sample. When a regression analysis was conducted in which measures of anxiety, depression, age, chronicity, and drinking practices were used as predictors of the NIS scores, there was some evidence that chronicity and consumption rate were related to ratings of impairment. Depression and anxiety scores, however, were most strongly predictive. Parsons (1987, p. 162) concluded:

> In summary, sober alcoholics do claim impairment of behaviours that are important to adapting to everyday life demands. The perceived lessened effectiveness in memory, cognitive/intellectual, language and communication and perceptual-motor behaviour is related to drinking behaviour; the higher the amount consumed, the greater the perceived impairment ... However, our data also suggest a caution to clinicians and researchers. The reported impairments ... were associated with the affective variables of depression and anxiety. In most analyses, these variables accounted for more variance than the drinking variables.

Further work on the relationship between symptom appraisal and actual performance on neuropsychological tests, using ratings from both relatives and patients, and treatment outcome would be of considerable interest.

RECOVERY

In this section, we examine the relationship between deficit and length of abstinence. The aim is to establish whether there is evidence from neuropsychological testing that the brain recovers its ability to perform cognitive operations once the alcoholic stops drinking. In earlier chapters neurophysiological studies of brain changes following abstinence have been considered. There is some evidence (see Chapter 4) that indices of atrophy measured on CT scans show improvement over a period of months following initial abstinence. Many neuropsychological investigations since the 1980s have focused on determining whether these biological changes are accompanied by improvements in cognitive functioning.

Superficially, conducting a recovery study may seem to be no great challenge; merely a matter of testing a group of alcoholics at various times after they cease drinking. Conducting a valid recovery study, however, requires the researcher to overcome some formidable obstacles. Many such studies reported in the literature provide disappointingly inconclusive data because of the neglect of various methodological precautions. For studies focusing on time since abstinence and recovery of function, the use of independent groups is important. This is because the repeated measures used in longitudinal designs are likely to confuse time-dependent recovery with practice or "carryover" effects. Repeated administration of the same test has been found to produce significant improvements in alcoholics' performance (Forsberg & Goldman, 1987) attributable to experience with a particular test. As we will see, this is an important finding in its own right because it supports the prospect of cognitive rehabilitative interventions to enhance recovery; however, such experimental designs do not help answer questions about the extent of time-dependent recovery. Constituting independent and matched groups of alcoholics at different stages of their recovery, as required by a cross-sectional design, is often difficult to achieve. For a variety of reasons, subject attrition from inpatient therapy programmes is often high, meaning that a random sample of patients tested in the first few days after detoxication is likely to differ substantially in demographic characteristics from a group randomly selected from a treatment programme 30 days later. Usually it is necessary to undertake *post hoc* matching of groups for age, education, and chronicity of alcoholism, although the groups may still differ on more subtle personality or motivational variables. When testing patients after long periods of abstinence—in excess of 12 months—problems in matching groups become even more pronounced. There is also the related problem of guaranteeing that alcoholics have been abstinent over the recovery period. As inpatient treatment progresses and patients become eligible for leave privileges, the opportunities for a relapse or "slip" become greater. There is no guarantee that any abstinence violation will be known to the clinical staff or researchers. Another problem in the interpretation of findings from recovery studies is that frequently no normal control group data are presented. Thus, although the results may demonstrate that alcoholic patients recover their functioning, the extent to which their performance can be characterised as normal cannot be determined. Independent group studies of alcoholics with control groups provide our most valuable information on time-dependent recovery of function. Unfortunately there have been few such studies.

There is considerable evidence that on a variety of neuropsychological tests the performance of alcoholics is impaired in the first week of abstinence relative to their performance up to a month later (Claiborn & Greene, 1981; Eckardt et al., 1978b; Eckardt, Ryback, & Pautler, 1980; Hester, Smith, & Jackson, 1980; Kish, Hagen, Woody, & Harvey, 1980; Page & Linden, 1974; Page & Schaub, 1977). Taken together, these studies suggest that alcoholics are most likely to be impaired soon after they enter treatment and to improve over the succeeding weeks. This finding is not particularly surprising. The effects of withdrawal from alcohol on a variety of physiological systems is dramatic. Newly detoxicated alcoholics have EEG abnormalities that take time to stabilise, and a variety of biochemical imbalances that take some time to correct. Withdrawal of alcohol, as we have seen in Chapter 2, has a variety of clinical and physiological consequences that are likely to exert an effect on cognition.

The time-dependent course of recovery in alcoholics has been most carefully charted in a series of studies by Goldman and colleagues. In this research, they have employed a design that has allowed them to separate time-dependent changes from the effects of experience (Goldman, 1986; 1987). They did this by integrating an independent groups cross-sectional design with a repeated measures format. How this was achieved will be described in more detail when experience and time-dependent recovery are contrasted later in this section. The first demonstration of time-dependent recovery by Goldman and his colleagues (Sharp, Rosenbaum, Goldman, & Whitman, 1977), employed the synonym learning test. This is a measure of ability to acquire new semantic information; the subject learns the synonyms for 10 words that they have previously been unable to define. Sharp et al. (1977) compared the learning performance over 10 trials for three matched and independent alcoholic groups tested either 5, 15, or 25 days after drinking had ceased. They found that the 5-day group was significantly impaired on this test relative to the other three groups, but that the 15- and 25-day groups had scores comparable to the performance of the normal controls. They concluded that verbal learning reached normal levels after a period of abstinence of about 10 to 14 days.

In a second study, Ellenberg, Rosenbaum, Goldman, and Whitman (1980) used the Stark test, which assessed visual and verbal paired-associate learning in two subtests matched for difficulty level in a group of head injured patients. The same basic experimental design was used: Matched groups of alcoholics were tested 5, 15, or 25 days after abstinence commenced. The results of this study confirmed their previous findings. Somewhere between 5 and 15 days, on both the verbal and visuospatial tasks, the alcoholics' performance returned to normal. One initial difficulty in the interpretation of the results of this study was to lead to a further refinement of their conclusions in subsequent studies. They found that the alcoholics that had been first tested at day 25 performed at an impaired level on the Stark visuospatial subtest, relative to the performance of both the control group and the 15-day alcoholics. This anomaly was resolved when results for older and younger groups were analysed separately. The 25-day group proved to contain more alcoholics over the age of 40, and the older alcoholics showed a pattern of consistent impairment on the visuospatial subtest at all three testing times.

This issue of age was explored further in a study using a repeated measures design (Goldman, Williams, & Klisz, 1983). They tested 31 alcoholics at weekly intervals over a 3-month period using a battery of tests previously shown to be sensitive to cognitive dysfunctions in alcoholics. Their alcoholic group was divided into three age groups (20–29, 30–39, and 40+ years). The effects of practice were assessed by the comparable repeated testing of normal subjects. Their results established the importance of age in the persistence of deficit. Alcoholics below the age of 40 showed no functional impairment after 2 to 3 weeks of abstinence; older alcoholics, however, showed performance decrements up to 3 months postabstinence on the TMT, the Digit Symbol subtest of the WAIS, and the grooved pegboard test. The sustained impairments seen on the neuropsychological tests were predicted solely by age; they were not related either to consumption or chronicity variables.

On the basis of these and other studies, Goldman (1987) was able to come to a number of conclusions about recovery during the first 6 months of abstinence from alcohol. It was apparent that verbal abilities of the kind assessed by vocabulary tests or the WAIS Verbal scale subtests were largely unimpaired, even early after detoxication. In contrast, on most other tasks, particularly those involving new learning or problem-solving, impairment could be found in the first 10 days or so of abstinence. Tasks using novel stimuli or requiring adaptation to new situations, or tests requiring complex skills particularly sensitive to any form of CNS decrement, were most likely to be impaired and to provide evidence of persistent deficit. Age also played an important part. Alcoholics over the age of 40 were more likely than younger patients to show signs of sustained loss. Goldman et al. (1983) suggested that these findings may indicate that the CNS becomes more vulnerable to the toxic effects of alcohol as it ages, a variant of the premature aging hypothesis that will be examined more closely later in this chapter. Goldman's studies provided information up to 6 months after abstinence; little is known about recovery beyond that time, apart from the study by Brandt et al. (1983), which showed that after 3 to 5 years of abstinence, the STM performance of alcoholics reaches normal levels.

Having shown that, as time passes, alcoholics may recover, Goldman and his fellow workers returned to explore the significance of some of the other findings in their earlier studies. The results of the initial testing at each of the three time intervals in the study by Ellenberg et al. (1980) have been already considered. However, in this study, subjects were also retested after the initial testing on some of the same measures. Ellenberg et al. observed that there was a marked practice effect; experience with the test improved alcoholics performance noticeably. Forsberg and Goldman (1985) examined this effect further. They recognised that this recovery effect, mediated simply by practice, might provide the basis for a strategy for the rehabilitation of neuropsychological deficits, and that enriching the environment of alcoholics by having them work on cognitive tasks could have beneficial effects for the process of recovery of functioning. First, however, it was necessary to establish the validity of the experience-dependent effect they had observed.

Forsberg and Goldman (1985) constituted two matched groups of 15 alcoholic men over the age of 40, assuming that these older subjects were most likely to show long-term residual deficits on a visuospatial memory test. They administered the verbal and visuospatial subtests of the Stark test beginning on day 4 for one group and day 16 for the other. Testing was then repeated, for each group, four times. This mixed longitudinal–cross-sectional design allowed the separate analysis of time-and-experience-dependent effects. In addition, at the final testing session, a matched alternate form of the two Stark subtests was given to allow the estimate of transfer of training effects. In this way, the specific improvements resulting from exposure to the same stimuli four times, could be separated from non-specific and generalised improvement in learning skills. The results of the repeated administration of Stark visuospatial stimuli are illustrated in Fig. 9.1. Note that there are no time-dependent differences in performance at days 4 and 16; there are, however, marked improvements in performance with practice. At each of

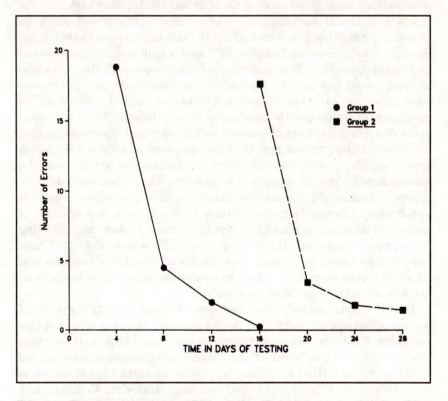

FIG. 9.1. Experience-dependent effects of visuospatial learning in alcoholics. From experience-dependent recovery of visuospatial functioning in older alcoholic persons by Forsberg, L.K., and Goldman, M.S. *Journal of Abnormal Psychology,* (1985). Copyright © 1985, American Psychological Association. Reprinted with permission.

the three testing sessions after the initial trail, the number of errors had decreased to normal levels. When the performance of the alcoholics on the transfer task was compared to the performance of a group of controls who had performed the task just the one time, it was apparent that the alcoholics' performance was in the normal range. Thus the experience of completing the Stark test four times generalised from one set of stimuli to another. The experience-dependent effect was not simply a consequence of becoming increasingly familiar with a constant set of specific stimuli.

Forsberg and Goldman (1987) replicated these findings in another carefully constructed study. This time they employed a battery of transfer tasks and both an alcoholic and a normal control group to assess baseline performance on the transfer task. The experimental design is somewhat complex and is best illustrated schematically (Table 9.10). Two groups of alcoholics were tested four times, with the transfer task battery being administered on a fifth occasion. Once again, the training task was the Stark visuospatial learning test. Generalisation was tested using an alternate form of the Stark task, the TMT, the Digit Symbol subtest, the Benton Visual Retention Test, the TPT, and a task testing judgement of line orientation. They hypothesised that experience with the Stark test training would improve the alcoholics' performance on all the transfer tests, except the TPT, which does not involve visuospatial processing. The results for the training on the Stark subtest were the same as are portrayed in Fig. 9.1. On the battery of transfer tasks, the two alcoholic groups that had received Stark training performed at an equivalent level. A MANOVA comparing the performance of these two remediated groups and the unremediated alcoholic group was significant. The remediated alcoholic groups outperformed the unremediated alcoholic group and were not significantly different from the controls. In short, there was evidence of transfer of training from the Stark test experience to other tests involving visuospatial processing. However, on the TPT, a spatial–tactual task requiring no visual processing, no evidence of transfer of training was found. The authors concluded that generalisation effects may be confined to transfer tasks using the same modality.

Thus Goldman and colleagues had demonstrated not only the power of practice effects on the performance of a repeated test, but also that this generalised both to other instances of the same task and to other visuospatial tests. The "training" strategy consisted simply of unstructured practice. In two further investigations, Goldman turned his attention to the usefulness of more structured training strategies. Goldman and Goldman (1988) used Part B of the TMT as their learning task and recruited two groups of alcoholics, one of which received remediation, the other did not. The training strategy involved practising the components of the TMT task—visual search, rapid alternation between letters and digits,

TABLE 9.10

Research Design for Establishing Transfer of Experience-Dependent Recovery (Forsberg & Goldman, 1987)

Group	No. of days following drinking														
	2	4	6	8	10	12	14	16	18	20	22	24	26	28	30
Alcoholic 1	01		02		03		04 T								
Alcoholic 2								01		02		03		04 T	
Alcoholic 3						T									T
Controls					T										T

01, 02, 03, and 04 refer to the first, second, third and fourth administrations, respectively, of the original Stark visuospatial training task; T refers to the six training tasks.

Non-alcoholic controls were tested once without reference to drinking cessation.

From Forsberg and Goldman (1987), reprinted with permission.

247

and the integration of the skills. They found that this cognitive intervention improved alcoholic performance to normal levels. Using a similar training strategy, applied to the WAIS Block Design subtest, Stringer and Goldman (1988) showed that the component remediation strategy worked; however, it was no better than unstructured practice.

In summary, research on the recovery of cognitive function in abstinent alcoholics has shown that alcoholics are most impaired during the first week after they stop drinking and that thereafter their functioning may return to normal. There are exceptions to this; on complex learning tasks, alcoholics over the age of 40 may not show time-dependent recovery during the first 6 months of abstinence. What is of interest, however, is that they do show improvement to normal levels as a result of repeated experience with a particular measure. What is more, Goldman and his colleagues have shown that this improvement in cognitive skill generalises to performance on other tasks in the same modality. These results offer specific encouragement for the use of cognitive retraining and rehearsal strategies with alcoholics during the recovery phase. Many therapeutic processes depend on understanding and acquiring complex treatment information. If there is a link between treatment failure and neuropsychologial deficit, a possibility we will consider in a later chapter, then demonstrations of experience-dependent learning in alcoholics offer the possibility that some of these deficits may be ameliorated.

PREDICTING NEUROPSYCHOLOGICAL IMPAIRMENTS

In the preceding sections of this chapter, evidence for a range of neuropsychological deficits in alcoholics has been detailed. It will be apparent from this review, however, that not all alcoholics display impairments on cognitive tests. In this section we will consider studies that have investigated factors that might help explain these individual differences in the incidence of neuropsychological damage.

The search for predictors of cognitive impairments in alcoholics is of interest because of the potential to find clues as to why alcoholics perform more poorly on neuropsychological tests in general. Failure on neuropsychological tests is generally assumed to be the endpoint of a process of systematic deterioration in the biological integrity of the brain caused by the neurotoxic effects of alcohol, as we have seen in Part 2. These CNS effects are compounded by the effects of liver disease, a greater incidence of cardiomyopathy, and disruption to endocrine functioning. If this is the case, one would expect an association between duration of alcoholism and biological damage on the one hand, and neuropsychological dysfunction on the other.

There are, however, other possible explanations of the cognitive deficits seen in alcoholics. Their poor cognitive skills may have predated their history of alcoholism. Although the evidence for genetic transmission is equivocal, it is apparent that the children of alcoholics are at an abnormally high risk of becoming alcoholics themselves. Being raised in a family where one or both parents are alcoholics may create disruptive effects resulting in poor educational achievement, disruption of learning, antisocial behaviour, or poor nutrition. Alcoholic mothers may pass on a subclinical fetal alcohol syndrome to their children. All these factors suggest that the children of alcoholics may be at a risk for developing alcoholism and may have a reduced capacity for cognitive skills, compared with children who have no such family history. Thus, the cognitive deficits seen in group comparison studies may be the product of pre-existing cognitive deficits in alcoholics with a positive family history of alcoholism. Another possibility is that the cognitive impairments are a result of the higher risk of neurological damage, independent of the neurotoxic effects of alcohol, amongst alcohol abusers. For example, as we have seen in Part 2 of this book, problem drinkers are more likely to be involved in motor vehicle accidents, fights, and falls. They may also be more prone to depression, which may serve to reduce their test performance levels. Neuropsychological impairments in alcoholics may therefore be the results of being at a higher risk of sustaining medical problems that affect cognition.

Another reason for examining predictors of impairment is that they may help explain inconsistencies in results between studies. One of the problems in comparing studies of cognitive deficit is the differences in the characteristics of samples of alcoholics. In some studies, subjects with neurological damage independent of alcohol effects are excluded; in others they are not. Samples differ in average age, education, and alcoholism history. All these factors help explain why the presence and severity of neuropsychological dysfunction can vary from one study to the next. Studies of predictors help to determine which factors are important and must be specified or controlled for, and which are not.

Age, duration, and consumption

One factor that is generally held to be of some significance in predicting neuropsychological damage is age. Alcoholics over the age of 40 are more likely to reveal cognitive deficits than those who are younger (Ellenberg et al., 1980; Goldman et al., 1983; Hesselbrock, Weidenman, & Reed, 1985; Tarter & Alterman, 1984; Tarter & Edwards, 1986; Tarter et al., 1986) and this is independent of duration of alcohol consumption. Although studies using sensitive measures have reported deficits in younger samples

(Bowden, 1988), an association between age and degree of alcoholic deterioration has commonly been observed. This has been recognised in the way the effects of alcoholism have been described in terms of premature ageing.

The relationship between length of alcoholism and neuropsychological test performance, in contrast, is more difficult to characterise. Sometimes an association between duration and deficit is found, sometimes not, and reconciling inconsistencies is difficult. In some cases, results from the same laboratory have not been consistent. Parsons (1987) outlines how duration of alcoholism was initially found to be related to HRB and WCST scores (Jones & Parsons, 1971; Tarter & Parsons, 1971), but was subsequently found to be unrelated to concept identification (Klisz & Parsons, 1977), WCST performance (Klisz & Parsons, 1979), and tests from the HRB (Fabian, Parsons, & Silberstein, 1981). Svanum and Schladenhauffen (1986) found duration was associated with HRB impairments; Tarter and Schneider (1976) found that duration did not predict Memory Quotient scores on the WMS. These inconsistencies are likely to be in part the result of the problems implicit in measuring a variable such as duration, which relies on the accuracy of the retrospective recall of patients known to have cognitive impairments. There are also variations in how alcohol abuse is defined and in the criteria for such variables as length of heavy drinking or alcohol abuse.

Another option is to look more closely at consumption variables; these are often more discriminating, easier to define, and more likely to be recalled accurately. Eckardt et al. (1979) found that recent drinking behaviour was correlated with cognitive deficits in the first week following abstinence. However, these impairments may have been primarily the result of withdrawal effects, likely to be closely related to heaviness of consumption, and therefore not applicable when alcoholics have had longer periods of abstinence. Adams and Grant (1984; 1986) used a number of consumption variables, including number of years ethanol consumption exceeded 560g/week, consumption in the heaviest drinking year, consumption in the year preceding testing, and lifetime consumption. Using both curvilinear and linear regression models, no evidence of a significant relationship between HRB scores and consumption variables was found for subjects tested after 3 weeks' or 18 months' abstinence.

In a study completed in his laboratory, described by Parsons (1987), multiple regression procedures were used to assess the effects of several consumption variables on clusters of cognitive test scores. Results from the neuropsychological tests were divided into clusters of verbal, learning/memory, abstraction/problem-solving, perceptual-motor skills, and general impairment. The best predictive measure of drinking practices was the product of the maximum quantity per session and frequency of sessions (MQF). Other predictor variables entered into the regression analyses were years education, age, chronicity, and state anxiety and depression scores, with each of the five clusters of cognitive variables serving as the criterion in turn. For the alcoholic group, MQF was a significant predictor in four of the five analyses (all except perceptual-motor) and education in all five. Age was significant in three cases, but chronicity in only one. Anxiety and depression did not emerge as significant at all. These findings suggest that the usual precaution of matching alcoholic groups for education level is important, and that both age and excessive levels of alcohol consumption play a significant part in determining severity of neuropsychological impairments.

Family history

The children of alcoholics are at a higher than average risk of becoming alcohol abusers themselves, although whether this is indicative of a genetic basis for alcoholism is unclear (Searles, 1988). In a number of studies the cognitive abilities of children with alcoholic parents have been contrasted with those of children who have no family history of alcoholism. This has been undertaken either by testing the children of alcoholics before they reach adulthood, or by dividing groups of adult alcoholics into those with or without a family background of alcoholism (Pihl, Peterson, & Finn, 1990). Evidence of reduced cognitive skills in the children of alcoholics tends to be inconsistent and difficult to interpret. Children of alcoholics have been consistently found to be more likely to be conduct disordered, hyperactive, or to have difficulties maintaining attention (Knop, Teasdale, Schulsinger, & Goodwin, 1985; Sher & Alterman, 1988; Schulsinger et al., 1986). This may be the result of genetic or congenital abnormalities, or it may be attributable to the disruptive family and school life of children who have an alcoholic parent. Whatever the reason, Pihl et al. (1990, p. 292) observed that the sons of male alcoholics "appear impaired in their ability to concentrate, to pay attention, and to control their motor behaviour sufficiently when required to, at least in structured situations, and they appear comparatively quick to resort to aggression in social situations ...".

In a study of 34 university students by Alterman, Bridges, and Tarter (1986), sons of male alcoholics were found to perform more poorly than matched controls on the Embedded Figure Test, but not on measures of maze solution, paired-associated learning, or mirror tracing. Hegedus, Alterman, and Tarter (1984) tested 41 white male delinquents with a mean age of 16 years, 16 of whom had a father who was alcoholic and 25 who did not. On measures of intelligence there was no difference between these groups; however, on a standardised measure of educational achievement—

the Peabody Individual Achievement Test—the alcoholics' sons performed more poorly on the Reading Comprehension and General Information subtests. No correlations were found between test performance and ratings of either family environment or level of behavioural disturbance. The authors concluded that the impairments in educational achievement reflected a vulnerability to alcoholism. Perhaps the strongest evidence for a relationship between a positive family history (FH+) and neuropsychological deficits in non-alcoholic subjects comes from a Danish longitudinal study of a large cohort of children followed from birth. Gabrielli and Mednick (1983) found that, at age 12, children who had either parent diagnosed as alcoholic had lower WISC verbal scores than matched controls, although their Performance IQs tended to be equivalent. At age 19 years, Drejer et al. (1985) compared 134 FH+ subjects from this sample with 70 low risk controls on 12 neuropsychological tests and found an overall significant difference between the groups. Univariate tests revealed that the FH+ subjects made more WAIS vocabulary and Category Test errors than those with a negative family history (FH–). There were no group differences on measures of paired associate learning, maze solution, word fluency, detection of embedded figures, picture recall, and digit span.

Tarter, Jacob, and Bremer (1989a,b) recruited alcoholic, normal, and depressed men through newspaper advertisements and selected from the families who responded, those who had a son aged between 8 and 17. The sons of alcoholics tended to be younger and in lower grades than the normal parents' sons, and accordingly covariance procedures were used in subsequent analyses to match the groups. The authors administered a variety of neuropsychological tests and computed some 37 one-way analyses of covariance, eight of which were significant, two at the 0.01 alpha level. Differences were found on measures of maze learning and planning and sequential analysis; however, the large number of unprotected group comparisons weakens the conclusions from this study. Better evidence comes from Whipple, Parker, and Noble (1988) who compared three groups of subjects: sons at a high risk of alcoholism (father alcoholic), sons with a non-alcoholic father, but a positive family history of alcoholism, and sons with a low risk history. The average age of the children was about 10. The high-risk sons had significantly poorer WISC-R PIQ scores, and also scored more poorly on the Rey AVLT and Embedded Figures Test. Differences were also found on neurophysiological measures of event-related potentials. Finally, Workman-Daniels and Hesselbrock (1987) compared two groups of 21 FH+ and FH– non-alcoholic subjects and found no significant differences on the WMS, HRB, and WAIS subtests.

Studies of the neuropsychological functioning of children with a positive family history of alcoholism are have generally provided inconsistent results. As Bates and Pandina (1992) observed, even reviewers of the available literature have been unable to agree on the trends in the research findings. For example, Searles (1988) concluded that there was no evidence for neurocognitive deficits in FH+ subjects, whereas Pihl et al. (1990) drew attention to substantial deficits on tests of verbal and abstract reasoning. Bates and Pandina (1992, p. 321) noted that "Disparate results have also obtained when virtually the same instruments and assessment procedures have been used with comparable samples". In an attempt to resolve these inconsistencies, Bates and Pandina tested 353 female and 324 male subjects, who were classified either as FH– or had varying degrees of positive family history for alcoholism, with the SILS, WAIS subtests, the TMT, and the Spatial Relations test from Thurstone's Primary Mental Abilities Test. In this large-scale investigation, family history was not associated with test scores; there were not even the predicted, but non-significant, trends in the results. These negative findings are consistent with results from several recent studies (Alterman & Hall, 1989; Gillen & Hesselbrock, 1992; Turner & Parsons, 1988). Gillen and Hesselbrock (1992) tested FH+ and FH– subjects on measures of motor co-ordination, the TMT, the CVLT, and the WMS. No significant differences emerged. However, they did find that differences in cognitive and motor performance emerged when their sample was divided into subjects with or without behavioural problems, consistent with a diagnosis of antisocial peronality disorder. Interactions between Personality Disorder and Family History were not significant. These results raise the possibility that the differences between FH+ and FH– groups may be a consequence of the over-representation of personality-disordered subjects in the FH+ samples.

The results have also been inconsistent when groups of alcoholics have been divided into those with a positive or negative family history, and compared on measures of neuropsychological performance. Alterman, Gerstley, Goldstein, and Tarter (1987) divided 81 alcoholics into FH+ or FH– groups using two different strategies: (1) conventional (no alcoholic relative, one or both parents alcoholic, other relatives alcoholic); and (2) unilineal–bilineal groupings. There were no significant differences on a range of neuropsychological tests, including the Category Test, paired-associate learning, Block Design, and the Porteus mazes. Similar negative findings come from a study by Reed, Grant, and Adams (1987), who divided 84 alcoholic males into four groups: (1) strong family history (parent plus another first degree relative alcoholic); (2) moderate family history (parent only); (3) weak family history (first degree relative only); and (4) no family history. No differences emerged on the WAIS Vocabulary and Digit Symbol subtests, the Category Test, the TPT and Rhythm test of the HRB, and subtests of the WMS. Reed et al. concluded that no influence of family history on cognition could be discerned where groups were matched carefully for education, drinking history, and medical risk.

Support for the importance of family history in determining deficits in alcoholics comes from Schaeffer, Parsons, and Errico (1988), who tested 130 subjects with an average age of 40 on tests assessing verbal skills, learning and memory, abstracting and problem-solving, and perceptual-motor skills. Sixty-eight of the subjects were alcoholic, 41 of whom were FH+ (parent, brother, or sister alcoholic), and 27 FH–. The normal group was also divided into those with FH+ or FH– backgrounds. Analyses showed that the alcoholics performed more poorly than the non-alcoholics, and that FH+ subjects were superior to FH–; however, there was no Family History × Alcoholism interaction. This suggests that family history was an important determinant of test scores for both the alcoholic and non-alcoholic subjects. The authors concluded (Schaeffer et al., 1988, p. 347) that alcoholism and family history may have independent and additive effects on cognitive and perceptual performance and that "future neuropsychological studies of alcoholism should consider the frequency of FH+ and FH– individuals in both alcoholic and control groups". Associations between positive family history and cognitive deficits have also been reported in groups of women alcoholics by Turner and Parsons (1988) and Wilson and Nagoshi (1988). On a cluster of non-verbal abstracting/problem-solving tests, Turner and Parsons (1988) found that alcoholic women performed more poorly than normal controls or FH– alcoholics. On the verbal tests FH+ and FH– alcoholics performed at equivalent levels, and more poorly than controls. Family history variables were not associated with test performance in the control group.

Once again, all that can be readily concluded from these studies is that results are inconsistent and difficult to reconcile. In a recent study of predictors of impairment, Schaeffer et al. (1991) found no evidence that family history predicted the performance of alcoholics on a brief battery of neuropsychological tests. They observed (Schaeffer et al., 1991, p. 659) that "… the failure of some studies, including the present one, to note significant differences between FH+ and FH– male alcoholics on cognitive tasks is puzzling and seemingly impervious to any simple explanation". It is difficult to disagree. In studies of alcoholics, family history has not emerged as a predictor of cognitive capacity. It may well be that differences apparent in persons who have a positive family history may be disguised by the later onset of heavy drinking. The neurotoxic effects of alcohol may be so potent as to wash out individual differences in neuropsychological test performance resulting from a family background of alcoholism.

Medical factors

Several lines of research have investigated the possibility that the degree of neurological damage as reflected in the biological and physical damage associated with alcoholism may predict degree of impairment. Tarter et al.

(1983) found that the occurrence of seizures during withdrawal was not associated with performance by alcoholics on the WAIS and HRB. Similarly, Tarter and Schneider (1976) found that male alcoholic inpatients with a high incidence of memory blackouts could not be distinguished from those with a low incidence on the WMS and another learning test. Franceshi et al. (1984) found no correlation between degree of liver damage and scores on Raven's Progressive Matrices. However, this negative finding has been countered by positive results from two recent studies. Tarter et al. (1986) looked at the association between neuropsychological test performance and integrity of liver functioning in 15 alcoholic patients who had undergone sliver biopsy for medical reasons. Some positive associations between test scores and indices of liver damage were reported. Schaeffer et al. (1991) found that liver function results predicted performance on neuropsychological tests at the time of admission, but not at discharge 4 weeks later or at the 3-month follow-up testing. These results suggest that liver functioning may be a significant indicator of alcoholism severity, and may be associated with degree of cognitive impairment in the earliest stages of abstinence.

Adams and Grant (1986) outlined a cluster of possible complications that might explain dysfunctional cognition in alcoholics as being a consequence of increased exposure to medical risks. These included neonatal developmental indicators, childhood illness, learning disability, head injury, toxicity risk (incidence of alcohol or drug-related blackouts, unconsciousness, withdrawal), occurrence of neurological symptoms (such as epilepsy), events such as necessity for cardiopulmonary resuscitation, or administration of general anaesthetics and concurrent illnesses (hypertension, liver disease, anaemia). They constituted two risk groups, one comprising subjects who endorsed one or more of the items of the medical risk questionnaire, the other endorsing no risk items. These alcoholic subjects were further divided into groups on the basis of age (above and below 40) and length of abstinence. Significant age effects emerged on the HRB, the Russell revision of the WMS, and the WAIS. There were, however, no group effects due to medical risk and only a non-significant trend for recently detoxified alcoholics to score more poorly than the controls and long-term abstinent alcoholics. There was, however, a Group × Medical Risks interaction, which was interpreted as indicating that recently detoxified alcoholics with a positive medical risk history performed neuropsychological tests more poorly than those with no such risk. Overall, this study suggests that medical complications play a relatively small part in determining deficits. Unfortunately, it was not possible to distinguish premorbid medical factors and complications resulting from alcoholism in the group comparisons.

Other factors

Several other variables have been proposed as predictors of neuropsychological dysfunction in alcoholics. One possible explanation for their poor performance is the presence of depression. Here again findings are mixed. Clark et al. (1984) found that depressive severity as measured by the BDI was not significantly associated with cognitive impairment on the Benton Visual Retention Test, SILS, and TMT. Schaeffer et al. (1991) found that depression ratings predicted test performance at admission and at the 3-month follow-up, but not after 1 months' abstinence. Depression levels may be an important predictor of performance, but only at certain stages in the intoxication–abstinence process. Affective changes presumably operate on test performance by inhibiting a person's motivation to succeed. Possible motivational factors were examined more closely by Sander, Nixon, and Parsons (1989), who looked at the relationship between pretest expectations of performance, actual performance, and post-test ratings of achievement, on a battery of tests assessing learning/memory, abstraction/problem-solving, and perceptual-motor performance. Although alcoholics performed more poorly than controls, and rated themselves less positively, there was no significant correlation between expectancies and actual performance.

Malloy et al. (1989) assessed 182 alcoholics and computed a BAQ score using subtests of the WAIS and HRB. They also administered the Russell version of the WMS. Their subjects were divided into two groups on the basis of their BAQ scores. Those alcoholics who had the higher BAQ impairment scores, were more likely to have features of an antisocial personality disorder, and were both older and had abused alcohol longer. Presence of personality disorder was, however, the strongest predictor of impairment and was independent of other factors. Thus, those alcoholics who tended to be characterised as being uninhibited, displaying maladaptive behaviours, and unconcerned with social consequences, showed greater evidence of cognitive impairment.

Conclusions

There is disappointingly little in the way of consistency in results from studies that have examined the correlation between factors differentiating individual alcoholics and neuropsychological performance. The literature is difficult to synthesise and hard to interpret meaningfully. In large part, this is attributable to variations in methodology and idiosyncratic choices in the measurement of particular variables. As a result, this research has not served to advance our understanding of the aetiology of alcoholism to any great degree. There are a number of provocative findings, but these are overwhelmed by a profusion of irreconcilable inconsistencies.

However, at least findings from these studies alert researchers to variables likely to be important in the constitution of subject samples. In this regard at least three variables are of unequivocal significance: (1) age; (2) premorbid educational achievement/premorbid IQ; and (3) length of abstinence. Younger and better-educated individuals and alcoholics who have been abstinent for several weeks perform better than those who have been recently detoxicated, have fewer years of schooling, and are over the age of 40 to 50 years. Drinking practices and quantities consumed may be important predictors, especially in the early stages of abstinence. The various consumption measures used appear to vary in sensitivity; measurement of frequency and quantity of recent drinking may provide the most sensitive index. Chronicity of heavy drinking or alcoholism has been employed as a predictor with mixed success. Variations in the definition of such terms as "heavy drinking" may have contributed to this. Family history of alcoholism has often been selected as a variable of interest. There is good evidence that the sons of male alcoholics show more disturbed personal behaviour and family background than sons of non-alcoholic parents. There are also inconsistent findings suggesting that these social deficits are accompanied by poorer educational and cognitive test performance. Alcoholics with a positive family history of alcoholism have also been found to perform more poorly than controls in some studies, but not all. It is possible that pre-existing deficits tend to be diminished by the acute and chronic effects of alcohol abuse, particularly in older and more impaired alcoholic samples.

There is no consistent evidence that signs of medical or neurological damage, associated with or independent of alcohol abuse, are predictive of cognitive deficit, although liver damage has been identified as possibly significant. Incidence of blackouts or seizures and other evidence of the toxic effect of alcoholism have not been shown to be predictive. There is little to suggest that independent premorbid or alcohol-related medical risk factors contribute to prediction of neuropsychology deficit. Finally, in a significant study, Schaeffer et al. (1991) have demonstrated that predictive factors may not be consistently useful at all phases of the recovery period. They found that age and WAIS vocabulary (used as an index of premorbid IQ) were related to test performance at admission, discharge, and follow-up, but that depression and liver damage had effects at different stages.

PATTERNS OF IMPAIRMENT

In this chapter we have seen that alcoholics display cognitive decrements that may persist in some individuals. Thus far, however, no attempt has been made to consider whether these neuropsychological deficits reflect any underlying pattern of systematic changes in brain functioning. For example, is it possible that some regions of the brain are more vulnerable to the effects of alcohol than others? Do changes in the CNS caused by alcohol abuse follow some predetermined sequence of deterioration? Two attempts to explain the deficits of alcoholics have focused on the proposed especial vulnerability of the right hemisphere to the effects of alcohol, and the related view that alcohol-induced impairments are an instance of premature ageing.

Right hemisphere hypothesis

The right hemisphere (RH) hypothesis (Bertera & Parsons, 1978; Miglioli, Butchtel, Campanini, & DeRisio, 1979) proposes that alcohol causes neurodegenerative or electrophysiological changes that are more pronounced on the right side of the brain. As a consequence, the pattern of neuropsychological deficits in alcoholics will be similar to those seen in brain damaged patients with predominantly right-sided lesions. A weaker version of the RH hypothesis posits that RH functioning is more susceptible to the effects of alcohol abuse than the left (Ellis & Oscar-Berman, 1989). Here the physiological signs of damage may be comparable in the two hemispheres, but the physiological processes mediated by the right hemisphere are more vulnerable to disruption than left hemisphere (LH) processes. Regardless of the form of the hypothesis, the underlying proposition is that tasks that measure RH functions are more likely to be impaired than those that measure LH functions, relative to normal controls. Evidence for the RH hypothesis comes primarily from measures of cognitive function in alcoholics. The results from the brain imaging, neuropathological, and neurophysiological studies reviewed in Part 2 provide no basis for expecting pathological asymmetries.

It should be noted at the outset that there are immense technical problems implicit in demonstrating that one hemisphere is impaired relative to the other. These include devising tasks that actually tap functions resident in one and not both hemispheres. The brain normally functions as a whole, and hemispheric specialisation for complex and higher order cognitive tasks is difficult to determine. Similarly, although it is possible to construct tasks that require semantic or verbal encoding, it is difficult to construct non-verbal (putative RH) stimuli that cannot be encoded semantically. For example, a geometric design can be regarded as a non-verbal stimulus, but the elements of the stimulus may still be encoded verbally, as "a square within a circle", for example. Furthermore, even if tasks are devised that are specific to the left or right hemispheres, any comparison of performance requires that the tasks be matched for discriminatory power. That is, the psychometric characteristics of the two contrasting tasks must be equivalent, in particular with respect to test reliability and difficulty levels. Meeting these requirements is seldom easy. In addition, as was detailed in Chapter 2, Chapman and Chapman (1988) have drawn attention to the fact that differences in absolute performances between two groups on any two tasks constrain the size of any index measuring the difference between the tasks. This has particular implications for laterality studies, where the two contrasted groups need to produce equivalent averages on the right and left hemisphere tests in the middle range of such scores. Needless to say, these requirements are seldom met, and constructing studies that produce unequivocal findings is a considerable challenge (Chapman & Chapman, 1988).

In the study of alcoholics, the RH hypothesis has typically been proposed as a postexperimental explanation for the pattern of findings on particular tests. Such studies are seldom able to exclude the possibility that the pattern of results is anything other than an artefact of the psychometric characteristics of the tests administered. Only recently have studies that test for specific RH deficits in a methodologically acceptable manner been designed. The results of earlier studies (reviewed earlier in the chapter) have often been cited as evidence of a RH deficit. For example, alcoholics show their greatest impairments on those subtests of the WAIS (Block Design, Digit Symbol, Picture Arrangement) that are often assumed by clinicians to involve RH visuospatial processing. However, these WAIS subtests are those that nearly every pathological group has difficulty with, regardless of the putative basis of the lesions causing the disorder. As had already been demonstrated, patients with a multifocal disorders like multiple sclerosis produce the same pattern of subtest results as do alcoholics. Payne (1960) presented results from a variety of groups from the forerunner of the WAIS, the Wechsler–Bellevue, that show the mean Digit Symbol performance of schizophrenics (a disorder often assumed to involve a LH deficit) as 7.07, versus the 9.2 of normal controls. Similarly, neurotic patients averaged 6 on the Digit Symbol as opposed to the 8.1 scored by their matched controls. It is likely that the pattern of deficits shown by alcoholics reflects nothing more than the differential difficulty level of the individual subtests to impairment, determined primarily by their content. In particular, the fact that the Performance subtests typically employ novel procedures, whereas the Verbal subtests use items and methods that are familiar to subjects, may render the latter less sensitive to brain impairment than the former.

Perhaps the most consistent contrast using psychometric tests is between visuospatial and verbal learning. Where non-verbal stimuli have been used, alcoholics have consistently shown memory deficits (Cutting, 1978b; Ellenburg et al., 1980; Ryan & Butters, 1980b), where learning of verbal material has been normal. A compelling example of this is provided by the study of Ellenberg et al. (reviewed in the section on recovery of functioning), who made use of the Stark tests, which contrast verbal and visuospatial paired-associate learning. The non-verbal stimuli are geometric designs; for example, a regular triangle is paired with an equilateral triangle as an easy response, and with an irregular four-sided figure as a difficult response. Ellenberg et al. (1980) found that although verbal paired-associate learning returned to normal levels, even in older alcoholics, after a short period of abstinence, visuospatial learning did not. On the face of it, this provides evidence that alcoholics have more problems with visuospatial than verbal processing, a finding that Stark (1961) had shown was associated with RH lesions. There are a number of methodological problems, however, that make interpretation of these results problematic. Stark's (1961) normative study contrasted two groups of 20 right and left unilateral lesion patients and produced a clear interaction: The left hemisphere lesion group made more errors on the verbal task, but performed normally on the non-verbal task, whereas the RH group were normal on the verbal task, but impaired on the visuospatial learning test. The control subjects performed at an equivalent level on both tasks, suggesting that the two Stark subtests were equivalent. Nevertheless, there are some problems in applying this evidence of equivalence to the situation currently being considered. At issue is the equivalence of the two tests when control subjects perform poorly, that is, what would happen if a group of diffusely damaged patients were tested? Would the psychometric equivalence of the tests be maintained? There is no reason to assume that tests that are matched for good control performance remain matched for "poor" control or bilaterally lesioned subjects.

On the whole, the evidence from standardised tests does not conclusively demonstrate a specific RH vulnerability in alcoholics. The results can be explained by the assumption that so-called RH tests are more sensitive to generalised impairments than verbal tests. There is also ample evidence that alcoholics do show impairments on verbal tests that are presumed to be mediated primarily by the LH. For example, Ryan and Butters (1980b) and Riege et al. (1984) have demonstrated verbal learning deficits in alcoholics; they found that if the tests are made sufficiently difficult or sensitive, then deficits do emerge. Similarly, alcoholics have been shown to have subtle language deficits on verbal fluency tests (Cutting, 1978a; Hewett, Nixon, Glenn, & Parsons, 1991) and other verbal measures (Parker, Chelune, Hamblin, & Kitchens, 1984) that are primarily sensitive to left-sided lesions.

Experimental tasks have also been employed to assess laterality deficits in alcoholics. In these studies, more rigorous attempts have been made to control for procedural differences in contrasted tasks. Further evidence for the RH hemisphere hypothesis came from a study by Bertera and Parsons

(1978), who measured speed of visual search for letter trigrams and 16-point random shapes. Some evidence consistent with the RH hypothesis emerged when it was found that alcoholics made more shape errors in the left visual field (controlled by the right hemisphere). However, a complex four-way interaction revealed that the control subjects had a right visual field–left hemisphere (RVF–LH) dominance for random shapes, making the overall results difficult to interpret (Ellis & Oscar-Berman, 1989). Jenkins and Parsons (1981) compared left and right handed performance on the Tactual Performance Test of the HRB. In this test, subjects assemble a formboard with either the left or right hands while blindfolded. A normal subject typically performs this task most rapidly with his/her left hand, which has direct connections with the right hemisphere. Jenkins and Parsons, however, found that the left hand superiority of normals was not seen in alcoholics when the standard version of the TPT was used. This suggested a RH impairment. However, modification to the task to make the shapes less regular and harder to encode verbally had the effect of making the task equivalent for the right and left hands of both the control and alcoholic subjects. It could be argued that, having matched the contrasted tasks for normal performance, differences in the specific deficit of the alcoholics disappeared.

Jenkins and Parson's study makes use of the fact that the right and left hemispheres may receive sensory input through discrete and separate channels. The left visual field projects directly to the right hemisphere, and sensation from the right hand to the LH. In a series of studies, Oscar-Berman and colleagues have exploited this property of the CNS to test the RH hypothesis. Oscar-Berman, Weinstein, and Wysocki (1983) tested the ability of alcoholic and control subjects to identify letter (verbal) or line (non-verbal) stimuli presented simultaneously to both hands. When different verbal stimuli are presented at the same time to the left and right hand, the right hand should dominate in identification of the letter. The reverse should occur for non-verbal stimuli. Oscar-Berman et al. (1983) found that the asymmetries of performance in alcoholics were the same as those of normal controls. No evidence for the RH hypothesis emerged from a similar study using information presented tachistoscopically to either the LVF–RH or RVF–RH (Oscar-Berman & Weinstein, 1985).

In a study of dichotic listening in 22 abstinent alcoholics and 22 normal volunteers, Ellis (1990) contrasted the RH hypothesis with the alternative "diffuse generalised" hypothesis. The dichotic listening paradigm involves presenting two different and competing auditory signals to the left and right ears. Asymmetries in function may be detected by comparing the speed of response to or accuracy of identification of the stimuli presented to both ears. It has been shown that auditory information received by one ear passes to both hemispheres, although contralateral dominate ipsilateral pathways. Hence information received by the left ear is transmitted primarily to the right hemisphere, which is assumed to be specialised for non-verbal sounds, such as musical tones. Similarly, verbal signals are processed most efficiently in the left hemisphere and, because contralateral pathways dominate, an advantage for the right ear should emerge. In normal subjects, therefore, there is a left-ear–right-hemisphere advantage for non-verbal sounds and a right-ear–left-hemisphere advantage for the sounds of language. If the right hemisphere is damaged, however, the left ear advantage for non-verbal sounds should be diminished significantly. The right-ear–left-hemisphere advantage for language sounds should strengthen. This is the pattern that would be expected if the RH hypothesis were valid: Alcoholics would show a stronger right ear advantage for language than normal and a weaker left ear advantage for non-verbal sounds.

Ellis (1990) used a tonal discrimination task known to produce a left-ear–right-hemisphere advantage in normals and a verbal discrimination task that conferred a right ear advantage in normals. He also administered the WAIS-R to his subjects and found the typical decrements on the performance subtests that have been reported previously. He then conducted a regression analysis to determine whether there was any relationship between functional asymmetry on his dichotic listening tasks and alcoholism. No significant effects emerged. Ellis concluded that there was no abnormality in hemispheric asymmetry in alcoholism and no evidence for the right hemisphere hypothesis. He suggested that the poorer performance of alcoholics on non-verbal or visuospatial tasks is a consequence of the psychometric sensitivity or unfamiliarity of these tests.

To date no evidence has emerged that the right hemisphere or right hemisphere functions are differentially sensitive to the effects of alcohol abuse. Laterality studies are notoriously difficult to conduct and the asymmetries that do emerge are prone to multiple *post hoc* interpretations. Although differences suggestive of the RH hypothesis have emerged from comparative studies with standardised tests, problems in ascertaining the equivalence of contrasted tests make these results uninterpretable. Experimental studies of asymmetrical processing of sensory information have produced normal results in alcoholics. At this time, there is no evidence for the right hemisphere hypothesis.

Premature ageing

From the time of the earliest studies of cognition in alcoholism, attention has been drawn to the possibility that ageing and alcohol abuse have parallel effects on the brain (Fitzhugh et al., 1965). This notion became explicit in the form of the premature ageing hypothesis. This hypothesis has two major variants. The first suggests that alcohol abuse accelerates the process of ageing such that alcoholics show evidence of the cognitive decline associated with ageing at an earlier stage than non-alcoholics. The accelerated ageing model (Holden, McLaughlin, Reilly, & Overall, 1988; Ryan & Butters, 1980a) implies that there is a constant difference in neuropsychological test performance across the age range. The second and alternative model can be described as the "age-sensitivity" hypothesis (Ellis & Oscar-Berman, 1989) and proposes that the CNS becomes increasingly vulnerable to the neurotoxic effects of alcohol as it ages. Thus alcoholism has little effect on the test scores of patients under the age of about 40; from then on, however, the performance of alcoholics becomes increasingly dysfunctional relative to age-matched controls. Seen in terms of an analysis of variance model, this second model implies an interaction between age and alcoholism on cognitive testing; in contrast, the accelerated ageing hypothesis predicts significant age and alcoholism main effects, but no interaction.

Several early studies provided support for the accelerated ageing version of the premature ageing hypothesis. For example, Blusewicz et al. (1977a,b) found that the pattern of decline on the WAIS and HRB were similar for both aged and alcoholic subjects. Data from studies reporting Reitan's BAQ index in alcoholic subjects reinforce the view that subtests sensitive to ageing are also sensitive to alcohol abuse. Ryan and Butters (1980b) found that the memory performance of alcoholics was similar to that of normal controls who were 10 to 15 years older. However, the accelerated ageing model has not received consistent support (Becker et al., 1983a,b; Shelton, Parsons & Leber, 1984). The vulnerability age-sensitive model has also been tested and found wanting in a number of investigations (Noonberg et al., 1985; Page & Cleveland, 1987; Ryan & Butters, 1980b).

Overall, it is the lack of consistency in findings from premature ageing research that has undermined the acceptability of the hypothesis. This can be illustrated by Becker et al's. (1983b) results. In this investigation, subjects were shown an initial list of three to seven items followed immediately by a second list comprising all except one of the items from the first list. There were three missing-item tests developed, using either face, digit, or word stimuli. In each case, the subject's task was to list all the items that appeared in both lists and then to identify the missing item. Becker et al. found that on all three tasks, there was a decline attributable to ageing. A similar decline was found for the alcoholic subjects on the missing digit and missing face tasks; however, the alcoholics' performance of the missing word task was normal. Thus, not all tasks that were sensitive to ageing were also sensitive to alcohol abuse. Further, on the missing digit task, the results were consistent with the age sensitivity model, with an interaction between age and alcoholism emerging. In contrast, in the missing faces condition, there was no such interaction, a result consistent with the generalised ageing effects model. This inconsistency suggests that either the effects of ageing and alcohol abuse are linked in some more complex way than is envisaged by the premature ageing model, or the theory has no real substance.

A number of studies also suggest that the effects of ageing and alcoholism are different and independent (Grant et al., 1984; Kramer, Blusewicz & Preston, 1989a; Riege et al., 1984). Kramer et al. (1989a) administered the California Verbal Learning Test (CVLT) to young and old alcoholics and to young and old healthy volunteers. The CVLT is a verbal learning procedure in which subjects receive five learning trials of a 16-word list comprised of four words from four different taxonomic categories. Learning is tested in a variety of ways resulting in indices of recall, recognition, error types, and degree of semantic clustering. The results failed to support consistently either variant of the premature ageing hypothesis. There was no support from the recall results of an Age × Alcoholism interaction. Although the recall data were consistent with the accelerated ageing variant, more detailed analysis of the performance of the subjects revealed that the normal elderly and the alcoholics performed the tests in different ways. For example, older normal subjects, although performing more poorly than younger subjects on the recall parts of the test, showed no deficits in recognition performance. Alcoholics performed both recognition and recall tests more poorly than the normals. There were also differences in the pattern of errors. In particular, Kramer et al. (1989a, p. 261) noted that the alcoholics were susceptible to the effects of interference, raising "the possibility that alcoholics tend to confuse information in episodic memory, perhaps as a consequence of insufficient processing of temporal features during encoding or a greater vulnerability to retroactive interference".

CONCLUSIONS

The pattern of deficits seen in alcoholics has been compared to that seen in patients with unilateral RH damage and to the declines seen in ageing. As Ellis & Oscar-Berman (1989) have observed, there are many parallels between the premature ageing and RH hypothesis. Although both of these views have stimulated research, the comparisons have proved to be superficial. Alcoholics have both right and left hemisphere damage and, when tasks comparing the severity of specific functional impairment arising from this damage are carefully matched, RH deficits do not predominate. There is emerging evidence that age and alcoholism have independent effects on neuropsychological functioning. Detailed analyses of the strategies that the healthly aged and alcoholics use to perform tasks, suggest that the parallel between these two causes of decline is not strong. At this stage it appears that alcohol neurotoxicity may cause a generalised and diffuse degree of brain damage, which is dissimilar to the general effects of ageing.

CHAPTER TEN

Neuropsychology of the Wernicke–Korsakoff Syndrome

> *Oh! as for that,*
>   *My memory is of two sorts, long and short:*
>   *With them who owe me aught it never fails;*
>   *My creditors indeed complain of it*
>   *As mainly apt to leak and lose its reckoning*
>
> Aristophanes, *The Clouds*

In this chapter, the neuropsychological deficits of those alcoholics who sustain severe acute or irreversible brain impairment are reviewed. In Chapter 2, the relationship between Wernicke's encephalopathy and Korsakoff's syndrome was outlined. These two disorders are linked by their common neuropathology: lesions in the grey matter surrounding the third and fourth ventricles. Patients in the chronic and residual state of alcoholic amnesia are typically diagnosed as having Korsakoff's syndrome or, if the range of cognitive impairment extends to the intellect, alcoholic dementia. At the outset, the lack of precision with which these terms are used must be acknowledged. Korsakoff's syndrome is most commonly used to describe patients who have severe amnesia, but relatively preserved functioning in other cognitive domains. In those patients where there is clinical evidence of a decline in intellectual functioning the term alcoholic dementia is more likely to be employed. None the less, there are no universally accepted criteria that distinguish between alcoholic Korsakoff's syndrome and alcoholic dementia. Indeed, from the neuropsychological perspective, surprisingly little is known about the natural history and progression of Wernicke–Korsakoff syndrome and related disorders; without doubt, this has contributed to the confusion over the appropriate nosology.

The neuropsychological study of patients with Wernicke–Korsakoff syndrome has focused almost entirely on their failure of memory. Alcoholic Korsakoff patients represent the largest group of profoundly amnesic patients available for study; work with these patients has contributed significantly to our understanding of normal human cognitive processes and the neuroanatomy of memory. To gain an appreciation of the limitations and implications of the work, it is useful to begin by reiterating that there is considerable variability in both the clinical presentation and underlying brain pathology in patients with Korsakoff's syndrome. The biological effects of alcohol on the nervous system have been considered in Part 2, and from that review the diversity of lesions seen in chronic brain damaged alcoholics will be apparent. There is similar variety in the presentation of patients with Wernicke–Korsakoff syndrome.

There is, perhaps, no better way of introducing the psychological consequences of Wernicke–Korsakoff syndrome than to begin with Talland's (1965) report on his six-year investigation of chronic amnesic patients. In *Deranged Memory* Talland described not only the clinical features of the disorder, but also the results of an extensive series of experimental studies. This work is particularly valuable because it represents one of the first attempts to describe systematically the neuropsychological performance of a range of amnesic alcoholics; hence his conclusions were largely uncluttered by a weight of previous evidence and expectations. Early in his monograph Talland (1965, p. 19) provides an acute description of the amnesic Korsakoff patient:

> Confronted with a chronic Korsakoff patient, the observer may not find any evidence of a mental disorder for quite a while, even though they engage in conversation ... However, as soon as the interview turns to questions about the patient's experiences, activities, or interests in the immediate past, his answers are certain to betray a characteristic derangement. In the first place the content is extraordinarily slender; the paucity of information far exceeds the limits that could be attributed to the restrictive social setting of a mental hospital. Patients either profess to have done nothing at all over stretches of weeks, months, or even years; or they report their activities in general terms and are unable to name specific instances ...

The impact of this profound memory loss on the interviewer is to give the impression that the patient's lifespan has contracted dramatically; Korsakoff patients appear to have memories from their earlier life but know little of their recent history. It as if "the flow of time experienced stopped some years back; experientially nothing has happened, nothing has changed" (Talland, 1965, p. 23). Accompanying this failure of memory is a loss of spontaneity and initiative. Korsakoff patients rarely respond to questions with elaboration or extension, thus their answers seem brief and superficial. There is little effort on the patients' part to maintain conversations and left to themselves, groups of Korsakoff patients rapidly sink into silence, with no sign that this causes any distress. There are, as Talland notes, exceptions to this. Some patients are more loquacious, but typically the content of their discourse is full of repetition, consisting of anecdotes or complaints against relatives and staff, aired over and over again.

Most Korsakoff patients are oriented for place and know that they are in hospital or living in care. With time they learn their way about the environs of the hospital and their ward. They nearly always misestimate the length of passing time and thus are completely unreliable when asked how long ago events have occurred. Most patients can give their date of birth, but without some laboured mental calculation, they usually cannot give their correct age. They remember their children and families, although their memories are often frozen in time, so that a 28-year-old son may be recalled as a child of just four or five. Few Korsakoff patients have any contact with their families or with friends in the community. They are usually isolated people, frequently as a consequence of their long careers in alcoholism; they are typically divorced and may not see their children. Asked about the other patients living alongside them in the hospital or care facility, their answers are often vague or evasive. Korsakoff patients may learn the names of some staff, although their performance is variable. Talland (1965, p. 27) observed that "Eight patients regularly recalled my name promptly; five others habitually substituted a close enough alternative; seven could never learn or retain it for 5 minutes".

Another striking consequence of Korsakoff syndrome is the patients' lack of insight into the origin and significance of their condition. "Asked the reason for their continued hospitalisation, most of them referred to some physical ailment; only a few would consider the possibility of their being afflicted with a mental disease, and none would consistently regard this as a permanent disabling condition" (Talland, 1965, p. 29). This lack of awareness extended to their amnesic state: "None realised the full extent of his amnesic disability; some would admit to poor memory for names or dates, others denied any memory disturbance even in the face of the most striking evidence" (Talland, 1965, p. 29). Most patients reveal little distress in the face of quite abject failure on tests of memory. This is a feature of their amnesic condition that Korsakoff patients share with demented patients, such as those with Alzheimer's disease, but which is not seen in all amnesics. For example, the severely amnesic surgical case, H.M., described by Milner and colleagues (Milner, Corkin, & Teuber, 1968) appears to have retained the ability to appraise with some accuracy his memory disabilities.

A tendency often ascribed to patients with Korsakoff's syndrome is *confabulation*. Although definitions of confabulation vary, the term is used to describe the propensity to fabricate memories. Confabulation is often seen during a Wernicke's episode; in response to a question about their personal history, patients may construct a gratuitously inaccurate accounts of recent events in their lives. For instance, a patient may invent a husband or wife, or talk of children that do not exist, embroidering a family history that may appear at first to be quite plausible. The chronic Korsakoff does not do this with the same facility. If confabulation is defined as the presentation of inaccurate accounts of personal history or recent occurrences, then this does happen on occasion. Korsakoff himself (Victor & Yakovlev, 1955, p. 399) described the characteristic pseudoreminiscences of such patients as follows:

> ... it must be noted that in this form of amnesia a slight degree of confusion is frequently present ... Thus, when asked to tell how he has been spending his time, the patient would very frequently relate a story altogether different from that which actually occurred, for example, he would tell that yesterday he took a ride into town, whereas in fact he has been in bed for two months, or he would tell of conversations which never occurred, and so forth.

As Talland notes, Korsakoff patients often seem to be transposing or condensing events that they can remember from their earlier life to apply to their present existence, rather than developing elaborate and novel occurrences or personal circumstances. The number of patients who produce even this restricted evidence of confabulation is small; most Korsakoff patients respond to questions about their recent past by acknowledging that they cannot remember and appear unperturbed by this admission. Occasionally a patient will develop a history of their past that is based on reality, but is patently untrue as it relates to their personal circumstances. For example, a patient may describe himself as convalescing after a tour of military duty and answer questions about the present, with reference to his time on active service. Such a story is presented consistently over time and many have the quality of a delusion; however, instances of confabulation to this degree are extremely unusual.

Kopelman (1987) has drawn attention to the possibility that there are two types of confabulation, *spontaneous* confabulation, which is seen as the fantastic and sustained production of a wide range of false memories arising without external prompting, and *provoked* confabulation, which consists of the plausible but inaccurate recall of recent or long-past events, which often seem to have been displaced from their correct temporal context, in response to questioning. Spontaneous confabulation occurs in patients with considerable frontal damage or advanced dementia; it may also be seen in patients with Wernicke's encephalopathy. Provoked confabulation is more typical of the kind of distortion of reminiscence found in Korsakoff patients. Kopelman has shown that the quality of such inaccurate reproductions is similar to that produced by normal subjects, when their recall is tested after long periods of delay. He concludes that the confabulatory symptoms commonly documented in Korsakoff patients represent the normal response to a grossly defective memory system. Thus, there is no justification of describing Korsakoff's syndrome as an "amnesic–confabulatory" disorder.

Table 10.1 details the cognitive deficits that Talland identified in his sample, on the basis of the results from his extensive battery of experimental tasks, together with a list of those functions that the Korsakoff patients performed normally. Some preliminary trends can be seen in this Table. First, Talland's Korsakoff patients showed evidence of impairment on some tasks that are not associated with learning and memory. In some cases, these deficits can be attributed to the neurological damage resulting from the effects of severe alcohol abuse; in particular, peripheral neuropathy and reduced sensory acuity have an influence on the expression of perceptual motor skills. However, the Korsakoff patients also showed pronounced deficits on tasks requiring the maintenance of complex cognitive sets or a degree of conceptual abstraction. One test that Talland used nicely illustrates the sequencing and conceptual problems his patients displayed. He set up two decks of playing cards to give 16 sequences of B(black)–B–R(red)–B–R–R cards. He then told the subjects that there was a simple pattern in the order of the cards and that their task was to uncover this. On each trial they were asked to predict whether the next card would be red or black. If the subject failed to learn the repeated six-card pattern to a criterion of three correct sequences, they were shown the pattern several times, and the testing process continued until either all 16 sequences had been administered or the subject reached criterion. Of the 20 Korsakoff patients tested, only two solved the problem initially and a further two were successful when shown the pattern. Ten of 20 controls, however, discovered the rule during the first run through the cards, and a further nine learned the rule after the pattern was demonstrated. Thus, the Korsakoff patients showed a severe impairment in this style of concept formation task. On some of the other perceptual or conceptual learning tasks, the Korsakoff patients showed deficits only when the tasks became more difficult. For example, some of the more demanding perceptual span tasks Talland devised were performed more

TABLE 10.1
Impaired and Preserved Skills in a Group of Korsakoff Patients
(Talland, 1965)

Preserved skills	Impaired skills
Verbal and motor performance	
Performing long-established motor skills	Verbal fluency
Comprehension and writing	Divided attention tasks
Knowledge and use of semantic associates	Letter cancellation
Simple and complex reaction time	
Fine manual skills	
Perception	
Immediate memory span	Maintenance of two concurrent sets
Recognition of objects	Sequential integration of input
Understanding causality	
Visual and auditory matching	
Intelligence	
Use of information acquired previously	Ability to assimilate or apply new or
Formal reasoning	unfamiliar data
Application of knowledge	Problem-solving in novel situations
	Concept formation
	Keeping competing hypothesis in mind
Learning and remembering	
Following instructions (unless interrupted)	Remote memory
	Acquisition of new verbal or visual material when tested by recognition, or recall
	More susceptible to interference
	Spatial memory

poorly by the Korsakoff's than the controls, and although their simple and complex reaction times were in the normal range, they performed the more challenging cross-modal response tasks more slowly than matched controls. The Korsakoff patients therefore showed deficits on a variety of tests, not all of which were dependent on the ability to acquire new information; they had particular difficulties with tasks often described as sensitive to frontal lobe deficits, for example, verbal fluency, maintenance of set, temporal sequencing, and concept formation. In sum, Talland found that Korsakoff patients, although primarily distinctive by virtue of their amnesia, had many other signs of cognitive failure.

Second, the amnesic Korsakoff patients performed best on untimed tasks where the stimuli remained exposed in front of them and no element of new learning was necessary. Further, tasks that depended on skills acquired during the course of formal education were also likely to be performed normally. For instance, the Korsakoff patients did not lose the capacity to use language or semantic associations that they had acquired when they first became proficient in the use of language. However, when faced with novel or unfamiliar tasks, decrements in performance relative to the controls soon became evident.

A third trend apparent in the results of Talland's many experiments was that his Korsakoff subjects displayed a broad range of severe memory impairments. In all the learning situations he created, the Korsakoff patients performed at a poor level. Yet there was evidence that the Korsakoff patients were not completely devoid of the capacity for new learning. Talland (1965, p. 203) observed, for example, that the "amnesic patients proved remarkably efficient in following instructions and in pursuing their tasks". Knowledge of what to do did not evaporate with the passing of time. Nevertheless, if there was any interruption, their work set was likely to be disrupted, and they would not be able to recommence where they left off. Thus, as long as the task before them required no explicit interrogation of memory, no internal "what was I doing?", their work proceeded effectively. In addition, motor learning was unimpaired. Talland (1965, p. 233) concluded that "All this agrees with the view that the learning and retention of mechanical skills and of problem-solving information involve different processes. For practical purposes, the results suggest that Korsakoff patients might be taught simple routine skills with reasonable success, but not the type of skill that involves the storage of information and its application in planned action".

Throughout Talland's (1965) monograph there are numerous illustrations of individual differences in his group of Korsakoff patients: on some tasks some of these patients performed normally; others did not. An exception was tests of memory and learning, where he found almost no overlap between amnesics and controls. Talland selected his patients for their relatively pure and severe expression of memory loss, free of marked intellectual impairment. Despite a degree of selectivity, on average his group were found to have deficits in most spheres of cognitive activity. Talland also emphasised the personality and emotional deficiencies in his patients, particularly their lack of responsiveness. He believed (1965, p. 304) that the "patients' passivity, lack of spontaneity, must be functionally related to their cognitive disturbance". He argued that amnesia might be explained by the failure to sustain the process of retrieval (Talland, 1965, p. 306) and "traced to a premature termination of an activating function". Talland's work was also important for his demonstrations that, under some circumstances, learning in amnesics was preserved. For example, he found that certain types of skill learning were normal in amnesia, introducing a line of evidence important in later notions of multiple memory systems. He made the distinction between overlearned and automaticised skills that amnesics performed well and memory tests that required recall of the episode of learning that they failed badly. This dichotomy was to be elaborated by Squire and his colleagues (e.g. Squire, 1986), who distinguished between the context-free acquisition of new skills (which they termed *procedural* learning) and the recall of context-bound information (*declarative* learning). This issue will be considered further later in this chapter.

RESEARCH CRITERIA FOR KORSAKOFF'S SYNDROME

The question of whom to class as having Korsakoff's syndrome is not readily answered. In the clinical context this may matter little; functional skills and availability of psychosocial support are more important in determining the management of Korsakoff patients inside or outside the hospital than their precise diagnosis. For research purposes, however, classification may be more important. In several studies it has been shown that the Korsakoff label is applied to a range of patients with varying degrees of amnesia and dementia. Talland (1965) selected his group of 29 patients from a larger sample of 40 and noted (1965, p. 8) that his group "did not constitute a representative sample of its parent population, Korsakoff patients committed to a mental hospital". For the purposes of studying memory loss the exclusion of dementing patients has commonly been practised by researchers since Talland's time, a methodological tactic that is justifiable when the research focus in on amnesia *per se*, but one leaving a stereotyped impression of the typical Korsakoff patient in the neuropsychological literature (Bowden, 1990).

What deficits might be found in an unselected group of Korsakoff patients? Jacobson and Lishman (1987) set out to answer this question with a detailed psychometric study of alcoholic Korsakoff patients using the WAIS, WMS, and NART (a measure that yields a premorbid estimate of WAIS IQ scores). They constituted a group of 38 patients with a clinical diagnosis of Korsakoff syndrome selected from the total of 50 Korsakoffs resident in psychiatric hospitals in London. They excluded four patients with clinical evidence of dementia (such as the occurrence of dysphasic or dyspraxic deficits, or motor perseveration) and eight patients who were over the age of 65 or who had a history of either another neurological disorder or drug abuse. They found that their patients had a range of IQ scores extending from 74 to 125, NART IQ estimates ranging from 91 to 128, and WMS Memory Quotients from 59 to 105. They plotted their index of memory loss (FSIQ–MQ) against NART–WAIS IQ differences, and for both indices chose 15 as the magnitude of discrepancy indicative of impairment. Their results can be seen in Table 10.2. From this Table, it is apparent that there was a wide distribution of scores; their sample was

TABLE 10.2

Classification of Intellectual and Memory Deficits In Korsakoff Patients
(Jacobson & Lishman, 1978)

NART IQ–FSIQ discrepancy	FSIQ–MQ discrepancy		
	15+	0–14	Total
0–14	Amnesic, no IQ decrement 24 (63%)	Not amnesic, no IQ decrement 8	32
15+	Amnesia with IQ decrement 2	Not amnesic, with IQ decrement 4 (11%)	6
Total	26	12	38

heterogeneous with respect to degree of current memory and intellectual functioning. The correlation between the two indices was –0.25, suggesting a non-significant trend for memory loss and intellectual decline to be inversely associated. There are problems with the two indices they employed, as has been detailed in Chapter 3. The MQ–IQ difference has an unknown distribution and is likely to be influenced by strong floor effects. The NART IQ estimates are typically error prone and Jacobson and Lishman found that some of their NART IQ–FSIQ discrepancies were negative, suggesting that in some patients current IQ exceeded premorbid IQ, an unlikely circumstance. Nevertheless, their data contain an important message: Selected Korsakoff samples are likely to include patients with psychometric evidence of dementia, as well as other patients who, despite being hospitalised with Korsakoff's syndrome, do not have an IQ–MQ deficit in excess of 15 points.

Although no explicit research criteria for Korsakoff's syndrome, giving quantified guidance about how much amnesia or how little dementia is consistent with the diagnosis, have been published, researchers now provide considerable detail about the Korsakoff samples used in neuropsychological research. In Table 10.3, the comprehensive criteria that Squire and his colleagues have used (Shimamura & Squire, 1989) are detailed. This Table not only demonstrates the way in which amnesia may be quantified, but also the manner in which patients with frank signs of dementia are excluded. Shimamura and Squire regard those Korsakoff patients with a score in the demented range of a comprehensive mental status examination such as the Dementia Rating Scale (Mattis, 1976) or who are unable to accurately complete simple tests of aphasia and apraxia, as being unsuitable for inclusion in amnesic samples. The results in Table 10.3 also give a perspective on the severity of amnesia seen in Korsakoff

TABLE 10.3
Description of a Korsakoff Patient Research Sample
(From Shimamura & Squire, 1989)

Variable	Mean
Demographic information	
age (years)	54.1
years education	13.3
average WAIS-R FSIQ	103.3
Documentation of amnesia	
Wechsler Memory Scale-Revised	
attention-concentration	95.8
verbal memory	74.0
visual memory	76.1
general memory	68.5
delayed memory	56.7
Recall of prose passage	
immediate (segments)	5.6
delayed (12 minute) (segments)	0
Rey Complex Figure Test	
copy	28.2/36
delayed recall	4.8/36
Paired-associate learning (3 trials)	0.7/10, 0.7/10, 1.8/10
Rey Auditory Verbal Learning Test (5 trials)	4.3, 5.3, 5.6, 5.7, 5.5 (max = 15)
Two-choice recognition (% correct)	21.8, 24.5, 25.1, 26.1, 27.2
Exclusion of dementing patients	132.2/144
Normal range score on the Dementia Rating Scale	
No signs of aphasia or apraxia	
Draw house and cube in perspective	

patients. For example, they were able to recall nothing of a prose passage after a delay of 12 minutes. They score at least two standard deviations below average on the WMS-R. After three trials they learned on average, only 1.8 of 10 noun-noun paired associates.

AMNESIA IN KORSAKOFF'S SYNDROME

Failure of memory is the deficit in Korsakoff's syndrome that has most attracted the interest of neuropsychologists. The study of amnesic Korsakoff patients has provided important insights into the working of memory. The initial work of Talland provided a broad outline of the changes in cognition occurring in Korsakoff's syndrome, and his investigation was followed by the extensive neuropathological survey of Victor, Adams, and Collins (1971), which located the lesions responsible for anterograde amnesia in Wernicke–Korsakoff patients in the midline structures of the diencephalon. These two major pioneering studies were subsequently followed by a stream of investigations seeking to clarify the cognitive processes responsible for the memory failure seen in alcoholic amnesia and to specify more precisely the lesions critical to the production of this deficit.

An important stimulus for the decade of research that followed was Warrington and Weiskrantz's (1968) demonstration that amnesic patients were able to remember previous events provided they were tested using a procedure they termed *partial information* cueing. Their results were somewhat surprising and suggested that amnesics did acquire new information, but were unable to locate or retrieve it. One of the cueing procedures they administered made use of a series of degraded pictures of line drawings of common objects and word stimuli. Each of the stimulus pictures was prepared by photographing it through a series of filters that randomly blanked-out sections of the drawing or word. Using this process, a series of progressively degraded stimuli ranging from the original unaltered stimulus through three intermediate stages to a very incomplete representation was constructed. The incomplete or fragmented versions of the stimuli were unrecognisable without exposure to the original, complete version. Warrington and Weiskrantz presented these fragmented stimuli in order from the most fragmented to the least, until the subject recognised the stimulus word or picture. Initially this required exposure to the complete version, but the amnesic patients gradually came to learn to recognise the fragmented pictures at an earlier and earlier stage. In a subsequent study, Warrington and Weiskrantz (1970) found that they could produce normal recall of previously exposed words when the partial information cue comprised the stem (first three letters, e.g. PLA ...) of the stimulus word (e.g. PLANK). In this study, the memory performance of amnesics (five out of six of whom were alcoholic Korsakoffs) was found to be equivalent to a group of controls using both the word-stem and the fragmented picture methods of partial cueing. The results of these studies were intrinsically interesting because they revealed an unexpected degree of preserved memory capability in amnesics. On the basis of their results, Warrington and Weiskrantz raised the possibility that amnesia was a consequence of retrieval failure. Their results, which demonstrated that supporting memory with appropriate cues enhanced recall, suggested that amnesics acquired memories normally, but were unable to return them to consciousness when required.

Debate on the merits of their view that amnesia was primarily the result of retrieval failure was to occupy memory researchers throughout the 1970s (Butters & Cermak, 1980). At this time several competing hypotheses about the fundamental deficit that produced severe anterograde amnesia in Korsakoff and other patients were advanced. The research programme of Butters, Cermak, and their colleagues led them to advance the notion that amnesia was primarily a defect in the ability to consolidate newly acquired information (Cermak, Butters, & Goodglass, 1971; Cermak & Reale, 1978). Their hypothesis was that the initial encoding of information in short-term memory prior to transfer into long-term storage was defective. As evidence for this they cited data from their research which showed that Korsakoff amnesics had deficits in short-term memory as revealed by the Brown–Peterson distractor task (Cermak & Butters, 1972, 1973; Cermak et al., 1971). The integrity of short-term memory (STM) in amnesia was a matter of some importance as normal STM was consistent with retrieval theories, while abnormal performance was more consistent with the consolidation hypothesis. This research will be considered in the section below on STM; at this stage we can note, however, that amnesics' level of performance on STM tasks remains a matter of some debate. Further evidence for defective STM processes in amnesia came from studies in which release from proactive interference was assessed in amnesia. Initial findings that Korsakoff patients failed to show a normal pattern of release were countered by results that showed that this was not an obligatory finding in amnesics of all aetiologies (Cermak, 1976). The encoding–consolidation hypothesis was also weakened by the failure of Cermak and colleages to find any evidence for normal performance by amnesic patients when depth of encoding was enhanced. Cermak and Reale (1978) found that although instructing amnesics to make detailed semantic analyses of verbal input improved their recall, their scores did not reach normal levels. They concluded (Cermak & Reale, 1978, p. 173) that failure of memory could not be entirely attributed to tendency on the part of amnesic patients to fail to encode input adequately and that "other factors, such as level of retrieval search, must be explored as further contributors the patients' overall memory problems".

Warrington and Weiskrantz's retrieval theory was the primary alternative view to the consolidation hypothesis. On the basis of their findings that cued recalled was differentially beneficial to amnesic subjects, they proposed (Warrington & Weiskrantz, 1968, p. 391) that the mechanism responsible for retrieval failure and hence anterograde amnesia was " ... an excess of interference among stored items". Their attempts to establish this specific mechanism as the one responsible for amnesia, however, were unsuccessful and they concluded from the results of studies presented in Warrington and Weiskrantz (1978) that there was no evidence that the cueing effects operated by the restriction of response alternatives. Warrington and Weiskrantz (1982) provided a somewhat different account of amnesia, which was based on the proposition that memory failure was a consequence of a disconnection between the frontal and temporal lobes, resulting in the isolation of semantic memory from the putative "cognitive mediational memory system" that was important for the retrieval of episodic memories. They used the term "cognitive mediation" to refer to the elaboration of input by means of imagery, embellishment, manipulation, and organisation. They suggested (Warrington & Weiskrantz, 1982, p. 242) that "the amnesic subject is impaired, not in the ability to engage in cognitive mediation as such, but in those memory tasks in which the stored benefits of mediation are normally important". Although they do not make this entirely explicit, there is a sense in which "cognitive mediation" memory is an aspect of the context of learning. This relates to another hypothesis advanced at this time, the idea that long-term memory deficit was the result of the failure of amnesics to encode contextual information accurately (Huppert & Piercy, 1976; Winocur & Kinsbourne, 1978). This approach focused on the inability of amnesics to recall such contextual information as the order, recency, or spatial characteristics of target memory items. This theory has emerged as influential more recently, and the failure of amnesic subjects on tests of contextual information, reported under a variety of conditions (Parkin, 1992), has provided evidence for this viewpoint. We will review some of these results when we consider the performance of amnesics on temporal sequencing and recency tasks.

While cognitive studies with Korsakoff patients and other amnesics were proceeding, knowledge of the brain structures involved in memory was accumulating. Scoville and Milner (1957) had earlier published an account of the amnesia that followed the bilateral excision of portions of the medial temporal lobes as a neurological intervention for the relief of epilepsy. One of their cases, H.M., who has been studied over the last 30 years, was left with a profound, but relatively circumscribed amnesia as a consequence of this operation. On the basis of these results, the medial temporal lobes were identified as a region of the brain of key significance in the operation of memory. This conclusion was strengthened by reports showing that other patients with similar bilateral damage in the temporal lobes, most notably those with lesions caused by herpes simplex encephalitis, were also often severely amnesic. Damage to a second region of the brain, the medial diencephalon, has also been implicated in the memory failure, as has already been seen in the neuropathological study of Korsakoff patients. Supporting evidence came from studies of other patients with amnesia following bilateral thalamic damage (Cramon, Hebel, & Schuri, 1985). Although the minimal lesions in either the diencephalon or the temporal lobes necessary to produce severe amnesia remain to be precisely delineated, considerable progress has been made in understanding the biological basis of memory.

In the discussion section of their 1982 paper, Warrington and Weiskrantz made a significant attempt to link the emerging understanding of the biological bases of amnesia with the existing data from neuropsychological investigations. In doing so, they signalled an emerging concern with lesion-specific differences in memory performance that was to become a focus of much of the research of the next decade. This is of particular relevance to our consideration of the amnesia of patients with Korsakoff's syndrome. It soon became apparent that although alcoholic amnesics had many deficits in common with amnesics of other aetiologies, some of their impairments were unique (Squire, 1982). Warrington and Weiskranz (1982) also emphasised the significance of learning situations in which amnesics performed normally. Subsequent demonstrations of the apparent integrity of semantic priming in amnesics were enormously influential in generating new conceptualisations of normal memory functioning. Much of the experimental work that followed gave new significance to the earlier findings of Talland (1965) and Warrington and Weiskrantz (1970).

The remainder of this section will discuss two major questions, which arise from the research on Korsakoff patients outlined thus far: First, what are the boundaries of the memory failure seen in Korsakoff's syndrome? In this regard, both those memory-related capabilities that are lost and those that are preserved are of significance. Second, can the memory deficits seen in Korsakoff's syndrome, which are attributed to diencephalic–frontal lesions, be distinguished from those seen in amnesics of different aetiologies? To provide a basis for discussing these questions, those lines of experimental investigation that have been most productive in providing insights into the nature of amnesia in Korsakoff's syndrome, are reviewed.

Short-term memory

In the passage opening his contribution to the George Talland Memorial Conference, A. D. Smith (1980, p. 23) observed that:

> To remember something requires three things. First, the information must be encoded or learned; second, the information must be stored during a retention interval anchored by original encoding on one end and the time of the test on the other; and third, the information must be retrieved at the time memory is tested.

This simple characterisation of the process and structure of memory underpinned the design of experiments with Korsakoff amnesics during the 1970s. The aim of much of this work was to answer the question that Warrington and Weiskrantz had posed—are amnesic subjects primarily defective in their ability to encode, store, or retrieve new information? Their conclusion, as we have seen, was that the locus of the deficit lay in the third of Smith's stages—retrieval. To show that this deficit was the primary source of amnesic failure, and not just a flow-on effect of previous deficits, they needed to demonstrate that the processes that preceded retrieval were undamaged in amnesics.

The conventional manner in which the memory system is described often makes a distinction between brief sensory storage, short-term memory (STM), and long-term memory (LTM). This tripartite division does not necessarily deny the possibility that memory is a holistic or unitary process, but this structural model has proved to be a convenient way of organising experimental work on memory processes. Kintsch (1977) drew attention to the fact that STM is often used in two senses, one to describe memory performance in situations where brief retention intervals are used, the other to describe a theoretical distinction between short- and long-term memory processes. This theoretical distinction dates back at least to Galton (1883) and William James (1890). It was James (1890) who introduced the distinction between primary and secondary memory (synonymous with STM and LTM), which many contemporary neuropsychologists prefer to use because of the lack of any explicit and ambiguous reference to the duration of any memory trace. James regarded primary memory as the information available in current consciousness. In contrast, secondary memory has been processed beyond this stage and requires an effortful process of recollection. Galton (1883) described primary memory graphically as the "presence chamber of my mind where full consciousness hold court, and where two or three ideas are at the same time in audience ..."

The Digit Span subtest from the WAIS-R is a traditional method of assessing the capacity of primary memory. It gives a measure of the number of elements that can be held in the forefront of consciousness at any one time. As Ebbinghaus (1885) noted, there is a sharp discontinuity between the time taken to acquire and recall six pieces of information, and the time to learn 10: Most people can reproduce about six words or digits in correct order, but when this span of apprehension is exceeded, recall of further elements from a list requires that they be administered repeatedly. In this context, primary memory is seen to have a capacity limited to about 7 ± 2 units; acquisition and recall of more information brings secondary memory into play. If the prospect that amnesic patients have impaired brief sensory-buffer storage capacity was set aside, Warrington and Weiskrantz's retrieval hypothesis depended on showing that the initial stage of encoding, storage, and recall of information from primary or short-term memory was intact. It was this that provided the initial incentive to examine STM in patients with Korsakoff's syndrome.

Several tests have been used to determine the capacity of STM in alcoholic Korsakoff patients. One is the Wechsler Digit Span task; this is usually normal in most Korsakoff patients and chronic alcoholics. Another is the Peterson–Brown distractor task, which we encountered in Chapter 9. In this latter procedure, the subject is given an array of information that does not exceed the capacity of primary memory, for instance, a word triad (BELL–SOAP–CARD) and is then engaged in a distracting task, for example, counting backwards. After a delay ranging from 0 to 30 seconds, recall of the study stimuli is tested. The usual result is a rapid decline in recall accuracy, which is interpreted as a measure of the rate of decay from STM. Comparison of these rates gives an indication of the efficiency of primary memory storage in different groups. A third strategy involves the examination of the serial position effect curve, a process that Jones and Jones (1977) used to examine the effects of intoxication (Chapter 6). Typically, if a word list of 10 items is read to a subject, they will remember items from the beginning and end of the list better than items in the middle. The result is the bow-shaped curve relating serial position on the list to probability of recall, which comprises two components. One is the recency part of the curve, which is affected by further filled delay, and is made up of items accurately retrieved from primary memory. The other is the first part of the curve, which is unaffected by further distraction and comprises items assumed to be stored in secondary memory. If primary memory is damaged, then the recency effect will be attenuated; amnesia, being a defect of secondary memory, should result in a loss of the primacy component of the serial position curve.

Baddeley and Warrington (1970) examined the serial position curve for a group of amnesic patients and found that there was no primacy effect, although their recency effect was normal, a result consistent with unimpaired primary memory. Cermak (1982) examined the slope of the recency effect for Baddeley and Warrington's amnesics and contended that this was greater than that of controls, a finding suggestive of more rapid decay from short-term storage. Results from the serial position experiments were therefore not capable of settling the issue conclusively, and evidence from the Peterson–Brown distractor task became crucial in determining the integrity of primary memory in amnesia. However, the findings from experiments using the distractor task were mixed. Both Baddeley and Warrington (1970) and Warrington (1982) reported normal rates of decay from primary memory in groups of patients that included Korsakoffs; Cermak et al. (1971) found a significant greater rate of decay in a group composed solely of alcoholic Korsakoffs. This discrepancy was discussed in the literature at the time and attributed to either procedural differences in the administration of distractor task, or differences in the pattern of deficits in the groups tested by the researchers in London and

Boston. A subsequent report by Cermak (1976) of normal Peterson–Brown performance in an encephalitic amnesic, suggested that abnormal rates of decay may only be characteristic of patients with amnesic lesions, such as Korsakoff patients, or patients with frontal lesions. Several further studies have been completed since that time. Kopelman (1985) found no significant differences between Korsakoff and control performance; in contrast Longmore and Knight (1988) found a marked discrepancy (see Fig. 10.1). The major procedural difference between these studies was in the nature of the distraction technique. Longmore and Knight instructed subjects to count backwards in 3s from a different randomly determined three-digit numbers on each delay trial; Kopelman used the same starting point for his backward counting process. It is possible that Kopelman's distraction technique was less successful at inhibiting the rehearsal of items in primary memory. Leng and Parkin (1989) contrasted the performance of temporal lobe and Korsakoff amnesics using a version of the Peterson–Brown task similar to that used by Longmore and Knight. They found that the Korsakoff patients performed more poorly on this task than

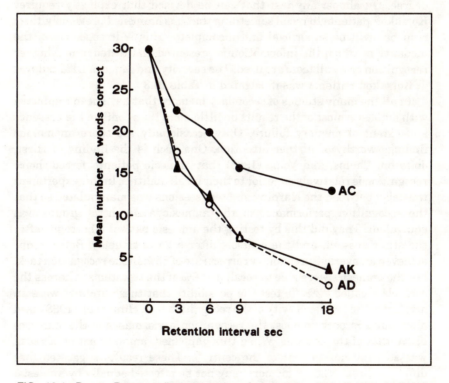

FIG. 10.1. Brown–Peterson distractor task performance by alcoholic Korsakoff (AK), alcohol demented (AD) and chronic alcoholic (AC) groups.

either the temporal lobe patients or the controls. Both Longmore and Knight (1988) and Leng and Parkin (1989) found no relationship between degree of intellectual decline in their amnesic patients and rate of decay from primary memory. Leng and Parkin did, however, find a marginally significant correlation between WCST and rate of decay.

It may be therefore, that both Warrington, and Butters and Cermak, are correct in their interpretation of results from their Peterson–Brown experiments. Rate of decay from primary memory may not be an obligatory feature of amnesia, but it may be a characteristic of many, if not all, Korsakoff patients. The results from Leng and Parkin's study suggest that individual differences in the performance of alcoholic amnesic patients may be related to degree of frontal lobe damage.

Long-term memory

From all that has been said about Korsakoff patients in this chapter, it will be clear that they have LTM or secondary memory failure of a profound degree. On almost any test that can be devised that explicitly requires Korsakoff patients to recall something that has happened previously, their response will be superficial and incomplete. This is irrespective of the modality in which the information is presented and tested, and whether recognition or recall tests are used. The severity and range of LTM failures in Korsakoff patients was illustrated in Table 10.3.

In all the many studies of secondary memory that have been conducted with amnesics most of the results do little more than confirm the presence and extent of memory failure. Only occasionally are there anomalous findings worthy of further attention. One such is the finding of Hirst, Johnson, Phelps, and Volpe (1988) that amnesic patients' forced-choice recognition is relatively superior to their recall abilities. In this experiment the delay between the learning and test sessions was manipulated so that the recognition performance of the amnesic and control groups was equivalent. They did this by testing the amnesic patient 30 seconds after the study session, and the controls after a 24-hour delay. Both groups achieved an average probability correct rate of 85% on the recognition task, but the amnesics were able to recall just 6% of the test items, whereas the controls recalled 22%. To test the possibility that these findings were an artefact of the low sensitivity of the recognition test, Hirst et al. (1988) used a similar approach to boost the recognition performance of the amnesics above that of the controls. When this happened, amnesic patients' recall was still inferior to that of the controls. These results suggested that different direct tests of memory may not be affected equally by amnesia. Hirst et al. explained the differentially superior performance of recognition tasks by amnesics in terms of a failure to link together individual mnemonic representations for a particular learning episode in a way that allows their retrieval. They (Hirst et al., 1988, p. 671) "suggest that amnesics may have difficulty supplying the glue that holds individual events together and creates a larger picture". This "glue" hypothesis can be regarded as a type of contextual theory of amnesia, since it implies that amnesia is the inability to create a sufficient context to allow the spontaneous recall of items from a word list. When such a context to some extent supplied, as in a forced-choice recognition test, amnesic performance is enhanced. Such results are consistent with a contextual memory explanation of amnesia.

The studies of Hirst and colleagues, however, used performance at one particular retention interval to match their amnesic and control groups. Haist, Shimamura, and Squire (1992) employed a more elaborate procedure for comparing recall, recognition, and confidence ratings in 12 amnesic patients of mixed aetiology (six of whom were Korsakoffs) and 12 control subjects; they tested the recall and recognition performance of each subject at intervals of, on average, 20 days. For the amnesic patients recall was tested at retention intervals of 15 sec, 1 min, 5 min, 10 min, 2 hr, and 1 day; recognition was tested at intervals of 15 sec, 1 min, 2 hr, 1 day, and 2 weeks. Both the recall and recognition of the control subjects was tested at intervals of 15 sec, 10 min, 2 hr, 1 day, 2 weeks, and 8 weeks. The recall test involved recall of prose passages, while the recognition test required subjects to select, from each of 20 word pairs, the word that had been presented in the study list. Subjects were also asked to rate each recognition response on a five-point confidence scale ranging from 1 (pure guess) to 5 (very sure). The aim was to match amnesic and control groups at different levels of recognition performance and then to see whether their scores on the recall tests, and their confidence ratings were also matched. If they were not, this would confirm Hirst et al.'s (1988) findings, and suggest that recall was differentially impaired in amnesia, possibly because the recognition performance of amnesics was at least in part supported by implicit memory processes undamaged in amnesia. On the other hand, matching of recall and recognition would show that these processes were equally dependent on the same direct memory systems. The results are illustrated in Fig. 10.2. When the overlap in recognition performance between amnesic and control memory scores on the recognition test was represented (as in the centre panel), the recall scores and confidence ratings proved to be matched. There was no evidence of a specific deficit in the recall performance of amnesics; the authors (Haist et al., 1988, p. 699) concluded that "... recall, recognition, and confidence ratings seem to be tightly linked functions", and that these findings applied equally to the Korsakoff patients in the sample (at least five of whom had frontal atrophy) as to the rest of the amnesics.

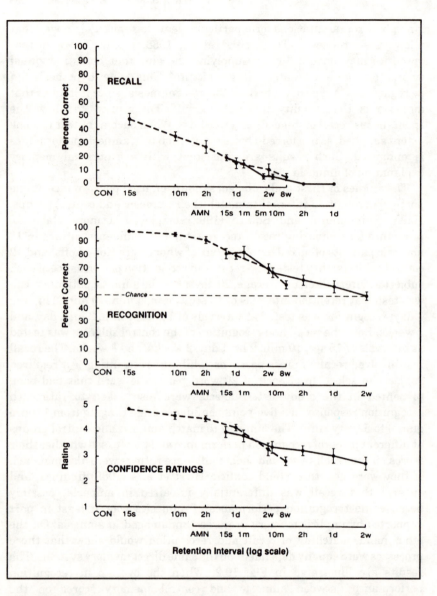

FIG. 10.2. Accuracy of recall and recognition performance and confidence ratings of amnesic patients (solid lines) and controls (dashed lines). The curves have been drawn such that the performance of the two groups on the recognition tests (middle panel) are equivalent. Amnesic recognition performance 15 sec, 1 min, and 10 min after learning was the same as control performance 1 day and 2 weeks after learning. When recognition scores were matched, the performance curves for free recall (top panel) and confidence ratings (bottom panel) also matched. Error bars indicate the standard error of the mean. From Haist, Shimamura, and Squire (1992). (In the public domain).

Release from proactive interference

Another task used extensively with amnesic patients, and which has revealed an intriguing pattern of results, is the release from proactive interference procedure, developed by Wickens (1970) and others. There are a number of versions of this task, but one that is convenient for use with brain damaged subjects involves the administration of five consecutive 12-word lists and testing immediate free recall. There are two conditions under which this occurs. In one—the shift condition—the first four lists come from the same taxonomic category (e.g. animals), but the fifth comes from a completely different category (e.g. vegetables). In the no-shift condition, the five trials use word lists from just the one taxonomic category. Normal performance on this task is detailed in Fig. 10.3. On successive trials with lists from the same categories, there is a gradual

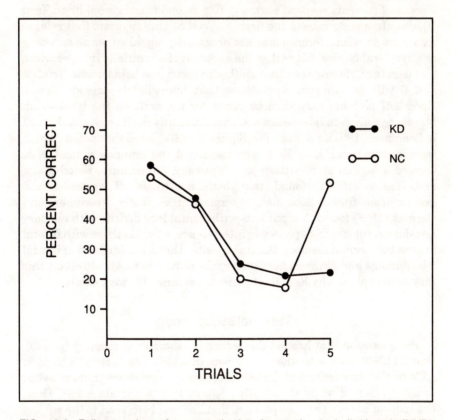

FIG. 10.3. Failure to release from proactive interference by alcoholic Korsakoff (KD) patients after a taxonomic shift on Trial 5. This is in contrast to the substantial shift of the normal control (NC) subjects.

decline in recall performance that can be attributed to a build up in proactive interference. With a switch in categories on the final trial in the shift condition, recall accuracy returns to the level of the first trial. Proactive interference has been released.

Cermak, Butters, and Moreines (1974) demonstrated that Korsakoff patients failed to show a release from proactive interference; It was as if the taxonomic change had passed without their notice. Cermak et al. (1974) cited these results as evidence for an encoding level deficit in Korsakoff patients. Several studies subsequently confirmed that amnesics, particularly Korsakoff patients, failed to show a normal taxonomic shift (Longmore & Knight, 1988; Squire, 1982; Warrington, 1982). Warrington (1982) concluded that failure to release was consistent with a retrieval interference hypothesis, although this is difficult to sustain in the light of Winocur, Kinsbourne, and Moscovitch's (1981) finding that amnesic Korsakoff patients respond normally to a second taxonomic shift on Trial 10, despite having missed the first, on Trial 5. This suggests that release from proactive interference may not necessarily signal either an encoding or a retrieval failure, but rather the adoption of an initially inappropriate metastrategy. Having seen that shifts can occur (the lists for both Trials 5 and 6 will be different from those that immediately precede them), Korsakoff patients may then be ready for the shift on the tenth trial. Moreover, failure to release is not seen consistently in all amnesics (Knight & Longmore, 1991). For example, Squire (1982) showed that patients with transient amnesia after ECT treatment and the amnesic patient N.A. showed a normal shift pattern and Janowsky, Shimamura, Kritchevsky, and Squire (1989a) found that both non-Korsakoff amnesics and non-amnesic frontal lobe patients released normally. Freedman and Cermak (1986) found that patients with frontal lobe deficits with memory loss did not release from proactive interference, whereas those with frontal lesions but normal memory did. It is possible that a combination of frontal lobe damage and amnesia is necessary for failure to release to occur; this may help explain why Korsakoff patients perform this task poorly.

Temporal sequencing

In the quotation that headed the section on short-term memory (p. 280), Smith (1980) drew attention to the way in which information is fixed in LTM by the time context of the learning episode. Questions that are asked to test memory directly are usually prefaced by a temporal context. Thus, the request to recall a prose passage that has just been read to the subject is couched in terms that identify a particular time at which the reading took place. The importance of time is recognised explicitly in Tulving's (1983) distinction between semantic and episodic memory. A failure of episodic memory with preserved semantic memory is another useful way of characterising amnesia. That is, although Korsakoff patients may not have lost their knowledge of language and related skills—the abilities Tulving regards as dependent on semantic memory—they fail when memory for recent events or learning episodes is tested. Part of the information that is encoded when particular learning episodes are consolidated in memory is the time that learning occurred. The ability to associate the temporal context of one episode to others has been attributed to processes located in the frontal lobes. Patients who sustain frontal lobe damage are frequently unable to report the correct temporal sequencing of events, even though their recall of such events may be normal.

In his 1889 paper describing a number of cases of patients with chronic amnesia, Korsakoff noted that the severity of memory failure was variable ranging from profound to mild. He observed that: "In milder degrees for example, there may be no complete abrogation of the memory of recent events, only the facts are remembered vaguely, unclearly. In some cases the facts themselves are remembered, but not the time that they occurred" (Victor & Yakovlev, 1955). We have already seen that confabulation provoked by questioning about past events is often attributed to the amnesic Korsakoffs' distortion of the temporal context of past occurrences (Kopelman, 1987). A number of researchers have proposed that the defective encoding or retrieval of contextual information may be the fundamental deficit underlying amnesia (Huppert & Piercy, 1976; Kinsbourne & Wood, 1975; Mayes, Meudell, & Pickering, 1985). In doing so they are making a distinction between memory for context and memory for targets (Parkin, 1992). Context memory is the ability to report the spatiotemporal location of a stimulus that has been exposed previously; target memory is ability recognise that a stimulus has been presented on a prior occasion. Testing context memory has been a recent focus of research interest and the ability to judge the temporal, spatial, and modality attributes of target stimuli have been investigated in Korsakoff patients.

Huppert and Piercy (1976) found that Korsakoff patients tended to confuse recency and frequency. They used a procedure in which a set of slides of pictures of paintings, scenes, objects, and people were shown to subjects, with half the slides being exposed just once and the remaining half three times. A second set of slides were shown a day later, again with half the slides exposed once and the balance three times. They were then able to assess recall of frequency by asking subjects whether they had seen the pictures once or three times, and recency by asking if they had seen the stimuli that day or the day before. They found that Korsakoff patients reported that the pictures that they had seen most recently were the ones they had actually been shown most frequently. Further, the amnesics' judgements of frequency were biased by the recency of the exposure of the stimuli. They tended to rate those pictures they had just seen as appearing more frequently. The propensity of Korsakoff amnesics to be biased in their recency judgements by the effects of frequency were confirmed by Meudell, Mayes, Ostergaard, and Pickering (1985), although they did not find as strong a biasing effect for recency on frequency. In this study they were also able to rule out the possibility that the confusion of recency and frequency was merely a characteristic of poor target memory. They tested the proposition that failure to retrieve context information accurately was a function of the degree of amnesia for the target items by assessing context memory in normal subjects whose memory had been weakened by a long period of delay between presentation of the target stimuli and the testing of their retention. They found that in this situation, decline in ability to recognise the target stimuli was not accompanied by a concurrent confusion of recency and frequency. Thus the effects they reported in amnesic Korsakoffs could not be explained by their poor memory for target stimuli.

Mayes et al. (1989) reported a study in which they investigated the biasing effects of frequency on recency discrimination in a group of non-Korsakoff amnesic patients (some with bitemporal or diffuse lesions following head injury, others with basal forebrain and frontal lesion consequent on aneurysmal rupture), and a group of non-amnesic patients with frontal lesions. They found the same pattern of results in their mixed-aetiology amnesic group as they had found in their Korsakoff patients. The patients with frontal lesions without amnesia performed normally. Although this study did not compare directly the degree of contextual confusion in diencephalic Korsakoff with that observed in other lesion-specific subgroups of amnesics, the implications of this study were that contextual memory failure is a deficit characteristic of organic amnesia irrespective of aetiology. This conclusion is not supported by results from other studies of recency discrimination in amnesics. Squire (1982) contrasted the ability of seven Korsakoff patients to make recency discriminations in a list learning paradigm. The subjects were shown one list of 12 sentences, and then a second list, 3 minutes later. Using a recognition procedure, subjects identified those sentences that were familiar to them and then indicated whether these sentences were part of the first or second lists. The Korsakoff patients and patients with amnesia induced by ECT did not differ in their recognition performance. However, the Korsakoff patients were markedly inaccurate in their identification of the list to which the words belonged; their performance being at chance levels (47% correct). Parkin, Leng, and Hunkin (1990) compared patients with amnesia following herpes simplex encephalitis (HSE), who have lesions that are primarily bitemporal and orbital–frontal, with Korsakoff patients on a task that required retention of the temporal context of a set of target items. They found a more marked degree of deficit in the Korsakoff patients than in HSE subjects. Parkin (1992) reported results showing that Korsakoff patients were more impaired in ability to encode temporal information than the HSE group, and that recency discrimination and target recognition were correlated for the Korsakoff group but not the HSE group. Shimamura et al. (1990) conducted two studies in which patients with frontal lesions, Korsakoff amnesics, and a group of amnesics with non-alcoholic aetiologies were tested for their ability to arrange in correct temporal sequence newly learned words, and famous events from the period 1941 to 1985. Both amnesic groups were significantly impaired in their ability to recall and temporally sequence the items tested. However, although their levels of target recognition were similar, patients with Korsakoff syndrome did worse on the temporal ordering component of the memory task than the other amnesics. The frontal patients were impaired in their ability to sequence items correctly, despite having a normal memory for the target items. Squire and colleagues concluded that it is the superimposed frontal lobe damage that causes the specific problems with temporal ordering seen in Korsakoff patients. They supported this conclusion by results from amnesic patients in the study, who had circumscribed diencephalic damage with no apparent frontal damage, but showed no deficits on the tests of temporal ordering.

Overall, both clinical and research evidence supports the view that the ability to order events in their correct temporal sequence is deficient in Korsakoff patients. Whether or not this deficit is found in amnesics of different aetiologies has not been conclusively determined. Contextual–memory deficit theories of amnesia (e.g. Pickering, Mayes, & Fairbairn, 1989), which propose that the intrinsic dysfunction in amnesia is a failure to encode the context of designated target information, have cited these results as evidence for their views. A context memory failure hypothesis provides a more compelling explanation for global amnesia if context memory failure is seen in all amnesics regardless of aetiology. The results reported by Parkin and colleagues are difficult to interpret, as Parkin (1992) acknowledges, in circumstances where the target recognition performance of two distinct amnesic groups are equal, but one shows an impairment in recalling context information relative to the other. In this situation, it is not clear what to conclude about the significance of the context deficit. If context memory failure underlies some forms of amnesia but not others, then one might expect that the HSE patients, with their normal context memory, would perform better on tests of target memory than Korsakoffs, who do not have normal context memory. As Parkin (1992, p. 127) has observed: "One might argue, on the grounds that target memory can arise from both target and context attributes, that the HSE patients should fare better on recognition, because their available target memory should be enhanced by the additional contextual memory that may be available". Alternatively, context memory failure may be a non-obligatory feature of amnesia, seen in some amnesics with diencephalic–frontal lesions but not in others. It may also be that the two amnesic groups do not in fact have equivalent levels of target memory deficit and that the matching recognition task is insensitive to real differences in severity. If this were the case, however, context memory impairments might be related to severity of anterograde amnesia. The relationship between poor temporal discrimination and explicit memory failure remains to be further elucidated.

Metamemory

Shimamura and Squire (1986a) came upon another memory task that Korsakoff patients performed more poorly than other groups of amnesics when they tested the accuracy of their feeling-of-knowing (FOK) judgements. Part of the process of mobilising effort to recall particular items of information involves having some sort of feeling that the information is known or is available. If a question is posed and the answer does not come automatically to mind, then devoting further energy to the recall of the information will depend on having a sense that the answer is somewhere to be found. FOK is often regarded as an instance of *metamemory* capacity, where metamemory refers to the awareness of one's memory performance. The validity of this feeling-of-knowing sensation has been tested in a number of paradigms. One commonly used procedure was developed by Nelson and colleagues (e.g. Nelson & Narens, 1980) and involves presenting a list of general knowledge questions (e.g. "What is the capital of Australia?" [Canberra]) to subjects and identifying a set of questions that they are unable to answer correctly. For each of these questions, subjects are asked to make FOK judgements on a four-point scale (1 = high feeling of knowing; 4 = pure guess), based on their estimate of how likely they would be to select the correct answer from amongst seven possible alternatives. Then, for each individual subject, a seven-choice recognition task is administered, based on a set of 12 or 24 questions not answered correctly, and the FOK ratings and outcome of the recognition test for each item are correlated. This resultant correlation is an estimate of the accuracy of feeling of knowing for each subject.

Shimamura and Squire (1986a) applied this experimental procedure to eight Korsakoff patients, four other amnesics, depressed patients with transient amnesia after receiving ECT, and matched control groups. Only the Korsakoff patients performed abnormally on Nelson's general information metamemory task. Shimamura and Squire also administered a new learning metamemory task. In this, the subjects were given a series of sentences to read (e.g. "At the museum we saw some relics made of clay") and their recall was then tested by providing them with the sentence, but with a noun omitted ("At the museum we saw some relics made of ——"). Sentences containing those missing words that the subjects could not recall correctly were then rated for FOK. The subjects were then given a seven-choice recognition task using a set of nouns that might plausibly complete the stimulus sentence. On this task the Korsakoff patients also performed poorly; indeed their average FOK-recognition correlation was –0.007. Even after a seven-day delay the performance of the control groups was superior to that of the Korsakoff patients. Overall, comparisons between the amnesic groups suggested to Shimamura and Squire (1986a, p. 458) that the Korsakoff patients "have a particular deficit in metamemory that cannot be explained as a result of their memory impairment". They went on to state (Shimamura & Squire, 1986a, p. 459) that "Presumably, Korsakoff's syndrome typically produces a more widespread cognitive deficit than is observed in other forms of amnesia".

Shimamura and Squire (1986a) concluded that impairment on metamemory tasks may not be an obligatory feature of amnesia. In a subsequent study, Janowsky, Shimamura, and Squire (1989b) found that patients with circumscribed frontal lobe lesions also showed deficits on the sentence recall metamemory task, when recall was tested after a one- to three-day delay. On general information metamemory tasks, however, the frontal lobe patients accuracy of FOK was unimpaired. Janowsky et al. (1989b) thus established that under some circumstances patients with frontal lobe lesions perform abnormally on metamemory tasks, despite having no significant degree of memory loss. The implication of these results is that the frontal lesions of Korsakoff patients render their performance on metamemory tasks distinctive from those of other amnesics. One caution, however, is in order. Squire's amnesic Korsakoff patients appear to have absolute memory performance decrements on the WMS that are greater than those of his comparison group of amnesics. The age-corrected average MQ score for the Korsakoff group was 78 (range 64 to 93), whereas the MQs for the four amnesics were 91, 81, 92, and 97. Although the amnesic samples may have had equivalent FSIQ–MQ decrements, the severity of the amnesia could be a factor in determining the presence of metamemory deficits.

Perceptual skill learning

In an elegant experiment, Cohen and Squire (1980) demonstrated that not only is motor skill learning preserved in amnesia, but new perceptual skills are also acquired and retained normally. A mirror-reading task was used whereby subjects were asked to read aloud as quickly as possible three low-frequency eight- to ten-letter nouns (e.g. grandiose–capricious–

bedraggle) that had been mirror-reversed. On half of the trials, the word trials were repeated, on the other half the words used occurred only once. This allowed Cohen and Squire to measure how rapidly the actual skill of reading mirror-reversed words was acquired, and the extent to which the subjects were able to benefit from the repetition of specific words. The results showed clearly that the Korsakoff patients were able to acquire the skill at a normal rate. There was no difference between the amnesic and control groups in the speed with which they read the non-repeated mirror-reversed word trials. On the repeated trials, however, there was a between-group difference. The authors found (Cohen & Squire, 1980, p. 208) that "the ability of amnesic patients to mirror read repeated words was inferior to the control rate, because amnesic patients, unlike the control subjects, could not remember the specific words that had been read". Cohen and Squire had found a clear dissociation between the ability to recall particular items of information and to learn a new perceptual skill. On the basis of these findings and similar results with motor skill learning tasks, they proposed a distinction between *declarative* ("knowing that") and *procedural* ("knowing how") memory that has become influential in characterising preserved skills in amnesia. By declarative memory they were referring to the storage of specific or data-based information; instances of procedural learning are provided by the acquisition of new skills or rules. They proposed that this latter ability was largely unaffected by the lesions causing amnesia as evidenced by studies that show normal motor skill learning in amnesics (Brooks & Baddeley, 1976).

Priming

In addition to skill learning, there is at least one other important instance of preserved learning in amnesics—normal semantic priming. We have already seen that semantic priming is also normal in chronic alcoholics. Priming refers to the situation where the exposure of one stimuli alters the availability or facilitates the subsequent analysis of a second stimuli. For example, the word BREAD will be read more quickly if it is preceded by the word BUTTER than if the prior word is COUPLET. Underlying this effect is the assumption that when a word is read, its representation and those of closely associated concepts in semantic memory are activated, making their availability temporarily more accessible. Thus, if subjects have recently read the word MOTEL, the cognitive schema for this word will have been activated, and they are more likely to respond to the instruction to complete the word stem MOT— with the primed word MOTEL, than with an alternative, such as MOTOR. One significant aspect of the priming phenomenon is that it precedes conscious awareness. The features of the word are activated automatically producing a bias in responding that the subject need not be aware of; no explicit reference to the previous exposure of the word is necessary for priming to occur.

An interesting test of semantic priming in amnesics was conducted by Jacoby and Witherspoon (1982). They asked five Korsakoff patients to answer a series of questions that contained a word that was one of a pair of homophones (words that sound the same but are spelt differently e.g. GRATE and GREAT). The questions were intended to create a bias towards the least frequently used member of the homophone pair. An example of a biasing question was "Name a musical instrument that employed a *reed*". They then conducted a spelling to dictation test that contained items that had appeared in the biasing questions (e.g. READ/REED). They found that the Korsakoff patients were just as likely as the controls to produce the homophone spelling biased by the initial questions. When they were tested for the ability to recognise the words they had been exposed to in the questions, however, the amnesics were severely impaired. Thus, although they were unaware of the priming episode, the Korsakoff patients' behaviour was influenced by its occurrence. Jacoby and Witherspoon (1982, p. 313) proposed that remembering and awareness might be dissociated and suggested "the possibility that amnesics have relatively normal memory for events but are incapable of aware forms of remembering".

These findings have many parallels with the results of Warrington and Weiskrantz's (1968; 1970; 1978) studies in which normal cued recall was found in amnesic patients. Warrington and Weiskrantz (1968) observed that some of their patients, when completing the fragmented pictures task, acted as if the exercise was a guessing game rather than a test of memory. This suggested that the patients were treating the recognition process as a perceptual task and were not aware of any prior learning episode; thus the enhanced performance of the amnesics may have resulted from something akin to a priming effect. The work of Warrington and colleagues was followed by several attempted replications in which other workers were unable to find a selective improvement due to partial information cueing with letter stems (e.g. Mayes, Meudell, & Neary, 1978; Mortensen, 1980; Squire, Wetzel, & Slater, 1978). Then, in 1984, Graf, Squire and Mandler reported a study that helped explain why the results of the replications and the original studies were not in accord. They found that the crucial factor in the cueing experimental procedure was the instructions. If these were devoid of any reference to a previous learning episode then Korsakoff amnesics and controls performed at equivalent levels. However, if the instructions referred to previous learning then amnesics were more likely to be impaired. Graf et al. (1984) suggested that these results might be evidence not for a retrieval-based deficit in amnesia as Warrington and Weiskrantz had suggested, but for the existence of more than one memory system.

The procedure that Graf et al. (1984) used required subjects to read a list of words and to rate them on a "liking" scale from 1 (dislike extremely) to 5 (like extremely). The object of the process of making the liking ratings, and other similar tasks, was to ensure that the word stimuli were encoded semantically. No reference was made to these stimuli being a part of any later memory test. A priming test was then administered in which subjects were presented with a list of three-letter word stems and asked to complete them with the first English word that came to mind. Half of these word stems could be answered using words exposed during the liking rating task; the remainder came from another word list that the subjects had not seen before and were used to determine baseline guessing rates. All the word stems used could make at least 10 common English words. Under the "first word into your mind" instructions, the bias towards the words from the primed list was the same for both normals and controls. In contrast, when the conventional cued recall instructions were used (stressing that subjects use each stem as a prompt to recall words from the rating list), Korsakoff patients were impaired relative to the controls. The Korsakoffs showed similar marked deficits on tests of free recall and recognition. Graf et al. (1984, p. 176) concluded that:

> The present results identify the important role of instructions in determining whether the performance of amnesic patients is normal or impaired. Performance is normal when the instructions define the task as one of word completion, but performance is impaired when the instructions define the task as one of cued recall. Word completion seems best understood as depending on a process, or a memory system, that is spared in amnesia and does not require the integrity of those brain regions damaged in amnesia.

Normal priming has been observed in amnesics in a number of studies and is a robust phenomenon (e.g., Cermak, Talbot, Chandler, & Wolbarst, 1985; Cermak et al., 1991; Graf, Shimamura, & Squire, 1985; Longmore & Knight, 1988). Priming has been found to be as long-lasting in amnesic patients as in normals (Cave & Squire, 1992), and to occur normally in amnesics following a wide variety of experimental manipulations (Musen & Squire, 1991; Smith & Oscar-Berman, 1990; Squire & McKee, 1992; Tulving, Hayman, & MacDonald, 1991). The effect is strongest for words or paired associates that are represented in semantic memory. Korsakoff patients do not prime for novel non-words (Cermak et al., 1985) and their performance is variable for newly acquired associations between previously unrelated words (Schacter & Graf, 1986). Both the severity of amnesia and the type of priming test appear to be important in demonstrating the integrity of the effect in memory-impaired patients. The success of Korsakoff patients on priming tasks has provided a major line of evidence in favour of a distinction between memory processes that are tested implicitly and those assessed explicitly. Word completion is a test where learning is tested by implicit or indirect instructions; cued recall involves explicit reference to previous learning. This distinction will be considered in more detail later in this chapter.

Retrograde amnesia

One of the principal weaknesses of a strong retrieval-based explanation of amnesia is that it does not appear to operate consistently across the full range of items stored in memory. It is a common observation that patients with Korsakoff's syndrome may recollect information from childhood or early adult life with some facility, whereas information for more recent occurrences is seemingly lost. Procedures for testing memory for public events were introduced in Chapter 9. On these tests of public information, a simple retrieval model would predict that retrograde amnesia was ungraded with respect to time; that is, items from the 1940s should be recalled as well (or as poorly in the case of Korsakoffs) as items from the 1980s. This assumes that the remote memory test has been constructed so that the subtests for the individual decades are psychometrically equivalent, and in particular, matched for level of difficulty.

There is no doubt that retrograde amnesia is a characteristic of Korsakoff's syndrome. Although some early studies suggested that there was an ungraded relationship between accuracy of recall and decades tested (e.g. Sanders & Warrington, 1971), there is now a consensus that most cases of Korsakoff's syndrome show a temporal gradient. Recall of memories from adolescence and early adulthood is superior to that of more recently acquired information (Albert, Butters, & Levin, 1979; Kopelman, 1989). This pattern of graded decline in memory is illustrated in Fig. 10.4. Clinical evidence for the graded and severe disturbance of remote memory in alcoholic amnesia dates back to Korsakoff's own writings (Victor & Yakovlev, 1955, p. 398):

> With all this, the remarkable fact is that, forgetting all events that have just occurred, the patients usually remember quite accurately past events which occurred long before the illness. What is forgotten usually proves to be everything that happened during the illness and a short time before the beginning of the illness. Such is the case in the more typical instances of the disease; in others, even the memory of remote events may be disturbed.

How is this pattern of graded deterioration best explained? One possibility is that the gradual onset of anterograde amnesia, through the course of the chronic alcohol abuse that usually precedes Korsakoff's

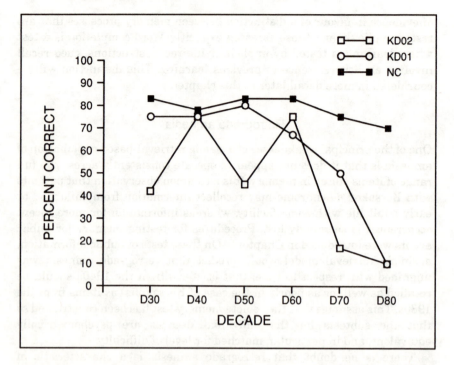

FIG. 10.4. Remote memory performance in two Korsakoff patients (KD01 and KD02) and a group of age-matched controls (NC).

syndrome, is responsible. The alcoholic lifestyle, combined with deficits in memory that become more obvious with age, cause a progressive decline in new learning, leaving the Korsakoff patient with a graded memory loss. If this were the case, however, one would expect to find that older impaired alcoholics would have as severe a level of retrograde amnesia as Korsakoff patients do for memories acquired many years before they were hospitalised with severe amnesia. The retrograde amnesia of Korsakoff's syndrome is more severe than can be explained solely by the chronic effects of alcohol abuse. Another possibility is that the episode of drinking preceding the onset of Korsakoff's syndrome, which may be characterised by symptoms of Wernicke's encephalopathy, has a "traumatic effect" that intensifies the degree of retrograde amnesia. Studies of remote memory performance in alcoholic and Korsakoff patients have provided important data against which theories suggesting a continuity of deterioration in alcoholic syndromes may be measured. We will return to this issue later in this chapter.

There has also been considerable interest in the relationship between anterograde and retrograde amnesia in Korsakoff patients. At issue is the

AMNESIA IN KORSAKOFF'S SYNDROME   299

question of whether these deficits are caused by the dysfunction of the same or different functional systems (Kopelman, 1989; Parkin,1991; Shimamura & Squire, 1986b). Correlations between remote memory test scores and results from verbal learning measures for groups of Korsakoff patients have generally been found to be negligible. An exception is that significant associations have been found for degree of anterograde deficit and memory for events in the most recent decades (Parkin, Montaldi, Leng, & Hunkin, 1990). These findings are not readily interpreted as evidence for or against distinct functional systems underpinning retrograde and anterograde amnesia. There is no theoretical reason why levels of one form of amnesia should be equivalent to another even if the failure of the same system underlies both (Parkin, 1991). More compelling evidence comes from a study that investigated the role of context in remote memory test performance. As we saw in the section above on temporal sequencing, it has been proposed that a specific deficit in encoding the context of target items is reponsible for anterograde amnesia (Mayes, 1988). Parkin et al. (1990) reasoned that the same deficit might underlie retrograde amnesia. They compared remote memory test performance under conditions of low context (a picture of the target devoid of any contextual identification) and high context (a picture with contextual information, for example, a singer with a guitar). The control subjects showed no temporal gradient in their performance and a consistent advantage for high over low context information across all decades. The Korsakoff patients, however, had a marked temporal gradient and the contextual cueing advantage was significantly less for more recent decades relative to the early decades. These results were not consistent with a context memory deficit account of retrograde amnesia, and suggested to Parkin (1991) that a storage deficit might provide a more plausible expanation of remote memory test failure.

At this stage, it is evident that an extensive and temporally graded retrograde amnesia is characteristic of patients with Wernicke–Korsakoff syndrome and that there are considerable individual variations in the extent of the memory loss and steepness of the resulting gradients. The correlations between performance on measures of new learning and memory for recent events suggests that anterograde amnesia plays some part in producing the more pronounced deficits seen in recalling events from recent decades. Individual differences in remote memory performance have not been found to correlate with either neuroradiological evidence of frontal lobe atrophy or performance on tests that assess frontal function (Kopelman, 1989). Cases where severe anterograde amnesia occurs without remote memory failure (e.g., Winocur et al., 1984), together with other evidence marshalled by Parkin and colleagues (Parkin, 1991; Parkin et al., 1990) provide some preliminary evidence for a dissociation between the functional systems subserving new learning and remote memory. The reason why temporal grading is more evident in some Korsakoff patients than others, and in alcoholic amnesics than in patients with Alzeheimer's disease (Kopelman, 1989), remains to be elucidated.

Conclusions

It is now nearly three decades since the publication of Talland's seminal work. A greater understanding of the nature of amnesic deficit in Wernicke–Korsakoff syndrome has emerged in that time. Experimental neuropsychological investigations of Korsakoff patients have made significant contributions to our understanding of how human memory works. However, no consensus has been reached about whether there is a fundamental cognitive deficit underpinning amnesia, and if so what it is. The precise role that storage, encoding, consolidation, retrieval, and contextual processes play in memory failure remains unclear. Findings from this research support two major conclusions. First, the lesions responsible for alcoholic Korsakoff's syndrome do not affect all memory-related skills and the discovery of preserved functions has been of importance in testing models of memory at both behavioural and biological levels. Second, Korsakoff patients differ in their memory performance from other groups of amnesics in ways that suggest that either diencephalic amnesias can be distinguished from those amnesias caused by temporal lobe lesions, or that concurrent frontal or cortical atrophy play a significant part in the pattern of symptoms of Korsakoff's syndrome.

Preserved and impaired learning. As we have already observed, Korsakoff patients show normal perceptual and motor skill learning, and semantic priming, despite profound impairments on all traditional tests of new learning. Those tasks that are normal in amnesia all have one important attribute in common: they involve learning without intentional reference to any prior learning episode (Johnson & Hasher, 1987). For example, it is possible to demonstrate acquisition of a new motor or perceptual skill by responding to stimuli without any conscious access to previous experiences with the same stimuli. Squire and his colleagues (Squire, 1986) distinguished between tasks amnesics could or could not perform normally with the terms procedural and declarative learning; similarly, Jacoby and Witherspoon (1982) made a distinction between learning with or without awareness. Perhaps the most influential dichotomy that has been proposed along these lines is between *explicit* and *implicit* memory. Schacter (1987, p. 501) offered the following definitions: "Implicit memory is revealed when previous experience facilitates performance on a task that does not require conscious or intentional recollection of those experiences; explicit memory is revealed when performance on a task requires conscious recollection of previous experiences". Schacter regarded the terms *unconscious* memory (Prince, 1914) or memory without awareness as being largely synonymous with implicit memory. An alternative dichotomy, *direct* versus *indirect* memory, has been suggested by Johnson and Hasher (1987). This distinction is based entirely on the nature of the test instructions and makes no reference to the actual memory processes subjects use to complete particular tasks. Direct measures have instructions that focus attention on a target event or episode of learning, whereas indirect tests have instructions that refer only to the present situation confronting the subject.

Table 10.4 illustrates the various dichotomised labels that have been used to characterise the normal and impaired performance of Korsakoff patients. For clinicians, although much of this distinction may seem to be of academic interest only, this research with amnesic patients has provided some basis for predicting what such patients may learn, in the course of any rehabilitation programme.

There is also the clear expectation that despite a profound amnesia, Korsakoff patients will be able to learn new skills. Although they may forget what they know, if they are engaged in a practised task their new skill will still be available.

Frontal lobe damage.   Is the amnesia seen in alcoholic Korsakoff's syndrome unique? Or, do all forms of amnesia, regardless of aetiology, result in the same pattern of deficits? It seems that the alcoholic amnesic performs differently to other amnesics on many memory tasks.

The reason for this does not appear to be a greater level of intellectual deficit in Korsakoff patients. Longmore and Knight (1988) showed that demented and purely amnesic alcoholics were equally deficient on such

TABLE 10.4

Dichotomised Terms Used to Label Preserved and Impaired Memory Functions in Amnesia

Normal	Impaired
Memory without awareness	Memory with awareness
Procedural memory	Declarative memory
Indirect tests	Direct tests
Incidental learning	Intentional learning
Semantic memory	Episodic memory
Implicit memory	Explicit memory
Unconscious memory	Conscious memory

memory tasks as release from proactive interference, recall and recognition, and the Peterson–Brown distractor technique. However, there is evidence that points to frontal lobe damage as the factor that determines the special quality of amnesia in Korsakoff patients. In this view, the amnesic deficits that are caused by diencephalic damage are superimposed on and complicated by lesions in the frontal lobes. The fact that Korsakoff patients have frontal damage has been reported by a number of researchers, including Shimamura, Jernigan, and Squire (1988) and Jacobson and Lishman (1987), who have conducted CT studies of Korsakoff patients. In order to demonstrate using neuropsychological tests that this damage has some behavioural consequences, it is necessary to show that Korsakoffs have cognitive deficits similar to those seen in frontal patients, but which are not seen in other amnesics. Any such demonstration requires overcoming a formidable series of methodological obstacles. Cognitive tests that provide a valid assessment of frontal damage need to be devised. The precise nature of the lesions in the amnesic and frontal groups need to be determined. Contrasted groups need to be matched for a variety of factors, such as premorbid IQ and age.

Janowsky et al. (1989a) have reported one such study. They identified seven patients with frontal lobe damage (three with left-sided, two right-sided and two with bilateral lesions). These patients were contrasted with a group of seven Korsakoffs and their six alcoholic controls, and with five non-Korsakoff amnesics and their eight healthy controls, on a variety of clinical and experimental neuropsychological tasks. One of their principal findings was that the frontal lobe patients were not amnesic and scored in the normal range on most of the memory tests. The general pattern of results on the memory tests is apparent in Table 10.5. The amnesic patients have markedly reduced scores on both the WMS and the WMS-R. On the WMS-R there is a dissociation between the performance of the 12 amnesic patients and the frontal patients whereby the amnesic perform better than the frontal group on the Attention–Concentration scale, but worse on the Delayed Memory scale. The performance of the two amnesic groups on the WMS and WMS-R were not contrasted statistically, but the Korsakoff patients performed more poorly on all the measures except the Delayed Memory index, where the scores are comparable. A similar pattern to that portrayed in Table 10.5 was found for the results from tests of paired-associate learning and story recall, the Rey AVLT, and the Complex Figure Test. The two amnesic groups performed at about the same level on these measures and were impaired relative to their control groups; the frontal patients were unimpaired on the memory tests with the exception of the recall procedure from the Rey AVLT.

On the WCST (Table 10.5), the non-Korsakoff amnesic group was significantly different in performance from the Korsakoff patients. Six of

TABLE 10.5
Comparison of Frontal Lobe Damaged Patients, Korsakoffs, and Other
Amnesics (From Janowsky et al. (1989))

	Frontal group	Korsakoffs	Other amnesics
Age	64.0	54.6	53.4
WAIS-R IQ	101.1	97.1	109.2
WMS MQ	107.4	81.3	93.0
WMS-R indices			
attention–concentration	83.8	90.1	105.4
verbal memory	100.7	70.6	77.8
visual memory	90.5	75.1	81.2
general memory	95.7	66.1	73.0
delayed memory	94.5	56.7	55.0
WCST			
categories	2.1	3.3	5.4
% perseverative errors	41.6	25.2	14.4

the frontal patients scored in the normative range for impairment on this
test. The alcoholic Korsakoffs also performed poorly, but did make on
average at least three category shifts. These results are compounded by
the higher average age of the frontal patients, nevertheless, the trend for
the Korsakoff patients to perform more poorly than the other amnesics
provides further evidence that Korsakoff patients have cognitive deficits
consistent with frontal atrophy and that they can be distinguished from
amnesics of other aetiologies for this reason. Joyce and Robbins (1991)
similarly found that Korsakoff patients made more errors on the WCST
and other tests known to be sensitive to frontal lobe lesions.

Janowsky et al. (1989a) also tested their subjects on a variety of other
tests. On the release from proactive interference task, only the Korsakoff
patients failed to release; the other amnesics and the frontal lobe damaged
subjects performed normally. This result is in contrast to Moscovitch's
(1982) report that frontal patients fail to release, but may be explained by
Freedman and Cermak's (1986) finding that only frontal lobe patients with
marked memory loss failed to release. The normal performance of
Janowsky et al.'s frontal group may be explained by their essentially
normal memory performance. On the verbal fluency test, only the frontal
patients with left-sided lesions were impaired; neither of the amnesic
groups showed any deficits. Finally, on the Perseveration–Initiation scale
of the Dementia Rating Scale (Mattis, 1976), both the Korsakoff and the
frontal damaged patients were impaired; the other amnesics performed
normally. Janowsky et al. (1989a, p. 558) came to the overall conclusion
that:

Taken together, the findings from our study suggest that certain features of Korsakoff syndrome may be attributed to frontal lobe dysfunction. Specifically, patients with Korsakoff's syndrome and patients with a frontal lobe pathology exhibited an impairment on the Wisconsin Card Sorting Test, and impairment on the Initiation–Perseveration subscale of the Dementia Rating Scale, and possibly a disproportionate deficit in recall performance.

There are other findings that suggest that the amnesia of Korsakoff's syndrome is specifically affected by frontal lobe damage. The remarkable apathy and lack of initiative seen in many Korsakoffs is also seen in patients with severe frontal lobe damage (Blumer & Benson, 1975). Further, Korsakoff patients are likely to have problems with temporal sequencing comparable to those of frontal patients. On metamemory tasks, patients with Korsakoff's syndrome are the only patient group to show deficits in general information feeling-of-knowing (FOK) judgements; similar deficits emerge for frontal patients on more difficult FOK judgement tasks testing new learning. The Peterson–Brown distractor task is another situation where Korsakoff performance is unlike that of amnesics (Leng & Parkin, 1989). A variable degree of deficit on the Peterson-Brown task seems to be a feature of the amnesia of Korsakoff's syndrome that other amnesics do not share.

Whether or not the quality of amnesia seen in Korsakoff patients can be attributed to concurrent frontal damage, there is little doubt that memory failure in alcoholic Korsakoff's syndrome is complicated by damage to aspects of cognition other than memory and by changes in emotionality, not seen in other amnesics. This is not unexpected, given that the Korsakoff patient often arrives at an amnesic state after years of alcohol abuse, nutritional insufficiency, and medical complications. In contrast, neurosurgical, anoxic, or viral cases all become amnesic after only a relatively brief transition and without necessarily having a long premorbid history of complications that might compromise cognitive functioning. Although these other conditions may result in a range of brain lesions, the damage to the brain tends to be more circumscribed than that seen in Korsakoff's syndrome.

THE CONTINUITY HYPOTHESIS

The chapters in Part 3 have been divided according to an implicit assumption that social drinking, alcoholism, and the Wernicke–Korsakoff syndrome represent discrete typologies. In part, this is encouraged by the way these groups are identified for study. Social drinkers live in the community, alcoholics are found in treatment programmes, and Korsakoff patients are usually either in hospital or some other dependent care facility.

The order in which the chapters have been presented, however, also suggests some degree of continuity in impairment. Social drinkers have only equivocal evidence of impairment and their deficits do not fall in the range typical of clinical brain damage. Alcoholics, on average, do show signs of cognitive dysfunction, but these deficits do not impede routine aspects of an independent lifestyle, although there may be some impact on their efficiency in the work setting. Wernicke–Korsakoff patients have a degree of neuropsychological deficit that does interfere with their everyday living and they therefore need to be cared for by others. There is, therefore, a progression in dysfunction from the early stages of alcoholism to a degree of irreversible dementia.

Ryback (1971) prepared a review of contemporary research on the cognitive effects of alcohol abuse that was organised in a manner similar in many respects to that presented in this book. He noted that alcohol acutely affects memory, which he termed the "cocktail party" effect, and from the few studies then available, he concluded that memory loss was a feature of chronic alcoholism. He also incorporated results from studies of Wernicke–Korsakoff syndrome. He proposed that a disturbance in short-term memory was "the specific deficit common to cocktail party drinking, alcoholic amnesia and Wernicke–Korsakoff". He then went on to add (Ryback, 1971, p. 1008) "Perhaps there is also a continuum among the latter three". This tentatively expressed proposition was the basis of what came to be known as Ryback's "continuity hypothesis".

It is clear that Ryback recognised the crucial objection to his continuum model, the fact that the aetiological basis for brain injury in alcoholism was attributed to neurotoxicity, while the Wernicke–Korsakoff syndrome was regarded as being the result of thiamine deficiency. Most clinicians at that time, as indeed they would now, considered that there was a discontinuity between chronic alcoholism and Wernicke–Korsakoff syndrome in terms of both the extent and cause of the typical brain lesions observed post-mortem. Ryback, however, questioned the evidence that the neuro-pathological lesions underlying Wernicke–Korsakoff syndrome were correctly attributed to thiamine deficiency. The lack of a precise understanding of the aetiology and biological basis of brain damage in Korsakoff and alcoholic patients still remains a major stumbling block to determining whether the continuum hypothesis has any validity. Recent post-mortem studies have made more salient some of Ryback's doubts about the validity of thiamine depletion as the principal causative factor in the production of the lesions responsible for amnesia.

The best recent statement of the evidence for and against the continuity hypothesis comes from Butters and Granholm (1987). Figure 10.5 presents representations of Ryback's continuity model and Butters and Granholm's modification, labelled the "trauma model". In essence, the trauma model

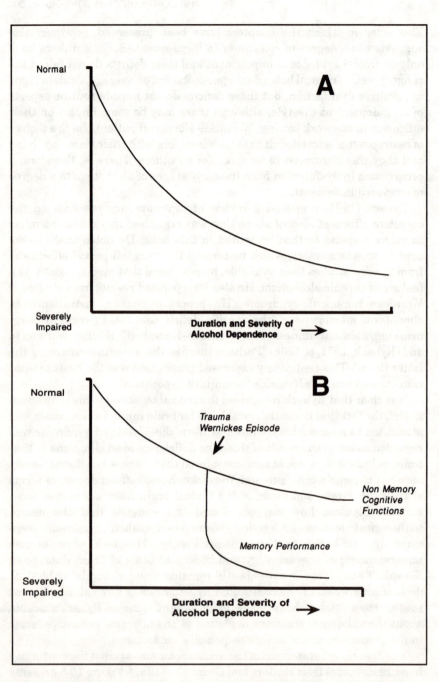

FIG. 10.5. Schematic representation of (A) Ryback's Continuity Model and (B) the Trauma Model of Butters and Granholm (1987).

implies that there is a continuity in the decline in some cognitive functions, but not in learning and retention, where there is a sharp discontinuity between alcoholism and Wernicke–Korsakoff syndrome. The severe amnesia of Wernicke–Korsakoff syndrome is the result of an acute traumatic incident, presumably an episode of Wernicke's encephalopathy, that produces substantial lesions in the diencephalic region. Butters and Granholm (1987, p. 193) observed that: "The Korsakoff patients' precipitous decline in memory performance would then represent the exceeding of a critical threshold of diencephalic damage for the maintenance of relative intact memory functions". Much of the evidence that Butters and Granholm marshall to support the trauma model has already been reviewed in preceding chapters. They concluded that patients with Korsakoff's syndrome show visuoperceptual and problem-solving impairments that are consistent with a history of alcoholism and fit with Ryback's notion of a graded continuum. Their amnesic deficits, however, are discontinuous with the memory problems displayed by alcoholics. The equivalence of visuoperceptive and problem-solving deficits in alcoholic and Korsakoff patients has been demonstrated in a number of studies. Both groups have difficulty with the WCST (Janowsky et al., 1989a; Parsons & Farr, 1981) and with maintaining a consistent hypothesis testing strategy (Becker, Rivoira, Butters, & Ciraulo, 1984, cited in Butters & Granholm, 1987; Oscar-Berman, 1973). Becker and his colleagues, using an experimental task similar to the familiar game of "20 questions", found that the quantitative and qualitative performance of alcoholic and Korsakoff patients were similar. In this task, subjects try to identify a predesigned object with a minimum number of questions. The two groups of patients had a similar and maladaptive approach to this game; unlike the normal controls "they seemed unable to initiate and maintain an optimal strategy for identifying the chosen objects" (Butters & Granholm, 1987, p. 181).

As we saw in Chapter 9, studies of memory and learning in alcoholics suggest that their average impairment is relatively minor (Brandt et al., 1983; Forsberg & Goldman, 1987; Ryan & Butters, 1980a) and does not approach the anterograde amnesia of the average Korsakoff patient. In addition, evidence from studies of retrograde amnesia provide some data that support the trauma model. Korsakoff patients typically produce a pattern of performance on remote memory tests that has a temporal gradient, although this gradient may not be as steep as that seen in other amnesics. One explanation for this graded remote memory loss is that retrograde amnesia begins to become apparent during the period of alcoholism that precedes the onset of Korsakoff's syndrome. The primary deficit may be the development of a anterograde amnesia and the consequent failure to consolidate new input in the years preceding the onset of Korsakoff's amnesia. This is consistent with the continuity hypothesis. Albert et al. (1980) have shown that although detoxified alcoholics do show a significant decrease in remote memory performance for the 10 years immediately prior to testing, this decrement is not of the extent of severity of that seen in Korsakoff patients.

Butters and Brandt (1985), in a single case study, provide some compelling evidence that the retrograde amnesia of Korsakoff's syndrome is greater than would be expected to occur simply as a consequence of an extensive history of alcoholism. Their patient, designated P.Z., was an eminent scientist who, some three years prior to a diagnosis of alcoholic Korsakoff's syndrome, published an autobiography giving a detailed account of his life and involvement in teaching and research. On the basis of this, Butters and Brandt were able to construct a personalised test of remote memory based on events and people mentioned in the book that the author was presumably familiar with only two years prior to the onset of the Korsakoff amnesia. P.Z. was found to have a profound degree of retrograde amnesia, with his ability to recall events described in his autobiography during the 1960s and 1970s being almost zero. His performance was compared with that of a similarly prominent scholar in the same discipline and the extent of the loss of recent autobiographical memories in P.Z. was dramatically apparent. This study illustrated Butters and Granholm's (1987) contention that the retrograde amnesia seen in Korsakoff's syndrome can not be attributed entirely to the anterograde amnesia deficits of alcoholism. Nevertheless, the memory loss seen in P.Z. had a marked temporal gradient, suggesting that recent memories were in some way less stable than early memories. This may or may not be a consequence of an alcohol-induced instability in consolidation during a premorbid period of alcohol abuse. Alternatively, the "trauma" that produces the Korsakoff's syndrome may have a retroactive effect that is independent of the degree of stability of the consolidated material.

The trauma model that Butters and Granholm (1987) propose fits much of the data available from neuropsychological research. However, there are problems in the uncritical acceptance of this hypothesis, which arise from the gaps in our knowledge of the biological basis of the "traumatic" event and from the representation in the model of a stereotyped view of the course of Wernicke–Korsakoff syndrome. These difficulties are anticipated in Bowden's (1990) review of attempts to distinguish the Wernicke–Korsakoff syndrome from the neurologically undamaged alcoholic.

The lesions generally held to be responsible for the clinical manifestations of Wernicke–Korsakoff syndrome are located in the grey matter around the third and fourth ventricles. These lesions are sometimes termed the Wernicke–Korsakoff complex. As both Bowden (1990) and Butters and Granholm (1987) observe, post mortem studies of alcoholics frequently revealed evidence of the Wernicke–Korsakoff complex in patients who in life did not show a severity of cognitive failure consistent with Wernicke–Korsakoff syndrome. On the basis of the research by Harper and colleagues (Harper & Kril, 1985; 1989) (which was considered in Chapters 3 and 4), Bowden concludes that many alcoholics found to have diencephalic lesions post-mortem may show no evidence of amnesia, or only mild deficits in memory and learning during the course of their lives. The implication of these post-mortem studies is that neurobiological damage resulting from alcohol abuse in the diencephalon is more common than is generally supposed. The extent of this damage might well be distributed in some continuous manner and, if this were the case, it is possible that the clinical effects of this damage on cognitive function may also be continuous. This possibility may be countered by assuming that increments in the amount of damage either cross some quantitative threshold as Butters and Granholm suggest, or eventually result in the destruction of a critical fibre tract or tracts. An alternative explanation is that the diencephalic damage plays only a part in the production of amnesia, and that damage in another critical region is necessary to produce the Wernicke–Korsakoff syndrome. Butters (1985) suggested that neuro-pathological damage to the nucleus basalis of Meynert may provide the biological basis of alcoholic amnesia. Although damage in this region has been reported in some Korsakoff patients (Arendt, Bigl, Arendt, & Tennstedt, 1983), this finding has not been replicated in other cases (Mayes et al., 1988). Although basal forebrain damage may well play a part in the expression of symptoms in some Korsakoff patients, the precise consequences of damage to the nucleus are presently unknown.

Studies of the lesions in alcoholic patients with and without Wernicke–Korsakoff syndrome have not provided an exact picture of the damage critical to producing amnesia, how this damage evolves, and the aetiological factors involved. Although thiamine deficiency consequent on malnutrition is assumed to cause the lesions responsible for amnesia, lack of thiamine, despite producing severe amnesia, does not produce an irreversible memory failure in patients who are not alcoholics. As Lishman (1987, p. 497) observed "... the rarity of a fully-fledged Korsakoff syndrome as a residue of thiamine deficiency in non-alcoholics raises the possibility that a direct neurotoxic action of alcohol may play some part in the evolution of the condition". Thus, the aetiological basis of the alcoholic Korsakoff amnesia is also not precisely understood. The evidence available from studies of patients with the Wernicke–Korsakoff lesion complex does rule out the possibility that both the extent of the brain damage and the clinical effects of this damage may be represented on a continuum, at least in some patients. To date this prospect has not been well evaluated because representative samples of alcoholic patients have not been tested.

The principal theme that emerges from Bowden's (1990) review is that the way Korsakoff patients are represented in neuropsychological research literature is stereotyped and unrepresentative. Because researchers have been concerned with studying amnesia, they have constituted groups of Korsakoff patients with severe amnesia that is uncomplicated, as far as possible, by other cognitive deficits. To do so they exclude patients with evidence of dementia or who have less severe memory deficits. For example, Weiskrantz (1985, p. 388) reported that "we have seen many patients who have been referred by hospital consultants as 'Korsakoff' amnesics; after screening these patients clinically we have rejected them prior to inclusion in any experimental investigations as being too mixed and/or mild ...". Similarly, Talland (1965) was selective in the group of Korsakoffs he studied, and Jacobson and Lishman (1987) tested only 38 of the 50 cases of Korsakoff's syndrome referred to them. The implication of this selectivity is that there are at least some patients who are classified as Korsakoff by clinicians, but who have an insufficiently severe amnesia for inclusion in research groups with this diagnosis. Similarly, selection of alcoholics for study typically involves eliminating those with clinical evidence of Korsakoff's syndrome. Thus there may be a group of memory impaired patients who provide the "missing link" in the continuity between the deficits of the average alcoholic and the amnesia of the highly selected Korsakoff. As data from a representative sample of alcoholics across the full range of impairment in memory and intellectual functioning are not available, there is no way of knowing whether the distribution of memory impairment is continuous or discontinuous. Similarly, there are no longitudinal studies that might document the transition from alcoholism to alcoholic amnesia.

At best the trauma model in Fig. 10.5 represents the course of a subgroup of alcoholic Korsakoff patients, those who develop the condition relatively abruptly, often after an episode of Wernicke's encephalopathy. Such patients may be genetically predisposed to be excessively sensitive to thiamine deficiency (Martin, McCool, & Singleton, 1993). For many other Korsakoffs, the disorder develops more insidiously over a considerable period of time, perhaps as a consequence of numerous subclinical episodes of Wernicke's encephalopathy (Harper, 1983) but without clear evidence of an abrupt traumatic episode. In this view, for some patients, the development of amnesia is the consequence of progressive disability and is likely to be complicated by other cognitive deficits. In addition, the trauma model ignores the possibility of profound dementia in Wernicke–Korsakoff patients. This is also, at least in part, the result of testing unrepresentative groups of Korsakoff patients. As Bowden (1990, p. 362) asserts:

If Korsakoff patients are selected for study on the basis of below-average memory capabilities but an IQ in the average range, it is hardly surprising that they then show general intellectual skills in the average range when tested with other measures. In other words, many neuropsychological accounts of Wernicke–Korsakoff syndrome suffer from an unacknowledged selection bias and, as a consequence, beg the question.

In sum, any comprehensive model of the progression of alcoholism needs to take account of different end points, and various possible courses the development of cognitive impairment may take. There are Korsakoff patients with circumscribed amnesia, but there are many more brain damaged alcoholics with a mixture of memory loss and signs of dementia. For some of the patients with Wernicke–Korsakoff syndrome, the transition from the relatively mild impairment seen in many alcoholics to severe cognitive dysfunction is relatively abrupt; in other cases there is a more insidious decline with no history of a Wernicke episode. The severity of both memory and intellectual impairment differs considerably between members of any group of patients with clinically diagnosed Wernicke–Korsakoff syndrome. At present there is no clear explication of how diencephalic, basal forebrain, and cortical (including frontal) lesions combine to produce the range of impaired alcoholics visible in any clinical setting. The sheer diversity of these lesions and of clinical patients suggests multiple pathways to different endpoints. Research on the continuity hypothesis is of particular value for highlighting the considerable gaps in our knowledge of the progress of alcoholism, and the relationship between the complex of lesions resulting from the disorder and their behavioural effects.

PART 4

IMPLICATIONS FOR PRACTICE

CHAPTER ELEVEN

Implications for the Treatment of Alcoholic Patients

The fact that we cannot easily alter the long-term course of alcoholism should be no reason for despair. If treatment as we currently understand it does not seem more effective than the natural healing processes then we need to understand those natural healing processes better than we do. We also need to understand the special role that clinicians can play.

Vaillant (1983, p. 316)

That long-term alcohol dependence results in cognitive impairments in a percentage of patients was evident from the literature reviewed in Chapter 9. With prolonged abstinence, many of these deficits disappear, although for some patients signs of dysfunction remain after months or even years after the patient stops drinking. For example, Fabian and Parsons (1983) found that alcoholic women who had been abstinent for 4 years, although not as impaired as alcoholics abstinent for only 30 days, differed significantly from controls on Digit Span and Memory for Designs tests. The outcome of the recovery process is extremely variable, however, as Fabian and Parsons (1983, p. 94) noted: "although recovering alcoholic women as a group may show impairment, individual alcoholics may perform as well as or better than individual control subjects and may demonstrate substantial improvement or even complete recovery with continued abstinence".

In this chapter we consider the implications of the findings outlined in the previous sections of this book for the treatment of alcoholics. We examine first the relationship between therapy success and neuro-psychological impairment. There are two basic ways in which neuro-psychological performance might be related to treatment outcome. Impaired patients, by virtue of their diminished cognitive capacity, may be less able to participate in, and thus benefit from, the therapeutic process. Most inpatient and community-based treatment programmes involve exposing clients to an educational process that includes information about the detrimental aspects of substance abuse and teaching new skills, attitudes, or cognitions. The acquisition of this input and competent participation in group and individual counselling sessions requires intact learning, memory, and problem-solving skills. It is reasonable to expect that there will be individual differences in these skills amongst recovering alcoholics. An additional possibility is that brain impairments may reduce the motivation or capacity of clients to make use of the skills or cognitions they have been taught after they are discharged. The brain-impaired alcoholic may achieve during an inpatient programme, for example, but these achievements may rapidly be overwhelmed by the demands of everyday life outside the hospital. Of course, the therapy skills may be both less successfully acquired and subsequently practised by brain impaired alcoholics. The predicted outcome, regardless of the cause, will be that neuropsychologically impaired alcoholics will show a lower rate of treatment success and more rapid relapse. In what follows, we review studies of therapy participation by alcoholics in which some account has been taken of neuropsychological status, and investigations of the power of neuropsychological test scores to predict relapse and treatment benefits. Before doing so, however, it is important to consider some of the problems in conducting research in this area.

METHODOLOGICAL ISSUES

Studies of the impact of neuropsychological status on treatment outcome are problematic both to conduct and to interpret for a variety of reasons; some of these difficulties have been addressed in Chapter 3. Militating against the prospects of establishing significant correlations between impairment and therapy success are problems in establishing the magnitude of an acquired deficit. Most correlational analyses use as measures of impairment current performance on a battery of tests. Where this has been done, premorbid and current performance cannot be separated and therefore the size of the acquired deficit cannot be determined. This creates problems because a deficit score is likely to be a more precise estimate of the effects of alcohol on cognitive function than a simple measure of current level of performance. Measures of impairment like the Brain Age Quotient, the Halstead Impairment Index, and the NART-IQ–WAIS-IQ discrepancy scores get around this problem to some extent by making some allowance for premorbid status. It is useful to remember, however, that estimates of current cognitive performance are not measures of acquired deficit and may have limited associations with therapy monitors for that reason.

Differences in therapy procedures and outcome goals are another difficulty. Treatment programmes inevitably have varied emphases, teaching methods, and lengths of therapy involvement or aftercare. The extent to which different programmes make intellectual demands on clients may well vary. In addition, the adequacy of aftercare services varies considerably, as does the ability of services to maintain follow-up contact with clients to assess therapy outcome. The assessment of outcome is subject to all the problems of the reliability and validity of measures of consumption and drinking practices considered in Chapter 3. The outcome goals and criteria for therapy success are not applied consistently in different treatment settings (Nathan & Skinstad, 1987). Controlled drinking in one context may be seen as a relapse in another.

Another important variable is the time at which the cognitive testing is completed. Impairments assessed early in a therapy programme may be largely the product of withdrawal effects and primarily reflect intensity of consumption prior to admission. Assessments completed later in therapy may be less predictive of the subject's ability to acquire information early in treatment. There is also the additional problem of deciding which test best reflects the cognitive skills necessary to consolidate and apply treatment-related skills. Most neuropsychological tests have little demonstrated ecological validity and are difficult to associate with the acquisition and application of the behavioural, affective, and cognitive changes integral to therapy success. There is an urgent need to harmonise neuropsychological testing procedures with the actual objectives or skills implicit in the therapy process. The useful application of particular neuropsychological tests to a specific prediction situation depends on their validity in that situation. Unless they are valid, then the search for meaningful predictors is doomed. Finally, the size of correlations between neuropsychological damage and therapy outcome may be restricted by the admission practices of therapy programmes. If impaired patients are excluded from treatment the range of abilities tested will be constrained and the size of resultant correlations attenuated.

In summary, a number of methodological issues that make the conduct of research on the implications of neuropsychological test results for therapy with alcoholics difficult have been identified. These include the general problem of specifying precisely the magnitude of a deficit both in terms of premorbid functioning and normative levels. In addition, the goals of treatment, the process of therapy, and the definition of relevant outcome criteria vary considerably. However outcome is measured, it is typically dependent on the trustworthiness of the verbal report of alcoholics and the testimony of collateral informants. In addition, existing neuro-psychological tests are not necessarily valid measures of the cognitive processes necessary for acquiring or using the skills, knowledge, or cognitions taught in therapy. Finally, differences in the constitution of individual samples of alcoholics may lead to variations in the magnitude of cognitive performance–outcome correlations.

PROGRESS DURING THERAPY

There are many approaches to the treatment of patients with alcohol dependence or abuse problems. However, the majority of inpatient programmes have abstinence as a treatment goal and employ the same general therapy format. After the first 3 to 5 days detoxification is complete, and thereafter patients attend ward meetings, are educated about the physical, social, and personal consequences of alcohol abuse, are confronted in individual or group sessions with aspects of denial, and may be involved in a variety of occupational therapy activities. Admission and discharge criteria vary considerably. Some programmes maintain close links with Alcoholics Anonymous, others run special evening groups for couples. There are also inpatient and outpatient treatment programmes that strongly emphasise learning new coping skills, which are based upon a cognitive social learning approach to psychopathology (Monti, Abrahams, Kadden, & Cooney, 1989). In this approach, treatment sessions focus on teaching clients to deal constructively with problems in living and to substitute the use of these new coping strategies for abusive consumption in aversive situations. The aim is to teach such interpersonal skills as appropriate assertive behaviours, how to refuse a drink, ways of building social support networks, and methods of enhancing close or intimate relationships. Clients may also be taught personal skills such as relaxation as a coping response, anger management, problem-solving and how to cope with thoughts about drinking. Part of this process involves planning for the possibility of relapse by teaching alcoholics to identify situations where they are personally at high-risk for drinking and to use alternative methods of coping (Marlatt & Gordon, 1985).

The common element in all the various treatment approaches to alcoholism, regardless of whether the underlying philosophy is derived from Alcoholics Anonymous or social learning therapy, is a process of educating the alcoholics about more constructive ways of thinking and behaving. There have been few studies investigating the impact of neuropsychological impairments on the success of the therapy process in alcohol dependent clients. This seems an important area to neglect; if patients have deficits that restrict their ability to acquire or process information, then it is likely that education-based therapy sessions or attempts to teach new life skills will be compromised. O'Leary, Donovan, Chaney, and Walker (1979a) administered the component tests that are used to compute Reitan's Brain Age Quotient (BAQ) to 30 alcoholic subjects at a time 9 to 14 days after they became abstinent. They then asked two clinical psychologists involved in the management of these patients to sort the patients into three categories of level of functioning in the therapy programme, based on the staff's observations of the patients' behaviour and cognitive skills. They found an association between the clinicians' ratings of the patients level of functioning while under treatment and actual BAQ scores. These results provided preliminary evidence that neuropsychological test scores were related to the way in which the patients participated in therapy activities during their hospital stay.

A more informative study was conducted by Leber, Parsons, and Nichols (1985). The objective of this study was to determine whether clinicians' judgements of patients' performance during therapy and subsequent predictions about their prognosis were related to neuropsychological test scores. This study was conducted with two independent samples of male alcoholics under treatment at the Oklahoma City Veterans Administration Medical Center. The testing took place between 20 and 30 days after therapy began and the clinician ratings were made at the end of the 9-week programme. The clinician rating scale was designed to tap a number of aspects of therapy progress and on the basis of factor analysis three relevant dimensions were identified. These three factors (with loadings for the significant items in brackets) were: Cognitive functioning— Ability to generalise (0.90), Reasoning by analogy (0.87), Plans for the future (0.61), Approach toward change (0.56); Interpersonal involvement— Participation in group (0.90), Involvement in therapy (0.67); Clinical improvement—Therapeutic benefit (0.88), Change in psychological functioning (0.85), Insight (0.47). In addition, a total of 19 test scores were computed from the battery of neuropsychological tests administered (which included the WCST, SILS, Memory for Designs, Raven's Progressive Matrices, and subtests from the WAIS and HRB). These 19 variables were correlated with the factor scores from the clinician rating scale data to produce a total of 57 correlations, 41 of which were significant ($P < 0.05$). The significant correlations were modest in magnitude, ranging from 0.24 to 0.54; 17 correlations with the Cognitive Functioning factor were significant, 10 correlations with the Interpersonal Involvement factor were significant, and there were 0.14 significant correlations with the Client

Improvement factor. These findings therefore provided support for the view that neuropsychological test performance was congruent with clinicians' ratings of impairment and therapy progress. Leber et al. (1985) also performed a number of multiple correlation analyses in order to identify the tests most predictive of the clinical ratings. A summary of these results is presented in Table 11.1

In a further analysis, Leber et al. (1985) divided the sample into those with either a clinical predicted good prognosis or with a poor prognosis (about 60% of the total sample). The poor prognosis group had a longer drinking history, but were matched with the good prognosis group in terms of age and education. The two subgroups were then compared on each of the 19 neuropsychological test variables, with duration of alcoholism treated as a covariate. There were five significant variables on which the groups varied, SILS-Verbal ($P < 0.05$), Memory for Designs ($P < 0.05$), Block Design ($P < 0.05$), WCST perseverative errors ($P < 0.001$), and Trails B ($P < 0.01$). Thus neuropsychological deficits underpinned the clinicians' ratings of the prognosis of the clients they had treated. Whether these predictions bore any relationship to actual outcome, however, was not reported.

These findings have been confirmed in two other studies by Parsons and colleagues reported in Parsons (1987). In the first, the same clinician rating scales used in the Leber et al. (1985) study were applied to a further group of 60 patients undergoing treatment for alcoholism on an inpatient basis. Each subject was also tested on a range of cognitive tasks that included three measures of problem-solving skills. It was found that high and low scores on these tests were significantly associated with ratings of cognitive functioning during therapy, some treatment behaviours (e.g. insight, future orientation, and therapeutic benefit, but not involvement in therapy and motivation), and predicted treatment outcome at 1 year (particularly

TABLE 11.1

Multiple Correlations Between the Best Neuropsychological Predictors and Clinicians' Ratings (from Leber et al. 1985)

	Cognitive functioning	Interpersonal involvement	Clinical improvement
R^2	0.58	0.48	0.49
Variables	Memory for designs Trails B Perseverative errors SILS-Verbal (WCST) Conceptual quotient (SILS)	Trails B Memory for designs Conceptual quotient (SILS) SILS-Verbal	

R^2 = Squared multiple correlation.

ratings of vocational status, cognitive functioning, and quality of life, but not length of abstinence and legal status). In the second study described by Parsons (1987), clinician ratings of ability to learn, memory, analogical reasoning, ability to plan and cognitive function during treatment were strongly associated with SILS-Verbal and Abstraction scores, but not to measures of learning, memory, or level of emotionality (Beck Depression Inventory and the State Trait Anxiety Inventory).

The studies that Parsons and colleagues have reported provide evidence of a moderate association between neuropsychological test scores and clinician perception of clients during treatment. This suggests that the way clients behave during the course of their inpatient programme is related to their actual cognitive abilities at the time of treatment. Lacking from these analyses is information about the ability of clients to acquire new skills or cognitions. Patients may be impaired, and this may be recognised by their therapists, but this may have no impact on the successful learning therapy objectives. It would also be interesting to know the relationship between actual therapy outcome and the predictions made by therapists. To what extent does mastery of the goals of a treatment programme, whatever these may be, predict the long-term outcome of a group of clients? These questions emphasise how little is known about the relationship between neuropsychological status and development of changed cognitions or new skills in alcohol abusers.

One study that goes some way towards attempting to answer these questions was reported by Smith and McCrady (1988), who administered the SILS, the CVLT and the BAQ subtests to 33 male alcoholics undergoing an inpatient abstinence-based programme. A component of this programme was skill training for drink refusal, based on Chaney, O'Leary, and Marlatt's (1978) approach to the moderation of abusive drinking. The Situational Competency Test (Chaney et al., 1978), which involves recording verbal responses to a series of alcohol-related role-play scenarios (four of which focus on drink refusal), was given to all subjects before and after treatment. Competence in drink refusal was determined by measuring verbal response latency and duration. They found that post-treatment latency of responses were associated with lower SILS Abstraction scores, although the effect was not strong ($P < 0.058$). This may have been a consequence of only 19 of the 33 competency test protocols being available because of accidental erasure of 14 tapes. No other individual test scores were significantly related to drink refusal competence. Smith and McCrady (1988) also found that subsequent attendance at aftercare sessions was correlated with high SILS-Abstraction scores. This study illustrates how neuropsychological test data can be used to examine ecologically relevant treatment parameters.

NEUROPSYCHOLOGICAL DEFICITS AND
TREATMENT OUTCOME

Several studies have been conducted in which the usefulness of neuropsychological status as a predictor of treatment outcome after discharge has been investigated. This research has important practical implications, as a positive association would suggest either that treatment procedures were not suitable for alcoholics with some degree of brain impairment or that the process of therapy did not make due allowance for patients with impairments.

A number of studies completed before 1980 suggested that psychometric evidence of neurological damage was associated with successful outcome. Berglund, Leijonquist, and Horlen (1977) were able to locate 40 of a group of 53 alcoholics an average of 3.7 years after discharge. Of the 13 missing at the time of follow-up, two refused to participate, two were intoxicated, two could not be traced, two had handicapping physical disorders, and five were deceased. The subjects were then classified into those who were improved (i.e. were abstinent, displayed controlled drinking, or had changed their drinking patterns) and those who were unimproved. The improved group were found to have scored more highly on tests administered during the course of treatment, including a measured paired-associate learning, the Benton Visual Retention Test, and a Block Design test. However, the association between outcome status and impairment was not strong, suggesting to the authors that cerebral dysfunction is not a strong barrier to abstinence. Guthrie and Elliott (1980) classified 92 alcoholics admitted to the Tayside Area Alcoholism Unit, in East Scotland, as either impaired or not impaired on the basis of their Benton Visual Retention and word-learning test scores. They found a significant association between attendance at outpatient groups after discharge and impairment on these tests 2 weeks after admission. Of the 19 unimpaired patients, 13 attended the outpatient group, as opposed to 23 of 63 impaired patients. Given that outpatient attendance is an index of the success of therapy, these results suggest an association between outcome and cognitive deficits.

In a study designed to identify predictors of relapse, Gregson and Taylor (1977) administered a complex computer-scored measure of subjects' ability to remember and correctly order an array of 10 symbols (the Patterned Cognitive Impairment Test) and the Elithorn Maze Test to 90 male alcoholics attending a residential treatment programme. Patients were contacted 10, 30, 90, and 180 days post-discharge and the minimum number of days between leaving hospital and resumption of drinking estimated from follow-up reports. After 6 months, 64% of the patients had relapsed. Multiple regression analyses were used to find the cognitive and sociodemographic factors that predicted relapse. When patients were divided into those with high, medium, or low scores on the Pattern Cognitive Impairment Test, it was found that after 6 months, 37% of the high, 70% of the medium, and 87% of the low scorers were drinking. The multiple regression analyses showed that the impairment test was the most significant predischarge predictor of relapse, ahead of social status, religious observance, marital status, number of prior hospitalisations, and measures of job and accommodation stability. Age was not a significant predictor. In a further study, Abbott and Gregson (1981) confirmed the importance of neuropsychological factors. They traced 103 patients who had completed treatment and contacted them 3 months and 1 year after discharge. After 12 months, 48 subjects had relapsed, 14 had controlled or moderated their consumption, and 38 were abstinent. Once again, the regression analyses showed that cognitive performance predicted relapse more strongly than measures of drinking behaviour or sociodemographic variables. These early studies suggested that cognitive deficits may play a part in treatment failure; however, the amount of variance accounted for was not large.

A series of reports by Walker, Donovan, and colleagues has come to much the same conclusion (O'Leary & Donovan, 1979; Walker, Donovan, Kivlahan, & O'Leary, 1983). Walker et al. (1983) conducted a study with 245 male veterans to investigate the relationship between length of stay in an inpatient programme, and achievement of an abstinence treatment goals. Walker et al. were also interested in determining those variables that might predict outcome, and included the Reitan BAQ index and the Group Embedded Figures Test in their assessment battery. Patients were assigned randomly to either 2- or 7-week treatment programmes at the Seattle Veterans Administration Medical Centre and followed up 3, 6, and 9 months after discharge. On the basis of their BAQ scores, the patients were divided into high, medium, and low neuropsychological performance subgroups. At the 9-month follow-up it was found that the high performance group, who showed least evidence of impairment, were significantly more likely to have remained abstinent and to be in full-time employment. Their average monthly income over the follow-up period was also significantly higher. Overall ratings of treatment success were also better for the high neuropsychological performance group, however, attendance at aftercare groups was not associated with neuropsychological status. The authors (Walker et al., 1983, p. 909) concluded that "This finding extends previous suggestive results on the modest predictive utility of neuropsychological functioning for subsequent treatment outcome".

In a further report, based on the same study, Donovan, Kivlahan, and Walker (1984) looked in more detail at the cognitive performance of their subjects during and after treatment. Their subjects were tested on average

24 days after their last drink and retested with the Block Design, Digit Symbol, Trails B, and Group Embedded Figures Test at a time 6 months after discharge. They found that cognitive performance at the time of admission was correlated with age, but not with measures of drinking practices. They also found that age was predictive of recovery of functioning between the initial and 6-month follow-up testing sessions. There was a significant difference on the four tests administered at both the initial and retest points between subjects who were employed and those who were not. The cognitive variables did not predict amount consumed during follow-up nor the number of days drunk, but they were correlated with amount of time worked. Block Design score was the only cognitive variable associated with the relapse–abstinence outcome criterion at 6 months. Donovan et al. (1984, p. 474) reported that although neuropsychological test scores had some association with outcome, they accounted "for less than 5% of the variance in the average number of drinks per day, and the number of heavy drinking days during the 90-day period prior to the 9-month follow-up".

In subsequent reports, Donovan and colleagues (Donovan, Kivlahan, & Walker, 1986; Donovan, Kivlahan, Walker, & Umlauf, 1985), turned their attention to the problem of defining specific subgroups of alcohol abusers within their sample of 245 alcoholics. The objective was to find distinctive groups of alcoholics on the basis of their demographic, behavioural, and neuropsychological profile, and to relate group membership to outcome variables. To achieve this, they used cluster analysis, a statistical procedure that identifies distinctive groups of individuals within a larger sample on the basis of the similarity of their profile of test scores. This statistical technique has been used on a number of occasions in research devoted to finding improved methods of describing the range of alcohol-dependent patients. For example, Shelley and Goldstein (1976) used a clustering procedure to classify alcoholics on the basis of their WAIS and HRB scores. They categorised their sample into five clusters, the most impaired of which comprised the oldest subjects who had the most evidence of neuropsychological impairment on testing. At the other end of the impairment continuum were a group of young, well-educated patients who showed little evidence of brain impairment.

Donovan et al. (1985) used cluster analytical procedures to investigate neuropsychological factors predictive of treatment outcome. They entered 13 scores from the neuropsychological tests they administered to their 245 male subjects into the cluster programme. From the results they identified three clusters of subjects that accounted for 92% of the total sample. The first cluster comprised 95 patients whose performance on the neuropsychological tests placed them in the average to above-average range. These subjects were unimpaired on the cognitive tests. Cluster 3 included 85 patients whose scores were average or below on the WAIS, or in the impaired range on both the Group Embedded Figures Test and the majority of the HRB test they administered. Cluster 2 was made up of 46 patients with average BAQ and SILS scores intermediate to those of Clusters 1 and 3, but WAIS Verbal scores higher than the other two clusters. The demographic characteristics and treatment outcome data for each of the three clusters were then computed; the results on selected variables are presented in Table 11.2. With respect to treatment outcome, the results were inconsistent; Cluster 2 appeared to have the most successful outcomes. However, the only significant difference to emerge from the statistical analysis was between the Cluster 2 and Cluster 3 patients involved in the 7-week programme. Cluster 2 also showed the highest rate of completion of the aftercare programme, and this was a significant difference for both the 7- and 2-week treatment groups. Cluster 1, made up of younger, less impaired, subjects had a success rate immediate to Clusters 2 and 3. Comparisons of Clusters 2 and 3, which were matched for average age and other demographic characteristics, showed that the percentage treatment success rates were higher for the less impaired Cluster 2. Overall, there was no consistent relationship between age and neuropsychological status on the one hand, and treatment outcome on the other.

TABLE 11.2

Neuropsychological Clusters and Treatment Outcome (from Donovan et al., 1985)

| | Cluster | | | |
	1	2	3	P
Neuropsychological scores				
BAQ	98.7	93.4	78.2	0.001
number of impaired BAQ scores	0.7	2.1	4.2	0.001
WAIS-Verbal IQ	110.7	117.4	102.4	0.001
WAIS-Performance IQ	112.6	112.4	98.4	0.001
SIL Conceptual Q	93.5	78.0	72.5	0.05
Demographic data				
age	37.3	51.1	51.1	0.001
education	12.6	12.6	11.8	ns
social position index	53.7	55.7	57.0	ns
mean monthly income	774.0	734.0	697.0	ns
years problem drinking	12.1	17.9	14.4	0.01
daily volume index	3.0	3.1	3.2	ns
Treatment outcome				
abstinence (n =175) (%)	47.8	53.8	35.8	ns
treatment success (n = 225) (%)	40.0	52.2	35.7	ns
aftercare completion (n = 224) (%)	28.4	52.2	34.1	0.05

Donovan et al. (1986) refined their cluster analytic procedures and included a more diverse set of variables in the analysis. Measures introduced into the clustering process included scores from an abbreviated MMPI, three measures of drinking behaviour, age, social position, BAQ, VIQ estimates, and hours worked per week. The analysis produced six clusters and a complex pattern of results. There was a significant association between cluster membership and both aftercare completion and employment status, but not treatment outcome. On the basis of the analyses of their data, Donovan, Walker, and Kivlahan (1987) concluded that their results challenged the view that neuropsychological status was an important predictor of treatment outcome with alcoholics who undergo conventional hospital-based therapy programmes. They observed that neuropsychological status was only one of a range of potent variables relevant to treatment success and that the most consistent associations were between test scores and employment status. By comparison, correlations between drinking behaviour after discharge and neuropsychological test data were more modest and less consistent.

These conclusions were reinforced by findings from Eckardt et al. (1988). They administered the Benton Visual Retention Test, SILS, WCST, and a number of HRB and WAIS subtests to 91 male alcohol abusers who had completed an inpatient treatment programme at a California VA medical centre. The patients were followed up over a 6-month period and both self-report and information from collaterals was used to estimate number of drinking occasions per month and the volume of alcohol consumed on each occasion after discharge. A series of multiple regression analyses were conducted to assess the predictive utility of neuropsychological impairment for treatment outcome. The relationships that emerged were described by the authors as "variable and fragile". Some tests were consistently related to outcome measures, but the overall pattern of results was inconsistent. Poor Block Design and Object Assembly performance predicted failure, but so also did better performance on Digit Span, Trails A, visual retention, TPT, and Speech Sounds perception. Thus the relationship between test scores and outcome had limited validity for the prediction of outcome in conventional alcoholism treatment programmes.

Alterman, Kushner, and Holahan (1990) assessed 87 primarily black alcohol-dependent patients involved in a 30-day rehabilitation programme. While in treatment they were tested on a number of cognitive measures that assessed language function, verbal learning, memory for prose passages, and complex cognitive functioning. In addition, they also administered a 21-item multichoice test designed to assess knowledge of the medical consequences of alcohol, an important component of the alcohol education programme. Outcome was assessed 1 and 6 months after discharge and was defined in terms of changes in the severity of medical, legal, employment, alcohol, drug, family, and psychological problems. Outcome at 6 months was predicted by age, complex cognitive functioning, and severity of pretreatment alcohol, drug, and family problems. Baseline severity of alcohol problems was found to be the most powerful predictor of changes after treatment. The measure of within-programme learning did not predict outcome at either the 1- or 6-month follow-up points.

The significance of neuropsychological impairments relative to other relapse predictors was investigated by Glenn and Parsons (1991). They recruited 58 male and 45 female alcoholics who had undergone inpatient treatment programmes based on the Alcoholics Anonymous philosophy. The authors identified five factors that had been shown to correlate with treatment outcome: (1) depressive symptomatology; (2) neuropsychological deficit; (3) psychosocial adjustment; (4) previous treatment history; and (5) a history of childhood attention deficit disorder. For each subject, a neuropsychological performance index was calculated based on the results from 11 tests. Glenn and Parsons also constructed two interview-based scales to assess psychosocial adjustment and previous treatment. The psychosocial adjustment scale comprised 10 items rated on a two-point scale that focused on employment, accommodation, and number of arrests. The four-item previous treatment scale elicited information about number of inpatient and outpatient treatment episodes over the past 6 months. Depressive symptoms were assessed using the Beck Depression Inventory, and attention deficit symptoms were assessed retrospectively on a self-report scale validated for use with alcoholic samples. Assessments were conducted at the end of treatment and patients followed-up 14 months later. At the time of the follow-up assessment, the former patients were classified as either abstainers ($n = 62$) or resumers ($n = 41$) on the basis of their self-report and information from collaterals.

Of the five factors investigated in this study, only the scores on the previous treatment scale did not significantly discriminate between abstainers and relapsers. Although the neuropsychological test scores were significant, the absolute difference between the groups was small. On an index with a scale mean of 50 and a deviation of 10, the mean of the resumers was 46.6 (SD = 6.93) versus 49.9 (SD = 6.64) for the abstainers. The largest absolute difference was for the BDI scores, where the mean for the resumers was 11.15 (SD = 7.61) versus 5.75 (SD = 5.12) for the abstaining group. Stepwise multiple regression procedures identified depressive symptomatology at the time of discharge as the most significant predictor of relapse. Other variables that contributed to the prediction of outcome were psychosocial maladjustment prior to admission and number of previous treatments; the amount of variance accounted for by the regression equations was just 27%. There was also a significant negative correlation between the neuropsychological index and BDI scores of −0.25.

The authors concluded that relapse prevention might be enhanced by specific treatment for patients with depressive symptom patterns.

THE ROLE OF NEUROPSYCHOLOGICAL TESTING IN THE TREATMENT OF ALCOHOLICS

The use of neuropsychological tests with clinical patients initially developed as an adjunct to the process of detecting and, where possible, localising neurological lesions. At first, psychologists adapted many of the tests they were familiar with for this new purpose. Measures like the Halstead battery and the Wechsler–Bellevue, constructed as means of assessing innate intellectual abilities, and the Bender–Gestalt, which was at first used as a projective test, were soon found to have value in the quantification of cognitive deficits. As psychologists became more intimately involved in working with neurologically impaired patients, a range of new neuropsychological procedures were constructed and validated in terms of their ability to detect known brain lesions. With the introduction of sophisticated and non-invasive brain scanning devices, the role of neuropsychological testing shifted away from a primary focus on detecting brain damage. Increasingly, testing is being used to document the consequences of known lesions on cognition, behaviour, and affect. At the same time, psychologists working in neurological settings have become more involved in patient management and aftercare, and a demand has developed for testing strategies relevant to these concerns.

This gradual evolution in the function of neuropsychological testing is evident in approaches to research and practice with alcoholic clients. The first concern in the research literature was to establish how alcoholics performed on standard measures of neuropsychological status, as a basis for determining the presence and extent of the brain damage caused alcohol abuse. As we have seen, a diffuse range of deficits have been identified, and the variable rates of recovery of these dysfunctions examined. Attention has turned to the implications of these findings for the successful management of clients with alcohol dependency problems. In this context the need for tests that are relevant to the practical deficits that these patients may display has become more apparent. Tests that attempt to measure an aspect of real-world functioning affected by the cognitive dysfunctions associated with alcoholism are often described as ecologically valid or relevant. Ecological validity is sometimes ascribed to tasks that involve testing practical skills, even though these may not be directly relevant to solving problems that typically confront alcoholics. For example, Nixon and Parsons (1991) described the use of a test that requires a consistent problem-solving strategy to determine the outcome of a particular treatment regime. They called this the Plant Test, and subjects were instructed to predict how a plant would respond to a particular combination of conditions (e.g. amount of water, type of plant food, etc.), given some examples of how variations in these conditions had affected other similar plants. The authors reported that alcoholics showed deficits in their reasoning abilities, although there was no group differences in the ability to predict outcome. In this instance ecological validity is being equated with "real-world" as opposed to laboratory-based problem-solving skills. The elements of the task have been couched in terms that have some direct relevance to everyday life; however, the task itself is not relevant to specific skills alcoholics must master. Of more interest is the use of tasks that measure skills that alcoholics must display to function successfully in therapy or in life after discharge.

An example of a measure that assesses everyday functioning in a manner relevant to treatment planning is the Rivermead Behavioural Memory Test (RBMT; Wilson, 1987; Wilson, Cockburn, & Baddeley, 1985). This test is primarily of value with impaired amnesic patients and has been validated on samples of patients with Wernicke–Korsakoff syndrome, as will be seen in Chapter 12. In several studies, practical memory tests have been employed with alcoholics. Becker et al. (1983b) measured rate of learning a series of face–name paired associates and found that alcoholics made more errors during the learning phase of the task, and were less likely to reach the learning criterion than the controls. In this case, a sensitive measure of cognitive deficit was used to test a function, learning names of direct relevance to everyday memory skills. Another example is provided by Becker and Jaffe's (1984) test of the recall and recognition performance of alcoholics and controls exposed to a film providing education about the effects of alcoholism. Sussman et al. (1986) assessed memory performance in alcoholics using pictures of products taken from magazine advertisements. They found that immediate recall of these products was more predictive of treatment success than a traditional memory-for-designs test. Similarly, Sanchez-Craig and Walker (1982) tested recall of treatment-relevant information in a group of alcoholics who had been taught coping skills in a halfway house project. They found that there were considerable deficits in the recall and application of these strategies one month after treatment. They also found that progress in the acquisition of these skills during treatment was correlated with scores on Trails B and the Wide Range Achievement Test. Here, neuropsychological tests and relevant treatment monitors were used in concert. Sanchez-Craig and Walker (1982, p. 47) observed that "clearly, future attempts at the development of didactic programmes for a chronic alcoholic population will require close attention to the specific nature of the cognitive deficits to be found within the population and to the appropriate timing of the programmes".

These comments imply an important role for neuropsychological testing in the monitoring of patients' capacity to be involved in skills or education-based treatment, and their acquisition of new information. This requires that the areas of cognitive skill that alcoholics need to return to the community can be identified and validly assessed. McCrady (1987) provided a list of some possible skills, which included effective problem selection, the ability to generate problem solutions in relapse risk situations, the ability to identify situations where drinking is a risk and to remember relapse prevention strategies, and the ability to learn about people one has just met, and to develop appropriate social support networks. "My own clinical experience suggests that neuropsychologically impaired alcoholics have more difficulty with each of these skills" (McCrady, 1987, p. 387). These sentiments are echoed by Glass (1991, p. 821) who observes that although the presence of brain damage is recognised in alcoholics, little is known about the implications of these findings. She asks: "What do we tell our patients, and what does what we tell them mean to them, and what is the natural history of the deficits? More specifically, how do we match treatment interventions more appropriately to the cognitive state of the recently abstaining alcoholic?" The role of the neuropsychologist could be to test individual patients for their ability to function in various alcohol-relevant skill areas so that appropriate behavioural targets and therapy progress monitors can be formulated. The challenge is to construct measures that are relevant to treatment objectives, sensitive to alcohol-induced deficits, and based on skills that are relevant to successful rehabilitation.

CONCLUSIONS

The primary concern of the present chapter has been the usefulness of knowing about neuropsychological deficits in the management of alcoholic clients. Most of the research considered has focused on the impact of cognitive dysfunction on response to therapy. With some exceptions, the amount of variance in treatment outcome explained by cognitive factors has been modest.

The prediction of individual alcoholics at risk for relapse would appear to been an important task. The identification of relevant predictor variables would make possible the screening of alcoholic treatment samples so that at-risk patients who required specialised treatment input or specific aftercare services might be referred appropriately. In general terms, prognostic factors can be divided into those that are intrinsic to the alcoholic clients and those that are extrinsic measures of the environment or circumstances to which the alcoholic returns. Relapse may well best be predicted by some complex interaction between intrinsic individual characteristics and external environmental factors. Neuropsychological performance at the time of treatment is one possible intrinsic factor that might explain outcome. Other internal variables that have been cited as possible determinants of treatment success include depression at the time of discharge (Caster & Parsons, 1977; Hatsukami & Pickens, 1982), pretreatment psychosocial stability (O'Leary et al., 1979a), history of hospitalisations (Gibbs & Flanagan, 1977; Glenn & Parsons, 1991; 1992), and childhood psychopathology (Tarter, 1988). There is no evidence, however, that these variables, or some combination of these variables (Glenn & Parsons, 1991), are strongly predictive of outcome. Correlations between tests of neuropsychological functioning and outcome, measured in a variety of ways, have typically been significant, but explained only a small amount of the variance in treatment benefit.

This failure to find strong associations between impairment and outcome could be accepted as evidence that treatment programmes operate in such a way that neuropsychological deficits are not greatly relevant. The level of functioning required for completion of education and skill-based components of therapy may be set well within the capacity of the impaired alcoholic. Individual counsellors may alleviate disadvantages caused by cognitive impairment when therapeutic procedures are applied. It may be that cognitive capacity is not an important factor in the assimilation of the active ingredients of therapy; above a certain threshold of gross impairment more or less cognitive ability may make little difference. It is also possible that relapse is more dependent on external environmental factors or on the mastery of certain skills that on patient characteristics. The family and work situations that face the alcoholic on discharge, the expectations and skills of caregivers, and the success of lifestyle changes may play a more important part in predicting outcome than differences in "person" variables such as cognitive skills (Billings & Moos, 1983; Moos, Finney, & Chan, 1981). Alternatively, it may be that the utility of neuropsychological measures in predicting relapse has been restricted by inadequate measurement validity. Such factors as preadmission selection criteria and unreliable measurement of outcome, which were considered in Chapter 3, may attenuate correlations.

One of the difficulties in determining the validity of predictors of relapse has been a lack of concern with how such variables affect outcome. The issue of how neuropsychological impairment might impact on treatment has seldom been considered, and models of relapse processes in alcoholism that incorporate neuropsychological factors are correspondingly oversimplistic. There are several ways in which treatment and cognitive dysfunction might be related, each of which has implications for measurement and for the management of individual cases. Some of the possibilities are considered below:

1. *Impact on treatment.* Neurologically impaired alcoholics may have more difficulty acquiring relevant treatment information and skills. With few exceptions (Alterman et al., 1990), mastery of treatment objectives has not been used as either an outcome predictor or as an indicator of therapy progress that neuropsychological testing might predict (McCrady, 1987). In many inpatient programmes the objectives of therapy are not expressed in terms of cognitive or behavioural skills, and accordingly are hard to assess. Where cognitive and behavioural changes can be specified, for example, in terms of acquisition of problem-solving strategies or methods of refusing alcoholic drinks, it is possible that neuropsychological tests might be associated with successful learning (Sanchez-Craig & Walker, 1982). It may be necessary, however, to devise testing and monitoring procedures that are more directly related to the teaching objectives. This prospect argues for the construction of ecologically valid neuropsychological assessment strategies for use with alcoholics.

2. *Interaction between deficits and staff response.* A psychological explanation for an association between outcome and cognitive dysfunction is the effect of the staff's awareness of the cognitive status of the patients in therapy. Leber et al. (1985) have demonstrated that clinicians' ratings of patients' cognitive abilities and prognosis are correlated with level of neuropsychological deficit. If staff are aware of deficits, then they may respond to patients in either a negative or a positive way. Positive strategies might include implementation of compensatory procedures to accommodate the needs of patients who learn more slowly. It is also likely, however, that staff may have negative expectations about the outcome of treatment for impaired patients, expend less time on their therapy, or convey negative expectations about prognosis to them.

3. *Post-discharge vulnerability.* It is possible that neuropsychological deficits result in vulnerability after the patient leaves hospital. Patients may be detoxified successfully and master the objectives of therapy, but their impairments may leave them more vulnerable to the vicissitudes of life outside hospital and thus lead to a more rapid relapse. Brain impairments may reduce the ability of patients to apply new skills to the management of stressful situations constructively or to adapt to new employment demands. Further, impairments may create negative reactions on the part of caregivers or employers. They may be less tolerant or engender negative expectations.

The above explanations suggest some causal role for neurological impairment in treatment failure. It is also possible that neuropsychological deficits are simply correlates of the factors that actually determine response to treatment. For example, impaired patients are generally older and may also have a more extensive history of dependency and treatment failure. There are other factors, such as polydrug abuse or affective disturbance, that may be related to both treatment outcome and neuropsychological functioning. A causal role for cognitive status in relapse has yet to be demonstrated convincingly.

To date, psychological approaches to treatment and the measurement of therapy outcome on the one hand, and neuropsychological testing on the other, have developed largely independently. Studies of the relationship between outcome and cognitive performance have focused on global issues and shown little concern for investigating the specific processes involved in therapy and relapse. If neuropsychological assessment is to have a role in the management of alcoholics this is likely to necessitate the construction of ecologically valid measures of the cognitive skills or attributes that treatment or alcohol education require. McCrady and Smith (1986) have perhaps specified most clearly the potential usefulness of neuropsychological testing in the ongoing management of alcohol dependent patients. They observed (McCrady & Smith, 1986, p. 147) that little account is taken in most inpatient programmes of individual differences in impairment and rate of recovery: "We expect all patients to learn and progress through treatment at approximately the same rate, whether or not they are able to do so". An important task for neuropsychologists is the development of valid procedures for determining readiness for treatment and the development of ongoing assessments of skill acquisition. Impaired patients should be given ample time to assimilate new information. Neuropsychologists can be involved in the detection of learning impairments and the preparation of procedures and material that are commensurate with patients' present skills. Thus, any resulting correlation between neuropsychological deficit and treatment outcome would be seen as a failure on the part of the treatment programme rather than the client.

Finally it should be emphasised that neuropsychological status is but one factor to consider in the total conceptualisation of any patient's alcohol dependency problem. The barriers to recovery include a powerful range of psychosocial disruptions and deficits that result from the lifestyle of the alcoholic. These include the stigma associated with legal problems, employment failure, and family disintegration. The alcoholic client typically has physical disabilities, marital or relationship problems, and a long history of social turmoil. The significance of neuropsychological impairments needs to be placed in this wider context. The challenge is to integrate the findings from neuropsychology with other social and treatment issues to specify effects and interactions with more precision and in ways of value to alcohol counsellors and therapists.

CHAPTER TWELVE

Rehabilitation of Patients with Alcohol-related Cognitive Impairment

Nothing can have value without being an object of utility.
Marx, *Capital* (1946, p. 179)

To the electron: May it never be of use to anybody.
Toast attributed to Lord Ernest Rutherford (Andrade, 1964, p. 5)

The primary goal of treatment of chronic alcoholic patients is focused on the reduction of alcohol consumption, preferably to a level of abstinence, particularly for those patients in whom cognitive impairment persists beyond the period of detoxication. Neuropsychological and neurobiological research showing significant recovery of structural and functional abnormalities after greatly reduced consumption provides support for the priority of this objective. Perhaps as a consequence of this, and the involvement of neuropsychologists in research and assessment rather than treatment planning, there are few neuropsychological studies relevant to the rehabilitation of the chronic alcoholic.

Most of the studies considered in this chapter have reported the outcome of efforts to rehabilitate chronic alcoholic patients; the term "rehabilitation", however, has been applied rather loosely to a wide variety of treatment strategies. In its broadest sense, it has meant any comprehensive treatment programme for chronic alcoholics. A narrower use has related to programmes developed to return long-term alcoholics with vocational, psychosocial, and cognitive deterioration to independent functioning in the community. Most specifically, the term has been applied to programmes of cognitive rehabilitation aimed at restoring neuropsychological functioning or at least ameliorating the effect of deficits by teaching substitute or compensatory functions. The terms cognitive rehabilitation and cognitive retraining have sometimes been used interchangeably. This chapter will place emphasis on the research reporting attempts at cognitive rehabilitation with chronic alcoholic patients. Before that, we will discuss the growing recognition that neuropsychological assessment procedures and programmes aimed at the amelioration of deficits have a place in the more general treatment and rehabilitation of alcohol abusers.

SCREENING FOR NEUROPSYCHOLOGICAL IMPAIRMENT

Despite the absence of research evidence assigning a large portion of the variance in alcoholism treatment outcome to neuropsychological status, there is an increasing awareness, at a clinical level, that some alcoholic patients have brain damage of sufficient severity that traditional treatments must be modified if they are to be effective. In other words, although neuropsychological status may not be a good outcome predictor in the treatment of unselected samples of younger, mildly impaired patients, in older patients with moderate to severe cognitive impairment, a negative outcome may be predicted unless special steps are taken. As we have discussed previously, most therapy for alcoholism, regardless of theoretical orientation, assumes that patients have the ability to acquire new knowledge, attitudes, skills, and patterns of behaviour. Furthermore, these must be generalised from the treatment setting to the psychosocial environment in which the patient lives. This requires spared memory and new learning functions, as well as intact abstraction and problem-solving abilities.

There are at least two patterns of alcohol-related brain damage that may render traditional programmes ineffective. The first involves severe impairment of memory and/or intellectual functions. This small group of patients with profound deficits usually receive diagnoses of alcoholic Korsakoff's syndrome or alcoholic dementia. Their disorientation and anterograde amnesia overshadow associated impairments in abstraction, problem solving, and visuospatial and perceptuomotor functions, which are usually also present. The second pattern is much more common. It is characterised by relatively subtle and less clinically obvious, but still disabling, impairments of problem-solving and abstracting ability, together with perceptuomotor deficits. Significant cognitive impairments may be overlooked in these patients as a result of the traditional view that the non-Korsakoff, middle-aged alcoholic is cognitively well preserved. The presence of intact conversational skills may enhance the clinical impression of preservation of psychological functions. Misplacement of patients with significant alcohol-related cognitive impairment in programmes from which they may be unable to benefit leads to costly treatment failure. In addition to the adverse implications for funding, there are countertherapeutic effects within the treatment settings themselves. Therapeutic failure may be misattributed to inadequate motivation or unconscious defence mechanisms, such as denial. Treatment staff may be perplexed and react adversely to perceived resistance which is, in large part, due to the unrecognised neuropsychological deficits.

McCrady (1987) has advocated a screening process that, after supervised withdrawal, assesses the ability of a patient to benefit from a traditional alcoholism treatment programme. An important element of the process is the assessment of health and nutritional status because of the association between body organ damage, endocrine dysfunction, and neuropsychological deficits. The next stage involves assessment of whether patients fit the criteria for primary alcoholism (De Obaldia & Parsons, 1984). At this stage, the presence of a history of learning disabilities is also assessed. These features have both been associated with a greater risk of cognitive impairment. McCrady (1987) argues that, as a result, patients over 40 years of age who meet these two criteria are likely to require a prolonged "preprogramme" period of physical care, with establishment of adequate nutrition, before being able to benefit from treatment.

Regardless of the validity of some of the criteria employed, McCrady's screening process directs attention to the likelihood that many alcoholics are simply misplaced in traditional inpatient treatment programmes, particularly immediately after a brief 2 to 3 day detoxification period. More careful assessment of their readiness to benefit from treatment is necessary if therapy is to have any chance of success. In a second phase of assessment, neuropsychological testing can be helpful in determining the range and severity of deficits present. It should be remembered that ongoing monitoring of these deficits is essential because in some patients most deficits will recover spontaneously whereas, in other patients, such as those with pre-existing deficits (perhaps due to cranial trauma) and coexisting psychopathology, they will not. In most patients, some recovery will occur, but the pattern of remaining deficits will only be accurately determined by repeated neuropsychological assessments. McCrady (1987) has taken up this point by suggesting that one phase of assessment be directed at "recovery relevant skills" which should be assessed with ecologically relevant measurement devices. Such skills include remembering and integrating into daily living the knowledge gained in the treatment programme, the ability to locate social support and follow-up treatment, new name learning, attention and concentration, identification of risk situations, problem-solving, ability to identify consequences, and social interaction skills. It is McCrady's view that active rehabilitation must proceed until mastery is achieved in each of these areas. The goal of mastery, however, will be beyond some patients at the severe end of the spectrum of alcohol-related brain damage, and such a goal also has very significant implications for the cost of services. Perhaps of greatest relevance in the present context, however, is the dearth of validated, ecologically relevant, measurement devices. Furthermore, there is a distinct lack of "rehabilitation" techniques of proven efficacy for promoting such mastery. We shall return to both of these problems later in this chapter.

TREATMENT OF ALCOHOLIC PATIENTS WITH BRAIN DAMAGE

Clinicians responsible for the treatment of alcoholics with brain damage have tended to set post discharge abstinence as the primary goal of treatment. For example, Lennane (1986) reported the outcome of a 10 to 12 week inpatient treatment programme for such patients. Neuropsychological assessment was conducted only once, at about the time of admission, and non-specific treatment goals were established in proportion to the degree and range of deficits. Of the 104 patients (aged between 45 and 60 years) who were treated, 73 were assessed fully. All of these showed impairment of both frontal functioning (problem solving, initiation, abstraction) and memory. A further six patients were too uncooperative or confused to be assessed. Therapy was based on the Alcoholics Anonymous (AA) philosophy, but had a high degree of externally imposed structure and repetition to take account of the patients' cognitive deficits. The post-discharge goals of the patients were also set according to the degree of cognitive impairment. For example, instead of planning to leave hospital, find a flat, and get a job independently, patients were assisted to obtain social security benefits and find suitable supervised accommodation.

During the inpatient programme, the patients' daily routine consisted of individual and group therapy, participation in an industrial therapy unit geared to their level of disability, and voluntary attendance at AA meetings. Patients received repeated reorientation, individually, in groups, and also by notices placed around the ward. They were also encouraged to use memory aids placed in a prominent location. The average length of stay of the 104 patients was 10.8 weeks. Once they were medically well, in receipt of a social security benefit, and had a well-established daily routine without alcohol, a living arrangement was worked out together with any family or friends they might have. Placement was conditional on the patient being able to return to the ward if this proved necessary. At follow-up, on average 16.4 months (range 8 to 24 months) later, 51% of the patients were known to be placed successfully, 10.6% were still in hospital, 4.8% were dead, 9.6% could not be contacted, and 24% were "lost". Patients in the last two categories were considered "probably failed" and "presumed failed", respectively. Of the 51% placed successfully, only one patient was drinking, and his intake was limited by financial constraints. Of the 53 successes, 73.6% were living in boarding houses where all meals were supplied and there was supervision of their hygiene and medication.

In a later study, Lennane (1988) provided further information about the relationship between neuropsychological status and long-term outcome of these patients. They were rated in terms of their impairment on tests of frontal lobe function and memory as follows. Frontal score ranged between 1 (decrease in test scores of up to 10%, some problems in organising complex material) and 4 (decrease of up to 100% on tests, difficulty organising even simple tasks, e.g. showering). Memory score ranged between 1 (decrease in test score of up to 10%, patient may have noticed some problem in memory) and 5 (retains no new information after 3 minutes). These data are presented in Table 12.1 and show that those lost to follow-up were less impaired at admission than those who had good outcome. Those patients who could not be discharged from hospital had the most severe impairment at admission. Difference in "frontal" scores between the "lost to follow-up" group and those still in hospital was significant, while the differences in "memory" scores between the "lost" group and both other groups were significant. The difference between those who did well and those still in hospital failed to reach significance on both scales.

TABLE 12.1
Relationship of Neuropsychological Test Scale Scores to Outcome

Outcome	Number	Mean "frontal" score (1–4)	Mean memory score (1–5)
Lost	25	2.7	2.9
Good outcome	34	3.1	3.8
Still in hospital	8	3.7	4.1
Dead	5	3.2	3.2

From: Patients with alcohol-related brain damage, by K.J. Lennane, *Australian Drug and Alcohol Review, 7,* 89–92. Copyright © 1988, Australian Medical and Professional Society on Alcohol and Other Drugs. Reprinted with permission.

The finding that those who are more cognitively impaired may do better in the long-term is familiar to clinicians and has been reported by others (e.g., Price et al., 1988). Explanations for this paradoxical outcome include the possibility that those with more severe impairment were more willing to accept a "sick" role and the need for external assistance including ongoing supervision. Sometimes, corresponding physical defects (e.g. cerebellar ataxia) may encourage those with more severe alcohol-related brain damage to accept that their problems are serious. Perhaps the most significant factor, however, is the limitation on independent functioning resulting from the severe impairment of new learning, initiation, motivation, and problem solving (Lennane, 1988). Even patients with frontal lobe dysfunction of sufficient severity to curtail insight may still do well if their motivation and initiative are so impaired that the pursuit of alcohol is no longer possible. It may be that slightly less damaged patients with impaired insight but intact motivation and initiative are most at risk for frequent relapse. At the extreme end of the spectrum of impairment are patients whose deficits are so severe that they require a degree of ongoing supervision and monitoring only available in an institutional setting.

Lennane (1986; 1988) has emphasised many important features of a comprehensive approach to the rehabilitation of brain-damaged alcoholics. Among these is the importance of establishing appropriate aftercare placement following discharge from hospital. Spittle (1991) adopted such a strategy in the rehabilitation of 61 older (57± 11 years) chronic, frequently hospitalised alcoholic patients, many of whom were severely disabled. Twenty-one were alcoholic amnesics and four had dementia associated with alcoholism. All patients had repeatedly received detoxication admissions and lengthy periods of hospitalisation followed by counselling, day therapy programmes and other standard procedures. Spittle (1991) added financial management to the existing therapy programmes by having the patients' incomes credited directly to their bank accounts. Access to their funds was only through a budget advisory officer, who retained a cheque book requiring both staff and patient signatures. This allowed money that would otherwise be spent on alcohol to be diverted to meet basic living requirements such as board, rent, electricity, telephone, television, meals, groceries, tobacco, clothing, and other items. Outcome of the financial management intervention was assessed by comparing the number of days of hospitalisation for the group during equal periods before and after its introduction. There was a very highly significant difference: During financial management the total duration of hospitalisation of these patients was 39 ± 64 days (range = 0–323), whereas for an equal period before this it was 285 ± 411 days (range = 0–1,795). The duration was reduced by 86%. Results were even more impressive for those patients who had been high consumers of hospitalisation (i.e. greater than 100 days) prior to the intervention.

Although these studies are of interest clinically, they do have limitations. Lennane assessed patients in the early stages of treatment only and her reports provide no information directly relating assessment results, specific aspects of the program, and outcome. The observed outcome may have been entirely unrelated to the reported neuropsychological deficits and the interventions for them. As Spittle (1991) has shown, disabled, relapsing alcoholics, many of whom had severe neuropsychological impairment, may be assisted by paternalistic interventions entirely unrelated to the neuropsychological aspects of their disorder. Furthermore, in the absence of a control group or an alternative methodology allowing direct comparison, the effectiveness of Lennane's rehabilitation programme is indeterminate. Spittle's (1991) study has a number of similar deficiencies. Although he employed before and after comparisons, Spittle failed to take advantage of the opportunity to relate the effectiveness of his programme to the neuropsychological status of the participants. No mention is made of whether the patients with severe impairment (e.g. Korsakoff's syndrome) had a different outcome to the other participants. Furthermore, some patients appear not to have been in hospital during the preprogramme assessment. For these patients, number of days spent in hospital after the intervention is an unhelpful measure of outcome. If anything, these studies tend to confirm one of the conclusions reached in the previous chapter; treatment programmes and measurement of their outcome have developed independently from the neuro-psychological study of alcohol abuse. We will now review the rather sparse literature reporting programmes designed by neuropsychologists to ameliorate cognitive impairments in patients with alcohol-related brain damage.

REHABILITATION OF CHRONIC ALCOHOLIC PATIENTS

Previous chapters have reviewed studies showing that although many cognitive functions in alcoholic patients recover spontaneously after detoxication, others seem to require practice with the task for recovery to occur (Goldman, 1986; 1987). It is also apparent from the studies reviewed in earlier chapters that older and more severely impaired patients have a less complete recovery after abstinence. It has been argued that these patients and other subgroups of alcoholics, so-called "primary" alcoholics in particular, may require special interventions. There are also a small number of patients with severe irreversible memory and new learning impairments who need specially constructed rehabilitation programmes. There is now general agreement that these patients are candidates for interventions aimed at improving cognitive functions (Goldstein, 1987; McCrady, 1987; Parsons, 1987). In this section, we will review the literature reporting the outcome of efforts by neuropsychologists to remediate memory, problem solving, and abstraction deficits by cognitive rehabilitation, including the methods sometimes referred to as cognitive retraining. The relatively small number of studies undertaken can be divided into two groups: (1) those reporting attempts to ameliorate the memory deficits of patients with Korsakoff's syndrome; and (2) those evaluating attempts to teach a broader range of cognitive skills to alcoholics with less severe cognitive impairment.

Cognitive rehabilitation of amnesic patients

Three of the six studies reporting cognitive retraining of alcoholic Korsakoffs have been uncontrolled single-case reports. Jaffe and Katz (1975) used first letter cues to teach the names of staff members to a Korsakoff patient by using a prompted recall technique. Davies and Binks (1983) used external aids, such as providing a preset signal to consult a set of commands, to support the independent functioning of a Korsakoff patient outside hospital. They also trained this patient to show a prompt card to social contacts in order to facilitate social interaction. They reported clinical evidence of improved initiative and motivation and, anecdotally, that the social interaction aid was still in use 1 year after discharge from hospital.

In a later single case report of an attempt to retrain the memory of a Korsakoff patient, Heinrichs (1989) used the selective reminding procedure of Kovner et al. (1983; 1985) to promote free-recall of information related to personal history. Heinrichs' patient, a severely amnesic (WMS MQ = 63) 49-year-old without significant ancillary neuropsychological deficits (WAIS-R IQ = 91; intact WCST and word fluency performance), was taught a narrative containing 10 to-be-remembered target words that were related directly to his personal history. These target words were linked together in a "chunked" meaningful personal narrative: "I have been at Queen *Street* Mental Health Centre for over a year; for many years I abused *alcohol*; as a result I became ill and went to *hospital* in London etc." (Heinrichs, 1989, pp. 153–154). During the initial trial of each session the story was read with the instruction to the patient to remember the emphasised target words. On the next three trials, the story was not read and the patient was asked to recount the narrative, with cues provided to elicit the target words when necessary. Then on a fifth and final trial, free-recall was tested without cueing. Thirty sessions were conducted over eight weeks and a written test of the patients' ability to fill in blanks with the target words was administered 12 months later. Immediate recall, assessed at the end of each session, improved to a plateau of 4/10 from session 13 onwards. Delayed recall, assessed at the beginning of each session never exceeded 0/10. Implicit learning was demonstrated by the patient's ability to correctly fill 9/10 blanks on the written test 12 months later. Despite this, and the observation that the patient appeared to require less cueing over time and showed general clinical improvement, success was very limited. He continued to require some cueing throughout and his delayed recall never improved, although there was a strong floor effect in the way delayed recall was tested. Perhaps of greatest significance was the fact that the patient remained disorientated with respect to time and showed little initiation or motivation. Heinrichs (1989) concluded that the methods previously reported as successful for amnesic patients (Kovner, Mattis, & Goldmeier, 1983; Kovner, Mattis, & Pass, 1985) may have failed to promote robust free recall with this particular patient because of the greater severity of his anterograde amnesia (MQ 63 vs Kovner et al.'s patients' MQs of 100 and 83).

Although the reports of uncontrolled single case studies are of interest in describing techniques with therapeutic potential, their results are often difficult to interpret for a number of reasons. The extent to which the case was representative is difficult to determine, the degree to which practice effects were operating cannot often be known, and the specific relationship between intervention and outcome cannot be determined because so many other variables may be operating. As Goldman and his colleagues have shown, overcoming these problems requires a complex methodology involving multiple groups.

Three studies of cognitive retraining involving small groups of Korsakoff and chronic alcoholic subjects have been reported. Cermak (1975) demonstrated that the use of visual imagery or verbal mediation was preferable to rote learning in the acquisition of verbal paired associates. Visual imagery appeared to have a slight advantage over verbal mediation when the test involved recognition memory rather than recall. Unfortunately, no data were reported regarding generalisation across time, or setting, and the clinical relevance of the gains was not specified. In an intervention study with a group of amnesic alcoholics, Godfrey and Knight (1985) attempted to teach their subjects to use imagery techniques for associating words in a list learning context. They used experimenter-generated imagery to illustrate the procedure. Examples of the way in which the words GIRAFFE–BATH, and RABBIT–MOTORBIKE might be associated are illustrated in Fig. 12.1. Howes (1983) showed that visual imagery techniques were superior to a no-instruction condition in promoting verbal paired-associate learning in 11 Korsakoff and 11 chronic alcoholic subjects. There appeared to be a slight advantage of

FIG. 12.1. Stimuli used in teaching the use of visual imagery with Korsakoff patients (from Godfrey & Knight, 1985).

subject-generated images over experimenter-generated images on tests of recall but not of recognition memory. Gains were maintained for 24 hours but the long-term efficacy of the techniques, and the generalisability and clinical significance of the gains were not reported.

In a group comparison study, Godfrey and Knight (1985) randomly assigned 12 hospitalised and chronic alcoholic patients (mean age 57 years) with moderate to very severe memory deficits to either experimental or activation control conditions. The patients had mixed diagnoses (seven alcoholic amnestics, two dementias associated with alcoholism, one amnesic syndrome, and two chronic alcohol dependents). There were no significant between-groups differences on relevant variables prior to entering an 8-week programme comprising 32 hours of memory retraining (experimental group) or an equivalent amount of non-specific activation (control group). The experimental group received training in visual associate learning tasks, reality orientation activities (Folson, 1968), picture recognition training, and retraining of memory for recent events experienced on trips outside the hospital. The control group spent an equivalent amount of time in social skills exercises, card and bingo games, discussion of news items, story writing, and delivering speeches. This group also had trips outside the hospital. One of the strengths of this study was that it employed a comprehensive selection of progress and outcome measures. In addition to six standardised laboratory measures involving learning and retention of visually presented material, the participants were also tested on six practical measures (e.g. memory for instructions). Subjects were also rated independently by two nurses using a validated observational method the Inpatient Memory Impairment Scale (IMIS; Knight & Godfrey, 1984b), and they also completed a 20-item questionnaire assessing temporal, topographical–spatial orientation, and memory for recent events. Two word-learning tests, two orientation questionnaires, and nurse clinical ratings were also employed as progress monitors at weekly intervals during the 4 weeks prior to treatment, during the 8 weeks of treatment, and for 4 weeks post-treatment. Outcome measures were administered by an independent psychometrician pretreatment, post-treatment, and 3 months later. Only four experimental subjects and five control subjects completed the entire programme and assessment battery.

The principal finding of this study was that, with only one exception, the control activation group made the same degree of improvement in memory test performance as the group who received 32 hours of training in specific memory skills. The memory intervention group showed significantly greater improvement on the orientation measures used to monitor progress and there was a trend for them to show greater improvement on the six laboratory-based memory tests, but this was not maintained at follow-up. Subjects in both groups demonstrated significant improvement in a composite total memory score and a practical memory test score and this was maintained at follow-up. No significant effects of the programme were found on the clinically relevant IMIS or the orientation questionnaire score. No evidence emerged from this study to support the view that specific retraining in memory skills was any more effective in promoting generalised recovery of memory function than was non-specific activation. There was no evidence for the generalisation of any treatment benefits to observed behaviour on the ward. Godfrey and Knight (1985, p. 557) concluded by suggesting that the cognitive rehabilitation strategy most likely to succeed with such patients would require clearly defined clinical goals and specific training designed to achieve them "... with little expectation that generalisation will occur spontaneously".

Godfrey, Knight, and Spittle (1985) investigated the clinical progress of these same patients 12 months later and reported that half of the experimental group and two-thirds of the activation control group had been discharged from hospital. This compared favourably with an equivalently impaired, similarly institutionalised, untreated group ($n = 4$), none of whom had been discharged. The authors concluded that cognitive rehabilitation efforts might be cost effective, but presented no data that associated treatment-related improvements in cognitive performance to successful postdischarge functioning. As we have discussed in an earlier part of this chapter, multiple extraneous variables such as financial control, availability of appropriate living arrangements, and family and social support, not to mention hospital policy, make important contributions to the variance in this measure of outcome.

One of the major strengths of the Godfrey and Knight study was its inclusion of ecologically relevant measures of everyday memory problems. Wilson, a leading researcher in the clinical assessment and remediation of memory problems (Wilson, 1981; 1982; 1985; 1987) has pioneered the development of a valid assessment battery for everyday memory functioning. The Rivermead Behavioural Memory Test (RBMT; Wilson et al., 1985) was designed to combine the strength of a standardised repeatable test with that of behaviourial assessment (Wilson, 1987). The RBMT is administered and scored in a standardised way, but uses items drawn from everyday life situations. In 11 subtests, patients are required to demonstrate skills needed for adequate independent functioning. The subtests include remembering a name, remembering the location of a hidden belonging, remembering an appointment, recognition memory for pictures, recall of prose, remembering a short route, remembering an error, orientation in time and place, recall of date, recognition memory for faces, and learning a new six-step skill (Wilson, 1987). All subtests performed correctly receive one credit point, except for remembering a name, on which two credits are possible. The test has been shown to discriminate between controls and various groups with cognitive impairment. Table 12.2 shows the scores of two alcoholic Korsakoff's patients and one alcoholic on the RBMT. These results highlight one of the most important aspects of the RBMT—its provision of information of direct relevance to the planning, implementation, monitoring, and outcome assessment of cognitive rehabilitation strategies. The Rivermead battery has been found to be sensitive to improvements following behavioural therapy; Wilson (1987) reported that the RBMT scores of alcoholic Korsakoff patients receiving group memory retraining improved significantly.

At this point it is worth extending our review of cognitive rehabilitation beyond amnesia of alcoholic aetiology so that we can describe some recent advances in the rehabilitation of memory disorders in general. Wilson and Cooper (cited in Wilson, 1987) studied the effects of memory retraining in groups on the general memory functioning of 20 patients with acquired brain injury of various aetiologies. The patients, ranging in age from 13 to 59 years, were mainly severe head injury cases, but four had had cerebrovascular accidents (strokes) and one had suffered encephalitis.

TABLE 12.2

Results of Two Alcoholic Korsakoff Patients and One Chronic Non-Amnesic Alcoholic on the Rivermead Behavioural Memory Test

Item	Korsakoffs T.F.	Korsakoffs D.B.	Chronic alcoholic
Remembering a name	0	1	1
Finding a hidden belonging	0	0	0
Remembering an appointment	0	1	1
Picture recognition	0	0	1
Route recall immediate	0	0	1
Route recall delayed	0	0	1
Immediate prose recall	0	0	1
Remembering to deliver a message	0	0	1
Orientation	1	0	1
Date	0	0	1
Delayed prose recall	0	0	1
Delayed route recall	0	0	0
Total	1	2	10

They were assigned randomly to memory or problem-solving training. Memory training involved playing memory games and practising memory exercises; group discussion and problem-solving techniques; introduction of external memory aids; practice in use of external aids; and practice in using visual images, mnemonics, and other internal aids. Problem-solving training involved completing a series of verbal and non-verbal problems, such as those from the Raven's Progressive Matrices and the Luria Neuropsychological Investigation. Wilson and Cooper obtained results similar to those of Godfrey and Knight (1985). There was a non-specific improvement on the RBMT in both the memory and problem-solving groups but no difference between the two groups. Only the RBMT seemed to be sensitive to the changes brought about by the cognitive rehabilitation programmes. In discussing her findings from an extensive programme of research in memory training of individuals and groups with severe impairments, Wilson (1987, p. 336) concluded:

> My own view is that individual memory therapy is a preferable method of treatment, but the aim should not be to improve or retrain memory skills. Rather, therapy should attempt (1) to teach patients ways to bypass their memory deficits as far as possible, and (2) to discover the most efficient way for individuals to retain new information.

Recently, Wilson (1992) reported that of 54 patients referred for rehabilitation of severe memory disorders in the previous 5 to 10 years, all but nine were living with relatives or friends rather than in long-term care. Wilson identified external memory aids and compensatory strategies applied within a framework derived from behavioural psychology as essential aspects of memory rehabilitation. Rather than attempting to restore "memory powers", Wilson prefers to identify precise deficits, define these behaviourally, and then pursue strategies that will lead to improvements in subjective well-being and adjustment to the demands of daily living. This is achieved by teaching the patient and their relatives or friends strategies that will enable them "to compensate for or bypass problems caused by impaired memory" (Wilson, 1992, p. 317). The specific methods include provision of relevant education about the effects of memory loss; encouraging the use of external aids, such as a diary; use of contingency management to reinforce use of memory aids; role-playing exercises to teach patients how to explain their memory disorders to others; and mnemonics and rehearsal strategies designed to make most efficient possible use of residual memory capacity. In a similar vein to Godfrey and Knight (1985), Wilson emphasised that generalisation or transfer of learning to the environment in which the patient will reside is essential.

Residual memory capacity and errorless learning

As we described in Chapter 10, patients with alcoholic Korsakoff's syndrome, like other patients with acquired organic amnesia, have some preserved learning and memory abilities. To summarise, these include the acquisition of skills in perceptual, motor, and cognitive domains that are learned gradually over many trials and priming of new verbal associations, when explicit recollection is not required. However, as Baddeley (1992) has pointed out, little use has been made of this consistent evidence of residual learning and memory ability in attempts to rehabilitate patients with memory disorders. An exception to this has been the work of Glisky, Schacter, and their colleagues (Glisky & Schacter, 1987, 1989; Glisky, Schacter, & Tulving, 1986) who attempted to utilise preserved priming effects to teach the vocabulary associated with computer use. They employed the method of vanishing cues which, briefly, involved presenting definitions of the items to be learned together with letter fragments of those target items. For example, the definition "to store a program on a disk" would be presented with S- for SAVE (Glisky & Schacter, 1989, p.108). Increasing numbers of letters were presented until the subject was able to guess the response. On the following learning trials the letter cues gradually "vanished" until the patient could provide the target item in their absence. In an impressive series of studies, Glisky and Schacter demonstrated the utility of this technique for teaching complex computer vocabulary to patients with severe memory impairments. In one case, H.D. (who became severely amnesic in her mid-20s after contracting encephalitis) was able to learn more than 250 discrete items of new information. Furthermore, she was able to use this information in the workplace to secure and retain a data entry job.

Several important issues have emerged from these studies. The first relates to whether successful application of these methods relies on implicit memory processes spared in organic amnesia, on residual capacity in the damaged explicit memory system, or on some combination of the two. The second question, which is in some ways related, is whether or not this type of learning is generalisable. The third issue surrounds the nature and severity of memory disorders present in patients who can learn sufficient new complex vocabulary to secure work or even function independently in the home. Glisky and Schacter (1989, p. 119) indicated that, although both implicit and explicit memory systems may be operating, the intervention was aimed at the preserved implicit memory system. They suggested that this may be one of the reasons that the new learning had a "hyperspecific" quality and transfer of training did not occur readily. Glisky and Schacter also noted that their highly successful patient H.D., "possesses excellent attentional skills that may be instrumental in her success". Furthermore, her amnesia was severe, but not profound, suggesting that some residual explicit memory capacity was present. While emphasising the success of this method, Glisky and Schacter (1989) have acknowledged the extensive requirement of time and effort, and the slow rate of learning achieved compared with normal subjects.

Baddeley (1992) has taken up a number of these points recently in an attempt to apply theoretical distinctions regarding preserved memory systems in amnesia to rehabilitation. Baddeley begins by arguing that one important aspect of the evolutionary value of our explicit memory system is that it prevents us from becoming "imprisoned" by our errors. Relying unduly on implicit memory, which simply accumulates and averages data or increases habit, the amnesic patient may be unable to escape errors once they are made. Unable to remember that an error was made on a previous trial, the amnesic simply continues to emit the strongest, "primed", response whether it is correct or incorrect. Baddeley and Wilson (in press) tested the hypothesis that amnesic subjects learn better when prevented from making errors during the learning process. They taught lists of the words to 16 amnesic patients of whom six had suffered from encephalitis, four from severe closed head injury, three from cerebral haemorrhages, and one each from thalamic stroke, carbon monoxide poisoning, and Korsakoff's syndrome. Two different learning conditions were employed. In the "errorful" condition, the subjects were given word stems and encouraged to produce the correct completion by guessing. The correct completion was provided after four incorrect guesses or 25 seconds. In the "errorless" condition, the subjects were given the correct completion and asked to record it without making any erroneous guesses. During nine test trials that followed subjects were asked to complete each of the stems with a word they had written down earlier with the same stem. All subjects were tested in each condition and their performance was compared with that of 16 young and 16 elderly controls. Results showed that amnesics performed significantly better in the "errorless" learning condition and that the benefits of this method were greater for them than for either control group (although there was a marked ceiling effect in the young control group). Analyses of the data suggested that, although errorless learning was particularly beneficial for amnesic subjects, there was little difference between the two conditions in the elderly control group. Baddeley and Wilson (in press) argued that amnesic patients rely much more heavily on implicit learning which is less well attuned to elimination of strong competing and erroneous responses. They have suggested that errorless learning may improve significantly the rate of learning and slow the rate of forgetting shown by amnesic patients in traditional cognitive rehabilitation programmes.

The general conclusion of the research reviewed in this section is that, under optimal conditions, patients with severe amnesia may be candidates for successful cognitive rehabilitation. There is some considerable doubt as to whether such techniques would have utility in the rehabilitation of representative samples of memory impaired chronic alcoholic patients. One reason for this is that the psychosocial circumstances of such patients are usually very unfavourable. Another reason to curb enthusiasm is that the amnesic deficits of chronic alcoholic patients are seldom circumscribed, often occurring in the presence of impairments of intellectual and cognitive functioning, which may also impede learning and enhance forgetting. On the other hand, Baddeley and Wilson (in press) have shown that "dysexecutive" patients with frontal lobe lesions in their amnesic sample performed similarly to those with "pure" memory deficits. The extent to which these methods are applicable to patients with alcohol-related memory impairment is worthy of empirical study.

Rehabilitation of chronic alcoholics

In this section we consider studies attempting to remediate chronic alcoholics who have a mild or moderate degree of alcohol-related brain damage that affects a range of their cognitive skills. Hansen (1980) trained a group of alcoholics with mild to moderate cognitive impairment in visuomotor co-ordination, attention and concentration, abstract problem solving, verbal functioning, and memory. The only measure of outcome— the patients' subjective reports—indicated improvements in memory and self-esteem. Binder and Schreiber (1980) showed that alcoholic inpatients could improve their recall of verbal paired-associates using visual imagery and verbal mediation. Both interventions were equivalent and superior to a control condition in which no training instructions were given. Neither study reported data regarding generalisation across time, setting, or type of memory assessment.

Despite the fact that residual memory impairment found in most young and middle-aged detoxified alcoholics is subtle (Brandt et al., 1983), such impairments feature prominently in the subjective reports of these patients (Parsons, 1987) and their relevance to long-term rehabilitation cannot be discounted. To investigate the impact of a group memory retraining programme, Hannon et al. (1989) assigned alcoholic patients to either memory retraining ($n = 14$) or control ($n = 15$) conditions. Although group assignment was based on willingness to participate in the programme, there were no significant differences between the two groups in age or education, duration of drinking, level of intake, or SILS vocabulary and Symbol Digit Modalities test scores. All the patients were participating in an inpatient rehabilitation programme and had been abstinent for at least 21 days prior to beginning the research programme groups. Before group assignment, subjects were assessed on the Boston Remote Memory test, Babcock Story Recall test, Hidden Objects test, the

Rey Auditory Verbal Learning test, and the Memory Matrix test, a non-verbal analogue of the RAVLT. Memory retraining was conducted in groups of three to six subjects for 1 hour per week over 8 weeks. The intervention used techniques described by Wilson and Moffat (1984) and employed in the Wilson and Cooper "memory training" condition (Wilson, 1987) described previously. Different stimulus items were used during training and assessment but there were similarities between the types of tasks and information employed. The subjects in the control condition received only pre- and post-testing. Results showed no significant between-groups difference on any test. There was improvement over time on the Memory Matrix test, but Babcock Story Recall was actually worse in both groups at post-test. On the Boston Remote Memory test there was a significant interaction between group and time; the memory training group improved while the control group deteriorated. This finding is particularly difficult to interpret as remote memory performance is perhaps the least likely skill to have been influenced by this memory retraining programme.

The negative findings of this study underscore two of the problems facing researchers in this area. First, most subjects scored at, or about, the average range on the tests employed prior to commencement of memory retraining, making sizeable score increments unlikely. It was also perhaps unfortunate that the RBMT was not employed. Wilson and Cooper had found that this was the only test in their battery sensitive to changes resulting from memory training. On the other hand, the RBMT is also subject to ceiling effects, a problem that has necessitated the development of a revised version. A second important point is the difficulty researchers in this area have in recruiting subjects. Hannon et al. (1989) resorted to a procedure likely to contribute significantly to biases arising from sampling error. When subject numbers are small, alternative methods such as single-subject designs (Wilson, 1987) may be more appropriate.

In a subsequent study, Wetzig and Hardin (1990) overcame these problems. They tested 62 voluntary male patients admitted for treatment of alcoholism on Nelson's modified version of the Wisconsin Card Sorting Test (N-WSCT). They enrolled 45 patients who achieved fewer than three (of a possible six) categories on this test in a cognitive retraining programme that utilised a hierarchical learning intervention, based on operant and cumulative learning principles, designed to facilitate the development of abstract reasoning and problem-solving strategies. The 45 subjects (mean age 33.66 years, range 18–55) were assigned randomly to groups receiving active treatment, practice, or assessment only. Groups were matched for race, age, and educational achievement. The group receiving active treatment learned how to perform component parts of the N-WCST. Initially, they were taught to sort fabric shapes according to colour and when this was mastered, the stimuli were turned plain side up and the subjects learned to sort according to shape. Finally, similar methods were employed to help them sort according to number and to acquire skills in shifting set. The practice group spent an equivalent amount of time (two 45-minute sessions) practising the N-WCST while the control group received only pre-, post-, and generalisation testing. Outcome was assessed by comparing the number of categories achieved on the N-WCST, and the numbers of perseverative and non-perseverative errors made in each group before and after the programme. A similar test employing position, pattern, and letter as categories to be sorted was administered to test generalisation of the cognitive processes augmented by training. Results showed that only the group receiving active cognitive training had improved performance. All members of this group passed the N-WCST post-test while none of the other two groups achieved three or more categories. Likewise, only the active cognitive training group subjects passed the generalisation test. The pattern of results was the same for both perseverative and non-perseverative errors. Wetzig and Hardin (1990, p. 228) concluded that the subjects had been trained: "... to plan and organise a strategy and to utilise environmental cues that they had previously neglected in order to organise incoming information into categories".

Alternative explanations exist, however. Equivalent activation was not present in the practice condition; these subjects spent two 45-minute sessions repeatedly failing an obscure test. The fact that the practice group's score decreased slightly between pre- and post-test may signify annoyance or boredom in some of these subjects. It was also disappointing that Wetzig and Hardin provided no information regarding the clinical relevance of the cognitive training gains or their relevance to behaviour during treatment or to post-treatment adjustment. The findings of this study provide the clinician working in alcoholism rehabilitation with further evidence to support the findings of Goldman and his colleagues (Goldman, 1986; Goldman et al., 1983, 1985) that retraining may assist the recovery of a range of cognitive functions in abstinent chronic alcoholics. However, unlike Goldman's findings with visualmotor deficits, the practice group in this study did not improve their abstract problem-solving skills by experience alone.

Perhaps the best study published to date reporting attempts to retrain a range of cognitive skills with abstinent chronic alcoholics is that of Yohman, Schaeffer, and Parsons (1988) who recruited 76 voluntary alcoholic patients receiving treatment at a milieu therapy facility in a study to test the efficacy of memory and problem-solving training. The patients were aged between 24 and 60 years (mean = 42.5) and all had SILS vocabulary age of at least 13 years. They were assessed at intake on a battery of memory, problem-solving, and perceptual motor tests sensitive to brain dysfunction and known to differentiate between chronic alcoholic and non-alcoholic subjects. Groups of three to seven subjects were randomly assigned to 12 hours of memory training (n = 25), problem-solving training (n = 26), or received only pre- and post-training assessment (n = 25). Subjects were assessed prior to training and again 3 weeks later by qualified psychometricians blind to group assignment. Instructors leading the groups taught both types of intervention depending on the condition assigned. Memory training focused on a variety of techniques including "chunking" and visual imagery for verbal stimuli, and verbal mediation for visual material. The process of memory training involved learning concentration skills, discussion of general strategies, and practice of specific memory skills, initially with instructor guidance. Problem-solving training involved similar general processes but focused on practising a particular strategy including identification of rules and goals, obtaining relevant information, problem simplification, utilisation of feedback, and pattern identification. A systematic "win–stay/lose–shift" strategy was taught and practised throughout. A mixture of laboratory-based and ecologically relevant tasks was included in the training process. Pre-testing established that the alcoholic groups were impaired, relative to age and education matched controls, on the tests of memory, problem solving, and perceptual motor function used to assess outcome. The level of performance on these test clusters did not differ between the groups receiving each of the three training conditions. Results showed that the group receiving memory training enjoyed no greater improvement on learning and memory tests than the other two groups; however, subsequent analysis revealed that memory training did facilitate memory test performance for the younger patients (less than 42.5 years). The group receiving problem- solving training improved more than the control group. However, the problem-solving group showed better performance than the memory group only on a difference score analysis of problem-solving performance. Neither group showed significant improvement in perceptual motor test performance. The authors speculated that the relative efficacy of problem-solving compared with memory training may have reflected the concentration of practice on one particular strategy in the former group and the relative spread of practice across a range of techniques in the latter group. They concluded that, in the light of the facilitative effect of memory training for younger subjects, more intensive practice may have yielded significant overall effects of memory training. Yohman et al. (1988) made an interesting distinction between training focusing on remediation strategies (restitution of skills that were once in the patient's repertoire) versus compensation strategies (learning new strategies to regain average everyday function). They suggested that the memory-training programme may have included more novel strategies than the problem-solving intervention, and that these may have been more difficult to learn than the remediation strategies comprising the bulk of the latter intervention. In evaluating their study, Yohman et al. (1988) acknowledged the need for follow-up data and information describing the relationship between the training procedures and post-treatment life adjustment. Despite these weaknesses, their results are promising given the brevity of the intervention. In addition, Yohman et al. (1988, p. 70) observed that: "As regards motivation and involvement in the training, many of the alcoholic subjects commented after the training on the improvement in their self-confidence; they enjoyed showing friends and relatives some of their new skills to prove that they were not 'burnt-out cases' ". At present, consumer satisfaction and non-specific improvements may be the major justification for providing cognitive rehabilitation to patients with chronic alcohol-induced organic mental syndromes. As is clear from the literature reviewed in this, and the previous section, it is premature to recommend them entirely on the basis of the empirical outcome literature.

PHARMACOLOGICAL APPROACHES

There has been interest in the neurochemical dysfunctions associated with alcohol-induced amnesia for some time, and work in this area has accelerated in the past decade. (Arendt, Bigl, Arendt, & Tennstedt, 1983; Butters, 1985; Kopelman & Corn, 1988). The discovery of excessive levels of major metabolites of important CNS neurotransmitters in the cerebrospinal fluid (CSF) of alcoholic Korsakoff's patients has been one of a number of findings that have stimulated attempts to ameliorate amnesic deficits pharmacologically.

McEntee and Mair (1980) studied the effects of three drugs designed to facilitate the activity of the central neurotransmitter noradrenalin on the memory performance of eight patients with alcoholic Korsakoff's syndrome. Based on the findings of an earlier study (McEntee & Mair, 1978) in which they reported increased levels of major noradrenalin metabolites in the CSF of six Korsakoff patients, they hypothesised that facilitation of central noradrenalin activity might ameliorate the severity of amnesia. Eight subjects between the ages of 40 and 58 years who had IQ–MQ differences of between 20 and 31 points were tested in a double-blind counterbalanced study. They received each of three drugs thought to facilitate noradrenalin activity by different pharmacological mechanisms. The drugs administered were clonidine, which is thought to stimulate both post-synaptic receptors and pre-synaptic autoreceptors, d-amphetamine, which is thought to stimulate release and block reuptake of noradrenalin, and methysergide, a putative serotonin blocker used in this study because of the suggested reciprocal relationship between the effects of noradrenalin and serotonin on learning. On a fourth occasion, each subject received a placebo. All drugs were administered for 2 weeks, with a 2-week "washout" period at the cross-over point. Order of administration was counterbalanced, with random assignment of subjects to order. Drugs were administered at 7.00 a.m. and 7.00 p.m. each day. Neuropsychological testing was conducted prior to and on the final day of each treatment block, 60 to 90 minutes after the final dose. The tests administered were the WMS, multiple-choice remote memory tests (Albert et al., 1979; Seltzer & Benson, 1974), the consonant trigram (CCC) version of the Peterson–Brown test (Butters & Cermak, 1975), the Digit Symbol subtest from the WAIS, an embedded figures test, and two tests of facial recognition. Results showed more consistent improvement in WMS and CCC test performance with clonidine than with either of the other drugs or the placebo. Performance on memory tasks placing a greater load on perceptual functioning (facial recognition memory tests) and performance on complex visuoperceptual tasks (embedded figures and digit symbol tests) did not improve. Performance on tests of retrograde amnesia was not facilitated by any drug. The authors suggested that this pattern of findings is consistent with a specific facilitation of memory by clonidine when tasks do not place demands on Korsakoff patients' impaired visual perceptual abilities. While significant improvement occurred on some tests, the memory performance of patients did not approach normal levels of functioning under any drug treatment. The authors provided no information about the clinical significance of the observed effects.

These findings were replicated and extended by Mair and McEntee (1986). In a similar study comparing the efficacy of clonidine with L-dopa and ephedrine, only clonidine had any significant effect on anterograde amnesia. Again, the WMS subtests Logical Memory and Visual Reproduction, and the CCC test were performed significantly better during clonidine treatment. As in the previous study (McEntee & Mair, 1980), severity of retrograde amnesia was not ameliorated and visuoperceptual performance did not improve. Clonidine, however, was also associated with improved Stroop interference score and faster habitation of acoustic startle response. Despite the fact that significant improvement on some memory tests occurred in these two studies, none of the patients showed significant clinical improvement or approached what would be accepted as normal memory performance. It should be noted that the experimental protocols did not allow for individual variation in doses and that each trial lasted only 2 weeks. Perhaps longer trials of individually titrated doses would improve clinical outcome. The application of measures of greater clinical and ecological relevance would be of value were such a trial to be undertaken.

Mention must be made at this point of potential adverse effects of clonidine on recovery of cognitive functions in some alcoholic patients. Herndon, Jackson, and Good (1991) studied the effect of clonidine on recovery of Wechsler Memory Scale performance of alcoholics undergoing acute withdrawal. Clonidine appeared to have an adverse effect on recovery of WMS performance, compared with placebo, during the first 24 hours. This finding has considerable clinical relevance as this drug is used widely in preference to benzodiazepines for the relief of sympathetic systemic symptoms and signs associated with the acute withdrawal of alcohol. Although the benefits of clonidine may outweigh its adverse effects on the recovery of memory function, clinicians should be aware of inhibiting effects and allow for them.

Another drug that has been reported to facilitate cognitive functioning in impaired alcoholics is piracetam. This drug is thought to operate by either increasing dopamine turnover or increasing acetylcholine release in the septum and hippocampus. Although there is considerable evidence to show that it results in statistically significant improvement in cognition of healthy volunteers, results with pathological groups have been inconsistent. As one of the reasons for this may be the variability in doses administered, Barnas et al. (1990) conducted a placebo-controlled dose-finding study of the effects of piracetam in patients with alcohol-induced organic impairment of cognitive function. Subjects were 52 male and eight female alcoholics with average ages of 44.3 and 42.4 years, respectively. All had diagnoses of alcohol dependence and were free of significant psychopathology or neuropathology. Subjects were randomly assigned to one of three groups—a placebo group and two groups receiving either 3g piracetam or 12g piracetam twice daily for 6 weeks. They were assessed at intake at least 7 days after ceasing alcohol intake and again 7, 14, 28, and 42 days later on a battery of cognitive tests. The focus of these tests was on attention, concentration, and organisation and memory. Results showed that all three groups improved on all tests during the 42 days of the trial. However, only the higher-dose piracetam group showed significant improvement in complex cognitive functions requiring organisational skills and memory, as well as speed. The authors concluded that it is this cognitive cluster that is of greatest clinical relevance. As in other studies, however, no data of direct clinical relevance is provided. It also seems highly likely that many of these patients were demonstrating spontaneous remission of their deficits.

Although there is still considerable debate about the relationship between the two chronic organic mental disorders associated with alcoholism (dementia associated with alcoholism and alcohol amnestic disorder, or Korsakoff's syndrome) the results of at least one study indicated that the two disorders may respond differently to pharmacotherapy. Martin et al. (1987) reported that fluvoxamine treatment was associated with improvement in episodic memory performance only in amnesic patients ($n = 6$) and not in patients with global intellectual decline ($n = 3$), or in a patient with cerebral impairment secondary to alcoholic liver disease.

Further research is required to establish whether or not pharmacotherapy has a role in the rehabilitation of patients with alcohol-related organic mental disorder. To date, there have been a number of promising findings with restricted doses of medication not specifically tailored to the needs of individual subjects. If pharmacotherapy is to become clinically relevant, future studies will need to incorporate measures that assess more than just improvement on laboratory memory test performance. As we have argued elsewhere, such measures are of little value in the planning or assessment of treatment programmes.

CONCLUSIONS

There are relatively few studies of rehabilitation of alcoholic patients with chronic organic mental disorders available for review and the quality of the extant literature is poor. Few studies have either homogeneous groups or large representative samples. The differences between group means reported disguise large within-group variation in treatment response. Only two studies have employed functional measures that could provide valid assessment of clinically relevant treatment gains. The results of these have suggested that general activation procedures have been as effective (or ineffective) as specific cognitive retraining methods.

There appears to be some evidence to suggest that specific retraining in problem-solving strategies may induce reliable improvements in performance on laboratory-based measures in alcoholic patients at the less severe end of the spectrum of organic mental disorders. This may be analogous to the experience dependent recovery reported by Goldman and his colleagues (Goldman, 1986), the clinical relevance of which is yet to be demonstrated. The efficacy of interventions for patients with alcohol amnestic disorder and dementia associated with alcoholism is very uncertain. When gains have been reported, these have not been linked to specific treatments or aspects of treatment. The improvements have not been related directly to post-treatment everyday functioning, except in anecdotal case reports. Pharmacotherapy approaches have, as yet, little more to recommend them.

Researchers in this area are dogged by a multiplicity of problems. The group of patients available for study is particularly heterogeneous. Patients with the most severe cognitive deficits, and those with chronic organic amnesia and/or dementia, are quite rare and difficult to engage in research. Until recently, few ecologically valid measures of cognitive impairment applicable for assessing outcome have been available. Fortunately, there is evidence from the studies reviewed in this chapter that this deficiency is being rectified, albeit slowly.

Finally, despite some worthwhile attempts at developing programmes of specific cognitive rehabilitation, it must be concluded that only relatively non-specific treatment effects have been demonstrated to date. With the exception of anecdotal case reports that are difficult to interpret, the contribution of improvements achieved in cognitive rehabilitation programmes to the enhancement of everyday independent functioning has not been demonstrated.

CHAPTER THIRTEEN

Concluding Comments

In this final section, we consider some of the research questions neuropsychologists have considered to date. We are also concerned to represent the view that to make a full contribution to the management of patients with alcohol problems, clinical neuropsychologists must take account of the patient's physical and psychosocial circumstances. Measurement and rehabilitation of the brain impairments caused by alcohol takes place against a background of concurrent medical, social, and personal dysfunction.

The history of medical involvement with alcoholic clients is one of a gradually developing awareness of the wide range of damage to the body that results from prolonged alcohol abuse. No functional system is entirely spared. For the clinical neuropsychologist this means that few patients with alcohol problems referred for assessment or advice on management are entirely spared from other medical complications. Organic damage is a significant factor to be taken into account when interpreting neuropsychological findings in the total context of the client's circumstances. The catalogue of non-neurological medical disorders in which an alcohol aetiology is implicated is a lengthy one. As the liver is the principal site for the metabolism of alcohol, few alcohol-dependent clients are entirely free of signs of liver damage, particularly in later life. Damage to the liver may be progressive, ranging from enlargement through the accumulation of fatty tissue, to an increased risk of carcinoma. Although regular intake of moderate amounts of alcohol reduces the risk of coronary heart disease and occlusive stroke, alcohol dependence is associated with increased incidence of elevated blood pressure, cerebral haemorrhage and infarction, and cardiomyopathy. Alcoholics typically also sustain damage to the digestive system, have a greater incidence of endocrine disorders, and run a higher than normal risk of developing many forms of cancer. All these medical factors complicate the treatment and rehabilitation of the alcoholic client and potentiate the adverse effects of neurological damage. It is likely that even if the brain were totally protected from the direct toxic effects of alcohol and from the malnutrition arising from the alcoholic's lifestyle, the indirect consequences of damage to other physical systems would result in some evidence of neuropsychological impairment. Recent evidence indicates that certain neuropsychological impairments attributable to the neurotoxic effects of alcohol are present in patients with liver cirrhosis but without a history of alcohol dependence. There are also important gender differences in susceptibility to these adverse effects. Preliminary evidence suggests that women are more prone to alcoholic liver disease and develop adverse neuroradiological changes after alcohol abuse of much briefer duration. This has been attributed to achievement of higher plasma levels at equivalent doses and has significant implications for the way alcohol consumption by women is viewed.

The brain, however, is not safe from the toxic effects of alcohol nor from the general hazards of the alcoholic's way of life. These latter perils include the poor nutrition and consequent vitamin deficiencies that have both acute and chronic consequences, the increased likelihood of accidents and brain trauma, and the probability that the alcoholic patient will at some time be a polydrug abuser and exposed to diseases such as hepatitis or HIV. That alcohol has a direct effect on brain function is apparent to anyone who has been intoxicated; alcohol consumption acutely impairs cognitive functioning and judgement. With prolonged alcohol abuse comes the increased prospect that acute amnesia or blackouts will occur, tolerance will increase, and withdrawal effects will result if alcohol is abruptly withdrawn. Most dependent alcoholics will show signs of withdrawal when admitted for treatment and they usually require close medical supervision while being detoxicated. The neuropsychologist asked to assess the newly admitted alcoholic patient will need to judge when this can be done without the test results being contaminated by the lingering effects of withdrawal. When withdrawal has resolved, residual neurological conditions may be exposed. The complex of symptoms labelled Wernicke–Korsakoff syndrome is perhaps the best known of these because of the interest it has excited in researchers concerned with understanding the psychological and biological bases of memory failure. Chronic alcoholic patients also typically show other signs of neurological damage, including peripheral neuropathy, cerebellar damage, and visual disturbances. In sum, the neuropsychological investigation and rehabilitation of the individual alcoholic client often presents against a background of medical disability and clinical evidence of nervous system damage.

Since the first reports on fetal alcohol syndrome (FAS) reached the literature in the 1970s, there has been considerable interest in the teratogenic effects of alcohol. Ethanol is not impeded by the placental barrier and it has become increasingly obvious that drinking during pregnancy increases the risk of fetal brain dysfunction. Research into FAS is difficult to conduct because of the problems involved in quantifying maternal intake accurately, especially retrospectively. It is thus difficult to set a safe level of consumption during pregnancy. There is, however, widespread acknowledgement by health-care professionals of the risks involved in drinking during pregnancy, and conveying this message as widely as possible is a priority for public health promotion. One of the most disabling aspects of FAS is mental retardation, which is often compounded by behavioural deficits and hyperactivity. This is an area of considerable practical significance to the clinical neuropsychologist. First, prenatal alcohol exposure may provide a diagnostic formulation for some children with developmental and behavioural deficits. Second, for the clinician working with an alcoholic family, the presence of one or more children with neurobehavioural symptoms is likely to provide additional stress. Third, there is an urgent need to investigate methods for managing children with the cognitive and behavioural deficits associated with FAS. There is no evidence to suggest children with FAS will make up their initial developmental delay, and special intervention programmes, taking full account of the psychosocial environment in which the children of an alcoholic parent live, may need to be developed. Neuropsychologists have a role to play in the design and evaluation of such interventions.

Following the early experimental studies of Talland and others, an increasingly vigorous research effort has been focused on the neuropsychological changes associated with alcohol consumption. This work ranges from the investigation of the effects of acute intoxication to the documentation of deficits in the alcoholic dement. This research work proceeds against a background of methodological challenges and limitations. An awareness of these issues is important in planning and evaluating neuropsychological studies in this area. The initial task that confronts both the practitioner and the clinician is the selection of neuropsychological instruments that have the psychometric credentials to fulfil the testing objectives. This an obvious consideration, but poor test selection is one of the major barriers to the collecting valid and useful data. Researchers often handicap themselves by using testing strategies that are insufficiently powerful to detect real experimental effects. Neglect of basic psychometric principles also leads to the publication of dissociations in task performance that are the spurious result of poor task matching. Most psychologists are well-versed in the need for careful matching of pathological and control groups. Few take similar care to match tasks. Tests are rarely constructed to be of entirely comparable reliability and difficulty. Standardising the resultant scores to a single normative scale only serves to disguise the absence of psychometric equivalence. These considerations are particularly important when the focus of research is on contrasting deficits to determine a specific impairment. An example of this is the proposal that alcoholics are more susceptible to right than left hemisphere damage. Only when tests of left and right hemisphere functioning are equivalent can this hypothesis be tested meaningfully.

Another decision that researchers need to make in most studies involving human subjects, is how best to document their subjects' drinking practices. An initial issue may be the reliable and accurate formulation of diagnoses for the sample under study. Research into the neuropsychological consequences of drinking has made an implicit distinction between social drinkers with no history of treatment for alcoholism, alcohol abusers in treatment, and alcohol-dependent patients with clinical evidence of neurological damage. There are no precise research diagnostic criteria for any of these groups. Alcohol dependence, for example, tends to be formulated in terms of the physiological and social consequences of drinking, which are entirely appropriate for most clinical purposes. However, there is no account taken of current and past consumption levels. Hence most groups involved in inpatient care are heterogeneous with respect to drinking pattern and lifetime consumption rates. This means that samples of alcoholics vary from study to study, depending on programme admission criteria, and that intrasample variability is likely to be high on many relevant clinical and performance variables. This would be the case even if consumption patterns could be measured reliably and validly. Inaccuracies in self-reported drinking practices and variations in the way in which such data are collected further contribute to error in the execution of research. Studies of the effects of drinking on neuropsychological performance are limited by the fact that participants in the research have been exposed to variable amounts of alcohol, under different psychosocial and health-related circumstances, for different periods of time. Attempts to quantify these conditions retrospectively can only be approximate. Despite all these problems it is possible to approach a number of important questions about the way in which drinking effects the nervous system and human behaviour. In what follows, some of the questions considered in previous chapters will be reviewed.

Does social drinking cause residual long-term cognitive deficits?

Most people who drink do so in moderation, and alcohol causes them no discernible medical or social difficulties. A study of Californian male social drinkers (Parker & Noble, 1977) attracted attention because it suggested an association between average quantity consumed per occasion and scores on measures of intellect and conceptual learning. This relationship is readily interpreted. It could be that alcohol affected cognition, or that less able people were more likely to drink. Alternatively, some third variable, such as personal stress or depression, might be responsible for both rate of consumption and current cognitive functioning. These results were supported by the findings of Bergman and colleagues that a Swedish community sample had CT-scan evidence of cortical and subcortical brain shrinkage that was significantly correlated with alcohol consumption.

Attempts to replicate Parker and Noble's original results produced inconsistent and equivocal results. In a 1987 review, Bowden concluded that the evidence available provided negligible evidence for an association between cognitive impairment and social drinking, and that the positive associations that had been uncovered were capable of alternative explanations and of no practical significance. This particular research effort has been hampered by many of the methodological limitations alluded to above. Quantification of consumption in social drinkers is problematic, the tests that can be administered to large samples, such as the Shipley Institute of Living Scale, have limited sensitivity to acquired neurological impairment, and results that are typically reported as large numbers of correlations can only be interpreted with considerable scepticism. There is therefore no conclusive answer to this first question and there is no strong justification to recommend that social drinking be classed as a health hazard. Nevertheless, acute intoxication does produce dramatic changes in cognitive performance and it would be surprising if repeated episodes of inebriation did not initiate some of the brain changes that become detectable in alcohol-dependent patients. Future research may more usefully focus on more specific questions, such as the identification of groups within the larger population who may be at early risk for developing impairments through heavy social drinking, on the basis of their medical, family, or racial backgrounds.

Does alcohol damage the brain and affect the cognitive performance of alcohol-dependent patients?

Although there remain many inconsistencies in the literature, there is a sufficient quantity of converging evidence to make an affirmative answer to this question. On measures of brain function, post-mortem analyses, and neuropsychological test batteries, dependent alcoholic patients show dysfunctions relative to healthy controls. Neuropsychological research in this area has turned from establishing that deficits occur, to documenting the extent, specificity, and reversibility of these impairments. A related issue concerns the specificity of the brain damage resulting from the action of alcohol. At this time there is no convincing evidence to dispute the view that, in the alcoholic, the damage is diffuse and affects a wide range of cognitive functions. It is possible that frontal lobe functioning is specifically impaired in alcoholics, but testing this hypothesis is difficult because of problems with the validity of tests of frontal functioning. For example, the WCST—traditionally viewed as a measure of frontal deficits—may also be failed by patients with non-frontal lesions. There is no evidence that the right hemisphere is more vulnerable than the left to alcohol; nor does the pattern of deficits caused by alcohol dependence entirely resemble premature ageing.

Does abstinence lead to recovery of neuropsychological functioning?

Evidence from the work of Mark Goldman and his colleagues into time-dependent recovery following abstinence during treatment suggests that age is an important factor in recovery. Under the age of 40, alcoholic patients' functioning on a variety of routine neuropsychological tests reaches normal after about 25 days abstinence. Patients over the age of 40, however, showed persistent deficits on some measures, particularly those involving novel learning or problem-solving, even after 6 months abstinence. Forsberg and Goldman (1985) went on to demonstrate that after practice on a particular task, normal levels of performance could be achieved by subjects who showed no sign of time-dependent recovery. They made an important distinction between time- and experience-dependent recovery, and suggested that their demonstration of the latter, in the absence of spontaneous improvement over time provided a basis for undertaking cognitive retraining with alcoholics. No large-scale investigations of the efficacy of specific cognitive retaining or rehearsal strategies have been reported.

The experimental literature would suggest, however, that at a practical level abstinent alcoholics should be capable of returning to normal premorbid levels of cognitive performance on most of the activities they were familiar with prior to treatment. It is possible, however, that routine experimental neuropsychological tests are not sufficiently sensitive to detect subtle deficits in complex learning situations or in maintaining attention over long periods of time. These dysfunctions may only become apparent when the alcoholic returns to a demanding occupation or when performance is evaluated over a lengthy period of time. Normal performance on standard neuropsychological tests is an encouraging indication of an improvement in function; the clinician should, however, expect that transition back into the work setting may reveal some changes in performance standards readily apparent to employers and colleagues.

What factors predict neuropsychological impairments?

The attempt to uncover factors associated with greater than average incidence of brain impairment in subgroups of alcoholics is important because of the clues that may be offered the process of brain impairment consequent on alcoholism. One factor that has been investigated is family history. Several studies have suggested that non-alcoholic subjects with a positive family history of alcoholism may score more poorly on tests of cognition than those with no such history. Similarly, alcoholics with a positive family history may be more impaired than those who do not have such a history. Neurophysiologists have also reported significant correlations between a family history of alcohol abuse and abnormalities of brain evoked responses in non-alcoholic subjects. There are several reasons why family history may be associated with signs of impairment. The family environment created by the presence of an alcoholic parent may lead to poor educational achievement, behavioural deficits, or poor nutrition. Alternatively some biological vulnerability to alcoholism and brain damage might be transmitted genetically or the deficits may be the long-term outcome of fetal alcohol exposure. There is some support for the hypothesis that the non-alcoholic children of alcoholic parents have neuropsychological impairments; however, the possibility that this due to educational deficits can not be excluded. A family history of alcoholism has emerged as only an inconsistent predictor of impairment in alcohol-dependent subjects.

Other factors where a more consistent association with brain impairment has been demonstrated are age and liver damage. Age has been found to be related to evidence of impairment independently of both drinking history and consumption practices. Apart from reports that patients with clinical evidence of liver disease perform more poorly than those without, no other medical risk factors have been identified. Blackouts, head-injury, hypertension, and developmental indicators have all drawn a blank.

What is the relationship between the neuropsychological deficits of chronic alcohol dependence and the Wernicke–Korsakoff syndrome?

The predominant current view of this relationship is that the characteristic lesions associated with the Wernicke–Korsakoff syndrome are superimposed on the diffuse, predominantly cortical lesions seen in dependent alcoholics. This two-stage model is best represented by Butters and Granholm's (1987) trauma model of the development of Korsakoff's syndrome. In this model, the diffuse lesions in alcoholics are caused primarily by the neurotoxic effects of alcohol and its metabolites, while the specific midline lesions associated with Wernicke–Korsakoff syndrome arise from chronic thiamine deficiency. The course of the slow decline in ability seen in alcoholics as they age may change abruptly to the irreversible amnesia of Korsakoff's syndrome following an episode of Wernicke's encephalopathy. This model fits the progressive development of cognitive dysfunction characteristic of many patients with Korsakoff's syndrome and is consistent with the typical neuropathological and radiological findings in Korsakoff's syndrome—grey matter lesions around the third and fourth ventricles and evidence of diffuse cortical and subcortical lesions.

The validity of the two-stage model of alcoholic brain damage has, however, been challenged. Neuropathological studies of alcoholics' brains post-mortem have revealed many cases where the characteristic midline lesions of the Wernicke–Korsakoff syndrome were present, but the patients did not show the clinical features of this condition during their lifetimes. One implication of these findings is that the same pathological processes may underlie both alcoholic impairment and the Wernicke–Korsakoff syndrome (Bowden, 1990). Profound amnesia may only occur in a small subgroup of patients because of a relative specific distribution of these midline lesions, disrupting critical neural tracts. An important consequence of this research has been to expose how little is known about the course of neurological and neuropsychological impairment in brain damaged alcoholics. The manner in which Korsakoff patients have been selected for research into the psychological basis of memory failure has promoted the view that Korsakoff patients represent a distinct nosological category. It is apparent, however, that there is a range of severe neuropsychological impairments in alcoholics.

Although there are cases with a relatively circumscribed amnesia and abrupt onset, for example the case P.Z. documented by Butters and his colleagues, there are also many patients where memory failure coexists with dementia. In some cases the history of the appearance of amnesia is relatively gradual and there is no evidence of an episode of Wernicke's encephalopathy. There may also be cases where there is a marked degree of cognitive failure, which extends beyond that seen in alcoholics, but which is not severe enough to warrant inclusion in the clinical diagnostic category of Wernicke–Korsakoff syndrome. Researchers selecting amnesic alcoholics typically go through the exercise of discarding potential subjects whose disorders are either too mild or complicated by dementia. This may serve to perpetuate the view that the amnesic symptoms of Korsakoff's syndrome are discontinuous with the memory impairments typical of chronic alcoholism.

Both the research literature on the clinical consequences of Wernicke–Korsakoff syndrome and practical experience working with brain-damaged alcoholics suggests that the clinical neuropsychologist should resist the assumption that there is a "typical" Korsakoff or brain damaged alcoholic patient. Clinicians are more likely to encounter patients with a range of neurological deficits, varying in severity, complicated by a variety of medical problems and psychosocial circumstances, and with vastly differing histories of alcohol abuse.

What is the biological basis for amnesia in Korsakoff's syndrome?

The precise pattern of lesions needed to produce memory failure in patients with Korsakoff's syndrome is not known. The necessary damage, however, has been localised to the midline diencephalic regions of the brain. The structures most likely to be implicated are the mammillary bodies, the medial nuclei of the thalamus, and the fibre tracts linking these bodies. However, the uncertainty about the precise location of the lesions provides some justification for speculation that other parts of the brain are involved. Butters and Granholm, for example, have suggested that lesions in the cholinergic nuclei of the basal forebrain may play a part in the causation or accentuation of alcoholic amnesia. Identifying the critical lesions has been complicated by the range of changes seen in the brains of Korsakoff patients post-mortem and the small number of such Korsakoff patients with well documented neuropsychological profiles that come to post-mortem. This research has, however, contributed significantly to the development of neuroanatomical models of memory.

Does the pattern of amnesia seen in alcoholic Korsakoff's syndrome differ from that of other amnesiacs?

There is a general consensus that the amnesia seen in alcoholic Korsakoff patients can be attributed primarily to midline diencephalic damage. Although the critical lesions necessary to produce the amnesia have not been determined, it is clear than the general area of damage is distinct from the other major site of amnesia-producing lesions—the medial temporal lobe area. Cases of amnesia resulting from discrete bilateral temporal damage are rare, which is not surprising given the geographical separation of the two temporal lobes. Do Korsakoff patients differ from amnesiacs with circumscribed temporal lesions? The general consensus is that they do, although the evidence remains equivocal. There are many difficulties involved in comparing amnesiacs of differing aetiologies. Most amnesiacs are not without lesions in areas of the brain that may play a part in the expression of some memory impairments. For example, encephalitic amnesiacs sometimes have damage not only in the temporal regions but also to the frontal lobes. Matching patients for level of amnesic deficit is another problem. If the level of amnesia is not equivalent in the contrasted subjects, then differences in the expression of amnesia may be attributable to differences in severity. Korsakoff amnesiacs tend to be more likely to show metamemory impairments, failures of short-term memory, and ungraded remote memory performance, and have less insight and more signs of confabulation than temporal lobe amnesiacs. The most likely explanations for these differences are either the severity of the alcoholic amnesic syndrome in Korsakoff patients or the higher probability of coexisting frontal or other cortical atrophy in amnesia with an alcoholic aetiology

Do neuropsychological test scores predict therapy progress or outcome?

The answer to this question is a qualified yes. The results of numerous investigations add up to a general finding that cognitive impairment is a weak and inconsistent predictor of long-term outcome and progress during therapy. More important than the findings that have emerged, is the way in which these studies have exposed a dearth of cognitive measures directly relevant to assessing the ability to assimilate therapy goals and educational processes. Having identified a range of neuropsychological deficits in alcohol-dependent subjects, there needs to be a follow-up development of tasks that identify the kind of cognitive skills that alcoholics need to participate in therapy.

Conclusions

The study of the neuropsychological deficits in alcoholics has contributed to the understanding of brain–behaviour relationships. For the clinical neuropsychologist there is the further task of translating these findings into better strategies for managing patients with alcohol-related problems. To date, neuropsychology has played a relatively circumscribed part in the practical treatment of alcoholics. This is principally because cognitive dysfunction is typically just one of the multifarious personal and social dysfunctions that constitute barriers to successful therapy. Further, developments in the management of alcoholics and the practice of neuropsychology have evolved without a great deal of contact. The result is that neuropsychological assessment in particular often appears to therapists and alcohol counsellors as irrelevant and of largely academic interest. If neuropsychological assessment is to have an impact on the management of alcoholics, findings need to be conveyed in terms that emphasise their practical implications and integrated into the totality of the patients' circumstances. Similarly, the initiation of any rehabilitation process to remediate brain impairments in alcoholics needs to take account of the patients' specific neurobehavioural deficits and the effect these have on everyday functioning. There has been little systematic research into the components of an effective rehabilitation programme for chronic alcoholics with cognitive impairment. The literature on recovery and rehabilitation after brain injury of other causes is growing steadily and the opportunity exists for the application of these findings to the alcohol abuse setting. In addition, neuropsychologists have much to contribute in the design of interventions that are capable of being assimilated by cognitively impaired patients. They can also contribute to the evaluation and reintegration of alcoholic clients in the workplace.

There has been little research reported on the rehabilitation of patients with alcoholic dementia or Korsakoff's syndrome. This is in contrast to the large number of neuropsychological investigations that these patients have been involved in. Early work on the remediation of patients with profound amnesia arose out of the results of cognitive studies and was very much grounded in this tradition. The emphasis was on teaching mnemonic techniques and rehearsing cognitive skills. Lately, these procedures have been supplemented by interventions that are more behavioural in orientation. The objective in the behavioural paradigm is to define deficits in terms of deficits in everyday functioning and to look for ways of remedying them. An example is the case of a woman with a mild memory impairment who works as a teacher. Knowing that she can learn 10 words out of 15 after 12 trials on a verbal memory test does not make explicit the everyday memory problems she has. One of these is the difficulty of remembering her pupils' names. An assessment strategy needs to be sufficiently practical to make salient the practical significance of these problems, of which the patient may be unaware. One way of attempting to remedy this deficit would be to teach her face–name mnemonic imagery techniques. However, such procedures are not always easy for the client to apply and require considerable motivation to learn. An alternative is to teach the children to identify themselves when they speak, a process that can be faded gradually as the names are acquired. With Korsakoff patients the objective of assessment is to identify the skills they lack to live in a particular environment, and to work to remedy these, either by changing the patient's limitations or by changing the environment. In some cases both the patient and environment need altering. For example, the environment can be changed to include external aids to memory, and the patient taught to identify and use these memory prostheses.

Future research of relevance to the practising neuropsychologist working with alcoholic patients might focus on defining more precisely the way cognitive deficits of mild to moderate severity impact on aspects of the patients' lives that are most important to maintaining treatment gains, such as work skills, family relationships, and the ability to live independently. Especially important is research that relates neuro-psychological deficit to skill components. Research on more fundamental aspects of the neuropsychological deficits in patients with alcohol-related brain damage is likely to continue to contribute to the body of knowledge about the workings of the brain. The aims of this research might include a more precise understanding of alcohol-induced deficits and their manifestation in different subgroups of alcoholics.

In reviewing the literature on alcohol and the brain, it is noticeable that much of the most fruitful and important research has involved collaboration between specialists from different medical and psychological specialties. Determining the critical lesions for amnesia, for example, requires neurological or neuropathological data to be combined with psychological test results. Collaborative studies of this kind require an appreciation of the significance and limitations of the data contributed by different disciplines. To be optimally effective, both clinical and research practice needs to be informed by the expertise of a range of specialists. We hope this book goes some small way towards meeting the objective of introducing the clinical neuropsychologist to the diversity of knowledge available.

References

Abbott, M. W., & Gregson, R. A. M. (1981). Cognitive dysfunction in the prediction of relapse in alcoholics. *Journal of Studies on Alcohol, 42*, 230–243.

Abel, E. L. (1979). Sex ratio in fetal alcohol syndrome. *Lancet, ii*, 105.

Abel, E. L., & Sokol, R. J. (1991). A revised conservative estimate of the incidence of FAS and its economic impact. *Alcoholism: Clinical and Experimental Research, 15*, 514–524.

Abrams, D., & Wilson, G. T. (1979). Effects of alcohol on social anxiety in women. *Journal of Abnormal Psychology, 88*, 161–173.

Acker, W., Ron, M. A., Lishman, W. A., & Shaw, G. K. (1984). A multivariate analysis of psychological, clinical, and CT scanning measures in detoxified chronic alcoholics. *British Journal of Addiction, 79*, 293–301.

Adams, K. M., & Grant, I. (1984). Failure of nonlinear models of drinking history variables to predict neuropsychological performance in alcoholics. *American Journal of Psychiatry, 141*, 663–667.

Adams, K. M., & Grant, I. (1986). Influence of premorbid risk factors on neuropsychological performance in alcoholics. *Journal of Clinical and Experimental Neuropsychology, 8*, 362–370.

Adams, R. D., Victor, M., & Mancall, E. L. (1959). Central pontine myelinolysis: A hitherto undescribed disease occurring in alcoholic and malnourished patients. *Archives of Neurology and Psychiatry, 81*, 154.

Aggleton, J. P., & Mishkin, M. (1983). Visual recognition impairment following medial thalamic lesions in monkeys. *Neuropsychologia, 21*, 189–197.

Albert, M. S., Butters, N., & Brandt, J. (1980). Memory for remote events in alcoholics. *Journal of Studies on Alcohol, 41*, 1071–1081.

Albert, M. S., Butters, N., & Levin, J. (1979). Temporal gradients in the retrograde amnesia of patients with alcoholic Korsakoff's disease. *Archives of Neurology, 36*, 211–216.

Alterman, A. I., Bridges, R., & Tarter, R. E. (1986). The influence of both drinking and familial risk statuses on cognitive functioning of social drinkers. *Alcoholism: Clinical and Experimental Research, 10*, 448–451.

Alterman, A. I., Gerstley, L. J., Goldstein, G., & Tarter, R. E. (1987). Comparisons of the cognitive functioning of familial and nonfamilial alcoholics. *Journal of Studies on Alcohol, 48*, 425–429.

Alterman, A. I., & Hall, J. G. (1989). Effects of social drinking and familial alcoholism risk on cognitive functioning: Null results. *Alcoholism: Clinical and Experimental Research, 13*, 799–803.

Alterman, A. I., Kushner, H., & Holahan, J. M. (1990). Cognitive functioning and treatment outcome in alcoholics. *Journal of Nervous and Mental Disease, 178*, 494–499.

Anastasi, A. (1988). *Psychological testing* (6th ed.). New York: Macmillan Publishing Company.

Anderson, D. (Ed.). (1989). *Drinking to your health: The allegations and the evidence.* London: Social Affairs Unit.

Anderson, S. W., Damasio, H., Jones, R. D., & Tranel, D. (1991). Wisconsin Card Sorting Test Performance as a measure of frontal lobe damage. *Journal of Clinical and Experimental Neuropsychology, 13*, 909–922.

Andrade, E.N. (1964). *Rutherford and the nature of the atom.* New York: Doubleday.

Annis, H. M. (1979). Self-report reliability of skid-row alcoholics. *British Journal of Psychiatry, 134*, 459–465.

Arendt, T., Bigl, V., Arendt, A., & Tennstedt, A. (1983). Loss of neurons in the nucleus basalis of Meynert in Alzheimer's disease, paralysis agitans, and Korsakoff's disease. *Acta Neuropathologica, 61*, 101–108.

Aristophanes (*circa* 400 BC/1962). *The clouds.* (B. B. Rogers, Trans.). London: William Heinemann.

Arria, A. M., Tarter, R. E., Kabene, M. A., Laird, S. B., Moss, H., & Van Thiel, D. H. (1991). The role of cirrhosis in memory functioning of alcoholics. *Alcoholism: Clinical and Experimental Research, 15*, 932–937.

Arria, A. M., Tarter, R. E., Starzl, T. E., & Van Thiel, D. H. (1991). Improvement in cognitive functioning of alcoholics following orthotopic liver transplantation. *Alcoholism: Clinical and Experimental Research, 15*, 956–962

Atkinson, L. (1991). Concurrent use of the Wechsler Memory Scale-Revised and the WAIS-R. *British Journal of Clinical Psychology, 30*, 87–90.

Atkinson, R. C., & Shiffrin, R. M. (1968). Human memory: A proposed system and its control processes. In K. W. Spence & J. T. Spence (Eds.), *The psychology of learning and motivation: Advances in research and theory* (Vol. 2, pp. 89–105). London: Academic Press.

Babor, T. F., Stephens, R. S., & Marlatt, G. A. (1987). Verbal report methods in clinical research on alcoholism: Response bias and its minimization. *Journal of Studies on Alcohol, 48*, 410–424.

Baddeley, A. D. (1986). *Working memory.* Oxford: Oxford University Press.

Baddeley, A. D. (1992). Implicit memory and errorless learning: A link between cognitive theory and neuropsychological rehabilitation? In L. R. Squire & N. Butters (Eds.), *Neuropsychology of memory* (2nd ed., pp. 309–314). New York: The Guilford Press.

Baddeley, A. D., & Warrington, E. K. (1970). Amnesia and the distinction between long- and short-term memory. *Journal of Verbal Learning and Verbal Behavior, 9*, 176–189.

Baddeley, A. D., & Wilson, B. A. (in press). When implicit memory fails: Amnesia and the problem of error elimination. *Neuropsychologia.*

Bailey, R. J., Krasner, N., Eddleston, A. L. W. F., Williams, R., Tee, D. E. H., Doniach, D., Kennedy, L. A., & Batchelor, J. R. (1976). Histocompatibility antigens, autoantibodies, and immunoglobulins in alcoholic liver disease. *British Medical Journal, 2,* 727–729.

Baldy, R. E., Brindley, G. S., Ewusi-Mensah, I., Jacobson, R. R., Reveley, M. A., Turner, S.W., & Lishman, W.A. (1986). A fully automated computer-assisted method of CT brain scan analysis for the measurement of cerebrospinal fluid spaces and brain absorption density. *Neuroradiology, 28,* 109–117.

Ballantyne, F. C., Clark, R. S., Simpson, H. S., & Ballantyne, D. (1982). High density and low density lipoprotein subfractions in survivors of myocardial infarction and in control subjects. *Metabolism: Clinical and Experimental, 31,* 433–437.

Barnas, C., Miller, C., Ehrmann, H., Schett, P., Gunther, V., & Fleishhacker, W. W. (1990). High versus low-dose piracetam in alcohol organic mental disorder: A placebo controlled study. *Psychopharmacology, 100,* 361–365.

Barona, A., Reynolds, C. R., & Chastian, R. (1984). A demographically based index of premorbid intelligence for the WAIS-R. *Journal of Consulting and Clinical Psychology, 52,* 885–887.

Bates, M. E., & Pandina, R. J. (1992). Familial alcoholism and premorbid cognitive deficit: A failure to replicate subtype differences. *Journal of Studies on Alcohol, 53,* 320–327.

Bates, M.E., & Tracy, J. I. (1990). Cognitive functioning in young "social drinkers": Is there impairment to detect? *Journal of Abnormal Psychology, 99,* 242–249.

Battey, L. L., Heyman, A., & Patterson, J. L. (1953). Effects of ethyl alcohol on cerebral blood flow and metabolism. *Journal of the American Medical Association, 152,* 6–10.

Bearcroft, C. P., Metcalfe, K., McCarthy, M. I., Almond, M. K., Chong, M. S., & Hitman, G. A. (1988). Clinical heterogeneity of central pontine myelinolysis. Letter. *Lancet, 17,* 688.

Becker, J. T., Butters, N., Hermann, A., & D'Angelo, N. (1983a). A comparison of the effects of long-term alcohol abuse and aging on the performance of verbal and non-verbal divided attention tasks. *Alcoholism: Clinical and Experimental Research, 7,* 213–219.

Becker, J. T., Butters, N., Hermann, A., & D'Angelo, N. (1983b). Learning to associate names and faces: Impaired acquisition on an ecologically relevant memory task by male alcoholics. *Journal of Nervous and Mental Disease, 171,* 617–623.

Becker, J. T., & Jaffe, J. H. (1984). Impaired memory for treatment relevant information in inpatient men alcoholics. *Journal of Studies on Alcohol, 45,* 339–343.

Beevers, D. G. (1977). Alcohol and hypertension. *Lancet, ii,* 114–115.

Begleiter, H., & Platz. A. (1972). The effects of alcohol on the central nervous system in humans. In B. Kissin & H. Begleiter (Eds.), *The biology of alcoholism* (Vol 2. pp. 293–343). New York: Plenum Press.

Begleiter, H., Porjesz, B., & Bihari, B. (1987). Auditory brain stem potentials in sons of alcoholic fathers. *Alcoholism: Clinical and Experimental Research, 11,* 477–480.

Begleiter, H., Porjesz, B., Bihari, B., & Kissin, B. (1984). Event-related potentials in boys at high risk for alcoholism. *Science, 225,* 1493–1496.

Begleiter, H., Porjesz, B., & Chou, C. L. (1981). Auditory brainstem potentials in chronic alcoholics. *Science, 211,* 1064–1066.

Begleiter, H., Porjesz, B., Chou, C. L., & Aunon, J. (1983). P[3] and stimulus incentive value. *Psychophysiology, 20,* 95–101.

Begleiter, H., Porjesz, B., & Tenner, M. (1980). Neuroradiological and neurophysiological evidence of brain damage in chronic alcoholics. *Acta Psychiatrica Scandinavica 62* (Suppl. 286), 3–13.

Begleiter, H., Porjesz, B., & Yerre-Grubstein, C. (1974). Excitability of somatosensory evoked potentials during experimental alcoholization and withdrawal. *Psychopharmacology, 37,* 15–21.

Benjamin, I. S., Imrie, C. W., & Blumgart, L. H. (1977). Alcohol and the pancreas. In G. Edwards & M. Grant (Eds.), *Alcoholism: New knowledge and new responses* (pp. 198–207). London: Croom Helm.

Bennett, A. E., Doi, L. T., & Mowery, S. L. (1956). The value of electroencephalography in alcoholism. *Journal of Nervous and Mental Disease, 124,* 27–32.

Benson, D. F., Kuhl, D. E., Hawkins, R. A., Phelps, M. E., Cummings, J. L., & Tsai, S. Y. (1983). The fluorodeoxyglucose 18F scan in Alzheimer's disease and multi-infarct dementia. *Archives of Neurology, 40,* 711–714.

Berg, E. A. (1948). A simple objective test for measuring flexibility in thinking. *Journal of General Psychology, 39,* 15–22.

Berglund, M. (1981). Cerebral blood flow in chronic alcoholics. *Alcoholism: Clinical and Experimental Research, 5,* 295–303.

Berglund, M., Hagstadius, S., Risberg, J., Johanson, A., Blinding, A., & Mubrin, Z. (1987). Normalization of regional cerebral blood flow in alcoholics during the first 7 weeks of abstinence. *Acta Psychiatrica Scandinavica, 75,* 202–208.

Berglund, M., & Ingvar, D. H. (1976). Cerebral blood flow and its regional distribution in alcoholism and Korsakoff's psychosis. *Journal of Studies in Alcohol, 37,* 586–597.

Berglund, M., Leijonquist, H., & Horlen, M. (1977). Prognostic significance and reversibility of cerebral dysfunction in alcoholics. *Journal of Studies on Alcohol, 38,* 1761–1770.

Berglund, M., & Risberg, J. (1981). Regional cerebral blood flow during alcohol withdrawal. *Archives of General Psychiatry, 38,* 351–357.

Bergman, H. (1985). Cognitive deficits and morphological cerebral changes in a random sample of social drinkers. In M. Galanter (Ed.), *Recent developments in alcoholism* (Vol. 3, pp. 265–275). New York: Plenum Press.

Bergman, H. (1987). Brain dysfunction related to alcoholism: Some results from the KARTAD project. In O. A. Parsons, N. Butters, & P. E. Nathan (Eds.), *Neuropsychology of alcoholism: Implications for diagnosis and treatment* (pp. 21–44). New York: Guilford Press.

Bergman, H., Borg, S., Hindmarsh, T., Idestrom, C-M., & Mutzell, S. (1980). Computed tomography of the brain and neuropsychological assessment of male alcoholic patients and a random sample from the general male population. *Acta Psychiatrica Scandanavica, 62*(Suppl. 286), 47–56.

Berkowitz, G., Holford, T., Kasl, S., & Kelsey, J. (1979). The epidemiology of pre-term delivery. *American Journal of Epidemiology, 110*(Abstract No. 3), 355.

Bertera, J. H., & Parsons, O. A. (1978). Impaired visual search in alcoholics. *Alcoholism: Clinical and Experimental Research, 2*, 9–14.

Billings, A. G., & Moos, R. H. (1983). Psychosocial processes of recovery among alcoholics and their families: Implications for clinicans and program evaluators. *Addictive Behaviors, 8*, 205–218.

Binder, L. M., & Schreiber, J. (1980). Visual imagery and verbal mediation as memory aids in recovering alcoholics. *Journal of Clinical Neuropsychology, 2*, 71–74.

Bird, J. M. (1982). Computerised tomography, atrophy and dementia: A review. *Progress in Neurobiology, 19*, 91–115.

Birnbaum, I. M., Johnson, M. K., Hartley, J. T., & Taylor, T. H. (1980). Alcohol and elaborative schemas for sentences. *Journal of Experimental Psychology: Human Learning and Memory, 6*, 293–300.

Birnbaum, I. M., & Parker, E. S. (1977). Acute effects of alcohol on storage and retrieval. In I.M. Birnbaum, & E.S. Parker (Eds.), *Alcohol and human memory* (pp. 99–108). Hillsdale, NJ: Lawrence Erlbaum Associates Inc.

Birnbaum, I. M., Parker, E.S., Hartley, J. T., & Noble, E. P. (1978). Alcohol and memory: Retrieval processes. *Journal of Verbal Learning and Verbal Behavior, 17*, 325–335.

Birnbaum, I. M., Taylor, T. H., Johnson, M. K., & Raye, C. L. (1987). Is event frequency encoded automatically? The case of alcohol intoxication. *Journal of Experimental Psychology: Learning, Memory and Cognition, 13*, 251–259.

Birnbaum, I. M., Taylor, H. T., & Parker, E. S. (1983). Alcohol and sober mood state in female social drinkers. *Alcoholism: Clinical and Experimental Research, 7*, 362–368.

Blandford, G. F. (1884). *Insanity and its treatment.* Edinburgh: Oliver and Boyd.

Blumer, D., & Benson, D. F. (1975). Personality changes with frontal and temporal lobe lesions. In D. F. Benson & D. Blumer (Eds.), *Psychiatric aspects of neurologic disease.* New York: Grune and Stratton.

Blusewicz, M. J., Dustman, R. E., Schenkenberg, T., & Beck, E. C. (1977a). Neuropsychological correlates of chronic alcoholism and aging. *Journal of Nervous and Mental Disease, 165*, 348–355.

Blusewicz, M. J., Schenkenberg, T., Dustman, R. E., & Beck, E. C. (1977b). WAIS performance in young normal, young alcoholic, and elderly normal groups: An evaluation of organicity and mental aging indices. *Journal of Clinical Psychology, 33*, 1149–1153.

Bohman, M., Sigvardsson, S., & Cloninger, C. R. (1981). Maternal inheritance of alcohol abuse: Cross-fostering analysis of adopted women. *Archives of General Psychiatry, 38*, 965–969.

Bornstein, R. A., Chelune, G. J., & Prifitera, A. (1989). IQ–Memory discrepancies in normal and clinical samples. *Psychological Assessment: A Journal of Consulting and Clinical Psychology, 1*, 203–206.

Bottetta, P., & Garfinkel, L. (1990). Alcohol drinking and mortality among men enrolled in an American Cancer Society Prospective Study. *Epidemiology, 1*, 342–348.

Bowden, S. C. (1987). Brain impairment in social drinkers? No cause for concern. *Alcoholism: Clinical and Experimental Research, 11*, 407–409.

Bowden, S. C. (1988). Learning in young alcoholics. *Journal of Clinical and Experimental Psychology, 10*, 157–168.

Bowden, S. C. (1990). Separating cognitive impairment in neurologically asymptomatic alcoholism from Wernicke–Korsakoff syndrome: Is the neuropsychological distinction justified? *Psychological Bulletin, 107*, 355–366.

Bowden, S. C., Walton, N. H., & Walsh, K. W. (1988). The hangover hypothesis and the influence of moderate social drinking on mental ability. *Alcoholism: Clinical and Experimental Research, 12*, 25–29.

Bowman, K. M., Goodhart, R., & Jolliffe, N. (1939). Observations on the role of vitamin B1 in the etiology and treatment of Korsakoff psychosis. *Journal of Nervous and Mental Disease, 90*, 569–575.

Branchey, M. H., Buydens-Branchey, L., & Lieber, C. S. (1988). Abnormal P3 in alcoholics with disordered mood and aggression. *Alcoholism: Clinical and Experimental Research, 12*, 334.

Brandt, J., Butters, N., Ryan, C., & Bayog, R. (1983). Cognitive loss and recovery in long-term alcohol abusers. *Archives of General Psychiatry, 40*, 435–442.

Brewer, B., & Perrett, L. (1971). Brain damage due to alcohol consumption: an air-encephalographic, psychometric and electro-encephalographic study. *British Journal of Addiction, 66*, 170–182.

Brooks, D. N., & Baddeley, A. D. (1976). What can amnesic patients learn? *Neuropsychologia, 14*, 111–123.

Brown, S. A., Christiansen, B. A., & Goldman, M. S. (1987). The Alcohol Expectancy Questionnaire: An instrument for the assessment of adolescent and adult alcohol expectancies. *Journal of Studies on Alcohol, 48*, 483–491.

Buck, K. J., & Harris, R. A. (1991). Neuroadaptive responses to chronic ethanol. *Alcoholism: Clinical and Experimental Research, 15*, 460–470.

Burbige, E. J., Lewis, D. R., & Halsted, C. H. (1984). Alcohol and the gastrointestinal tract. *Medical Clinics of North America, 68*, 77–89.

Butters, N. (1985). Alcoholic Korsakoff's syndrome: Some unresolved issues concerning the etiology, neuropathology, and cognitive deficits. *Journal of Clinical and Experimental Neuropsychology, 7*, 181–210.

Butters, N., & Brandt, J. (1985). The continuity hypothesis: The relationship of long-term alcoholism to the Wernicke–Korsakoff syndrome. In M. Galanter (Ed.), *Recent developments in alcoholism* (Vol. 3, pp. 207–229). New York: Plenum.

Butters, N., & Cermak, L. S. (1975). Some analyses of amnesic syndromes in brain damaged patients. In K. Pribram & R. L. Isaacson (Eds.), *The Hippocampus* (Vol. 2). New York: Plenum.

Butters, N., & Cermak, L. S. (1980). *Alcoholic Korsakoff's syndrome: An information processing approach to amnesia*. New York: Academic Press.

Butters, N., Cermak, L. S., Montgomery, K., & Adinolfi, A. (1977). Some comparisons of the memory and visuoperceptive deficits of chronic alcoholics and patients with Korsakoff's disease. *Alcoholism: Clinical and Experimental Research, 1*, 73–80.

Butters, N., & Granholm, E. (1987). The continuity hypothesis: Some conclusions and their implications for the etiology and neuropathology of alcoholic Korsakoff's syndrome. In O. A. Parsons, N. Butters, & P. E. Nathan (Eds.), *Neuropsychology of alcoholism* (pp. 176–206). New York: Guilford Press.

Cahalan, D., Cisin, I. H., & Crossley, H. M. (1969). *American Drinking Practices*. New Brunswick, NJ: Rutgers Center of Alcohol Studies.

Cala, L. A., Jones, B., Burns, P., Davis, R. E., Stenhouse, N., & Mastaglia, F. L. (1983). Results of computerised tomography, psychometric testing and dietary studies in social drinkers, with emphasis on reversibility after abstinence. *Medical Journal of Australia, 2,* 264–269.

Cala, L. A., Jones, B., Mastaglia, F. L., & Wiley, B. (1978). Brain atrophy and intellectual impairment in heavy drinkers: A clinical, psychometric and computerized tomography study. *Australian and New Zealand Medical Journal, 8,* 147–153.

Camargo, C. A. (1989). Moderate alcohol consumption and stroke: The epidemiological evidence. *Stroke, 20,* 1611–1626.

Carlen,. P. L., Wilkinson, A., & Kiraly, L. T. (1976). Dementia in alcoholics: A longitudinal study including some reversible aspects. *Neurology, Minneapolis, 26,* 355.

Carlen, P. L., Wortzman, G., Holgate, R. C., Wilkinson, D. A., & Rankin, J. G. (1978). Reversible atrophy in recently abstinent chronic alcoholics measured by computed tomography scans. *Science, 200,* 1076–1078.

Caster, D. U., & Parsons, O. A. (1977). Locus of control in alcoholics and treatment outcome. *Journal of Studies on Alcohol, 38,* 2087–2095.

Cave, C. B., & Squire, L. R. (1992). Intact and long-lasting repetition priming in amnesia. *Journal of Experimental Psychology: Learning, Memory, and Cognition, 18,* 509–520.

Cermak, L.S. (1975) Imagery as an aid to retrieval for Korsakoff patients. *Cortex, 11,* 163–169.

Cermak, L. S. (1976). The encoding capacity of a patient with amnesia due to encephalitis. *Neuropsychologia, 14,* 311–326.

Cermak, L. S. (1982). *Human memory and amnesia.* Hillsdale, NJ: Lawrence Erlbaum Associates Inc.

Cermak, L. S., & Butters, N. (1972). The role of interference and encoding in the short-term memory deficits of Korsakoff patients. *Neuropsychologia, 10,* 89–95.

Cermak, L. S., & Butters, N. (1973). Information processing deficits of alcoholic Korsakoff patients. *Quarterly Journal of Studies on Alcohol, 34,* 1110–1132.

Cermak, L. S., Butters, N., & Goodglass, H. (1971). The extent of memory loss in Korsakoff patients. *Neuropsychologia, 9,* 307–315.

Cermak, L. S., Butters, N., & Moreines, J. (1974). Some analyses of the verbal encoding deficit of alcoholic Korsakoff patients. *Brain and Language, 1,* 141–150.

Cermak, L. S., & Peck, E. (1982). Continuum versus premature aging theories of chronic alcoholism. *Alcoholism: Clinical and Experimental Research, 6,* 89–95.

Cermak, L. S., & Reale, L. (1978). Depth of processing and retention of words by alcoholic Korsakoff patients. *Journal of Experimental Psychology: Human Learning and Memory, 4,* 165–174.

Cermak, L. S., & Ryback, R. S. (1976). Recovery of verbal short-term memory in alcoholics. *Journal of Studies on Alcohol, 37,* 46–52.

Cermak, L. S., Talbot, N., Chandler, K., & Wolbarst, L. (1985). The perceptual priming phenomenon in amnesia. *Neuropsychologia, 23,* 615–622.

Cermak, L. S., Verfaellie, M., Milberg, W., Letourneau, L., & Blackford, S. (1991). A further analysis of perceptual identification priming in alcoholic Korsakoff patients. *Neuropsychologia, 29,* 725–736.

Chaney, E. F., O'Leary, M. R., & Marlatt, G. A. (1978). Skill training with alcoholics. *Journal of Consulting and Clinical Psychology, 46,* 1092–1104.

Chapman, L. J., & Chapman, J. P. (1973). Problems in the measurement of cognitive deficit. *Psychological Bulletin, 79,* 380–385.

Chapman, L. J., & Chapman, J. P. (1988). Artifactual and genuine relationships of lateral difference scores to overall accuracy in studies of laterality. *Psychological Bulletin, 104,* 127–136.

Charness, M. E. (1993). Brain lesions in alcoholics. *Alcoholism: Clinical and Experimental Research, 17,* 2–11.

Chick, J. D., Smith, M. A., Engleman, H. M., Kean, D. M., Mander, A. J., Douglas, R. H. B., & Best, J. J. K. (1989). Magnetic resonance imaging of the brain in alcoholics: Cerebral atrophy, lifetime alcohol consumption, and cognitive deficits. *Alcoholism: Clinical and Experimental Research, 13,* 512–518.

Christie, J. E., Kean, D. M., Douglas, R. H. B., Engleman, H. M., St Clair, D., & Blackburn, I. M. (1988). Magnetic resonance imaging in pre-senile dementia of the Alzheimer type, multi-infarct dementia and Korsakoff's syndrome. *Psychological Medicine, 18,* 319–329.

Claiborn, J. M., & Greene, R. L. (1981). Neuropsychological changes in recovering men alcoholics. *Journal of Studies on Alcohol, 42,* 757–765.

Clark, D. C., Pisani, V. D., Aagensen, D. O., Sellers, D., & Fawcett, J. (1984). Primary affective disorder, drug abuse, and neuropsychological impairment in sober alcoholics. *Alcoholism: Clinical and Experimental Research, 8,* 399–404.

Clarren, S. K. (1986). Neuropathology in the fetal alcohol syndrome. In J. West (Ed.), *Alcohol and Brain Development* (pp. 158–165). New York: Oxford University Press.

Clarren, S. K., & Bowden, D. M. (1984). Measures of alcohol damage in utero in the pigtailed macaque (*Macaca nemestrina*). Ciba Foundation Symposium 105, *Mechanisms of alcohol damage in utero* (pp. 157–168). London: Pitman.

Clarren, S. K., & Smith, D. W. (1978). The fetal alcohol syndrome. *New England Journal of Medicine, 19,* 1063–1067.

Cloninger, C. R. (1983). Genetic and environmental factors in the development of alcoholism. *Journal of Psychiatric Treatment and Evaluation, 5,* 487–496.

Cloninger, C. R., Bohman, M., & Sigvardsson, S. (1981). Inheritance of alcohol abuse: Cross-fostering analysis of adopted men. *Archives of General Psychiatry, 38,* 861–868.

Coates, R. A., Halliday, M. L., Rankin, J. G., Feinman, S. V., & Fisher, M. M. (1984). Risk of fatty infiltration to ethanol consumption: A case-control study. *Hepatology, 4,* 1015.

Coger, R. W., Dymond, A. M., Serafetinedes, E. A., Lowenstein, I., & Pearson, D. (1976). Alcoholism: Averaged visual evoked response amplitude–intensity slope and symmetry in withdrawal. *Biological Psychiatry, 11,* 435–443.

Cohen, J. (1962). The statistical power of abnormal-social psychological research: A review. *Journal of Abnormal and Social Psychology, 65,* 145–153.

Cohen, J. (1977). *Statistical power analysis for the social sciences.* New York: Academic Press.

Cohen, N. J., & Squire, L. R. (1980). Preserved learning and retention of pattern analyzing skill in amnesia: Dissociation of knowing how and knowing that. *Science, 210,* 207–209.

Coid, J. (1979). Mania a potu: A critical review of pathological intoxication. *Psychological Medicine, 9,* 709–719.

Collins, R. L., & Searles, J. S. (1988). Alcohol and the balanced-placebo design: Were the experimenter demands in expectancy really tested? Comment on Knight, Barbaree, and Boland (1986). *Journal of Abnormal Psychology, 97,* 503–507.

Conry, J. (1990). Neuropsychological deficits in fetal alcohol syndrome and fetal alcohol effects. *Alcoholism: Clinical and Experimental Research, 14,* 650–655.

Courville, C. B. (1955). *The effects of alcohol on the nervous system of man.* Los Angeles: San Lucas Press.

Craik, F. I. M. (1977). Similarities between the effects of aging and alcoholic intoxication on memory performance, construed within a "level of processing" framework. In I. M. Birnbaum & E. S. Parker (Eds.), *Alcohol and human memory.* Hillsdale, NJ: Lawrence Erlbaum Associates Inc.

Craik, F. I. M., & Lockhart, R. S. (1972). Levels of processing: A framework for memory research. *Journal of Verbal Learning and Verbal Behaviour, 11* 671–684.

Cramon, D. Y. V., Hebel, N., & Schuri, U. (1985). A contribution to the anatomical basis of thalamic amnesia. *Brain, 108,* 993–1008.

Crawford, J., Parker, D., & McKinlay, W. (Eds.). (1992). *A handbook of neuropsychological assessment.* Hillsdale, NJ: Lawrence Erlbaum Associates Inc.

Crawford, J. R., Parker, D. M., Stewart, L. E., Besson, J. A. O., & DeLacy, G. (1989a). Prediction of WAIS IQ with the National Adult Reading Test: Cross-validation and extension. *British Journal of Clinical Psychology, 28,* 267–273.

Crawford, J. R., Stewart, L. E., Cochrane, R. H. B., Foulds, J. A., Besson, J. A. O., & Parker, D. M. (1989b). Estimating premorbid IQ from demographic variables: Regression equations derived from a UK sample. *British Journal of Clinical Psychology, 28,* 275–278.

Crawford, J. R., Stewart, L-E., & Moore, J. W. (1989c). Demonstration of savings on the AVLT and development of a parallel form. *Journal of Clinical and Experimental Neuropsychology, 11,* 975–981.

Cutting, J. (1978a). Specific psychological deficits in alcoholism. *British Journal of Psychiatry, 133,* 119–122.

Cutting, J. (1978b). The relationship between Korsakov's syndrome and "alcoholic dementia". *British Journal of Psychiatry, 132,* 240–251.

Cynn, V. E. H. (1992). Persistence and problem-solving skills in young male alcoholics. *Journal of Studies on Alcohol, 53,* 57–62.

Czarnecki, D. M., Russell, M., Cooper, M. L., & Salter, D. (1990). Five-year reliability of self-reported alcohol consumption. *Journal of Studies on Alcohol, 51,* 68–76.

Davidson, R. (1987). Assessment of the alcohol dependence syndrome: A review of self-report screening questionnaires. *British Journal of Clinical Psychology, 26,* 243–255.

Davies, D. M., & Binks, M. G. (1983.) Supporting the residual memory of a Korsakoff patient. *Behavioural Psychotherapy, 11,* 62–74.

Davis, P. A., Gibbs, F. A., Davis, H., Jetter, W. W., & Towbridge, L. S. (1941). The effects of alcohol upon the electroencephalogram (brain waves). *Quarterly Journal of Studies in Alcohol, 1,* 626–637.

Day, N. L., Goldschmidt, L., Robles, N., Richardson, G., Cornelius, M., Taylor, P., Geva, D., & Stoffer, D. (1991a). Prenatal alcohol exposure and offspring growth at 18 months of age: The predictive validity of two measures of drinking. *Alcoholism: Clinical and Experimental Research, 15*, 914–918.

Day, N. L., Robles, N., Richardson, G., Gena, D., Taylor, P., Scher, M., Stoffer, D., Cornelius, M., & Goldschmidt, L. (1991b). The effects of prenatal alcohol use on the growth of children at three years of age. *Alcoholism: Clinical and Experimental Research, 15*, 67–71.

de la Monte, S. M. (1988). Disproportionate atrophy of cerebral white matter in chronic alcoholics. *Archives of Neurology, 45*, 990–992.

D'Elia, L., Satz, P., & Schretlen, D. (1989). Wechsler Memory Scale: A critical appraisal of the normative studies. *Journal of Clinical and Experimental Neuropsychology, 11*, 551–568.

Delis, D. C., Freeland, J., Kramer, J. H., & Kaplan, E. (1988). Integrating clinical assessment with cognitive neuroscience: Construct validation of the California Verbal Learning Test. *Journal of Consulting and Clinical Psychology, 56*, 123–130.

Delis, D. C., Kramer, J. H., Kaplan, E., & Ober, B. A. (1987). *The California Verbal Learning Test.* New York: Psychological Corporation.

De Makis, J. G., Proskey, A., Rahimtoolay, S. H., Jamil, M., Sutton, G. C., Rosen, K. M., Gunnar, R. M., & Tobin, J. R. (1974). The natural course of alcoholic cardiomyopathy. *Annals of Internal Medicine, 80*, 293–297.

De Obaldia, R. D., & Parsons, O. A. (1984). Reliability and validity of the primary/secondary alcoholism classification questionnaire and the HK/MBD childhood symptoms checklist. *Journal of Clinical Psychology, 40*, 1257–1263.

De Wardener, H. E., & Lennox, B. (1947). Cerebral beri beri (Wernicke's encephalopathy). *Lancet, i*, 249–252.

de Wit, H., Metz, J., Wagner, N., & Cooper, M. (1990). Behavioral and subjective effects of ethanol: Relationship to cerebral metabolism using PET. *Alcoholism: Clinical and Experimental Research, 14*, 482–489.

Donovan, D. M., Kivlahan, D. R., & Walker, R. (1984). Clinical implications of neuropsychological testing in predicting treatment outcome among alcoholics. *Alcoholism: Clinical and Experimental Research, 8*, 470–475.

Donovan, D. M., Kivlahan, D. R., & Walker, R. D. (1986). Alcoholic subtypes based on multiple assessment domains: Validation against treatment outcome. In M. Galanter (Ed.), *Recent developments in alcoholism* (Vol. 4, pp. 207–222). New York: Plenum Press.

Donovan, D. M., Kivlahan, D. R., Walker, R. D., & Umlauf, R. (1985). Derivation and validation of neuropsychological clusters among men alcoholics. *Journal of Studies on Alcohol, 46*, 205–211.

Donovan, D. M., Walker, R. D., & Kivlahan, D. R. (1987). Recovery and remediation of neuropsychological functions, implications for alcoholism rehabilitation process and outcome. In O. A. Parsons, N. Butters, & P. E. Nathan (Eds.), *Neuropsychology of alcoholism* (pp. 339–360). New York: Guilford Press.

Drejer, K., Theilgaard, A., Teasdale, T. W., Schulsinger, F., & Goodwin, W. (1985). A prospective study of young men at high risk for alcoholism: Neuropsychological assessment. *Alcoholism: Clinical and Experimental Research, 9*, 498–502.

Duara, R., Grady, C., Haxby, J., Ingvar, D., Sokoloff, L., Margolin, R. A., Manning, R. G., Cutler, N. R., & Rapoport, S. I. (1984). Human brain glucose utilization and cognitive function in relation to age. *Annals of Neurology, 16,* 702–713.

Ebbinghaus, H. (1885). *Über das Gedächtnis* [On cognition] Leipzig: Dunker (Trans. H. Ruyer & C.E. Bussenius, 1913, *Memory.* New York: Teachers College, Columbia University.)

Eckardt, M. J., & Matarazzo, J. D. (1981). Test–retest reliability of Halstead Impairment Index in hospitalized alcoholic and nonalcoholic males with mild to moderate neuropsychological impairment. *Journal of Clinical Neuropsychology, 3,* 257–269.

Eckardt, M. J., Parker, E. S., Nobel, E. P., Feldman, D. J., & Gottschalk, L. A. (1978). Relationship between neuropsychological performance and alcohol consumption in alcoholics. *Biological Psychiatry, 13,* 551–565.

Eckardt, M. J., Parker, E. S., Noble, E. P., Pautler, C. P., & Gottschalk, L. A. (1979). Changes in neuropsychological performance during treatment for alcoholism. *Biological Psychiatry, 14,* 943–954.

Eckardt, M. J., Rawlings, R. R., Graubard, B. I., Faden, V., Martin, P. R., & Gottschalk, L. A. (1988). Neuropsychological performance and treatment outcome in male alcoholics. *Alcoholism: Clinical and Experimental Research, 12,* 88–93.

Eckardt, M. J., Rohrbaugh, J. W., Rio, D. E., & Martin, P. R. (1990). Positron Emission Tomography as a technique for studying the chronic effects of alcohol on the human brain. *Annals of Medicine, 22,* 341–345.

Eckardt, M. J., Ryback, R. S., & Pautler, C. P. (1980). Neuropsychological deficits in alcoholic men in their mid thirties. *American Journal of Psychiatry, 137,* 932–936.

Edwards, C., & Gross, M. M. (1976). Alcohol dependence: Provisional description of a clinical syndrome. *British Medical Journal, 1,* 1058–1061.

Edwards, G. (1977). The alcohol dependence syndrome: Usefulness of an idea. In G. Edwards & M. Grant (Eds.), *New knowledge and new responses.* London: Croom Helm.

Edwards, G. (1986). The alcohol dependence syndrome: A concept as stimulus to enquiry. *British Journal of Addiction, 81,* 71–84.

Edwards, G. (1987). *The treatment of drinking problems: A guide for the helping professions* (2nd ed.). Oxford: Blackwell Scientific.

Eich, J. E. (1977). State-dependent retrieval of information in human episodic memory. In J. M. Birnbaum & E. S. Parker (Eds.), *Alcohol and human memory.* Hillsdale, NJ: Lawrence Erlbaum Associates Inc.

Eich, J. E., Weingartner, H., Stillman, R. C., & Gillin, J.-C. (1975). State-dependent accessibility of retrieval cues in the retention of a categorized list. *Journal of Verbal Learning and Verbal Behavior, 14,* 408–417.

Ellenberg, L., Rosenbaum, G., Goldman, M. S., & Whitman, R. D. (1980). Recover ability of psychological functions following alcohol abuse: Lateralization effects. *Journal of Consulting and Clinical Psychology, 48,* 503–510.

Ellis, R. J. (1990). Dichotic asymmetries in ageing and alcoholic subjects. *Alcoholism: Clinical and Experimental Research, 14,* 863–871.

Ellis, R. J., & Oscar-Berman, M. (1989). Alcoholism, aging, and functional cerebral asymmetries. *Psychological Bulletin, 106,* 128–147.

Elmasion, R., Neville, H., Woods, D., Shuckit, M., & Bloom, F. (1982). Event-related potentials are different in individuals at high risk for developing alcoholism. *Proceedings of the National Academy of Sciences, U.S.A., 79,* 7900–7903.

Emmerson, R. Y., Dustman, R. E., Heil, J., & Shearer, D. F. (1988). Neuropsychological performance of young non drinkers, social drinkers, and long- and short-term sober alcoholics. *Alcoholism: Clinical and Experimental Research, 12,* 625–629.

Engel, G. L., Webb, J. P., & Ferris, E. B. (1945). Quantitative electroencephalographic studies of anoxia in humans; comparison with acute alcoholic intoxication and hypoglycaemia. *Journal of Clinical Investigation, 24,* 691–697.

Eppinger, M. G., Craig, P. L., Adams, R. L., & Parsons, O. A. (1987). The WAIS-R Index for estimating premorbid intelligence: Cross-validation and clinical utility. *Journal of Consulting and Clinical Psychology, 55,* 86–90.

Epstein, P. S., Pisani, V. D., & Fawcett, A. J. (1977). Alcoholism and cerebral atrophy. *Alcoholism: Clinical and Experimental Research, 1,* 61–65.

Erikson, R. C., & Scott, M. L. (1977). Clinical memory testing: A review. *Psychological Bulletin, 84,* 1130–1149.

Ervin, C. S., Little, R. E., Streissguth, A. P., & Beck, D. E. (1984). Alcoholic fathering and its relation to a child's intellectual development: A pilot investigation. *Alcoholism: Clinical and Experimental Research, 8,* 362–365.

Eslinger, P. J., & Damasio, A. R. (1985). Severe disturbance of higher cognition after bilateral frontal lobe ablation. *Neurology, 35,* 1731–1741.

Fabian, M. S., & Parsons, O. A. (1983). Differential improvement of cognitive functions in recovering alcoholic women. *Journal of Abnormal Psychology, 92,* 87–95.

Fabian, M. S., Parsons, O. A., & Shelton, M. D. (1984). Effects of gender and alcoholism on verbal and visual-spatial learning. *Journal of Nervous and Mental Disease, 172,* 16–20.

Fabian, M. S., Parsons, O. A., & Silberstein, J. A. (1981). Impaired perceptual–cognitive functioning in women alcoholics. *Journal of Studies on Alcohol, 42,* 217–229.

Farkas, T., Ferris, S. H., Wolf, A. P., DeLeon, M. J., Christman, D. R., Reisberg, B., Alavi, A., Fowler, J. S., George, A. E., & Reivich, M. (1982). 18F-2-deoxy-2-fluoro-d-glucose as a tracer in the positron emission tomographic study of senile dementia. *American Journal of Psychiatry, 139,* 352–353.

Ferrer, S., Santibanez, I., Castro, M., Krauskopf, D., & Saint-Jean, H. (1969). Permanent neurological complications of alcoholism. In R. E. Popham (Ed.), *Alcohol and alcoholism.* Toronto: University of Toronto.

Fisk, A. D., & Scerbo, M. W. (1987). Automatic and control processing approach to interpreting vigilance performance: A review and reevaluation. *Human Factors, 29,* 653–660.

Fitzhugh, L. C., Fitzhugh, K. B., & Reitan, R. M. (1965). Adaptive abilities and intellectual functioning in hospitalized alcoholics. *Quarterly Journal of Studies on Alcohol, 26,* 402–411.

Folson, J. C. (1968). Reality orientation for the elderly mental patient. *Journal of Geriatric Psychiatry, 1,* 291–307.

Forsberg, L. K., & Goldman, M. S. (1985). Experience-dependent recovery of visuospatial functioning in older alcoholics. *Journal of Abnormal Psychology, 94*, 519–529.

Forsberg, L. K., & Goldman, M. S. (1987). Experience-dependent recovery of cognitive deficits in alcoholics: Extended transfer of training. *Journal of Abnormal Psychology, 96*, 345–353

Fox, J. H., Ramsey, G., Huckman, M. S., & Proske, A. E. (1976). Cerebral ventricular enlargement in chronic alcoholics examined by computerised tomography. *Journal of the American Medical Association, 236*, 365–368.

Foy, A., March, S., & Drinkwater, V. (1988). Use of an objective clinical scale in the assessment and management of alcohol withdrawal in a large general hospital. *Alcoholism: Clinical and Experimental Research, 12*, 360–364.

Franceschi, M., Truci, G., Comi, G., Lozza, L., Marchinettini, P., Galardi, G., & Smirne, S. (1984). Cognitive deficits and their relationship to other neurological complications in chronic alcoholic patients. *Journal of Neurology, Neurosurgery, and Psychiatry, 47*, 1134–1137.

Freedman, M., & Cermak, L. S. (1986). Semantic encoding deficits in frontal lobe disease and amnesia. *Brain and Cognition, 5*, 108–114.

Freedman, R., & Nagamoto, H. (1988). Brain evoked potentials as predictors of risk. *Recent Developments in Alcohol, 6*, 323–331.

Friedland, R. P., Budinger, T. F., Koss, E., & Ober, B. A. (1985). Alzheimer's disease: Anterioposterior and lateral hemispheric alterations in cortical glucose utilization. *Neuroscience Letters, 53*, 235–240.

Frierichs, F. T. (1858). *A clinical treatise on liver disease.* (C. Murchoson Trans., 1879). New York: William Wood.

Freund, G. (1973). Chronic central nervous system toxicity of alcohol. *Annual Review of Pharmacology, 13*, 217–227.

Freund, G., & Ballinger, W. E. (1988a). Loss of cholinergic muscarinic receptors in the frontal cortex of alcohol abusers. *Alcoholism: Clinical and Experimental Research, 12*, 630–638.

Freund, G., & Ballinger, W. E. (1988b). Decrease of benzodiazepine receptors in the frontal cortex of alcoholics. *Alcohol, 5*, 275–282.

Freund, G., & Ballinger, W. E. (1989a). Neuroreceptor changes in the Putamen of alcohol abusers. *Alcoholism: Clinical and Experimental Research, 13*, 213–218.

Freund, G., & Ballinger, W. E. (1989b). Loss of muscarinic cholinergic receptors from the temporal cortex of alcohol abusers. *Metabolic Brain Disorders, 4*, 121–141.

Fukui, Y., Mori, M., Kohga, M., Tadai, T., Tanaka, K., & Katoh, N. (1981). Reassessment of CNS effects of acute ethanol administration with auditory evoked response: A comparative study of brain stem auditory evoked response, middle latency response and slow vertex response. *Japanese Journal of Alcohol and Drug Dependence, 16*, 9–32.

Gabrielli, W. F., & Mednick, S. A. (1983). Intellectual performance in children of alcoholics. *Journal of Nervous and Mental Disease, 171*, 444–447.

Galambos, J. T. (1972a). Alcoholic Hepatitis : Its therapy and prognosis. In H. Popper & D. Schaffner (Eds.), *Progress in liver diseases* (Vol. 4, pp. 567–588). New York: Grune and Stratton.

Galambos, J. T. (1972b). Natural history of alcoholic hepatitis. III. Histological changes. *Gastroenterology, 63*, 1026–1035.

Gallant, D. M., & Head-Dunham, R. (1991). Noncirrhotic liver dysfunction and neuropsychologic impairment. *Alcoholism: Clinical and Experimental Research, 15*, 899–901.

Galton, F. (1883). *Inquiries into human faculty and its development*. London: MacMillan.

Gibbs, L., & Flanagan, J. (1977). Prognostic indicators of alcoholism treatment outcome. *International Journal of Addictions, 12,* 1097–1141.

Gill, J. S., Shipley, M. J., Tsementzis, S. A., Hornby, R. S., Gill, S. K., Hitchcock, E. R., & Beevers, D. G. (1991). Alcohol consumption—A risk factor for hemorrhagic and non-hemorrhagic stroke. *American Journal of Medicine, 90*, 489–497.

Gillen, R., & Hesselbrock, V. (1992). Cognitive functioning, ASP, and family history of alcoholism in young men at risk for alcoholism. *Alcoholism: Clinical and Experimental Research, 16*, 206–214.

Glass, I. (1991). Alcoholic brain damage: What does it mean to patients? *British Journal of Addiction, 86,* 819–821.

Glenn, S. W., & Parsons, O. A. (1991). Prediction of resumption of drinking in post-treatment alcoholics. *International Journal of Addictions, 26*, 237–254.

Glenn, S. W., & Parsons, O. A. (1992). Neuropsychological efficiency measures in male and female alcoholics. *Journal of Studies on Alcohol, 53,* 546–553.

Glisky, E. L., & Schacter, D. L. (1987). Acquisition of domain specific knowledge in amnesia: Training for computer related work. *Neuropsychologia, 25*, 893–906.

Glisky, E. L., & Schacter, D. L. (1989). Extending the limits of complex learning in organic amnesia: Computer training in a vocational domain. *Neuropsycholgia, 27*, 107–120.

Glisky, E. L., Schacter, D. L., & Tulving, E. (1986). Computer learning by memory impaired patients: Acquisition and retention of complex knowledge. *Neuropsychologia, 24*, 313–328.

Goddard, G. V., McIntyre, D. C., & Leech, C. K. (1969). A permanent change in brain function resulting from daily electrical stimulation. *Experimental Neurology, 25*, 295–330.

Godfrey, H. P. D., & Knight, R. G. (1985). Cognitive rehabilitation of memory functioning in amnesic alcoholics. *Journal of Consulting and Clinical Psychology, 53*, 555–557.

Godfrey, H. P. D., Knight, R. G., & Spittle, B. J. (1985). Cognitive rehabilitation of amnesic alcoholics: A twelve month follow-up study. *New Zealand Medical Journal, 15*, 650–651.

Golden, C. J., Osman, D. C., Moses, J. A., & Berg, R. A. (1981). *Interpretation of the Halstead–Reitan Battery: A casebook approach*: New York: Grune & Stratton.

Goldman, M. S. (1983). Cognitive impairment in chronic alcoholics: Some cause for optimism. *American Psychologist, 38,* 1045–1054.

Goldman, M. S. (1986). Neuropsychological recovery in alcoholics: Endogenous and exogenous processes. *Alcoholism: Clinical and Experimental Research, 10,* 136–144.

Goldman, M. S. (1987). The role of time and practice in recovery of function in alcoholics. In O. A. Parsons, N. Butters, & P. E. Nathan (Eds.), *Neuropsychology of alcoholism: Implications for diagnosis and treatment* (pp. 291–321). New York: Guilford Press.

Goldman, M. S., Klisz, D. K., & Williams, D. L. (1985). Experience-dependent recovery of cognitive function in young alcoholics. *Addictive Behaviors, 10,* 169–176.

Goldman, M. S., Williams, D. L., & Klisz, D. K. (1983). Recoverability of psychological functioning following alcohol abuse: Prolonged visual-spatial dysfunction in older alcoholics. *Journal of Consulting and Clinical Psychology, 51,* 370–378.

Goldman, R. S., & Goldman, M. S. (1988). Experience-dependent cognitive recovery in alcoholics: A task component strategy. *Journal of Studies on Alcohol, 49,* 142–148.

Goldstein, G. (1987). Recovery, treatment, and rehabilitation in chronic alcoholics. In O. A. Parsons, N. Butters, & P. E. Nathan, (Eds.), *Neuropsychology of alcoholism: Implications for diagnosis and treatment* (pp. 361–380). New York: Guilford Press.

Goodwin, D. W. (1971). Two species of alcohol "blackout". *American Journal of Psychiatry, 127,* 1665–1670.

Goodwin, D. W. (1977). The alcoholic blackout. In I. M. Birnbaum & E. S. Parker (Eds.), *Alcohol and human memory.* Hillsdale, NJ: Lawrence Erlbaum Associates Inc.

Goodwin, D. W., Crane, J. B., & Guze, S. B. (1969a). Alcoholic blackouts: A review and clinical study of 100 alcoholics. *American Journal of Psychiatry, 126,* 191–198.

Goodwin, D. W., Crane, J. B., & Guze S. B. (1969b) Phenomenological aspects of alcoholic "blackouts". *British Journal of Psychiatry, 115,* 1033–1038

Goodwin, D. W., Powell, B., Bremer, D., Hoine, H., & Stern, J. (1969c). Alcohol and recall: State-dependent effects in man. *Science, 163,* 1358–1360.

Goodwin, D. W., Schulsinger, F., Hermansen, L., Guze, S. B., & Winokur, G. (1973). Alcohol problems in adoptees raised apart from alcoholic biological parents. *Archives of General Psychiatry, 28,* 238–243.

Gorelick, P. B. (1989). The status of alcohol as a risk factor for stroke. *Stroke, 20,* 1607–1610.

Gorham, D. R. (1956). A Proverbs Test for clinical and experimental use. *Psychological Reports, 1,* 1–12.

Graf, P., Shimamura, A. P., & Squire, L. R. (1985). Priming across modalities and priming across categories: Extending the domain of preserved functioning in amnesia. *Journal of Experimental Psychology: Learning, Memory, and Cognition, 11,* 385–395.

Graf, P., Squire, L. R., & Mandler, G. (1984). The information that amnesic patients do not forget. *Journal of Experimental Psychology: Learning, Memory, and Cognition, 10,* 164–178.

Graham, F. K., & Kendall, B. S. (1960). Memory-For-Designs-Test: Revised general manual [Monograph]. *Perceptual and Motor Skills, 11,* 147–188.

Grant, B. F., & Harford, T. C. (1990). The relationship between ethanol intake and DSM-III-R alcohol dependence. *Journal of Studies on Alcohol, 51,* 448–456.

Grant, I. (1987). Alcohol and the brain: Neuropsychological correlates. *Journal of Consulting and Clinical Psychology, 55,* 310–324.

Grant, I., Adams, K., & Reed, R. (1979). Normal neuropsychological abilities of alcoholic men in their late thirties. *American Journal of Psychiatry, 136,* 1263–1269.

Grant I., Adams, K., & Reed, R. (1984). Aging, abstinence and medical risk factors in the prediction of neuropsychological deficit amongst chronic alcoholics. *Archives of General Psychiatry, 41,* 710–718.

Grant, I., Reed, R., & Adams, K. M. (1987). Diagnosis of intermediate-duration and subacute mental disorders in abstinent alcoholics. *Journal of Clinical Psychiatry, 48,* 319–323.

Greene, T., Ernhart, C. B., Sokol, R. J., Martier, S. Marler, M. R., Boyd, T. A., & Ager, J. (1991). Prenatal alcohol exposure and preschool physical growth: A longitudinal analysis. *Alcoholism: Clinical and Experimental Research, 15,* 905–913.

Gregson, R. A. M., & Taylor, G. M. (1977). Prediction of relapse in men alcoholics. *Journal of Studies on Alcohol, 34,* 1749–1760.

Gross, M. M., Lewis, E., & Nagarajan, M. (1973). An improved quantitative system for assessing the acute alcoholic psychoses and related states (TSA & SSA). In M. M. Gross (Ed.), *Advances in Experimental Medicine and Biology* (Vol. 35, pp. 365–376). New York: Plenum Press.

Gudeman, H. E., Craine, J. F., Golden, C. J., & McLaughlin, D. (1977). Higher cortical dysfunction associated with long-term alcoholism. *International Journal of Neuroscience, 8,* 33–40.

Gustafson, R. (1986). Effects of moderate doses of alcohol on simple auditory reaction time in a vigilance setting. *Perceptual and Motor Skills, 62,* 683–690.

Gustafson, R., & Kallmen, H. (1990). Effects of alcohol on cognitive performance measured with Stroop's color word test. *Perceptual and Motor Skills, 71,* 99–105.

Guthrie, A., & Elliott, W. A. (1980). The nature and reversibility of cerebral impairment in alcoholism: Treatment implications. *Journal of Studies on Alcohol, 41,* 147–155.

Haist, F., Shimamura, A. P., & Squire, L. R. (1992). On the relationship between recall and recognition memory. *Journal of Experimental Psychology: Learning, Memory, and Cognition, 18,* 691–702.

Halmesmaki, E. (1988). Alcohol counselling of 85 pregnant problem drinkers: Effect on drinking and fetal outcome. *British Journal of Obstetrics and Gynaecology, 95,* 243–247.

Hamilton, P., & Copeman, A. (1970). The effect of alcohol and noise on components of a tracking and monitoring task. *British Journal of Psychology, 61,* 149–156.

Hannon, R., Butler, C. P., Day, C. L., Khan, S. A., Quitoriano, L. A., Butler, A. M., & Meredith, L. A. (1987). Social drinking and cognitive function in college students: A replication and reversibility study. *Journal of Studies on Alcohol, 48,* 502–506.

Hannon, R., Day, C. L., Butler, A. M., Larson, A. J., & Casey, M. B. (1983). Alcohol consumption and cognitive functioning in college students. *Journal of Studies on Alcohol, 44,* 283–298.

Hannon, R., de la Cruz-Schmedel, D. E., Cano, T. C., Moreira, K., Nasuta, R., & Staub, G. V. (1989). Memory retraining with adult male alcoholics. *Archives of Clinical Neuropsychology, 4,* 227–232.

Hansen, L. (1980). Treatment of reduced intellectual functioning in alcoholics. *Journal of Studies on Alcohol, 41,* 156–158.

Harper, C. G. (1983). The incidence of Wernicke's encephalopathy in Australia: A neuropathological study of 131 cases. *Journal of Neurology, Neurosurgery, and Psychiatry, 46,* 593–598.

Harper, C. G., & Blumberg, P. C. (1982). Brain weights in alcoholics. *Journal of Neurology, Neurosurgery, and Psychiatry, 45,* 838–840.

Harper, C. G., Giles, M., & Finlay-Jones, R. (1986). Clinical signs in the Wernicke–Korsakoff complex: A retrospective analysis of 131 cases diagnosed at necropsy. *Journal of Neurology, Neurosurgery, and Psychiatry, 49,* 341–345.

Harper, C. G. & Kril, J. J. (1985). Brain atrophy in chronic alcoholic patients: A quantitative pathological study. *Journal of Neurology, Neurosurgery, and Psychiatry, 48,* 211–217.

Harper, C. G. & Kril, J. J. (1989). Patterns of neuronal loss in the cerebral cortex in chronic alcoholic patients. *Journal of the Neurological Sciences, 92,* 81–89.

Harper, C. G., Kril, J. J., & Daly, J. M. (1987). Are we drinking our neurones away? *British Medical Journal, 294,* 534–536.

Harper, C. G., Kril, J. J., & Daly, J. M. (1988). Brain shrinkage in alcoholics is not caused by changes in hydration: A pathological study. *Journal of Neurology, Neurosurgery, and Psychiatry, 51,* 124–128.

Harper, C. G., Kril, J. J., & Holloway, R. L. (1985). Brain shrinkage in chronic alcoholics: A pathological study. *British Medical Journal, 290,* 501–504.

Hartley, J.T., Birnbaum, I.M., & Parker, E.S. (1978). Alcohol and storage deficits: Kind of processing? *Journal of Verbal Learning and Verbal Behavior, 17,* 635–647.

Hasher, L., & Zacks, R. T. (1984). Automatic processing of fundamental information. *American Psychologist, 39,* 1372–1388.

Hashtroudi, S., Parker, E. S., De Lisi, L. E., & Wyatt, R. J. (1983). On elaboration and alcohol. *Journal of Verbal Learning and Verbal Behavior, 22,* 164–173.

Hashtroudi, S., Parker, E. S., De Lisi, L. E., Wyatt, R. J., & Mutter, S. A. (1984). Intact retention in acute alcohol amnesia. *Journal of Experimental Psychology: Learning, Memory, and Cognition, 10,* 156–163.

Hashtroudi, S., Parker, E. S., Luis, J. D., & Reisen, C. A. (1989). Generation and elaboration in older adults. *Experimental Aging Research, 15,* 73–78.

Hatsukami, D., & Pickens, R. W. (1982). Post-treatment depression in an alcohol and drug abuse population. *American Journal of Psychiatry, 139,* 1563–1566.

Haug, J. O. (1968). Pneumoencephalographic evidence of brain damage in chronic alcoholics. *Acta Psychiatrica Scandinavica,* (Suppl. 203), 135–143.

Haut, J. S., Beckwith, B. E., Petros, T. V., & Russell, S. (1989). Gender differences in retrieval from long-term memory following acute intoxication with ethanol. *Physiology and Behavior, 45,* 1161–1165.

Hegedus, A. M., Alterman, A. I., & Tarter, R. E. (1984). Learning achievements in sons of alcoholics. *Alcoholism: Clinical and Experimental Research, 8,* 330–333.

Heinrichs, R. W. (1989). Attempted clinical application of a technique for promoting robust free recall to a case of alcoholic Korsakoff's syndrome. *Brain and Cognition, 9,* 151–157.

Herndon, R. R., Jackson, R. L., & Good, D. C. (1991). Effects of clonidine on short-term memory: A double-blind study. *Alcoholism Treatment Quarterly, 8,* 101–112.

Hesselbrock, M. N., Weidenman, M. A., & Reed, H. B. (1985). Effects of age, sex, drinking history and antisocial personality on neuropsychology of alcoholics. *Journal of Studies on Alcohol, 46,* 313–320.

Hester, R. D., Smith, J. W., & Jackson, T. R. (1980). Recovery of cognitive skills in alcoholics. *Journal of Studies on Alcohol, 41*, 363–367.

Hewett, L. J., Nixon, S. J., Glenn, S. W., & Parsons, O. A. (1991). Verbal fluency deficits in female alcoholics. *Journal of Clinical Psychology, 47*, 716–720.

Hightower, M. G., & Anderson, R. P. (1986). Memory evaluation of alcoholics with Russell's revised Wechsler Memory Scale. *Journal of Clinical Psychology, 42*, 1000–1005.

Hill, S. Y. (1983). Alcohol and brain damage: Cause or association? *American Journal of Public Health, 73*, 487–489.

Hillbom, M., & Kaste, M. (1990). Alcohol abuse and brain infarction. *Annals of Medicine, 22*, 347–352.

Hirst, W., Johnson, M. K., Phelps, E. A., & Volpe, B. T. (1988). More on recognition and recall in amnesics. *Journal of Experimental Psychology: Learning, Memory, and Cognition, 14*, 758–762.

Hochla, N. N., Fabian, M. S., & Parsons, O. A. (1982). Brain-age quotients in recently detoxified alcoholic, recovered alcoholic and nonalcoholic women. *Journal of Clinical Psychology, 38*, 207–212.

Hochla, N. A. N., & Parsons, O. A. (1982). Premature aging in female alcoholics. *Journal of Nervous and Mental Disease, 170*, 241–245.

Holden, K. L., McLaughlin, E. J., Reilly, E. L., & Overall, J. E. (1988). Accelerated mental aging in alcoholic patients. *Journal of Clinical Psychology, 44*, 286–289.

Holland, T. R., & Watson, C. G. (1980). Multivariate analysis of WAIS-MMPI relationships among brain-damaged, schizophrenic, neurotic, and alcoholic patients. *Journal of Clinical Psychology, 36*, 352–359.

Holmberg, G., & Martens, S. (1955). Electroencephalographic changes in man correlated with blood alcohol concentration and some other conditions following standardized ingestion of alcohol. *Quarterly Journal of Studies in Alcohol, 16*, 411–424.

Horn, J. L., Wanberg, K. W., & Forster, F. M. (1974). *The Alcohol Uses Inventory*. Colorado: Center for Alcohol Abuse Research and Evaluation.

Horsley, V., & Sturge, M. D. (1911). *Alcohol and the human body: An introduction to the study of the subject and a contribution to national health* (4th ed.). London: Macmillan.

Howe, G. O., Rohan, T., Decarli, A., Iscovich, J., Kaldor, J., Katsouyanni, K. Marubini, E., Miller, A., Riboli, E., Toniolo, P., & Trichopoulos, D. (1991). The association between alcohol and breast cancer risk: Evidence from the combined analysis of six dietary case-control studies. *International Journal of Cancer, 47*, 707–710.

Howes, J. L. (1983). Effects of experimenter and self-generated imagery on the Korsakoff patient's memory performance. *Neuropsychologia, 21*, 341–249.

Hull, J. G., & Bond, C. F. (1986). Social and behavioral consequences of alcoholic consumption and expectancy: A meta analysis. *Psychological Bulletin, 99*, 347–360.

Huppert, F. A., & Piercy, M. (1976). Recognition memory in amnesic patients: Effect of temporal context and familiarity of material. *Cortex, 12*, 3–20.

International Agency for Research on Cancer (1988). IARC Monographs on the evaluation of carcinogenic risks to humans. *Alcohol Drinking* (Vol 44). Lyon: WHO IARC.

Isbell, H., Fraser, H. F., Wickler, A., Belleville, R. E., & Eisenman, A. J. (1955). An experimental study of the etiology of "rum fits" and delirium tremens. *Quarterly Journal of Studies on Alcohol, 16*, 1–33.

Ishak, K. G., Zimmerman, H. J., & Ray M. B. (1991). Alcoholic liver disease: Pathologic, pathogenetic & clinical aspects. *Alcoholism: Clinical and Experimental Research, 15*, 45–66.

Jackson, R., Scragg, R., & Beaglehole, R. (1991). Alcohol consumption and risk of coronory heart disease. *Bristish Medical Journal, 303*, 211–216.

Jacobson, R. (1986). Female alcoholics: A controlled CT brain scan and clinical study. *British Journal of Addiction, 81*, 661–669.

Jacobson, R., & Lishman, W. A. (1990). Cortical and diencephalic lesions in Korsakoff's syndrome: A clinical and CT scan study. *Psychological Medicine, 20*, 63–75.

Jacobson, R. R., & Lishman, W. A. (1987). Selective memory loss and global intellectual deficits in alcoholic Korsakoff's syndrome. *Psychological Medicine, 17*, 649–655.

Jacoby, L. L., & Witherspoon, D. (1982). Remembering without awareness. *Canadian Journal of Psychology, 36*, 300–324.

Jaffe, P. G., & Katz, A. N. (1975). Attenuating anterograde amnesia in Korsakoff's psychosis. *Journal of Abnormal Psychology, 84*, 559–562.

James, W. (1890). *The principles of psychology*. New York: Holt & Co.

Janowsky, J. S., Shimamura, A. P., Kritchevsky, M., & Squire, L. R. (1989a). Cognitive impairment following frontal damage and its relevance to human amnesia. *Behavioral Neuroscience, 103*, 548–560.

Janowsky, J. S., Shimamura, A. P., & Squire, L. R. (1989b). Memory and metamemory: Comparisons between patients with frontal lobe lesions and amnesic patients. *Psychobiology, 17*, 3–11.

Jellinek, E. M. (1946). Phases in the drinking history of alcoholics. *Quarterly Journal of Studies on Alcohol, 7*, 1.

Jellinek, E. M. (1952). Phases of alcohol addiction. *Quarterly Journal of Studies on Alcohol, 13*, 673–684.

Jellinek, E. M. (1960). *The disease concept of alcoholism*. New Haven, CT: Hillhouse Press.

Jellinek, E. M. (1976). Drinkers and alcoholics in ancient Rome. *Journal of Studies on Alcohol, 37*, 1718–1741.

Jellinek, E., & McFarland, R. (1940). Analysis of psychological experiments on the effects of alcohol. *Quarterly Journal of Studies on Alcohol, 1*, 272–371.

Jenkins, R. L., & Parsons, O. A. (1981). Neuropsychological effect of chronic alcoholism on tactual–spatial performance and memory in males. *Alcoholism: Clinical and Experimental Research, 5*, 26–33.

Jernigan, T. L., Butters, N., Di Taglia, G., Schafer, K., Smith, T., Irwin, M., Grant, I., Schuckit, M., & Cermak, L. S. (1991a). Reduced cerebral grey matter observed in alcoholics using magnetic resonance imaging. *Alcoholism: Clinical and Experimental Research, 15*, 418–427,

Jernigan, T. L., Pfefferbaum, A., & Zatz, L. M. (1986). CT correlates in alcoholism. In I. Grant (Ed.), *Neuropsychiatric correlates in alcoholism* (pp. 21–36). Washington, DC: American Psychiatric Association.

Jernigan, T. L., Schafer, K., Butters, N., & Cermak, L. S. (1991b). Magnetic resonance imaging of alcoholic Korsakoff patients. *Neuropsychopharmacology, 4*, 175–186.

Johannesson, G., Berglund, M., & Ingvar, D. H. (1982). Reduction of blood flow in cerebral white matter in alcoholics related to hepatic function: A CBF and EEG study. *Acta Neurologica Scandinavica, 65*, 190–202.

Johnson, M. K., & Hasher, L. (1987). Human learning and memory. *Annual Review of Psychology, 38*, 631–638.

Jolliffe, N., Wortis, H., & Fein, H. D. (1941). The Wernicke syndrome. *Archives of Neurology and Psychiatry, Chicago, 46*, 569–597.

Jones, B., & Parsons, O. A. (1971). Impaired abstracting ability in chronic alcoholics. *Archives of General Psychiatry, 24*, 71–75.

Jones, B. M. (1973). Memory impairment on the ascending and descending limbs of the blood alcohol curve. *Journal of Abnormal Psychology, 82*, 24–32.

Jones, B. M., & Jones, M. K. (1976). Alcohol effects in women during the menstrual cycle. *Annals of the New York Academy of Sciences, 273*, 576–587.

Jones, B. M., & Jones, M. K. (1977). Alcohol and memory impairment in male and female social drinkers. In I. M. Birnbaum & E. S. Parker (Eds.), *Alcohol and human memory* (pp. 127–138). Hillsdale, NJ: Lawrence Erlbaum Associates Inc.

Jones, B. M., & Vega, A. (1972). Cognitive performance measured on the ascending and descending limb of the blood alcohol curve. *Psychopharmacologia, 23*, 99–114.

Jones, K. L., & Smith, D. W. (1973). Recognition of the fetal alcohol syndrome in early infancy. *Lancet, ii*, 999–1001.

Jones, K. L., Smith, D. W., Streissguth, A. P., & Myrianthoupolis, N. C. (1974). Outcome in offspring of chronic alcoholic women. *Lancet, i*, 1076–1078.

Jones, M. K., & Jones, B. M. (1980). The relationship of age and drinking habits to the effects of alcohol on memory in women. *Journal of Studies on Alcohol, 41*, 179–186.

Jones-Saumty, D. J., & Zeiner, A. R. (1985). Psychological correlates of drinking behavior in social drinker college students. *Alcoholism: Clinical and Experimental Research, 9*, 158–163.

Jorge, M. R., & Masur, J. (1985). The use of the Short-form Alcohol Dependence Questionnaire (SADD) in Brazilian alcoholic patients. *British Journal of Addiction, 80*, 301–306.

Joyce, E. M., & Robbins, T. (1991). Frontal lobe function in Korsakoff and non-Korsakoff alcoholics: Planning and spatial working memory. *Neuropsychologia, 29*, 709–723.

Kannel, W. B., Wolf, P. A., Verter, J., & McNamara, J. (1970). Epidemiologic assessment of the role of blood pressure in stroke: The Framingham Study. *Journal of the American Medical Association, 214*, 301–310.

Kaplan, H. L., Sellers, E. M., Hamilton, C., Naranjo, C. A., & Dorian, P. (1985). Is there acute tolerance to alcohol at steady state. *Journal of Studies on Alcohol, 46*, 253–256.

Kapur, N., & Butters, N. (1977). Visuoperceptive deficits in long-term alcoholics and alcoholics with Korsakoff's psychosis. *Journal of Studies on Alcohol, 38*, 2025–2035.

Keller, M. (1966). Alcohol in health and disease: Some historical perspectives. *Annals of the New York Academy of Sciences, 133*, 820–827.

Keshavarzian, A., Polepalle, C., Iber, F. L., & Durkin, M. (1990). Esophageal motor disorder in alcoholics: Result of alcoholism or withdrawal? *Alcoholism: Clinical and Experimental Research, 14*, 561–567.

Kessler, R. M., Parker, E. S., Clark, C. M., Martin, P. R., George, D. T., Weingartner, H., Sokoloff, L., Ebert, M. H., & Mishkin, M. (1984). *Society for Neuroscience Abstracts, 10*, 541.

Kety, S. S., & Schmidt, C. F. (1948). Nitrous oxide method for the quantitative determination of cerebral blood flow in man: Theory, procedure and normal values. *Journal of Clinical Investigation, 27*, 476–483.

Kinsbourne, M., & Wood, F. (1975). Short-term memory processes and the amnesic syndrome. In D. Deutsch & J. A. Deutsch (Eds.), *Short-term memory*. New York: Academic Press.

Kintsch, W. (1977). *Memory and Cognition*. New York: Wiley.

Kish, G. B., Hagen, J. M., Woody, M. M., & Harvey, H. L. (1980). Alcoholics' recovery from cerebral impairment as a function of duration of abstinence. *Journal of Clinical Psychology, 36*, 584–589.

Kivlahan, D. R., Sher, K. J., & Donovan, D. M. (1989). The Alcohol Dependence Scale: A validation study among inpatient alcoholics. *Journal of Studies on Alcohol, 50*, 170–175.

Klatsky, A. K., Friedman, G. D., Sieglaub, A. B., & Gérard, M. J. (1977). Alcohol consumption and blood pressure: Kaiser-Permanente Multiphasic Health Examination data. *New England Journal of Medicine, 296*, 1194–2000.

Klatsky, A. L., Armstrong, M. A., & Friedman, G. D. (1990). Risk of cardiovascular mortality in alcohol drinkers, ex-drinkers and non-drinkers. *American Journal of Cardiology, 66*, 1237–1242.

Kleinknecht, R. A., & Goldstein, S. G. (1972). Neuropsychological deficits associated with alcoholism: A review and discussion. *Quarterly Journal of Studies on Alcohol, 33*, 999–1019.

Klisz, D. K., & Parsons, O. A. (1977). Hypothesis testing in younger and older alcoholics. *Journal of Studies on Alcohol, 38*, 1718–1729.

Klisz, D. K., & Parsons, O. A. (1979). Cognitve dysfunction in alcoholics and social drinkers: Problems in assessment and remediation. *Journal of Studies on Alcohol, 88*, 268–276.

Knight, L. J., Barbaree, H. E., & Boland, F. J. (1986). Alcohol and the balanced-placebo design: The role of experimenter demands in expectancy. *Journal of Abnormal Psychology, 95*, 335–340.

Knight, L. J., Barbaree, H. E., & Boland, F. J. (1988). Experimenter demands in the balanced-placebo design: Reply to Collins and Searle. *Journal of Abnormal Psychology, 97*, 508–509.

Knight, R. G. (1992). *The neuropsychology of degenerative brain diseases*. Hillsdale, NJ: Lawrence Erlbaum Associates Inc.

Knight, R. G., & Godfrey, H. P. D. (1984a). Assessing the significance of differences between subtests on the WAIS-R. *Journal of Clinical Psychology, 40*, 808–810.

Knight, R. G., & Godfrey, H. P. D. (1984b). Reliability and validity of a scale for rating memory impairment in hospitalized anmesics. *Journal of Consulting and Clinical Psychology, 52*, 769–773.

Knight, R. G., Godfrey, H. P. D., & Shelton, E. J. (1988). The psychological deficits associated with Parkinson's disease. *Clinical Psychology Review, 8*, 391–410.

Knight, R. G., & Longmore, B. E. (1991). What is an amnesic? In M. C. Corballis, K. G. White, & W. C. Abraham (Eds.), *Memory mechanisms: A tribute to G. V. Goddard* (pp. 149–174). Hillsdale, NJ: Lawrence Erlbaum Associates Inc.

Knop, J., Teasdale, D. W., Schulsinger, F., & Goodwin, D. W. (1985). A prospective study of young men at high risk for alcoholism: School behavior and achievement. *Journal of Studies on Alcohol, 46*, 273–278.

Kopelman, M. D. (1985). Rates of forgetting in Alzheimer-type dementia and Korsakoff's syndrome. *Neuropsychologia, 23*, 623–638.

Kopelman, M. D. (1987). Two types of confabulation. *Journal of Neurology, Neurosurgery and Psychiatry, 50*, 1482–1487.

Kopelman, M. D. (1989). Remote and autobiographical memory, temporal context memory, and frontal atrophy in Korsakoff and Alzheimer patients. *Neuropsychologia, 27*, 437–460.

Kopelman, M. D., & Corn, T. H. (1988). Cholinergic "blockade" as a model for cholinergic depletion: A comparison of the memory deficits with those of Alzheimer type dementia and the alcoholic Korsakoff's syndrome. *Brain, 111*, 1079–1110.

Kovner, R., Mattis, S., & Goldmeier, E. (1983). A technique for promoting robust free recall in chronic organic amnesia. *Journal of Clinical Neuropsychology, 5*, 65–71

Kovner, R., Mattis, S., & Pass, R. (1985). Some amnesic patients can freely recall large amounts of information in new contexts. *Journal of Clinical and Experimental Neuropsychology, 7*, 395–411.

Kramer, J. H. (1990). Guidelines for interpreting WAIS-R subtest scores. *Psychological Assessment: A Journal of Consulting and Clinical Psychology, 2*, 202–205.

Kramer, J. H., Blusewicz, M. J., & Preston, K. A. (1989a). The premature aging hypothesis: Old before its time? *Journal of Consulting and Clinical Psychology, 57*, 257–262.

Krein, S., Overton, S., Young, M., Spreier, K., & Yolton. J. (1987). Effects of alcohol on event-related brain potentials produced by viewing a simulated traffic signal. *Journal of the American Optometric Association, 58*, 474–477.

Kuhl, D. E., Metter, E. J., & Riege, W. H. (1984). Patterns of local cerebral glucose utilization determined in Parkinson's disease by the [18F] fluorodeoxyglucose method. *Annals of Neurology, 15*, 419–424.

Laberg, J. C., & Loberg, T. (1989). Expectancy and tolerance: A study of acute alcohol intoxication using the balanced placebo design. *Journal of Studies on Alcohol, 50*, 448–455.

Lamberty, G. J., Beckwith, B. E., & Petros, T. V. (1990). Post-trial treatment with ethanol enhances recall of prose narratives. *Physiology and Behavior, 48*, 653–658.

Landesman-Dwyer, S., Ragozin, A. S., & Little, R. E. (1981). Behavioural correlates of prenatal alcohol exposures: A four-year follow-up study. *Neurobehavioural Toxicology and Teratology, 3*, 187–193.

LaPorte, R. E., Cresanta, J., & Kuller, L. H. (1981). Public health implications of moderate alcohol consumption. *Journal of Public Health, 21*, 198–223.

Lassen, N. A., & Ingvar, D. H. (1961). The blood flow of the cerebral cortex determined by radioactive krypton-85. *Experimentia, 17*, 42–50.

Leber, W. R., Jenkins, R. L., & Parsons, O. A. (1981). Recovery of visual-spatial learning and memory in chronic alcoholics. *Journal of Clinical Psychology, 37*, 192–197.

Leber, W. R., Parsons, O. A., & Nichols, N. (1985). Neuropsychological test results are related to ratings of men alcoholics' therapeutic progress: A replicated study. *Journal of Studies on Alcohol, 46,* 116–121.

Lee, F. I. (1966). Cirrhosis and hepatoma in alcoholics. *Gut, 7,* 77–85.

Leigh, B. C. (1989). In search of the seven dwarves: Issues of measurement and measuring in alcohol expectancy research. *Psychological Bulletin, 105,* 361–373.

Lelbach, W. K. (1975). Cirrhosis in the alcoholic and its relation to the volume of alcohol abuse. *Annals of the New York Academy of Science, 252,* 85–105.

Lemmens, P., Knibbe, R. A., & Tan, F. (1988). Weekly recall and diary estimates of alcohol consumption in a general population survey. *Journal of Studies on Alcohol, 49,* 131–135.

Leng, N. R. C., & Parkin, A. J. (1989). A etiological variation in the amnesic syndrome: Comparisons using the Brown–Peterson task. *Cortex, 25,* 251–260.

Lennane, K. J. (1986). Management of moderate to severe alcohol-related brain damage. *Medical Journal of Australia, 145,* 136–143.

Lennane, K. J. (1988). Patients with alcohol-related brain damage: Therapy and outcome. *Australian Drug and Alcohol Review, 7,* 89–92.

Lezak, M. (1983). *Neuropsychological assessment* (2nd ed.). New York: Oxford University Press.

Lieber, C. S. (1973). Hepatic and metabolic effects of alcohol (1966–1973). *Gastroenterology, 65,* 821–846.

Lieber, C. S. (1975a). Alcohol and malnutrition in the pathologenesis of liver disease. *Journal of the American Medical Association, 233,* 1077–1082.

Lieber, C. S. (1975b). Liver disease and alcohol: Fatty liver, alcoholic hepatitis, cirrhosis and their inter-relationships. *Annals of the New York Academy Science, 252,* 63–84.

Lieber, C. S. (1982). Medical disorders of alcholism: Pathogenesis and treatment. In L. H. Smith (Ed.), *Major problems in internal medicine* (Vol. XXII). Philadelphia: W. B. Saunders Co.

Lishman, W. A. (1981). Cerebral disorders in alcoholism: Syndromes of impairment. *Brain, 104,* 1–20.

Lishman, W. A. (1987). *Organic Psychiatry: The psychological consequences of cerebral disorder* (2nd ed.). Oxford: Blackwell Scientific Publications.

Lishman, W. A., Jacobson, R. R., & Acker, C. (1987). Brain damage in alcoholism: Current concepts. *Acta Medica Scandanavica* (Suppl. 717), 5–17.

Lishman, W. A., Ron, M. A., & Acker, W. (1980). Computed tomography and psychometric assessment of alcoholic patients. In D. Richter (Ed.), *Addiction and brain damage* (pp. 215–227). London: Croom Helm.

Liskow, B. I., Rinck, C., Campbell, J., & De Souza, C. (1989) Alcohol withdrawal in the elderly. *Journal on Studies of Alcohol, 50,* 414–421.

Lisman, S. A. (1974). Alcoholic "blackout": State-dependent learning? *Archives of General Psychiatry, 30,* 46–53.

Lister, R. G., Gorenstein, C., Risher-Flowers, D., Weingartner, H., & Eckardt, M. J. (1991). Dissociation of the acute effects of alcohol on implicit and explicit memory processes. *Neuropsychologia, 29,* 1205–1212.

Little, H. J. (1991). Mechanisms that may underlie the behavioural effects of ethanol. *Progress in Neurobiology, 36,* 171–194.

Little, R. E., & Sing, C. F. (1986). Association of father's drinking and infant's birthweight. *New England Journal of Medicine, 314,* 1644.

Littleton, J. (1989). Alcohol intoxication and physical dependence: A molecular mystery tour. *British Journal of Addiction, 84,* 267–276.

Lloyd, G. E. R. (1978). *Hippocratic writings.* London: Penguin.

Loberg, T. (1980). Alcohol misuse and neuropsychological deficits in man. *Journal of Studies on Alcohol, 41,* 119–128.

Lochry, E. A., & Riley, E. P. (1980). Retention of passive avoidance and T-maze escape in rats exposed to alcohol prenatally. *Neurobehavioural Toxicology, 2,* 107–115.

Lockwood, A. H. (1989). Hepatic encephalopathy and other neurological disorders associated with gastrointestinal disease. In M. J. Aminoff (Ed.), *Neurology and General Medicine. The neurological aspects of medical disorders* (pp. 211–230). New York: Churchill Livingstone.

Long, J. A., & McLachlen, J. F. C. (1974). Abstract reasoning and perceptual-motor efficiency in alcoholics. *Quarterly Journal of Studies on Alcohol, 35,* 1220–1229.

Longmore, B. E., & Knight, R. G. (1988). The effect of intellectual deterioration on retention deficits in amnesic alcoholics. *Journal of Abnormal Psychology, 97,* 448–454.

Longmore, B. E., Knight, R. G., Menkes, D. B., & Hope, A. (1988). The experimental investigation of a case of alcohol induced frontal lobe atrophy. *Neuropsychology, 2,* 77–86.

Longnecker, M. P., Berlin, J. A., Orza, M. J., & Chalmers, T. C. (1988). A meta-analysis of alcohol consumption in relation to risk of breast cancer. *Journal of the American Medical Association, 260,* 652–656.

Lorenz, K. (1966). *On aggression.* London: Methuen.

Lowe, G. (1982). Alcohol induced state dependent learning: Differentiating stimulus and storage hypotheses. *Current Psychological Research, 2,* 215–222.

Lowenfels, A. B., & Zevola, S. A. (1989). Alcohol and breast cancer: An overview. *Alcoholism: Clinical and Experimental Research, 13,* 109–111.

Lukas, S. E., Lex, B. W., Slater, J. P., Greenwald, N. E. et al. (1989). A microanalysis of ethanol-induced disruption of body sway and psychomotor performances in women. *Psychopharmacology, 98,* 169–175.

Lukas, S. E., Mendelson, J. H., Woods, B. T., Mello, N. K., & Teoh, S. K. (1989). Topographic distribution of EEG alpha activity during ethanol induced intoxication in women. *Journal of Studies on Alcohol, 50,* 176–185.

Lynch, M. J. G. (1960). Brain lesions in chronic alcoholism. *Archives of Pathology, 69,* 342–353.

MacVane, J., Butters, N., Montgomery, K., & Farber, J. (1982). Cognitive functioning in men social drinkers: A replication study. *Journal of Studies on Alcohol, 43,* 81–95.

Mair, R. G., & McEntee, W. J. (1986). Cognitive enhancement in Korsakoff's psychosis by clonidine: A comparison with L-dopa and ephedrine. *Psychopharmacology, 88,* 374–380.

Mair, W. G. P., Warrington, E. K., & Weiskrantz, L. (1979). Memory disorder in Korsakoff's psychosis: A neuropathological and neuropsychological investigation of two cases. *Brain, 102,* 749–783.

Maisto, S. A., & O'Farrell, T. J. (1985). Comment on the validity of Watson et al.'s "Do alcoholics give valid self-reports"? *Journal of Studies on Alcohol, 46,* 447–450.

Maisto, S. A., Sobell, L. C., & Sobell, M. B. (1979). Comparison of alcoholics' self-reports of drinking behaviour with reports of collateral informants. *Journal of Consulting and Clinical Psychology, 47*, 106–112.

Majewski, F., & Goeke, T. (1982). Alcohol embryopathy: Studies in Germany. In E. L. Abel, (Ed.), *Fetal alcohol syndrome, human studies* (Vol. 2, pp. 65–88). Boca Raton: CRL Press.

Malamud, N., & Skillicorn, S. A. (1956). Relationship between the Wernicke and the Korsakoff syndrome. *Archives of Neurology and Psychiatry, 76*, 585–596.

Malerstein, A. J., & Belden, E. (1968). WAIS, SILS, and PPVT in Korsakoff syndrome. *Archives of General Psychiatry, 19*, 743–750.

Mallet, B. L., & Veall, N. (1963). Investigation of cerebral blood flow determination by 133 Xe inhalation and external recording. *Lancet i*, 1080–1082.

Malloy, P., Noel, N., Rogers, S., Longabaugh, R., & Beattie, M. (1989). Risk factors for neuropsychological impairment in alcoholics: Antisocial personality, age, years of drinking and gender. *Journal of Studies on Alcohol, 50*, 422–426.

Mancall, E. L. (1989). Nutritional disorders of the nervous system. In M. J. Aminoff (Ed.), *Neurology and general medicine. The neurological aspects of medical disorders* (pp. 323–340). New York: Churchill Livingstone.

Mann, K., Batra, A., Gunther, A., & Schroth, G. (1992). Do women develop alcoholic brain damage more readily than men. *Alcoholism: Clinical and Experimental Research, 16*, 1052–1056.

Marlatt, C. G.., & Rosenhow, D. J. (1980). Cognitive processes in alcohol use: Expectancy and the balanced-placebo design: In N. K. Mello (Ed.), *Advances in substance abuse: Behavioral and biological research* (Vol. 1, pp. 159–199). Greenwick, CT: JAI Press.

Marlatt, G. A., & Gordon, J. R. (1985). *Relapse prevention.* New York: Guilford Press.

Marmot, M., & Brunner, E. (1991). Alcohol and cardiovascular disease : The status of the U-shaped curve. *British Medical Journal, 303*, 565–568.

Marmot, M. G., Rose, G., Shirley, M. J., & Thomas, B. (1981). Alcohol and mortality: A U-shaped curve. *Lancet, i*, 580–582.

Martin, P. R., Adinoff, B., Bone, G. A. H., Stapleton, J. M., Eckardt, M. J., & Linnoila, M. (1987). Fluroxamine treatment of alcoholic chronic organic brain syndromes. *Clinical Pharmacology and Therapeutics, 41*, 211.

Martin, P. R., McCool, B. A., & Singleton, C. K. (1993). Genetic sensitivity to thiamine deficiency and development of alcoholic organic brain disease. *Alcoholism: Clinical and Experimental Research, 17*, 31–37.

Martini, G. A., & Bode, C. H. (1970). The epidemiology of cirrhosis of the liver. In A. Engel & T. Larsson, (Eds.), *Alcoholic cirrhosis and other toxic hepatopathies* (pp. 315–335). Stokholm: Nordiska Bokhandelins Forlag.

Marx, K. (1889/1946). *Das Kapital: Kritik der politischen Oekonomie* [Capital: A critique of political economy]. (Trans. S.L. Trask). London: Allen & Unwin.

Matarazzo, J. D., & Prifitera, A. (1989). Subtest scatter and premorbid intelligence: Lessons from the WAIS-R standardization sample. *Psychological Assessment: A Journal of Consulting and Clinical Psychology, 1*, 186–191.

Matthew, R. I., & Wilson, W. H. (1986). Regional cerebral blood flow changes associated with ethanol intoxication. *Stroke, 17*, 1156–1159.

Mattis, S. (1976). Mental status examination for organic mental syndromes in the elderly patient. In L. Bellack & T. B. Karasu (Eds.), *Geriatric psychiatry* (pp. 77–121). New York: Grune & Stratton.

Mattson, S. N., Riley, E. P., Jernigan, T. L., Ehlers, C. L., Delis, D. C., Jones, K. L., Stern, C., Johnson, K. A., Hesselink, J. R., & Bellugi, U. (1992). Fetal alcohol syndrome: A case report of neuropsychological, MRI, and EEG assessment of 2 children. *Alcoholism: Clinical and Experimental Research, 16*, 1001–1003.

Mayes, A. R. (1988). *Human organic memory disorders*. Cambridge: Cambridge University Press.

Mayes, A. R., Baddeley, A. D., Cockburn, J., Meudell, P. R., Pickering, A., & Wilson, B. (1989). Why are amnesic judgements of recency and frequency made in a qualitatively different way from those of normal people? *Cortex, 25*, 479–488.

Mayes, A. R., Meudell, P. R., Mann, D., & Pickering, A. (1988). Location of lesions in Korsakoff's syndrome. Neuropsychological and neuropathological data on two patients. *Cortex, 24*, 367–388.

Mayes, A. R., Meudell, P., & Neary, D. (1978). Must amnesia be caused by either encoding or retrieval disorders? In M. M. Gruneberg, P. E. Morris, & R. N. Sykes (Eds.), *Practical aspects of memory* (pp. 712–719). London: Academic Press.

Mayes, A. R., Meudell, P. R., & Pickering, A. (1985). Is organic amnesia caused by a selective deficit in remembering contextual information? *Cortex, 21*, 167–202.

Mayfield, D., McLeod, G., & Hall, P. (1974). The CAGE questionnaire: Validation of a new alcoholism screening test. *American Journal of Psychiatry, 131*, 1121–1123.

Maylor, E. A., Rabbitt, P. M. A., & Kingstone, A. (1987). Effects of alcohol on word categorization and recognition memory. *British Journal of Psychology, 78*, 233–239.

McCrady, B. S. (1987). Implications of neuropsychological research findings for the treatment and rehabilitation of alcoholics. In O. A. Parsons, N. Butters, & P. E. Nathan, (Eds.), *Neuropsychology of alcoholism: Implications for diagnosis and treatment* (pp. 381–391). New York: Guilford Press.

McCrady, B. S., & Smith, D. E. (1986). Implications of cognitive impairment for the treatment of alcoholism. *Alcoholism: Clinical and Experimental Research, 10*, 145–149.

McDowell, J. R., & LeBlanc, H. J. (1984). Computed tomographic findings in Wernicke–Korsakoff syndrome. *Archives of Neurology, 41*, 453–454.

McEntee, W. J., & Mair, R. G. (1978). Memory impairment in Korsakoff's psychosis: A correlation with brain noradrenergic activity. *Science 202*, 905–907.

McEntee, W. J., & Mair, R. G. (1980). Memory enhancement in Korsakoff's psychosis by clonidine: Further evidence for a noradrenergic deficit. *Annals of Neurology, 7*, 466–470.

Meier, S. E., Brigham, T. A., & Handel, G. (1987). Accuracy of drinkers' recall of alcohol consumption in a field setting. *Journal of Studies on Alcohol, 48*, 325–328.

Melgaard, B., Danielsen, U. T., Sorensen, H., & Ahlgren, P. (1986). The severity of alcoholism and its relation to intellectual impairment and cerebral atrophy. *British Journal of Addiction, 81*, 77–80.

Melton, A. W. (1963). Implications of short-term memory for a general theory of memory. *Journal of Verbal Learning and Verbal Behavior, 2*, 1–21.

Mendelson, J. H. (1978). Fetal alcohol syndrome. *New England Journal of Medicine, 299*, 556.

Mensing, J. W. A., Hoogland, P. H., & Slooff, J. L. (1984). Computed tomography in the diagnosis of Wernicke's encephalopathy: A radiological–neuropathological correlation. *Annals of Neurology, 16*, 363–365.

Mercer, P. W., & Khavari, K. A. (1990). Are women drinking more like men? An empirical examination of the convergence hypothesis. *Alcoholism: Clinical and Experimental Research, 14*, 461–466.

Messing, R. O. & Greenberg, D. A. (1989). Alcohol and the nervous system. In M. J. Aminoff (Ed.), *Neurology and general medicine: The neurological aspects of medical disorders* (pp. 533–548). New York: Churchill Livingstone.

Metter, E. J., Riege, W. H., Kameyama, M., Phelps, M. E., & Kuhl, D. E. (1982). Correlational differences of regional glucose metabolism in Huntingdon, Parkinson and Alzheimer diseases. *Annals of Neurology, 12*, 88–94.

Metz, J., Yasillo, N., & Cooper, M. (1987). Cerebral metabolism and EEG: Relations to cognitive task. *Society of Neuroscience Abstracts, 13*, 1413.

Meudell, P. R., Mayes, A. R., Ostergaard, A., & Pickering, A. (1985). Recency and frequency judgements in alcoholic amnesics and normal people with poor memory. *Cortex, 21*, 487–511.

Michaelis, E. K. (1990). Fetal alcohol exposure : Cellular toxicity and molecular events involved in toxicity. *Alcoholism: Clinical and Experimental Research, 14*, 819–826.

Miglioli, M., Butchtel, H. A., Campanini, T., & De Risio, C. (1979). Cerebral hemispheric lateralization of cognitive deficits due to alcoholism. *Journal of Nervous and Mental Diseases, 167*, 212–217.

Miller, G. J., & Miller, N. E. (1975). Plasma high-density-lipoprotein concentration and development of ischaemic heart-disease. *Lancet, i*, 16–19.

Miller, M. E., Adesso, V. J., Fleming, J. P., Gino, A., & Lauerman, R. (1978). Effects of alcohol on the storage and retrieval processes of heavy social drinkers. *Journal of Experimental Psychology: Human Learning and Memory, 4*, 246–255.

Miller, W. R., Heather, N., & Hall, W. (1991). Calculating standard drink units: International comparisons. *British Journal of Addiction, 86*, 43–48.

Miller, W. R., & Orr, J. (1980). Nature and sequence of neuropsychological deficits in alcoholics. *Journal of Studies on Alcohol, 41*, 325–337.

Milner, B. (1963). Effects of different brain lesions on card sorting. *Archives of Neurology, 9*, 90–100.

Milner, B., Corkin, S., & Teuber, H.-L. (1968). Further analyses of the hippocampal amnesic syndrome: A 14-year follow-up study of H. M. *Neuropsychologia, 6*, 215–234.

Mitchell, M. C. (1985). Alcohol induced impairment of central nervous system function: Behavioral skills involved in driving. *Journal of Studies on Alcohol* (Suppl.), *10*, 109–116.

Mittenberg, W., Thompson, G. B., & Schwartz, J. A. (1991). Abnormal and reliable differences among Wechsler Memory Scale-Revised subtests. *Psychological Assessment: A Journal of Consulting and Clinical Psychology, 3*, 492–495.

Mohs, R. C., Tinklenberg, J. R., Roth, W. T., & Kopell, B. S. (1978). Slowing of short-term memory scanning in alcoholics. *Journal of Studies on Alcohol, 39,* 1908–1915.

Monti, P. M., Abrahams, D. B., Kadden, R. M., & Cooney, N. L. (1989). *Treating alcohol dependence.* New York: Guilford Press.

Moos, R. H., Finney, J. W., & Chan, D. A. (1981). The process of recovery from alcoholism. I. Comparing alcoholic patients with matched community controls. *Journal of Studies on Alcohol, 42,* 383–402.

Morgan, M. Y. (1982a). Sex and Alcohol. *British Medical Bulletin, 38,* 43–52.

Morgan, M. Y. (1982b). The effects of moderate alcohol consumption on male fertility. In M. Langer, L. Chiandusse, J. Chojora, & L Martini (Eds.), *The endocrines and the liver* (pp. 157–158). Serono Symposium No. 51. London: Academic Press.

Morgan, M. Y., & Sherlock, S. (1977). Sex-related differences among 100 patients with alcoholic liver disease. *British Medical Journal, 1,* 939–941.

Mortensen, E. L. (1980). The effects of partial information in amnesic and normal subjects. *Scandinavian Journal of Psychology, 21,* 75–82.

Moscovitch, M. (1982). Multiple dissocations of function in amnesia. In L. Cermak (Ed.), *Human memory and amnesia* (pp. 337–370). Hillsdale, NJ: Lawrence Erlbaum Associates Inc.

Moskowitz, H., & Burns, M. (1971). Effect on alcohol on the psychological refractory period. *Quarterly Journal of Studies on Alcohol, 32,* 782–790.

Moskowitz, H., & Burns, M. (1973). Alcohol effects on information processing time with an overlearned task. *Perceptual and Motor Skills, 37,* 835–839.

Moskowitz, H., Burns, M. M., & Williams, A. (1985). Skills performance at low blood alcohol levels. *Journal of Studies on Alcohol, 46,* 482–485.

Moskowitz, H., & Murray, J. (1976). Alcohol and backward masking of visual information. *Journal of Studies on Alcohol, 37,* 40–45.

Moskowitz, H., & Roth, S. (1971). Effects of alcohol on response latency in object learning. *Quarterly Journal of Studies on Alcohol, 32,* 969–975.

Musen, G., & Squire, L. R. (1991). Normal acquisition of novel verbal information in amnesia. *Journal of Experimental Psychology: Learning, Memory, and Cognition, 17,* 1095–1104.

Mutzell, S., & Tibblin, G. (1989). High alcohol consumption, liver toxic drugs and brain damage—a population study. *Upsala Journal of Medical Science, 94,* 305–315.

Muuronen, A., Bergman, H., Hindmarsh, T., & Telakivi, T. (1989). Influence of improved drinking habits on brain atrophy and cogntive performance in alcoholic patients: A 5-year follow-up study. *Alcoholism: Clinical and Experimental Research, 13,* 137–141.

Nakano, M., & Lieber, C. S. (1982). Ultrastructure of initial stages of perivenular fibrosis in alcohol fed baboons. *American Journal of Pathology, 106,* 145–155.

Nanson, J. L. (1992). Autism in fetal alcohol syndrome: A report of 6 cases. *Alcoholism: Clinical and Experimental Research, 16,* 558–565.

Nanson, J. L., & Hiscock, M. (1990). Attention deficits in children exposed to alcohol prenatally. *Alcoholism: Clinical and Experimental Research, 14,* 656–661.

Nathan, P. E., & Skinstad, A-H. (1987). Outcomes of treatment for alcohol problems: Current methods, problems, and results. *Journal of Consulting and Clinical Psychology, 55,* 332–340.

Needle, R., McCubbin, H., Lorence, J., & Hochhauser, M. (1983). Reliability and validity of adolescent self-reported drug use: A methodological report. *International Journal of the Addictions, 18,* 901–912.

Nelson, H. E. (1982). *The National Adult Reading Test.* Windsor: NFER-Nelson.

Nelson, T. O., McSpadden, M., Fromme, K., & Marlatt, G. A. (1986). Effects of alcohol intoxication on metamemory and on retrieval from long term memory. *Journal of Experimental Psychology: General, 115,* 247–254.

Nelson, T. W., & Narens, L. (1980). A new technique for investigating the feeling of knowing. *Acta Psychologica, 46,* 69–80.

Neubuerger, K. T. (1957). The changing neuropathological picture of chronic alcoholism. *Archives of Pathology, Chicago, 63,* 1–6.

Newlin, D. B., Golden, C. J., Quaife, M., & Graber, B. (1982). Effect of alcohol ingestion on regional cerebral blood flow. *International Journal of Neuroscience, 17,* 145–150.

Nilsson, L. G., Backman, L., & Karlsson, T. (1989). Priming and cued recall in elderly alcohol intoxicated and sleep deprived subjects: A case of functionally similar memory deficits. *Psychological Medicine, 19,* 423–433.

Nixon, S. J., Kujawski, A., Parsons, O. A., & Yohman, J. R. (1987). Semantic (verbal) and figural memory impairment in alcoholics. *Journal of Clinical and Experimental Neuropsychology, 9,* 311–322.

Nixon, S. J., & Parsons, O. A. (1991). Alcohol-related efficiency deficits using an ecologically valid test. *Alcoholism: Clinical and Experimental Research, 15,* 601–606.

Nixon, S. J., Parsons, O. A. Schaeffer, K. W., & Hale, R. L. (1988). Subject selection biases in alcoholic samples: Effects on cognitive performance. *Journal of Clinical Psychology, 44,* 831–836.

Noonberg, A., Goldstein, G., & Page, H. A. (1985). Premature aging in male alcoholics: "Accelerated aging" or "increased vulnerability"? *Alcoholism: Clinical and Experimental Research, 9,* 334–338.

Nylander, I. (1960). Children of alcoholic fathers. *Acta Paediatrica Scandinavica, 49,* 1–134.

O'Donnell, W. E., & Reynolds, D. M. (1983). *Neuropsychological impairment scale manual.* Annapolis, MD: Annapolis Psychological Service.

O'Farrell, T. J., Cutter, H. S. G., Bayog, R. D., Dentch, G., & Fortgang, J. (1984). Correspondence between one-year retrospective reports of pretreatment drinking by alcoholics and their wives. *Behavioral Assessment, 6,* 263–274.

O'Leary, M. R., & Donovan, D. M. (1979). Male alcoholics: Treatment outcome as a function of length of treatment and level of current adaptive abilities. *Evaluation and the Health Professions,2,* 373–384.

O'Leary, M. R., Donovan, D. M., Chaney, E., & Walker, R. D. (1979a). Cognitive impairment and treatment outcome with alcoholics: Preliminary findings. *Journal of Clinical Psychiatry, 40,* 397–398.

O'Leary, M. R., Donovan, D. M., Chaney, E. F., Walker, R. D., & Shau, E. J. (1979b). Application of discriminant analysis to level of performance of alcoholics and nonalcoholics on Wechsler–Bellevue and Halstead–Reitan subtests. *Journal of Clinical Psychology, 35,* 204–208.

O'Leary, M. R., Speltz, M. L., Donovan, D. M., & Walker, R. D. (1979c). Implicit preadmission screening criteria in an alcoholism treatment program. *American Journal of Psychiatry, 136,* 1190–1193.

O'Malley, S. S., & Maisto, S. A. (1985). Effects of family drinking history and expectancies on responses in alcohol in men. *Journal of Studies on Alcohol, 46,* 289–297.

Oscar-Berman, M. (1973). Hypothesis testing and focusing behavior during concept formation by amnesic Korsakoff patients. *Neuropsychologia, 11,* 191–198.

Oscar-Berman, M., & Ellis, R. J. (1987). Cognitive deficits related to memory impairments in alcoholism. In M. Galanter (Ed.), *Recent developments in alcoholism* (Vol. 5, pp. 59–80). New York: Plenum Press.

Oscar-Berman, M., & Weinstein, A. (1985). Visual processing, memory and lateralization in alcoholism and aging. *Developmental Neuropsychology, 1,* 99–112.

Oscar-Berman, M., Weinstein, A., & Wysocki, D. (1983). Bimanual tactual discrimination in aging alcoholics. *Alcoholism: Clinical and Experimental Research, 7,* 398–403.

Ouellette, E. M., Rosett, H. L., Rossman, N. P., & Weiner, L. (1977). Adverse effects on offspring of maternal alcohol abuse during pregnancy. *New England Journal of Medicine, 297,* 528–530.

Page, R. D., & Cleveland, M. F. (1987). Cognitive dysfunction and aging among male alcoholics and social drinkers. *Alcoholism: Clinical and Experimental Research, 11,* 376–384.

Page, R. D., & Linden, J. D. (1974). Reversible organic brain syndrome in alcoholics. *Quarterly Journal of Studies on Alcohol, 35,* 98–107.

Page, R. D., & Schaub, L. H. (1977). Intellectual functioning in alcoholics during six months abstinence. *Journal of Studies on Alcohol, 38,* 1240–1246.

Parker, D. A., Parker, E. S., Brody, J. A., & Schoenberg, R. (1983). Alcohol use and cognitive loss among employed men and women. *American Journal of Public Health, 73,* 521–526.

Parker, E. S. (1982). Comments on "Cognitive functioning in men social drinkers: A replication study". *Journal of Studies on Alcohol, 43,* 170–177.

Parker, E. S., Alkana, R. L., Birnbaum, I. M., Hartley, J. T., & Noble, E. P. (1974). Alcohol and the disruption of cognitive processes. *Archives of General Psychiatry, 31,* 824–828.

Parker, E. S., Birnbaum, I. M., Boyd, R. A., & Noble, E. P. (1980a). Neuropsychologic decrements as a function of alcohol intake in male students. *Alcoholism: Clinical and Experimental Research, 4,* 330–334.

Parker, E. S., Birnbaum, I. M., Weingartner, H., Hartley, J. T., Stillman, R. C., & Wyatt, R. J. (1980b). Retrograde enhancement of human memory with alcohol. *Psychopharmacology, 69,* 219–222.

Parker, E. S., Morishisa, J. M., Wyatt, R. J., Schwartz, B. L., Weingartner, H., & Stillman, R. C. (1981). The alcohol facilitation effect on memory: A dose–response study. *Psychopharmacology, 74,* 88–92.

Parker, E. S., & Noble, E. (1977). Alcohol consumption and cognitive functioning in social drinkers. *Journal of Studies on Alcohol, 38,* 1224–1232.

Parker, E. S., & Noble, E. P. (1980). Alcohol and the aging process in social drinkers. *Journal of Studies on Alcohol, 41,* 170–178.

Parker, E. S., Parker, D. A., Brody, J. A., & Schoenberg, R. (1982). Cognitive patterns resembling premature aging in male social drinkers. *Alcoholism: Clinical and Experimental Research, 6,* 46–52.

Parker, E. S., Parker, D. A., & Harford, T. C. (1991). Specifying the relationship between alcohol use and cognitive loss: The effects of frequency of consumption and psychological distress. *Journal of Studies on Alcohol, 52*, 366–373.

Parker, E. S., & Weingartner, H. (1984). Retrograde facilitation of human memory by drugs. In H. Weingartner & E. S. Parker (Eds.), *Memory consolidation: Psychobiology of cognition*. Hillsdale, NJ: Lawrence Erlbaum Associates Inc.

Parker, J. B., Chelune, G. J., Hamblin, D. K., & Kitchens, E. M. (1984). Verbal impairment in alcoholics. *Addictive Behaviors, 9*, 287–290.

Parkin, A. J. (1991). The relationship between autograde and retrograde amnesia in alcoholic Wernicke–Korsakoff syndrome. *Psychological Medicine, 21*, 11–14.

Parkin, A. J. (1992). Functional significance of etiological factors in human amnesia. In L. R. Squire & N. Butters (Eds.), *Neuropsychology of memory* (2nd ed.), (pp. 122–129). New York: Guilford Press.

Parkin, A. J., Leng, N. R. C., & Hunkin, N. (1990). Differential sensitivity to contextual information in duencephalic and temporal lobe amnesia. *Cortex, 26*, 373–380.

Parkin, A. J., Montaldi, D., Leng, N. R., & Hunkin, N. M. (1990). Contextual cueing effects in the remote memory of alcoholic Korsakoff patients and normal subjects. *Quarterly Journal of Experimental Psychology: Human Experimental Psychology, 42*, 585–596.

Parsons, O. A. (1986). Cognitive functioning in sober social drinkers: A review and critique. *Journal of Studies on Alcohol, 47*, 101–114.

Parsons, O. A. (1987). Do neuropsychological deficits predict alcoholics treatment course and posttreatment recovery? In O. A. Parsons, N. Butters, & P. E. Nathan (Eds.), *Neuropsychology of alcoholism* (pp. 273–290). New York: Guilford Press.

Parsons, O. A., & Fabian, M. S. (1982). Comments on "Cognitive functioning in men social drinkers: A replication study". *Journal of Studies on Alcohol, 43*, 178–182.

Parsons, O. A., & Farr, S. P. (1981). The neuropsychology of drug and alcohol abuse. In S. B. Filskov & T. J. Boll (Eds.), *Handbook of clinical neuropsychology* (pp. 320–365). New York: Wiley Interscience.

Parsons, O. A., & Leber, W. R. (1981). The relationship between cognitive dysfunction and brain damage in alcoholics: Casual interactive, or epiphenomenal? *Alcoholism: Clinical and Experimental Research, 5*, 326–343.

Parsons, O. A., & Prigatano, G. P. (1977). Memory functioning in alcoholics. In I. M. Birnbaum & E. S. Parker (Eds.), *Alcohol and memory* (pp. 185–194). Hillsdale, NJ: Lawrence Erlbaum Associates Inc.

Parsons, O. A., Sinha, R., & Williams, H. L. (1990). Relationships between neuropsychological test performance and event related potentials in alcoholic and normal samples. *Alcoholism: Clinical and Experimental Research, 14*, 746–755.

Paton, W. R. (1916). *The greek anthology*, Vol. 1. London: William Heinemann.

Paulson, M. J., & Lin, T. T. (1970). Predicting WAIS IQ from Shipley–Hartford scores. *Journal of Clinical Psychology, 26*, 453–461.

Payne, R. W. (1960). Cognitive abnormalities. In H. J. Eysenck (Ed.), *Handbook of abnormal psychology*. London: Pitman Medical.

Peck, D. F. (1970). The conversion of Progressive Matrices and Mill Hill Vocabulary raw scores into deviation IQs. *Journal of Clinical Psychology, 26,* 67–70.

Persson, J. (1991). Alcohol and the small intestine. *Scandinavian Journal of Gastronterology, 26,* 3–15.

Peterson, J. B., Rothfleisch, J., Zelazo, P. D., & Pihl, R. O. (1990). Acute alcohol intoxication and cognitive functioning. *Journal of Studies on Alcohol, 51,* 114–122.

Petros, T. V., Kerbel, N., Beckwith, B. E., Sacks, G., & Sarafolean, M. (1985). The effects of alcohol on prose memory. *Physiology and Behavior, 35,* 43–46.

Pfefferbaum, A., Horvath, T. B., Roth, W. T., Clifford, S. T., & Kopell, B. S. (1980). Acute and chronic effects of ethanol on event related potentials. *Advances in Experimental Medicine and Biology, 126,* 625–639.

Pfefferbaum, A., Horvath, T. B., Roth, W. T., & Kopell. B. S. (1979). Event-related potential changes in chronic alcoholics. *Electroencephalography and Clinical Neurophysiology, 47,* 637–647.

Pfefferbaum, A., Lim, K. O., Zipursky, R. B., Mathalon, D. H., Rosenbloom, M. J., Lane, B., Chung, N. H., & Sullivan, E. V. (1992). Brain grey and white matter loss accelerates with aging in chronic alcoholics: A quantitative MRI study. *Alcoholism: Clinical and Experimental Research, 16,* 1078–1089.

Pfefferbaum, A., Rosenbloom, M., Crusan, K., & Jernigan, T. L. (1988). Brain CT changes in alcoholics: Effects of age and alcohol consumption. *Alcoholism: Clinical and Experimental Research, 12,* 81–87.

Phelps, M. E., Huang, S. C., Hoffman, E. J., Selin, C., Sokoloff, L., & Kuhl, D. E. (1979). Tomographic measurement of local cerebral glucose metabolic rate in humans with (F-18)2-fluoro-2-deoxy-D-glucose: Validation of method. *Annals of Neurology, 6,* 371–388.

Phillips, S. G., Harper, C. G., & Kril, J. J. (1987). A quantitative histological study of the cerebellar vermis in alcoholic patients. *Brain, 110,* 301–314.

Pickering, A. D., Mayes, A. R., & Fairbairn, A. F. (1989). Amnesia and memory for modality information. *Neuropsychologia, 27,* 1249–1259.

Pihl, R. O., Peterson, J., & Finn, P. R. (1990). Inherited predisposition to alcoholism: Characteristics of sons of male alcoholics. *Journal of Abnormal Psychology, 99,* 291–301.

Plutarch (circa 81AD/1928). *Moralia.* (F. C. Babbitt, Trans.). Vol. 2. London: William Heinemann.

Pokorny, A., Miller, B. A., & Kaplan, H. B. (1972). The brief MAST: A shortened version of the Michigan Alcoholism Screening Test. *American Journal of Psychiatry, 129,* 342–345.

Pollock, V. E., Teasdale, T. W., Gabrielli, W. F., & Knop, J. (1986). Subjective and objective measures of response to alcohol among young men at risk for alcoholism. *Journal of Studies on Alcohol, 47,* 297–304.

Pollock, V. E., Volavka, J., Goodwin, D. W., Mednick, S.A., Gabrielli, W. F., Knop, J., & Schulsinger, F. (1983). The EEG after alcohol administration in men at risk for alcoholism. *Archives of General Psychiatry, 40,* 857–861.

Pollock, V. E., Volavka, J., Goodwin, D. W., Gabrielli, W. F., Mednick, S. A., Knop, J., & Schulsinger, F. (1988). Pattern reversal visual evoked potentials after alcohol administration among men at risk for alcoholism. *Psychiatry Research, 26,* 191–202.

Porjesz, B., & Begleiter, H. (1975). Alcohol and bilateral evoked brain potentials. *Advances in Experimental Medicine and Biology, 59*, 553–567.

Porjesz, B., & Begleiter, H. (1983). Brain dysfunction and alcohol. In B. Kissin & H. Begleiter (Eds.), *The biology of alcoholism* (Vol. 7, pp. 415–483). New York: Plenum Press.

Porjesz, B., & Begleiter, H. (1987). Evoked brain potentials and alcoholism. In O. A. Parsons, N. Butters, & P. E. Nathan (Eds.), *Neuropsychology of alcoholism: Implications for diagnosis and treatment* (pp. 45–63). New York: Guilford Press.

Porjesz, B., Begleiter, H., & Garozzo, R. (1980). *Visual evoked potential correlates of information processing deficits in chronic alcoholics.* In H. Begleiter (Ed.), *Biological effects of alcohol* (pp. 603–623). New York: Plenum Press.

Potter, J. F., McDonald, I. A., & Beevers, D. G. (1986). Alcohol raises blood pressure in hypertensive patients. *Journal of Hypertension, 4*, 435–441.

Potter, J. F., Watson, R. D. S., Skan, W., & Beevers, D. G. (1986). The pressor and metabolic effects of alcohol in normotensive subjects. *Hypertension, 8*, 625–631.

Pratt, O. E. (1984). What do we know of the mechanisms of alcohol damage in utero? In Ciba Foundation Symposium 105, *Mechanisms of alcohol damage in utero* (pp. 1–7). London: Pitman.

Pratt, O. E., & Doshi, R. (1984). Range of alcohol-induced damage in the developing central nervous system. In Ciba Foundation Symposium 105, *Mechanisms of alcohol damage in utero* (pp. 142–156), London: Pitman.

Price, J., Mitchell, S., Wiltshire, B., Graham, J., & Williams, G. (1988). A follow-up study of patients with alcohol-related brain damage in the community. *Australian Drug and Alcohol Review, 7*, 83–87.

Prigatano, G. P. (1977). Wechsler Memory Scale is a poor screening test for brain dysfunction. *Journal of Clinical Psychology, 33*, 772–776.

Prince, M. (1914). *The unconscious.* New York: Macmillan.

Query, W. T., & Berger, R. A. (1980). AVLT memory scores as a function of age among general medical, neurologic, and alcoholic patients. *Journal of Clinical Psychology, 36*, 1009–1012.

Raistrick, D. S., Dunbar, G., & Davidson, R. J. (1983). Development of a questionnaire to measure alcohol dependence. *British Journal of Addiction, 78*, 89–95.

Randall, C. L. (1987). Alcohol as a teratogen: A decade of research in review. *Alcohol and Alcoholism* (Suppl. 1), 125–132.

Randall, C. L., Ekblad, U., & Anton, R. F. (1990). Perspectives on the pathophysiology of fetal alcohol syndrome. *Alcoholism: Clinical and Experimental Research, 14*, 807–812.

Redman, S., Sansom-Fisher, R. W., Wilkinson, C., Fahey, P. P., & Gibberd, R. W. (1987). Agreement between two measures of alcohol consumption. *Journal of Studies on Alcohol, 48*, 104–108.

Reed, R. J., Grant, I., & Adams, K. M. (1987). Family history of alcoholism does not predict neuropsychological performance in alcoholics. *Alcoholism: Clinical and Experimental Research, 11*, 340–344.

Reitan, R. M., & Davison, L. A. (1974). *Clinical neuropsychology: Current status and applications.* New York: Hemisphere.

Riege, W. H., Tomaszewski, R., Lanto, A., & Metter, E. J. (1984). Age and alcoholism: Independent memory decrements. *Alcoholism: Clinical and Experimental Research, 8*, 42–47.

Renault, B., Ragot, R., Lesevre, N., & Redmond, A. (1982). Brain events: Their onset and offset as indices of mental chronometry. *Science, 215*, 1413–1415.

Rimm, E. B., Giovannucci, E. L., Willett, W. C., Colditz, G. A., Ascherio, A., Rosner, B., & Stampfer, M. J. (1991). Prospective study of alcohol consumption and risk of coronary disease in men. *Lancet, 338*, 464–468.

Risberg, J., & Berglund, M. (1987). Cerebral blood flow and metabolism in alcoholics. In O. A. Parsons, N. Butters, & P. E. Nathan (Eds.), *Neuropsychology of alcoholism: Implications for diagnosis and treatment* (pp. 64–75). New York: Guilford Press.

Ritter, W., Ford, J. M., Gaillard, A. W. K., Harter, M. R., Kutas, M., Naatanen, R., Polich, J., Renault, B., & Rohrbaugh, J. (1984). Cognition and event-related potentials: I. The relation of negative potentials to cognitive processess. *Annals of the New York Academy of Sciences, 425*, 24–38.

Robins, L. N., Helzer, J. E., Croughan, J., & Ratliffe, K. S. (1981). National Institute of Mental Health Diagnostic Interview Schedule. *Archives of General Psychiatry, 38*, 381–389.

Ron, M. A. (1983). The alcoholic brain: CT scan and psychological findings. *Psychological Medicine* (monograph Suppl. 3), 1–33.

Ron, M. A. (1987). The brain of alcoholics: An overview. In O. A. Parsons, N. Butters, & P. E. Nathan (Eds.), *Neuropsychology of alcoholism: Implications for diagnosis and treatment* (pp. 11–20). New York: Guilford Press.

Ross, H. E., Gavin, D. R., & Skinner, H. A. (1990). Diagnostic validity of the MAST and the Alcohol Dependence Scale in the assessment of DSM-III alcohol disorders. *Journal of Studies on Alcohol, 51*, 506–513.

The Royal College of Physicians (1987). *A great and growing evil: The medical consequences of alcohol abuse.* London: Tavistock.

Rubin, E. (1979). Alcoholic myopathy in heart and skeletal muscle. *New England Journal of Medicine, 301*, 28–33.

Russell, E. W. (1975). A multiple scoring method for the assessment of complex memory functions. *Journal of Consulting and Clinical Psychology, 43*, 800–809.

Russell, E. W. (1982). Factor analysis of the Revised Wechsler Memory Scale tests in a neuropsychological battery. *Perceptual and Motor Skills, 54*, 971–974.

Russell, E. W. (1988). Renorming Russell's version of the Wechsler Memory Scale. *Journal of Clinical and Experimental Neuropsychology, 10*, 235–239.

Russell, E. W., Neuringer, C., & Goldstein, G. (1970). *Assessment of brain damage. A neuropsychological key approach.* New York: Wiley Interscience.

Russell, M. (1977). Intra-uterine growth in infants born to women with alcohol-related psychiatric disorders. *Alcoholism: Clinical and Experimental Research, 1*, 225.

Russell, M. (1982). The epidemiology of alcohol-related birth defects. In E. L. Abel (Ed.), *Fetal Alcohol Syndrome, Volume II Human Studies* (pp. 89–126). Boca Raton, FL: CRC Press.

Russell, M., Czarnecki, D. M., Cowan, R., McPherson, E., & Mudar, P. J. (1991). Measures of maternal alcohol use as predictors of developments in early childhood. *Alcoholism: Clinical and Experimental Research, 15*, 991–1000.

Ryan, C., & Butters, N. (1980a). Further evidence for a continuum-of-impairment encompassing male alcoholic Korsakoff patients and chronic alcoholic men. *Alcoholism: Clinical and Experimental Research, 4*, 190–198.

Ryan, C., & Butters, N. (1980b). Learning and memory impairments in young and old alcoholics: Evidence for the premature-aging hypothesis. *Alcoholism: Clinical and Experimental Research, 4*, 288–293.

Ryback, R. (1971). The continuum and specificity of the effects of alcohol on memory: A review. *Quarterly Journal of Studies on Alcohol, 32*, 995–1016.

Sachs, H., Russell, J. A. G., Christman, D. R., & Cook, B. (1987). Alteration of regional cerebral glucose metabolic rate in non Korsakoff chronic alcoholism. *Archives of Neurology, 44*, 1242–1251.

Samson, Y., Baron, J-C., Feline, A., Bories, J., & Crousel, C. (1986). Local cerebral glucose utilisation in chronic alcoholics: A positron tomography study. *Journal of Neurology, Neurosurgery, and Psychiatry, 46*, 1165–1170.

Sanchez-Craig, M., & Walker, K. (1982). Teaching coping skills to chronic alcoholics in a coeducational halfway house. I. Assessment of programme effects. *British Journal of Addiction, 77*, 35–50.

Sander, A. M., Nixon, S. J., & Parsons, O. A. (1989). Pretest expectancies and cognitive impairment in alcoholics. *Journal of Consulting and Clinical Psychology, 57*, 705–709.

Sanders, H. I., & Warrington, E. K. (1971). Memory for remote events in amnesic patients. *Brain, 94*, 661–668.

Savolainen, K., Pentillä, A., & Karhunen, P. J. (1992). Delayed increases in liver cirrhosis mortality and frequency of alcoholic liver cirrhosis following an increment and redistribution of alcohol consumption in Finland: Evidence from mortality statistics and autopsy survey covering 8533 cases in 1968–1988. *Alcoholism: Clinical and Experimental Research, 16*, 661–664.

Schacter, D. L. (1987). Implicit memory: History and current status. *Journal of Experimental Psychology: Learning, Memory, and Cognitive, 13*, 501–518.

Schacter, D. L., & Graf, P. (1986). Preserved learning in amnesic patients: Perspective from research on direct priming. *Journal of Clinical and Experimental Neuropsychology, 8*, 727–743.

Schaeffer, K. W., Parsons, O. A., & Errico, A. L. (1988). Abstracting deficits and childhood conduct disorder as a function of familial alcoholism. *Alcoholism: Clinical and Experimental Research, 8*, 347–351.

Schafer, K., Butters, N., Smith, T., Irwin, M., Brown, S., Hanger, P., Grant, I., & Schuckit, M. (1991). Cognitive performance of alcoholics : Longitudinal evaluation of the role of drinking history, depression, liver function nutrition, and family history. *Alcoholism: Clinical and Experimental Research, 15*, 653–660.

Schenker, S., Becker, H. C., Randall, C. L., Phillips, D. K., Baskin, G. S., & Henderson, G. I. (1990). Fetal alcohol syndrome: Current status of pathogenesis. *Alcoholism: Clinical and Experimental Research, 14*, 635–647.

Schmidt, W. (1977). The epidemiology of cirrhosis of the liver: A statistical analysis of mortality data with special reference to Canada. In M. M. Fisher & J. G. Rankin, (Eds.), *Alcohol and the Liver* (pp. 1–26). New York: Plenum Press.

Schroth, G., Naegele, T., Klose, U., Mann, K., & Petersen, D. (1988). Reversible brain shrinkage in abstinent alcoholics, measured by MRI. *Neuroradiology, 30*, 385–389.

Schulsinger, F., Knop, J., Goodwin, D. W., Teasdale, T. W., & Mikkelson, U. (1986). A prospective study of young men at high risk for alcoholism: Social and psychological characteristics. *Archives of General Psychiatry, 43*, 755–760.

Scoville, W. B., & Milner, B. (1957). Loss of recent memory after bilateral hippocampal lesions. *Journal of Neurology, Neurosurgery, and Psychiatry, 20*, 11–21.

Searles, J. S. (1988). The role of genetics in the pathogenesis of alcoholism. *Journal of Abnormal Psychology, 97*, 153–167.

Seidman, H., Stellman, S. D., & Mushinski, M. H. (1982). A different perspective on breast cancer risk factors: Some implications of the nonattributable risk. *A Cancer Journal for Clinicians, 32*, 301–313.

Seltzer, B., & Benson, D. F. (1974). The temporal pattern of retrograde amnesia in Korsakoff's disease. *Neurology, 24*, 527–530.

Selzer, M. L. (1971). Michigan Alcoholism Screening Test. The quest for a new diagnostic instrument. *American Journal of Psychiatry, 127*, 1653–1658.

Seneca (circa 63AD/1920). *Epistulae Morales* [*The epistles of Seneca*, Vol. 2]. (R.M. Grummere, Trans.). London: William Heinemann.

Sharp, J. R., Rosenbaum, G., Goldman, M. S., & Whitman, R. D. (1977). Recoverability of psychological functioning following alcohol abuse: Acquisition of meaningful synonyms. *Journal of Consulting and Clinical Psychology, 45*, 1023–1028.

Shaw, J. M., Kolesar, G. S., Sellers, E. M., Kaplan, H. L., & Sandor, P. (1981). Development of optimal treatment tactics for alcohol withdrawal. I. Assessment and effectiveness of supportive care. *Journal of Clinical Psychopharmacology, 1*, 382–389.

Shaw, T. G. (1987). Alcohol and brain function: An appraisal of cerebral blood flow data. In O. A. Parsons, N. Butters, & P. E. Nathan (Eds.), *Neuropsychology of alcoholism: Implications for diagnosis and treatment* (pp. 129–147). New York: Guilford Press.

Shau, E. J., & O'Leary, M. R. (1977). Adaptive abilities of hospitalized alcoholics and matched controls. *Journal of Studies on Alcohol, 38*, 403–409.

Shelley, C. H., & Goldstein, G. (1976). An empirically derived typology of hospitalized alcoholics. In G. Goldstein & C. Neuringer (Eds.), *Empirical studies of alcoholism*. Cambridge: Ballinger.

Shelton, M. D., & Parsons, O. A. (1987). Alcoholics' self-assessment of their neuropsychological functioning in every day life. *Journal of Clinical Psychology, 43*, 395–403

Shelton, M. D., Parsons, O. A., & Leber, W. R. (1984). Verbal and visuospatial performance in male alcoholics: A test of the premature-aging hypothesis. *Journal of Consulting and Clinical Psychology, 52*, 200–206..

Sher, K. J., & Alterman, A. I. (1988). The HK/MBD questionnaire: Replication and validation of distinct factors in a nonclinical sample. *Alcoholism: Clinical and Experimental Research, 12*, 233–238.

Sherlock, S. P. V. (1989). Diseases of the liver and biliary system. *Alcohol and the liver* (8th ed.). Oxford: Blackwell Scientific Publications.

Shillito, M. L., King, L. E., & Cameron, C. (1974). Effects of alcohol on choice reaction time. *Quarterly Journal of Studies on Alcohol, 35*, 1023–1034.

Shimamura, A. P., Janowsky, J. S., & Squire, L. R. (1990). Memory for the temporal order of events in patients with frontal lobe lesions and amnesic patients. *Neuropsychologia, 28*, 803–813.

Shimamura, A. P., Jernigan, T. L., & Squire, L. R. (1988). Korsakoffs syndrome: Radiological (CT) findings and neuropsychological correlates. *Journal of Neuroscience, 8*, 4400–4410.

Shimamura, A. P., & Squire, L. P. (1986a). Memory and meta-memory: A study of feeling-of-knowing phenomenon in amnesic patients. *Journal of Experimental Psychology: Learning, Memory, and Cognition, 12*, 452–460.

Shimamura, A. P., & Squire, L. R. (1986b). Korsakoff's syndrome: The relationship between anterograde amnesia and remote memory impairment. *Behavioral Neuroscience, 100*, 165–170.

Shimamura, A. P., & Squire, L. R. (1989). Impaired priming of new associations in amnesia. *Journal of Experimental Psychology: Learning, Memory, and Cognition, 15*, 721–728.

Shipley, W. C. (1940). A self-administering scale for measuring intellectual impairment and deterioration. *Journal of Psychology, 9*, 371–377.

Silberstein, J. A., & Parsons, O. A. (1981). Neuropsychological impairment in female alcoholics: Replication and extension. *Journal of Abnormal Psychology, 90*, 179–182.

Simpura, J., & Poikolainen, K. (1983). Accuracy of retrospective measurement of individual alcohol consumption in men: A reinterview after 18 years. *Journal of Studies on Alcohol, 44*, 911–917.

Sinha, R., Bernardy, N., & Parsons, O. A. (1992). Long term test–retest reliability of event related potentials in normals and alcoholics. *Biological Psychiatry, 32*, 992–1003.

Sivyer, G. (1989). Evidence of limited repair of brain damage in a patient with alcohol–tobacco amblyopia: letter. *Medical Journal of Australia, 151*(9), 541.

Skinner, H. A., & Allen, B. A. (1982). Alcohol dependence syndrome: Measurement and validation. *Journal of Abnormal Psychology, 91*, 199–209.

Smith, A. D. (1980). Age differences in encoding, storage, and retrieval. In L. W. Poon, J. L. Fozard, L. S. Cermak, D. Arenberg, & L. W. Thompson (Eds.), *New directions in memory and aging: Proceedings of the George A. Talland Memorial Conference*. Hillsdale, NJ: Lawrence Erlbaum Associates Inc.

Smith, D. E., & McCrady, B. S. (1988). Cognitive impairment among alcoholics: Impact on drink refusal skill acquisition and treatment outcome. *Addictive Behaviors, 16*, 265–274.

Smith, H. H., & Smith, L. S. (1977). WAIS functioning of cirrhotic and non-cirrhotic alcoholics. *Journal of Clinical Psychology, 33*, 309–313.

Smith, J. W., Burt, D. W., & Chapman, R. F. (1973). Intelligence and brain damage in alcoholics: A study in patients of middle and upper social class. *Quarterly Journal of Studies on Alcohol, 34*, 327–368.

Smith, M. E., & Oscar-Berman, M. (1990). Repetition priming of words and pseudowords in divided attention and in amnesia. *Journal of Experimental Psychology: Learning, Memory, and Cognition, 16*, 1033–1042.

Sneyd, M. J., Paul, C., Spears, G. F. S., & Skegg, D. C. G. (1991). Alcohol consumption and risk of breast cancer. *International Journal of Cancer, 48*, 812–815.

Sobell, L. C., Maisto, S. A., Sobell, M. B., & Cooper, M. A. (1979). Reliability of alcohol abusers self-reports of drinking behaviour. *Behaviour Research and Therapy, 17*, 157–160.

Sobell, L. C., & Sobell, M. B. (1978). Validity of self-reports in three populations of alcoholics. *Journal of Consulting and Clinical Psychology, 46*, 901–907.

Sobell, L. C., Sobell, M. B., Riley, D. M., Schuller, R., Pavan, D. S., Cancilla, A., Klajner, F., & Leo, G. I. (1988). The reliability of alcohol abusers' self-reports of drinking and life events that occurred in the distant past. *Journal of Studies on Alcohol, 49*, 225–232.

Sobell, M. B., Sobell, L. C., Khajner, F., Pavan, D., & Basian, E. (1986). The reliability of the timeline method for assessing normal drinker college students' recent drinking history: Utility for alcohol research. *Addictive Behaviors, 11*, 149–161.

Sokol, R. J., & Clarren, S. K. (1989). Guidelines for use of terminology describing the impact of prenatal alcohol on the offspring. *Alcoholism: Clinical and Experimental Research, 13*, 597–599.

Sokol, R. J., Miller, S. I., & Reed, G. (1980). Alcohol abuse during pregnancy: An epidemiological study. *Alcoholism: Clinical and Experimental Research, 4*, 135–145.

Sournia, J. G. (1990). *A history of alcoholism*. Oxford: Blackwell.

Spillane, J. D. (1947). *Nutritional disorders of the nervous system*. Edinburgh: E & S Livingstone Ltd.

Spittle, B. J. (1991). The effect of financial management on alcohol-related hospitalization. *American Journal of Psychiatry, 148*, 221–223.

Spohr, H. L., & Steinhausen, H. C. (1984). Clinical, psychopathological and developmental aspects in children with the fetal alcohol syndrome: A four-year follow-up study. In Ciba Foundation Symposium 105, *Mechanisms of alcohol damage in utero* (pp. 197–217). London: Pitman.

Squire, L. R. (1982). Comparisons between forms of amnesia: Some deficits are unique to Korsakoff's syndrome. *Journal of Experimental Psychology: Learning, Memory, and Cognition, 8*, 560–571.

Squire, L. R. (1986). Mechanisms of memory. *Science, 232*, 1612–1619.

Squire, L. R., & McKee, R. (1992). Influence of prior events on cognitive judgements in amnesia. *Journal of Experimental Psychology: Learning, Memory, and Cognition, 18*, 106–115.

Squire, L. R., Wetzel, C. D., & Slater, P. C. (1978). Anterograde amnesia following ECT: An analysis of the beneficial effects of partial information. *Neuropsychologia, 16*, 339–348.

Squires, K. C., Chu, N. S., & Starr, A. (1978). Auditory brain stem potentials with alcohol. *Electroencephalography and Clinical Neurophysiology, 45*, 577–584.

Stampfer, M. J., Sacks, F. Salvini, S., Willett, W. C., & Hennekens, M. (1991). A prospective study of lipids and apolipoproteins and risk of myocardial infarction. *New England Journal of Medicine, 325*, 373–381.

Stark, R. (1961). An investigation of unilateral cerebral pathology with equated verbal and visual–spatial tasks. *Journal of Abnormal and Social Psychology, 62*, 282–287.

Steinhausen, H. C., Gobel, D., & Nestler, V. (1984). Psychopathology in the offspring of alcoholic parents. *Journal of American Academy of Child Psychiatry, 23*, 465–471.

Sternberg, S. (1966). High speed scanning in human memory. *Science, 153*, 652–654.

Stockwell, T., Hodgson, R., Edwards, G., Taylor, C., & Rankin, M. (1979). The development of a questionnaire to measure severity of alcohol dependence. *British Journal of Addiction, 77*, 287–296.

Stockwell, T., Murphy, D., & Hodgson, R. (1983). The Severity of Alcohol Dependence questionnaire: Its use reliability and validity. *British Journal of Addiction, 78*, 145–155.

Storm, T., & Caird, W. K. (1967). The effects of alcohol on serial verbal learning in chronic alcoholics. *Psychonomic Science, 9*, 43–44.

Strauss, M. B. (1935). The etiology of "alcoholic" polyneuritis. *American Journal of Medical Science, 189*, 378–382.

Streissguth, A. P. (1976). Maternal alcoholism and the outcome of pregnancy: A review of the fetal alcohol syndrome. In M. Greenblatt & M. Schuckit (Eds.), *Alcoholism problems in women and children* (pp. 251) New York: Grune & Stratton.

Streissguth, A. P. (1977). Maternal alcoholism and the outcome of pregnancy: Implications for child mental health. *American Journal of Orthopsychiatry, 47*, 422–431.

Streissguth, A. P. (1986). The behavioural teratology of alcohol: Performance, behavioural and intellectual deficits in prenatally exposed children. In J. R. West (Ed.), *Alcohol and brain development* (pp. 3–44) New York: Oxford University Press.

Streissguth, A. P. (1988). Long term effects of fetal alcohol syndrome. In G. Robinson (Ed.), *Alcohol and child and family health* (pp. 135). Vancouver, BC: Vancouver Children's Hospital.

Streissguth, A. P., Barr, H. M., Martin, D. C., & Herman, C. S. (1980). Effects of maternal alcohol, nicotine and caffeine use during pregnancy on infant development at 8 months. *Alcoholism: Clinical and Experimental Research, 4*, 152–158.

Streissguth, A. P., Barr, H. M., & Sampson, P. D. (1990). Moderate prenatal alcohol exposure: Effects on child IQ and learning problems at age 7 1/2 years. *Alcoholism: Clinical and Experimental Research, 14*, 662–669.

Streissguth, A. P., Clarren, S. K., & Jones, K. L. (1985). Natural history of the fetal alcohol syndrome: A 10 year follow-up of the eleven patients. *Lancet, i*, 85–92.

Streissguth, A. P., Herman, C. S., & Smith, D. (1978). Intelligence, behaviour and dysmorphogenesis in the fetal alcohol syndrome: A report on 20 clinical cases. *Journal of Paediatrics, 92*, 363–367.

Streissguth, A. P., Martin, D. C., Barr, H. M., Sandman, B. M., Kirschner, G. L., & Darby, B. L. (1984a). Intrauterine alcohol & nicotine exposure: Attention and reaction time in 4 year old children. *Developmental Psychology, 20*, 533–541.

Streissguth, A. P., Martin, D. C., Barr, H. M., Sandman, B. M., Kirschner, G. L., & Darby, B. L. (1984b). Intrauterine alcohol exposure and attentional decrements in 4 year old children. *Alcoholism: Clinical and Experimental Research* (Abstract).

Streissguth, A. P., Sampson, P. D., & Barr, H. M. (1989). Neurobehavioural dose–response effects of prenatal alcohol exposure in humans from infancy to adulthood. *Annals of The New York Academy of Science, 562*, 145–158.

Stringer, A. Y., & Goldman, M. S. (1988). Experience-dependent recovery of block design performance in male alcoholics: Strategy training versus unstructured practice. *Journal of Studies on Alcohol, 49*, 406–411.

Strohmetz, D., Alterman, I., & Walter, D. (1990). Subject selection bias in alcoholics volunteering for a treatment study. *Alcoholism: Clinical and Experimental Research, 14*, 736–738.

Sullivan, J. T., Sykora, K., Schneiderman, J., Naranjo, C. A., & Sellers, E. M. (1989). Assessment of alcohol withdrawal: The revised clinical institute withdrawal assessment for alcohol scale (CIWA-AR). *British Journal of Addiction, 84*, 1353–1357.

Sussman, S. Rychtarik. R. G., Mueser, K., Glynn, S., & Prue, D. M. (1986). Ecological relevance of memory tests and the prediction of relapse in alcoholics. *Journal of Studies on Alcohol, 47*, 305–310.

Svanum, S., & Schladenhauffen, J. (1986). Lifetime and recent alcohol consumption among male alcoholics: Neuropsychological implications. *Journal of Nervous and Mental Disease, 174*, 214–220.

Swanson, J. M., & Kinsbourne, M. (1979). State-dependent learning on retrieval: Methodological cautions and theoretical considerations. In J. F. Kihlstrom & F. J. Evans (Eds.), *Functional disorders of memory*. Hillsdale, NJ: Lawrence Erlbaum Associates Inc.

Sweet, J. J., Moberg, P. J., & Tovian, S. M. (1990). Evaluation of Wechsler Adult Intelligence Scale–Revised premorbid IQ formulas in clinical populations. *Psychological Assessment: A Journal of Consulting and Clinical Psychology, 2*, 41–44.

Talland, G. A. (1965). *Deranged memory*. New York: Academic Press.

Tarquini, D., & Masullo, C. (1981). Cognitive impairment and chronic alcohol abuse: A neuropsychological study. *Drug and Alcohol Dependence, 8*, 103–109.

Tarter, R. E. (1970). Dissociative effects of ethyl alcohol. *Psychonomic Science, 20*, 342–343.

Tarter, R. E. (1988). Are there inherited behavioral traits that predispose to substance abuse? *Journal of Consulting and Clinical Psychology, 56*, 189–196.

Tarter, R. E., & Alterman, A. I. (1984). Neuropsychological deficits in alcoholics: Etiological considerations. *Journal of Studies on Alcohol, 45*, 1–9.

Tarter, R. E., & Edwards, K. L. (1986). Multifactorial etiology of neuropsychological impairment in alcoholics. *Alcoholism: Clinical and Experimental Research, 10*, 128–135.

Tarter, R. E., Goldstein, G., Alterman, A., Petrarulo, E. W., & Elmore, S. L. (1983). Alcoholic seizures: Intellectual and neuropsychological sequelae. *Journal of Nervous and Mental Disease, 171*, 123–125.

Tarter, R. E., Hegedus, A. M., Van Thiel, D.H., Gavaler, J. S., & Schade, R. R. (1986). Hepatic dysfunction and neuropsychological test performance in alcoholics with cirrhosis. *Journal of Studies on Alcohol, 47*, 74–77.

Tarter, R. E., Jacob, T., & Bremer, D. (1989a). Cognitive status of sons of alcoholic men. *Alcoholism: Clinical and Experimental Research, 13*, 232–235.

Tarter, R. E., Jacob, T., & Bremer, D. L. (1989b). Specific cognitive impairment in sons of early onset alcoholics. *Alcoholism: Clinical and Experimental Research, 13*, 786–789.

Tarter, R. E., & Jones, B. M. (1971). Absence of intellectual deterioration in chronic alcoholics. *Journal of Clinical Psychology, 27*, 453–454.

Tarter, R. E., Jones, B. M., Simpson, C. D., & Vega, A. (1971). The effects of task complexity and practice on performance during acute alcohol intoxication. *Perceptual and Motor Skills, 33*, 307–318.

Tarter, R. E., & Parsons, O. A. (1971). Conceptual shifting in chronic alcoholics. *Journal of Abnormal Psychology, 77,* 71–75.

Tarter, R. E., & Schneider, D. U. (1976). Blackouts. Relationship with memory capacity and alcoholism history. *Archives of General Psychiatry, 33,* 1492–1496.

Tarter, R. E., Van Thiel, D. H., Arria, A. M., Carra, J., & Moss, H. (1988). Impact of cirrhosis on the neuropsychological test performance of alcoholics. *Alcoholism: Clinical and Experimental Research, 12,* 619–621.

Tharp, V. K., Rundell, O. H., Boyd, K. L., Lester, B. K., & Williams, H. L. (1974). Alcohol and information processing. *Psychopharmacologia, 40,* 33–52.

Thomas, D. (1954). *Under Milkwood: A play for voices.* London: J.M. Dent & Sons.

Tofler, O. B. (1985). *The heart of the social drinker.* London: Lloyd-Luke.

Torvik, A., Lindboe, C. E., & Rodge, S. (1982). Brain lesions in alcoholics: A neuropathological study with clinical correlations. *Journal of Neurological Sciences, 56,* 233–248.

Tuck, R. R., & Jackson, M. (1991) Social, neurological and cognitive disorders in alcoholics. *Medical Journal of Australia, 155,* 225–229.

Tulving, E. (1983). *Elements of episodic memory.* Oxford: Clarendon Press.

Tulving, E., Hayman, O. A. G., & MacDonald, C. A. (1991). Long-lasting perceptual priming and semantic learning in amnesia: A case experiment. *Journal of Experimental Psychology: Learning, Memory, and Cognition, 17,* 595–617.

Turner, C. (1990). How much alcohol is in a "standard drink"? An analysis of 125 studies. *British Journal of Addiction, 85,* 1171–1175.

Turner, C., & Anderson, P. (1990). Is alcohol a carcinogenic risk? *British Journal of Addiction, 85,* 1409–1415.

Turner, J., & Parsons, O. A. (1988). Verbal and nonverbal abstracting–problem-solving abilities and familial alcoholism in female alcoholics. *Journal of Studies on Alcohol, 49,* 281–287.

Ulleland, C. N. (1972). The offspring of alcoholic mothers. *Annals New York Academy of Science, 197,* 167.

Vaillant, G. E. (1983). *The natural history of alcoholism.* Cambridge, MA: Harvard University Press.

Victor, M., & Adams, R. D. (1953). Effect of alcohol on the nervous system. *Research Publication of the Association for Research on Nervous Mental Disabilities, 32,* 526.

Victor, M., Adams, R. D., & Collins, G. H. (1971). *The Wernicke–Korsakoff syndrome.* Oxford: Blackwell Scientific Publications.

Victor, M., & Yakovlev, P. I. (1955). S. S. Korsakoff's psychic disorder in conjunction with peripheral neuritis: A translation of Korsakoff's original article with brief comments on the author and his contribution to clinical medicine. *Neurology, 5,* 394–406.

Volkow, N. D., Mullani, N., Gould, L., Adler, S. S., Guynn, R. W., Overall, J. E., & Dewey, S. (1988). Effects of acute alcohol intoxication on cerebral blood flow measured with PET. *Psychiatry Research, 24,* 201–209.

Vuchinich, R. E., & Sobell, M. B. (1978). Empirical separation of physiological and expected effects of alcohol on complex perceptual motor performance. *Psychopharmacology, 60,* 81–85.

Wagman, A. M. I., Allen, R. P., Funderbuck, F., & Upright, D. (1978). EEG measures of functional tolerance to alcohol. *Biological Psychiatry, 13,* 719–728.

Walker, R. D., Donovan, D. M., Kivlahan, D. R., & O'Leary, M. R. (1983). Length of story, neuropsychological performance, and aftercare: Influences on alcohol treatment outcome. *Journal of Consulting and Clinical Psychology, 51*, 900–911.

Waller, J. A. (1972). Factors associated with alcohol and responsibility for fatal highway crashes. *Quarterly Journal of Studies on Alcohol, 33*, 160–170.

Waller, N. G. & Waldman, I. D. (1990). A reexamination of the WAIS-R factor structure. *Psychological Assessment: A Journal of Consulting and Clinical Psychology, 2*, 139–144.

Warner, R. H., & Rosett, H. L. (1975). The effects of drinking on offspring: An historical survey of the American and British literature. *Journal of Studies on Alcohol, 36*, 1395–1398.

Warrington, E. K. (1982). The double dissociation of short- and long-term memory deficits. In L. S. Cermak (Ed.), *Human memory and amnesia* (pp. 61–76). Hillsdale, NJ: Lawrence Erlbaum Associates Inc.

Warrington, E. K., & Weiskrantz, L. (1968). A new method of testing long-term retention with special reference to amnesic patients. *Nature, 217*, 972–974.

Warrington, E. K., & Weiskrantz, L. (1970). Amnesic syndrome: Consolidation or retrieval? *Nature, 228*, 628–630.

Warrington, E. K., & Weiskrantz, L. (1978). Further analysis of the prior learning effect in amnesic patients. *Neuropsychologia, 11*, 169–177.

Warrington, E. K., & Weiskrantz, L. (1982). Amnesia: A disconnection syndrome. *Neuropsychologia, 20*, 233–248.

Watson, C. G. (1985). More reasons for a moratorium: A reply to Maisto and O'Farrell. *Journal of Studies on Alcohol, 46*, 450–453.

Watson, C. G., Tilleskjor, C., Hoodecheck-Schow, E. A., Pucel, J., & Jacobs, L. (1984). Do alcoholics give valid self-reports? *Journal of Studies on Alcohol, 45*, 344–348.

Webb, G. R., Redman, S., Sanson-Fisher, R. W., & Gibberd, R. W. (1990). Comparison of a quantity–frequency method and a diary method of measuring alcohol consumption. *Journal of Studies on Alcohol, 51*, 271–277.

Webster, W. S., Walsh, D. A., McEwen, S. E., & Lipson, A. H. (1983). Some teratogenic properties of ethanol and acetaldehyde in implications for the study of fetal alcohol syndrome. *Teratology, 27*, 231–243.

Wechsler, D. (1917). A study of retention in Korsakoff patients. *Psychiatric Bulletin of the New York State Hospital, 2*, 403–451.

Wechsler, D. (1987). *Wechsler Adult Intelligence Scale—Revised: Manual*. New York: The Psychological Corporation.

Weingartner, H., & Faillace, L. A. (1971). Alcohol state-dependent learning in man. *Journal of Nervous and Mental Disease, 153*, 395–406.

Weingartner, H., Faillace, L. A., & Markley, H. G. (1971). Verbal information retention in alcoholics. *Quarterly Journal of Studies on Alcohol, 32*, 293–303.

Weintraub, J. (Ed.). (1967). *The wit and wisdom of Mae West*. New York: G.P. Putnam.

Weiskrantz, L. (1985). Issues and theories in the study of the amnesic syndrome. In N. M. Weinberger, J. L. McGaugh, & G. Lynch (Eds.), *Memory systems of the brain* (pp. 380–415). New York: Guilford Press.

Werch, C. E. (1990). Two procedures to reduce response bias in reports of alcohol consumption. *Journal of Studies on Alcohol, 51*, 327–330.

Wernicke, C. (1881/1973). Acute hemorrhegic superior polioencephalitis. In R. H. Wilkins & I. A. Brody (Eds.). *Neurological classics*. New York: Johnson Reprint Corporation.

Wetzig, D. L., & Hardin, S. I. (1990). Neurocognitive deficits of alcoholism: An intervention. *Journal of Clinical Psychology, 46*, 219–229.

Whipple, S. C., Parker, E. S., & Noble, E. P. (1988). An atypical neurocognitive profile in alcoholic fathers and their sons. *Journal of Studies on Alcohol, 49*, 240–244.

White, H. R., & Labouvie, E. W. (1989). Towards the assessment of adolescent problem drinking. *Journal of Studies on Alcohol, 50*, 30–37.

Wickens, D. D. (1970). Encoding categories of words: An empirical approach to meaning. *Psychological Review, 77*, 1–15.

Wik, G., Borg, S., Sjogren, I., Wiesel, F-A., Blomqvist, G., Borg, J., Greitz, T., Nyback, H., Sedvall, G., Stone-Elander, S., & Widen, L. (1988). PET determination of regional cerebral glucose metabolism in alcohol dependent men and healthy controls using sup-1-sup-1C-glucose. *Acta Psychiatrica Scandinavica, 78*, 234–241.

Wikler, A., Pescor, F. T., Fraser, H. F., & Isbell, H. (1956). Electroencephalographic changes associated with chronic alcoholic intoxication and the alcohol abstinence syndrome. *American Journal of Psychiatry, 113*, 106–114.

Wilkinson, D. A. (1985). Neuroradiologic investigations of alcoholism. In R. E. Tarter & D. H. Van Thiel (Eds.), *Alcohol and the brain: Chronic effects* (pp. 183–216). New York: Plenum Press.

Wilkinson, D. A. (1987). CT scan and neuropsychological assessments of alcoholism. In O. A. Parsons, N. Butters, & P. E. Nathan (Eds.), *Neuropsychology of alcoholism: Implications for diagnosis and treatment* (pp. 76–102). New York: Guilford Press.

Wilkinson, D. A., & Carlen, P. L. (1980). Relationship of neuropsychological test performance to brain morphology in amnesic and non-amnesic chronic alcoholics. *Acta Psychiatrica Scandinavica, 62* (Suppl. 286), 89–103.

Williams, H. L. (1987). Evoked brain potentials and alcoholism: Questions, hypotheses, new approaches. In O. A. Parsons, N. Butters, & P. E. Nathan (Eds.), *Neuropsychology of alcoholism: Implications for diagnosis and treatment* (pp. 103–128). New York: Guilford Press.

Williams, H. L., & Rundell, O. H. (1984). Effect of alcohol on recall and recognition as functions of processing levels. *Journal of Studies on Alcohol, 45*, 10–15.

Williams, R., & Davis, M. (1977). Alcoholic liver diseases—basic pathology and clinical variants. In G. Edwards & M. Grant (Eds.), *Alcoholism: New knowledge and new responses* (pp. 157–178). London: Croom Helm.

Williams, R. M., Goldman, M. S., & Williams, D. L. (1981). Expectancy and pharmacological effects of alcohol on cognitive and motor performance: The compensation for alcohol effect. *Journal of Abnormal Psychology, 90*, 267–270.

Willshire, D., Kinsella, G., & Prior, M. (1991). Estimating premorbid WAIS-R IQ from the National Adult Reading Test: A cross-validation. *Journal of Experimental and Clinical Neuropsychology, 13*, 204–216.

Wilson, B. (1981). Teaching a patient to remember people's names after removal of a left temporal lobe tumour. *Behavioural Psychotherapy, 9*, 338–344.

Wilson, B. (1982). Success and failure in memory training following a CVA. *Cortex, 18*, 581–594.

Wilson, B. (1985). An investigation into the effectiveness of group training on memory functioning in patients with acquired brain damage. In B. Wilson (Ed.), *Rehabilitation of memory* (pp. 89–111). New York: Guilford Press.

Wilson, B. (1987). Identification and remediation of everyday problems in memory-impaired patients. In O. A. Parsons, N. Butters, & P. E. Nathan (Eds.), *Neuropsychology of alcoholism: Implications for diagnosis and treatment* (pp. 322–338). New York, London: Guilford Press.

Wilson, B., Cockburn, J., & Baddeley, A. D. (1985). *The Rivermead Behavioural Memory Test*. Reading, UK: Thames Valley Test Company.

Wilson, B., & Moffat, N. (1984). *Clinical management of memory problems*. London: Croom Helm.

Wilson, B. A. (1992). Rehabilitation and memory disorders. In L. R. Squire & N. Butters (Eds.), *Neuropsychology of memory* (2nd ed. pp. 315–321). New York: Guilford Press.

Wilson, J. R., & Nagoshi, C. T. (1988). Adult children of alcoholics: Cognitive and psychomotor characteristics. *British Journal of Addiction, 83*, 809–820.

Winocur, G., & Kinsbourne, M. (1978). Contextual cuing as an aid to Korsakoff amnesics. *Neuropsychologia, 16*, 671–682.

Winocur, G., Kinsbourne, M., & Moscovitch, M. (1981). The effect of cuing on release from proactive interference in Korsakoff amnesic patients. *Journal of Experimental Psychology: Human Learning and Memory, 7*, 56–65.

Winocur, G., Oxbury, S., Roberts, R., Agnetti, V., & Davis, C. (1984). Amnesia in a patient with bilateral lesions to the thalamus. *Neuropsychologia, 22*, 123–143.

Workman-Daniels, K. L., & Hesselbrock, V. M. (1987). Childhood problem behavior and neuropsychological functioning in persons at risk for alcoholism. *Journal of Studies on Alcohol, 48*, 187–193.

Yohman, J. R., & Parsons, O. A. (1985). Intact verbal paired-associate learning in alcoholics. *Journal of Clinical Psychology, 41*, 844–851.

Yohman, J. R., Parsons, O. A., & Leber, W. R. (1985). Lack of recovery in male alcoholics' neuropsychological performance one year after treatment. *Alcoholism: Clinical and Experimental Research, 9*, 114–117.

Yohman, R. J., Schaeffer, K. W., & Parsons, O. A. (1988). Cognitive training in alcoholic men. *Journal of Consulting and Clinical Psychology, 56*, 67–72.

Yuille, J. C., & Tollestrup, P. A. (1990). Some effects of alcohol on eyewitness memory. *Journal of Applied Psychology, 75*, 268–273.

Zipursky, R. B., Lim, K. O., & Pfefferbaum, A. (1989). MRI study of brain changes with short-term abstinence from alcohol. *Alcoholism: Clinical and Experimental Research, 13*, 664–666.

Glossary of Abbreviations

AA	Alcoholics Anonymous
AAAI	Annual Absolute Alcohol Index
AC	Alcoholic group
ADD	Attention Deficit Disorder
ADH	Alcohol dehydrogenase
ADS	Alcohol Dependency Scale
AE	Alcohol embryopathy
AP	Alcohol–placebo condition in studies of state dependent learning
AST	Aspartate aminotransferase
AWIS	Alcohol Withdrawal and Intoxication Scale
BAL	Blood alcohol level
BAQ	Brain-Age Quotient
BSP	Brain stem potential
CAGE	Acronym based on the keywords from the four items of the CAGE questionnaire
CBF	Cerebral blood flow
CCC	Consonant trigram
CI	Cerebral infarction
CIWA	Clinical Institute Withdrawal Assessment
$CMRO_2$	Cerebral metabolic rate of oxygen

CMRglu	Cerebral Glucose Utilisation Rate
CNS	Central Nervous System
CQ	Conceptual Quotient
CSF	Cerebrospinal fluid
CT	Computed tomography
CVLT	California Verbal Learning Test
DEQ	Drug Effects Questionnaire
DIS	Diagnostic Interview Schedule
DP	Drug–placebo condition in studies of state dependent learning
DSM-III	Diagnostic and Statistical Manual – III
DSM-III-R	Diagnostic and Statistical Manual – III – Revised
ECG	Electrocardiograph
ECT	Electroconvulsive therapy
EEG	Electro-encephalography
EP	Evoked potential
ERP	Event related potential
ES	Effect size
FAE	Fetal Alcohol Effects
FAS	Fetal Alcohol Syndrome
FDG	Fluorine-18 incorporated into 2-deoxy-D-glucose
FH	Family history
FM	Frequency of maximum amount consumed
FOK	Feeling of knowing
FSIQ	Full Scale Intelligence Quotient
FU	Usual frequency of drinking
GABA	Gamma-aminobutyric acid
GGT	Gamma-glutamyl transferase
GI	Gastrointestinal
HDL	High density lipoprotein
HRB	Halstead–Reitan Battery
ICD	International Classification of Disease
ICH	Intracerebral haemorrhage
KD	Korsakoff's disease
LH	Left hemisphere
LTM	Long-term memory
LVF-RH	Left Visual Field – Right Hemisphere
MAST	Michigan Alcoholism Screening Test
MEOS	Metabolic enzyme oxidising system
MQ	Memory Quotient

MQF	Product of the maximum quantity per session and frequency of sessions
MR	Magnetic resonance
MRI	Magnetic resonance imaging
N-WCST	Nelson's (modified version) Wisconsin Card Sorting Test
NART	National Adult Reading Test
NC	Normal controls
NIMH	National Institute of Mental Health
NMR	Nuclear Magnetic Resonance
OA	Old alcoholic group
ON	Old normal group
PASAT	Paced Auditory Serial Addition Test
PD	Placebo–drug condition in studies of state dependent learning
PEG	Pneumo-encephalography
PET	Positron emission tomography
PICS	Pericerebral space
PIQ	Performance Intelligence Quotient
PM	Progressive Matrices
POMS	Profile of Mood States
PP	Placebo–placebo condition in studies of state dependent learning
QPO	Quantity per occasion
RAVLT	Rey Auditory Verbal Learning Test
RBMT	Rivermead Behavioural Memory Test
rCBF	Regional cerebral blood flow
rCMRglu	Regional cerebral glucose utilisation rate
REM	Rapid eye movement
RH	Right hemisphere
ROI	Regions of interest
RT	Reaction Time
RVF-LH	Right Visual Field – Left hemisphere
SADD	Short-form Alcohol Dependence Data Questionnaire
SADQ	Severity of Alcohol Dependence Questionnaire
SAH	Subarachnoid haemorrhage
SDL	State dependent learning
SILS	Shipley Institute of Living Scale
STM	Short-term memory
TMT	Trail Making Test
TPT	Tactual Performance Test
VA	Annual volume consumed

VIQ	Verbal Intelligence Quotient
VM	Maximum amount per occasion
VU	Usual amount per occasion
WAIS	Wechsler Adult Intelligence Scale
WAIS-R	Wechsler Adult Intelligence Scale – Revised
WCST	Wisconsin Card Sorting Test
WMS	Wechsler Memory Scale
WMS-R	Wechsler Memory Scale – Revised
YA	Young alcoholic group
YC	Young controls group

Author Index

Subject Index